CREATING MINNESOTA

CREATING MINNESOTA

a History from the Inside Out

ANNETTE ATKINS

MINNESOTA HISTORICAL SOCIETY PRESS

"The Shape of Water and the Feel of Trees" was published in Richard Sisson, Christian Zacher, and Andrew R. L. Cayton, eds., *The American Midwest: An Interpretive Encyclopedia* (Bloomington: Indiana University Press, 2007).

www.mhspress.org

The Minnesota Historical Society Press is a member of the Association of American University Presses.

Manufactured in Canada

10 9 8 7 6 5 4 3 2 1

∞ The paper used in this publication meets the minimum requirements of the American National Standard for Information Sciences — Permanence for Printed Library Materials, ANSI Z39.48-1984.

International Standard Book Number
ISBN 13: 978-0-87351-596-2 (cloth)
ISBN 10: 0-87351-596-X (cloth)

Library of Congress Cataloging-in-Publication Data

Atkins, Annette, 1950–
    Creating Minnesota : a history from the inside out /
    Annette Atkins.
        p.   cm.
Includes bibliographical references and index.
ISBN-13: 978-0-87351-596-2 (cloth : alk. paper)
ISBN-10: 0-87351-596-X (cloth : alk. paper)
    1. Minnesota—History.
    2. Minnesota—Biography.
    3. Minnesota—Social conditions.
    4. Minnesota—Politics and government.
    I. Title.
F606.A87 2007
977.6—dc22
2007021565

Maps on pages viii–ix by Map Hero—Matt Kania.
Lake City bird's-eye view on page 75 courtesy Library of Congress.
All other illustrations from MHS collections.

For my colleagues and students,
for lessons learned and a life made more interesting.

The Minnesota Historical Society, the first grantee of the ELMER L. AND ELEANOR J. ANDERSEN FOUNDATION, *publishes this book in celebration of Minnesota's sesqui-centennial and the Foundation's fiftieth anniversary, and in honor of its founders, Elmer L. and Eleanor J. Andersen.*

CREATING MINNESOTA

Preface: The State I'm In — xi

1 The Shape of Water and the Feel of Trees: A South Dakotan in Minnesota — 3

2 Dancing the Rice — 11

3 Campbell Country — 26

4 Playing with the Future — 34

5 One Mixed-Blood Family Looks for Its Place — 49

6 The War Touched Us All — 61

7 Not Drawn to Scale — 72

8 Making a Living, Making a Life — 84

9 The Fairbrothers' Christmas — 100

10 Becoming Better and Becoming American — 107

11 The Look of the 1920s — 119

12 Hanging on for Dear Life — 170

13 We Never Had Enough Sugar — 192

14 Style Comes to Staples — 205

15 "The House That Hubert Built" — 219

16 Walleye Quesadilla and the New Minnesota — 236

Timeline: Dates Tell a Story, Too — 251

Epilogue: Synecdoche — 265

A Word to the Wise: Thank You — 267

Notes — 269

Index — 303

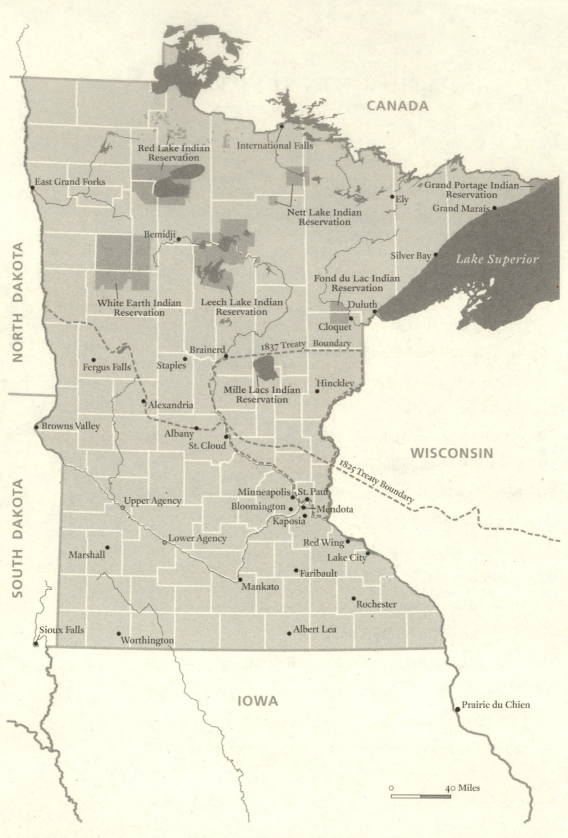

CANADA

Red Lake Indian
Reservation

International Falls

East Grand Forks

Ely

Grand Portage Indian
Reservation

Grand Marais

Nett Lake Indian
Reservation

Bemidji

Silver Bay

Lake Superior

NORTH DAKOTA

White Earth Indian
Reservation

Leech Lake Indian
Reservation

Fond du Lac Indian
Reservation

Duluth

Cloquet

Brainerd

1837 Treaty Boundary

Fergus Falls

Staples

Hinckley

Mille Lacs Indian
Reservation

Alexandria

Browns Valley

Albany

St. Cloud

WISCONSIN

1825 Treaty Boundary

SOUTH DAKOTA

Upper Agency

Minneapolis

St. Paul

Bloomington

Mendota

Kaposia

Lower Agency

Marshall

Red Wing

Lake City

Faribault

Mankato

Rochester

Sioux Falls

Albert Lea

Worthington

IOWA

Prairie du Chien

0   40 Miles

Minnesota: The Sites of Some of Our Stories

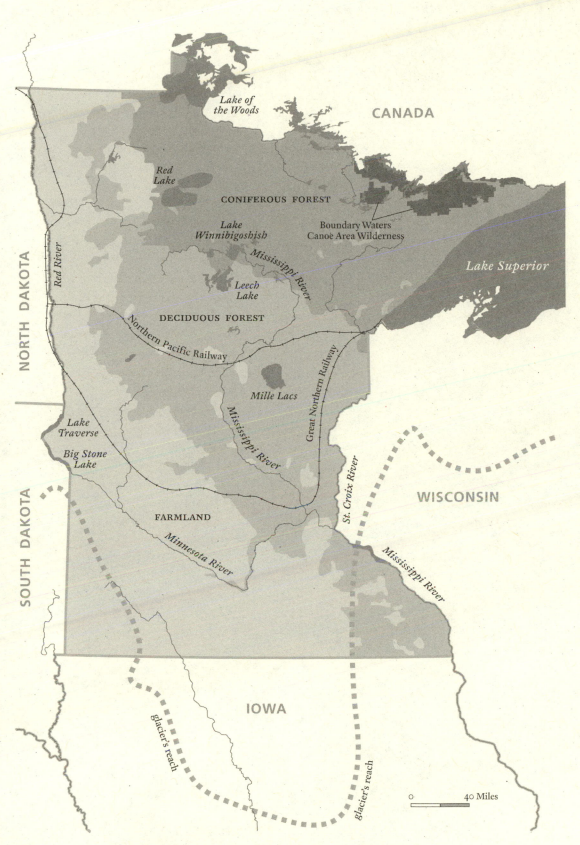

Minnesota: Natural Features and Railroads

PREFACE

The State I'm In

AFTER WORKING SOME YEARS on a project that demanded close reading of domestic and private documents, I yearned to read across a broader spectrum. Besides, I had been teaching state history for nearly two decades and had long wished for a different kind of central book than was available. Finally, I wanted (and still want) to bridge the increasingly wide divide between professional historians and readers interested in history. So I decided to write a one-volume history of the state of Minnesota that is based on extensive primary research and attempts to reimagine what state history is and can be.

The state has three excellent—though different—histories by twentieth-century writers. I had imagined initially that I would start with those, read broadly and deeply in the secondary literature, which in Minnesota is especially rich and varied, and make quick work of writing a new synthesis of the state's story. I wasn't more than a few months into the project when I realized that there would be no "quick work" and that maybe it wasn't even synthesis I wanted, but perhaps a different enterprise entirely.[1]

State history is a field born and raised in the great state-making days of our country's past. Like the national story, the overarching state narrative traditionally focused on great individuals, showed political and economic growth, and celebrated the bravery, ingenuity, perseverance, and marvels of the journey from a simpler past to a more complex and sophisticated present. These books honored the dead ("how did they do it?") and sought to identify and celebrate the first, the best, the most, the distinctive. Theodore Blegen's *Minnesota: A History of the State* is a fine example of this genre. Comprehensive, full of interesting detail and valuable references, Blegen's book appeared in 1963, in (belated) honor of Minnesota's one hundredth anniversary of statehood. More triumphalist than analytic, it tells how Minnesota over the years got better, richer, and smarter. Perhaps because Blegen himself was a scholar of

American immigration history, he was especially aware of what a powerful role and influence immigrants played (and play) in state building, so he went beyond the political narrative and paid particular attention, in addition, to education and the arts in Minnesota.

At almost the same moment that Blegen's book appeared, an earthquake began shaking the foundations of American society as well as the academic discipline of history (and other fields). Over the next decade, the civil rights, women's, and antiwar movements shifted the tectonic plates of American life and threw into question a century of intellectual work. These shifts destroyed many well-worn paths—including the single and common political narrative for nation or state—and created a new landscape for women and men, for marriages, for cities and schools, for laws and Congress, for race relations. In this new landscape, one after another historian asks, "yes, but what about . . ." women, laborers, African Americans, sexuality, the environment, material culture, pop music, patriarchy, racism, genocide? The list of previously overlooked and understudied topics was and is long and growing; so is the enthusiasm of new historians for asking new questions and exploring new answers.

The new historical scholarship delighted those who long felt their stories had been marginalized or distorted in the dominant narrative but dismayed and even alienated some more traditional historians and many lay readers of history because this new literature abandoned celebration for analysis and inserted theory and tables where narrative had once reigned. Schooled by antiwar and other social movements, many historians redefined the role of scholarship as the duty to ask questions and to shine light into dark corners. We asked new questions, explored new sources, and found new relationships and connections. In our enthusiasm to identify and explore and add more and more subgroups, we've built dozens of camps on the historical landscape and written hundreds of fine monographs.[2]

Using these—and other monographs—I have long been able to cobble together a "History of Minnesota" course and have offered variations of it for twenty-five years. I straddled the gap between old and new by holding primarily (if uncomfortably) to a political narrative while making a good-faith effort to include as many of the "yes, but . . ." groups as I could.

Somehow, however, when I tried to write a history of the state, this cobbling didn't work. I needed a structure, a guiding principle—indeed, a narrative. I also needed to grapple with several basic questions: What is the responsibility of a historian in general and a state historian in particular? What is a state (and how and when does it matter)? If I talk about Minnesotans as "we," whose point of view am I assuming? What's important to tell and what's not? Who am I talking about? For? To?

The issue of audience has especially concerned me. Many professional historians have long since conceded the audience for history books to journalists and other specialist writers. Writing in prose that is often intelligible only to other professional historians, we have lost our ability or sometimes even our desire to tell stories, as if storytelling isn't a serious enough pursuit.[3]

I have pinned to the wall over my writing desk a quotation from the folklorist Henry Glassie:

> The way to study people is not from the top down or the bottom up, but from the inside out, from the place where people are articulate to the place where they are not, from the place where they are in control of their destinies to the place where they are not.
>
> Soldiers on the battlefield, artists in the studio: generously we study some people in terms of their own excellence. All people deserve comparable treatment. Decent, serious study begins on the inside, where people are articulate, and powerful and in control.[4]

I began my rethinking by taking Glassie to heart. I remain grateful to other state historians—especially to William Watts Folwell, Theodore Blegen, and William Lass—but to find the Minnesota "where people are articulate, and powerful and in control," I had to listen for many forms of articulation and redefine power and what it means to be in control. I had to find the stories that conveyed essential and important things about "Minnesota." The secondary sources could point me to and the monographs could help me understand those articulations, but I would have to go to the primary sources to hear them and to hear them for myself. I had to ask new questions: How *did* people experience this place in the past, what did it mean to them, how did they understand it? How can we allow them and their stories to be as complex and nuanced as we allow ourselves and our contemporaries to be?

I also learned enormously from the staff of the Minnesota Historical Society and other friends and colleagues in public history. Public historians teach us how to think about audience, about the limitations of text and the different possibilities of objects for telling stories. Not just illustrations or sidebars, objects and images can be the central device for cracking open and looking into parts of the past we can't see by looking only at words. These lessons profoundly shaped how I approach state history—and now all of the history that I write and teach.

Students, too, in their impatience with theory and their enthusiasm for particulars, have pushed me to speak in more metaphors as well as in a language more connected to theirs. They push to have course work made more "relevant" and meaningful to them. They also give me one last chance—before they leave their formal education behind—to catch them up in the power of history to explain our—and other people's—lives.

So now the Minnesota Historical Society has published and you are holding in your hands my book, the product of these many forces. It's a work that moves (mostly) chronologically from then to now, that recognizes that the state is a political unit and that Minnesota is America, too. I've aimed to engage with current historical issues, including whiteness, modernization, material culture, environmental history, gender analysis. A few heroes show up, but not many traditional ones. Politics don't provide the backbone of this state story, but why a state develops in one direction rather than another are political questions that command our attention.

No single straight line (either up or down) runs through the past to the present in my account. Are women better off now than then? It depends. Is factory labor better than hand labor? For whom? Does urban life represent progress over rural? For whom was the move from territory to state an improvement?

Finally, my picture highlights not how Minnesota is unique but how American it is. Borderlands (American Southwest) historians are increasingly insisting that American history really starts there more truly than it does in Virginia and Massachusetts. Daniel Richter, in a brilliantly conceived and researched book, *Looking East from the Indian Country,* tells American history from the receiving side. Studying Minnesota's past reminds us that Colonial Williamsburg and the Mississippi River Valley both throbbed with life in the eighteenth century and that both places shaped what America was and is. Wherever we live and work, it ought to be possible to teach American history by teaching state history. Professor Jack P. Greene would call this a federalist approach, to distinguish it from what has largely been the nationalist approach of American history narratives.

Here's the idea I came to and the one that structures this book: I've set out to identify who holds the story-making power in the state at any given time. By "story-making power" I mean who or what in the state commands the state's attention, dominates its concerns, claims center stage? Like a baton in a relay race, the ability to define and tell the state's story never stays in the same place for long. Sometimes it's carried by an individual or a family or a group; sometimes by an economic person or place or force; sometimes by an idea, a Christmas tree, a chair, a fish.

The biographers of Ignatius Donnelly, of Harold Stassen, of Hubert Humphrey could well complain that I give these men short shrift. The yes-but historians may object to my giving these middle-class white men as much space as I do. Some might argue that I should simply label Henry Sibley a perpetrator of genocide and be done with it. Some traditional historians might think it trivial to anchor the story of the 1820s and 1830s in the lives of a mixed-blood couple. Do seamstresses or maps really carry the most important stories of other Minnesota decades? In my research and in my approach to state history, the answer is yes. Emphatically, insistently, and persistently yes. The 1862 Dakota War was a story of Wood Lake, and Camp Release, and soldiers and warriors. Its deeper—and, I would argue, more telling—story, however, is articulated in its explosive and shattering effects on the Campbell family.

I begin the story with my own experience of Minnesota, from being an outsider and seeing into this other place. I also begin with myself, in part, to invite all of us to think about the ways that we all "create" Minnesota—not only in our contributions to this place but in our knowing, telling, and remembering stories about our past. Every time we talk about the "good old days" or the "bad old days" or our families or the Vietnam War or how our mothers made grape jelly or chip dip, we're constructing the stories that give meaning and context to our lives. History is never a "given"; it is always a "creation."

The remaining stories in this book constitute the narrative of a place where Native people, then mixed bloods, controlled the story for a time. In the 1840s and 1850s, statemakers competed over the state's definition, outline, and future. The Dakota War erupted and proved to be one of the most important Indian/white wars in the American past; it demonstrated the movement from a many-dimensioned relationship among whites and Native Americans to a two-sided "us" and "them" catastrophe. The Civil War and the 1870s saw thousands of individuals inventing ways of being in and seeing this new place; the 1880s were primarily about making a living. The 1890s connect Minnesotans to the rest of the world and the rest of the world to Minnesota by means of railroads, commercial agriculture, advertising, and oranges.

At the turn of the century the defining story in the state does become political: what kind of government do Americans want? An activist government can do good and ill and did both. The 1920s signaled a turn to a new way—more urban in the nation's population and more "modern" in its self-definition. People in the many rural parts of Minnesota and America took pictures and had their pictures taken; they could and did look at themselves and each other in new ways. The 1930s depression pushed thousands of people to their limits and brought thousands of others in from the margins. Middle-class people felt what the poor had long felt; artists and writers got assistance as railroads and businesses long had. World War II sent thousands of men and women away—to service, to jobs, to adventures—and turned many at home to rationing and limitation. The 1950s found people without nostalgia and eager for the new—especially cars and television sets, lawn furniture and convenience foods. Hubert Humphrey took over the 1960s, and politics defined Minnesota (and the nation) in the Kennedy, Johnson, and Nixon years. In the most recent period in Minnesota—and national—history, sports and leisure, eating out, and new technologies have moved to center stage. This is the story that these stories tell.

These different stories require different methods. I use the tools of the biographer and genealogist, the playwright and social historian, the cultural historian of photos and objects. For each chapter I've asked two main questions: "What's the story here?" and "What are the best sources for telling it?" Then I have employed the method required by the answers to those two questions and a lurking third: How can I best invite the reader to understand or perhaps to rethink this period? I've used a variety of sources—newspapers, objects, letters, places, speeches, maps, census enumerations, photographs, art, travel books, fiction. Each set constitutes a legitimate historical source and each invites us into different ways of understanding and telling stories.

As a social historian, I find that social history is my default mode. Insofar as the state is a political entity, much of its narrative is constructed in the arena of formal politics, so I take up politics where it seems to matter most. Furthermore, why a state develops one political culture rather than another, why Gene McCarthy came from Minnesota and Joe McCarthy from Wisconsin, requires consideration of the nature of power and its exercise, both formally and informally. No matter what approach I take or source I use, however, my goal is to understand the nature of people's lives and choices, their opportunities and limitations, their public and secret selves, their roles, their safety nets, their failures— "from the inside out." I presume not that the important things happen elsewhere but that important things happen here, in this place and this time and to and through the agency of these people.

Finally, I hope with this narrative to invite readers into the complexity of the past, into the difficulty of making good decisions, into the ambiguous consequences of sincerity and good intention. I want the stories to remind us that no one ever acts from a single motive—not then, not now. The work of historians is not to heal the wounds of the past but to understand them enough to allow nuance and detail to cloud the easy answers. To make the complex simple and the simple complex, to widen our view and sharpen our vision—these are the goals of this book and the real and essential functions of history, even state history.

CREATING MINNESOTA

Hydrographical Basin of the Upper Mississippi River by Joseph Nicollet, 1843

1

The Shape of Water and the Feel of Trees: A South Dakotan in Minnesota

WHEN I WAS GROWING UP IN SIOUX FALLS, SOUTH DAKOTA, it was possible to believe I occupied a "corner of the world." I lived on a square block—twelve to the mile—lined on four sides with square houses with straight walls. The block was divided into two equal rectangles by the alley giving onto squared-off garages that in the 1950s housed squared-off cars. I could stand at the corner nearest my house at Eighth and Summit and see in a straight line in all four directions. So, square it was, and square it mostly is. In the 1960s, developers laid out curved streets in the south end of Sioux Falls, but not in my neighborhood, not in my time.

The first time I visited Scotland, I discovered those squares were etched into my psyche. In the seaside village of Ullapool I tried—in vain, but repeatedly nonetheless—to go around the block. I hadn't thought "Okay, I'll go around the block": I just found myself deeply and peculiarly puzzled when I couldn't find the square to take me back to where I'd started.

The Land Ordinance of 1785 established a system for surveying and dividing the United States into six-mile squares, counted westward from a point on the Ohio/Pennsylvania border. Subsequent land-law refinements divided those squares into thirty-six one-mile-square sections, then each of those into four 640-acre quarter sections, and so on down to my house's lot on my square block.[1]

The land division system, invented in New England, imposed order and predictability whatever the lay of the land. The grid lines lie awkwardly across the landscape in much of the country, but just west of Sioux Falls the lines match the flat contour of the landscape. I always ask for a window seat when flying into and out of Sioux Falls, just for the pleasure of seeing those squares. They define South Dakota.

They also describe the southwestern corner of Minnesota as well as a swath of western Minnesota counties stretching from Iowa to Canada, over one-third of the state. This area in the eastern Dakotas and western Minnesota was flattened by departing glaciers and by the 365,000-square-mile lake that formed when part of a glacier stalled and melted. Lake Agassiz, long since dried up, left in central Canada, eastern Dakota, and Minnesota a fertile, flat, and dry lakebed. Driving from Ortonville, Minnesota, across the Minnesota River to Milbank, South Dakota, you still can see the shorelines. You can see them even better farther north at Breckenridge. Here, in this fertile riverbed, the biggest, richest, so-called bonanza farms of the late nineteenth and early twentieth centuries flourished.[2]

The glaciers left behind a landscape only occasionally interrupted by trees. It's not the rainfall so much as the type and depth of soil that accounts for the presence or absence of trees. Prairie Minnesota has soil rich enough for grasses and crops, mostly uninterrupted by trees. Before whites showed up, native people burned the land to keep the trees down and the land open for animals. Later, Euro-Americans cleared the prairie for farming, then planted trees elsewhere for firewood, shade, and protection, perhaps some decoration around the house, but not enough to interfere with the crops.

Southwestern Minnesota has more trees now than a century ago. The U.S. Congress passed the Timber-Culture Act in 1873—an amendment to the Homestead Act of 1862—to encourage planting. The legislators hoped that trees would modify the harsh climate and increase rainfall. The lawmakers also judged trees to be more civilized than open land. Largely unsuccessful at changing the climate—or civilizing the inhabitants—the law was repealed by the early 1890s.

The State of Minnesota went further. From 1873 it paid bounties—up to twenty-five dollars per year—to farmers planting at least an acre's worth of trees not more than twelve feet apart and keeping them alive for six years. E. A. Running, for example, in Chippewa County (two over from the Minnesota–South Dakota border) planted a total of 6.25 acres of trees in 1874, 1875, and 1880. When grasshoppers damaged the trees, he replanted to assure his bounty. Minnesotans planted more than 25,000 acres of trees in the first decade of bounty distribution.[3]

After the turn of the nineteenth century, farmers planted trees as shelterbelts and windbreaks, recognizing the wind's proclivity to pile up snow in the winter and whip away soil the rest of the time. The drought years of 1910–11, and then the dusty 1920s and 1930s, added urgency to their need for wind protection. The new trees clustered on the windward side of a farmhouse or in a straight line along a fencerow. Driving through the southwestern and western counties, you see squared-off "islands of trees" in the "rolling seas of sod," as one forestry official described. Even where abandoned farmhouses have fallen, trees still interrupt the wind and hold the soil.[4]

The farmers who wanted a few more trees also wanted less water; many worked concertedly to drain it away. Wetlands, announced the state drainage commission in the early 1900s, "have impeded the progress of development." Drained land could be farmed into prosperity in dry years. In the first three decades of the century, Minnesotans in the southwest drained between 5 and 6 million acres of marsh and wetlands. The net effect of the effort made this part of the state more what it was—dry, with occasional trees.[5]

Despite the contour, aridity, and vegetation of this part of the state, Minnesota's identity is steeped in water: from the state's name, for muddy or sky-tinted waters, to its slogan "Land of 10,000 Lakes," even to its shape. Big Stone and Traverse lakes and the Red River of the North make up most of the western border. Lake of the Woods, Rainy and Namakan lakes, Lac La Croix, a string of other lakes, and the Pigeon River form most of the northern boundary. Lake Superior and the St. Croix and Mississippi rivers mark the eastern border. The state lines enclose 92,000 miles of river and "more shoreline than California, Florida, and Hawaii combined," the *Star Tribune* reckoned.[6]

Indians in northern Minnesota got around in elegantly graceful canoes. White explorers came and went by water. Fur traders and trade routes depended on water. Water-powered milling was the state's first industry. Dakota and Anishinaabe people contested control of water at Mille Lacs and at Leech, Cass, and Red lakes. The first three generations of white families arrived in the territory by water.

The same huge ice hands—Rainy, Superior, Des Moines, and Wadena—that flattened western Minnesota shaped the northeast and eastern third of the state into other patterns. There the glaciers left heaps of debris (moraines), thin soil (good for growing pines, cedars, and spruce but not for farming), too many trees to clear, and thousands of orphan glaciers that melted into lakes. Then there is the "driftless area" in southeastern Minnesota, where no glaciers reached at all.[7]

Roseau County, in the northwestern prairie part of the state, reports three lakes; its neighbor Pennington has one. Pipestone County in the southwest prairie has one; Rock County, two—and both of those are man-made reservoirs, so they don't really count. By contrast, Itasca County in northeastern Minnesota has 945.[8]

For most of my adult life I've lived in central Minnesota—in the zone between the two regions—coming to understand how deeply and fully water and trees define the state. No matter that half the state has little water and few trees: it's a state formed by water and trees. That's their story, and they're sticking to it.

And there's something to it.

My husband and I live in a house as square as anything in South Dakota. But here that squareness rebukes the undulating landscape around it. My Sioux Falls house was at home in its landscape. This one is at war with it. The builder, John Pueringer, took round, rough stones and turned them into two-foot-thick, straight walls, a barricade against the outside. Built just over a century ago, the house expresses a nineteenth-century farmer's yearning to escape the elements, to find refuge in the dark interior, safe from sun and storm.

We have put an addition on the back of the house—all windows. Unlike Mr. Pueringer, we're indoor people who want protection only from mosquitoes, wood ticks, tornados, and blizzards. I love the addition, but I still feel a little claustrophobic. I can't see anything; all those hills and trees get in the way. But this is my Minnesota-born husband's dream house, especially since he can better see the hills, trees, and water.

Our house stands on the line that divides the Minnesota without trees from the one with trees.* The low rises and distant hills are what geologists call a terminal moraine. They are made of debris, dropped as if by snowplow at the farthest extent of an ice lobe. It also means the soil is rich for growing trees especially and better for animals and pastures than crops because of the land's roll. Out the back window is another glacial remain—a pond. Too small to have a name, it's too shallow to support fish (freezes solid in winter) and doesn't qualify as one of the state's 10,000 lakes (11,400 according to the Department of Natural Resources; 11,800 by the count of the Minneapolis *Star Tribune*). But there are at least a dozen lakes—with names—within a mile.[9]

The nearest is Lake Sagatagan, at the heart of the campus that is home to Saint John's Abbey, University, Prep School, and Liturgical Press. The admissions counselors report that if they can just get students to see the campus, the natural surroundings will do the recruiting.

The sisters of Saint Benedict's Monastery—four miles away—have held a peculiarly Minnesota kind of grudge for more than a century against the monks of Saint John's Abbey, who stole the money intended for them by their Bavarian King Ludwig and bought this property—leaving the nuns to settle on the prairie nearby. The monks got the choice land—hilly, wooded, laked. The sisters got flat, dry land of a kind considered by many Minnesotans—and Americans—boring and empty. To my South Dakota eye, that land, full of grasses and crops, of mountains

*

In the three-part division of the state, we're in the deciduous trees region; the U.S. Geological Survey calls this a "tension zone," that is, the area between "two floristic provinces."

of hay, is a vista worth a linger. Neither sisters nor monks would agree.[10]

The "Sag"—the largest (170 acres) of the monks' five lakes—is alive with activity all year. Students, monks, and a few neighbors swim almost as soon as the ice goes out. In winter, the hockey teams practice indoors, but the hardier cross-country skiers, snowshoers, and amateur skaters take to lake ice. The really intrepid set up fish houses or upturn buckets to fish through the ice. Brother Paul Jasmer, OSB, who doesn't care much for fishing, receives callers and serves tea in his fish house. In the summer, neighbors fish, swim, canoe, listen to the loons, and enjoy the lake's beauty. These activities—minus the tea, I imagine—occur on thousands of lakes in the state.

The lakes have fostered an ice-hockey culture, allowing towns like Eveleth to boast that no other place its size "has produced as many quality players or has contributed more to the growth and development of the sport in the United States." Eveleth hosts the U.S. Hockey Hall of Fame. In this "national shrine," you can watch, endlessly, native sons leading the U.S. hockey team to victory over the USSR in the 1980 Winter Olympics.[11]

There are lakes in South Dakota, muddy and unattractive in my experience. For years I swam nearly every summer day at the Terrace Park city pool, and I still prefer pools to lakes. I like seeing the bottom, knowing where the edges are. And no fish, either. Minnesotans, though, prefer swimming in lakes.

Wherever one lives in Minnesota, "going to the lake" is a sacred ritual. No one concludes there's just one lake; still, most Minnesotans refer only to "the lake." Oddly, they never mean the really big lake, Superior; they call that the "North Shore," even though it's actually the lake's western shore, but never mind. It's all the other lakes they call "the lake." Maybe they figure there are just too many lakes—and so many with the same name—that it's not worth identifying their particular one. I mean, look, if you said you were going to Lake Alice, you could be going to one in Clearwater, Hubbard, Olmsted, Otter Tail, Pope, St. Louis, Washington, or Wilkin counties. What good would it do, then, to say Lake Alice? It would only require more explanation.

And Alice isn't anywhere close to being one of the most common lake names. Nearly one hundred are called some version of Mud and another hundred Long. Sixty-eight are called Rice (nine in Itasca County alone) and forty-eight are named Bass (ten of those in Itasca County, too). There are twelve Andersons, six Idas, two Mabels and two Ethels, three Josephines, four Johns, three Jacks and one Hungry Jack, five Potato

Lakes and two Pomme de Terre. My favorite names are Lost Honeymoon, the hopeful Fullof-Fish, and the despairing Dead (four of them).[12]

Mrs. George H. Davis and her daughters, Alice and Kate, made a chronicle of their lake summers, not unlike those many Minnesotans keep or wish they had. The Davises started going to the lake in 1912 or 1913, at first renting Spruce Cottage at the Pines, a small resort run by a Mrs. Osborne at Lake Hubert. (There is only one Lake Hubert—in Crow Wing County, north of Brainerd.) In 1915, Mrs. Davis had a cabin built two lakes away, on Clark (three of that name).

On June 10, she, Kate, and Alice arrived for a long, languorous summer at their new cabin, outhouse and all (that was part of the charm). There the Davises entertained friends and relatives including Aunt Bert (Mrs. Davis's sister from New York), Grace Hoyt, Helen Hull, Sally Williams, and Amy Hickok Dresser. They swam, took walks, did needlepoint, rowed, made Christmas wreathes, and took pictures. Women weren't the only vacationers, but no Mr. Davis, Sr., ever showed up. Neither did Kate and Alice's brother, Dr. Fred Davis, from Faribault. In 1935 a carload of relatives from Tacoma, Washington, made the drive to the cabin; Mrs. Davis recounted in her book, "To us their stay seemed all too short."

The Davises kept their "Summers at Clark Lake" book intermittently, despite their best intentions. In 1950 they took to the book with vigor, detailing a summer that anyone who's stayed at a lake would recognize:

> June 21   *baked cake*
> June 22   *to Brainerd for shopping*
> *thunderstorm*
> *Mr. and Mrs. Bane called*
> June 25   *to Lake Edward*
> June 26   *Kate fell down stairs*
> June 30   *Drove to dump*
> July 1   *1st row on lake, saw blue heron*
> July 4   *quiet day to ourselves . . .*
> July 19, 20, 21   *blueberrying 8 quarts*
> Aug. 1   *canned blueberries and made watermelon pickles*

In 1954 sister Kate reported—in the only entry for that year—that the girls were "late getting up this year because of ACD's arthritis." They held on for three more years, but in 1957 the sisters sold the cabin to a Marthena Drybread. In the final scrapbook entry Kate recalled, "Built in 1915 used by KG and AD 42 summers." Not a South Dakota story, this is a familiar one in Minnesota.[13]

As a South Dakotan, I'm also at a disadvantage in Minnesota because

I don't know trees. In my part of South Dakota there are some trees, of course: Dutch elms stood in front of our house until disease took them, three big evergreens in the back, a giant catalpa next door that shed petals we could turn into fingernails, an apple tree across the street. The South Dakota mode, though, is a tree here and a tree there, not the Minnesota mass of green that ruins the view.*

It came as a surprise that there are so many trees—worth looking at in themselves. My husband can recount red cedars, bur oaks, and several kinds of pine along the route from Minneapolis to Collegeville. I've driven that same route three times a week for more than a decade; I've noticed the lilacs. He also knows every tree on the Collegeville property. While I'm scouting for trees that we might cut down so that I can see something, he and the nurseryman have long conversations about which new tree to plant where. When they ask what I want, I remember a friend once oohed over a mountain ash, so I say, "Why not a few mountain ash?"—the only one I can think of. Now we have three flourishing mountain ash outside our windows.

Thirty-five species of trees are commonly found in Minnesota. I'm embarrassed to say I have a hard time remembering the difference between coniferous and deciduous trees (since in reading for this piece I finally made the connection between cones and coniferous I should be all right from now on). I'm not really slow; it's just that my consciousness is neither leafed nor treed. After twenty-five years in the state, I can now identify mountain ash, box elder (if there are box elder bugs around), maples, willows, cottonwoods, birches, and aspen. The other common trees—locust, walnut, hickory, oak, elm, ironwood, hackberry, basswood, balsam, poplar, and cherry—probably identifiable to "real" Minnesotans, are beyond me. The evergreens, including the tamarack (which isn't evergreen), cedars, pines, firs, and spruce, remain part of the green mass.

While Minnesotans in the southwest and west madly planted trees during the dirty 1930s, Civilian Conservation Corps workers in northeastern Minnesota thinned, pruned, and cleared trees. There were six CCC camps in Itasca County alone. The thinners were only slightly more successful than the planters at changing the natural environment.[14]

Outsiders often mock Minnesota—and the rest of the Midwest—as remote. Minnesotans both deny and make a virtue of it. They also distinguish among and between remotenesses. In the state imagination, the southwestern and western parts of Minnesota are the essence of remote. The remote of the north and northeast, however, is heaven.

I went to college in Marshall, Minnesota, expecting to find language classes and history and literature, philosophy and chemistry. I did not expect to discover nature or to find different ways of looking at or feel-

*

Except for the Black Hills in western South Dakota, of course.

ing about the landscape. My friends came from exotic-sounding places: Silver Lake, Bird Island, Sleepy Eye, Mountain Lake. They knew birds, wildflowers, and trees. They knew about glacial Lake Agassiz and how its melting created a riverbed far too big for the Minnesota River that currently runs through it. They even gave me words for what I had not previously seen: Robert Bly's description of trees in a valley as "heavy green smoke close to the ground"; Robert Frost's view of spring: "Nature's first green is gold, Her hardest hue to hold."[15]

Perhaps my discovery was an accident, perhaps the natural result of college life in a rural place. But I've come to believe it was the work of Minnesota itself, through my friends—Minnesotans, every one. They lived out a Minnesota relationship to the land, intense and immediate and, in that place, full of longing.

They shared a soulful yearning to be elsewhere. In southwestern Minnesota, many seemed to feel they were exiled to some domestic Siberia. Not because of the cold (we all had that) and not from a hunger for Los Angeles or New York or even Minneapolis. They pined, instead, for a place with more water and trees.

"Up North" including Lake Superior looks like the real Siberia including Lake Baikal—forests, bogland, lakes, more lakes. But exile? The heart of Minnesota beats strong amid these trees and lakes, on the rivers and in the woods. It's an end of the earth where many Minnesotans would prefer to live—if only . . .

Ely, International Falls, Grand Marais, Superior National Forest, Chippewa National Forest, the Boundary Waters Canoe Area Wilderness—they're all remote, but when you get there you're somewhere magical. Up North nurtures dreams and fires the imagination.

After college I left Minnesota for the East Coast and graduate school. I'd caught the disease, though, so I wrote my dissertation on a Minnesota topic to be sure I'd find my way back. I've lived here, more or less, since 1980. I love to go to the lake. I've learned how to garden. I've even taken to walking in the woods. But I'm still not quite a Minnesotan. When I drive down to see my dad in Sioux Falls, I feel myself start to breathe easier as the landscape flattens out and opens up, as those trees get out of my way and big, flat farm fields take over. My claustrophobia lifts. I relax. I'm reminded that I'm a South Dakotan at heart by how good I feel getting out of the woods and back into the open.

Minnesotans, by contrast, have an impulse to hike, camp, canoe, fish, boat, ski, hunt—anything that gets them into the woods and onto the water. It's this passion, this visceral connection to trees and water, that informs Minnesota history, identity, and life. It's the impulse that makes Minnesotans Minnesotans.[16]

2

Dancing the Rice

THE PEOPLES WHO LIVED ON THE CONTINENTS that came to be called North and South America and in the place now named Minnesota differed from one another in language and loyalties, in foodways and marriage patterns, in practices for honoring the spirits, and in their daily and annual rounds. In North America alone, the term "Indian" includes people who ate salmon, built adobe dwellings, raised their dead on platforms, stampeded buffalo, picked berries, lived in long houses. In Minnesota the term includes Mdewakanton, Wahpeton, Sisseton, and Wahpekute—all Dakota people—and the Anishinaabe or Ojibwe, who often identify themselves by place (Pillager, Mississippian, East Laker, Lake Lena) and more publicly refer to themselves by reservation affiliation (Red Lake, Nett Lake, White Earth, Mille Lacs, Grand Portage). The Ho-Chunk (previously called Winnebago) were deported to Minnesota from Wisconsin in the nineteenth century, then largely again to Dakota Territory, then to Nebraska after 1862.[1]*

Significant cultural, spiritual, and practical differences distinguished hundreds of bands and tribes in North America. Many of these groups fought fierce wars, competing for land and resources. They also forged strategic alliances, cooperated, intermarried, and traded with each other. Any generalization about Indians is certain to have its exceptions. Nonetheless, historian Donald Fixico has argued there is such a thing as "Indian thinking," or " 'seeing' things from a perspective emphasizing that circles and cycles are central to the world and that all things are related within the universe"—what Clara Sue Kidwell has described as "a world that can be alive with intent and will."[2]

The mistake European explorers and early observers made in thinking about the native people is that Indians were always as the whites saw them upon first contact. The Europeans made a common ahistorical mistake: feeling (and then presuming it to be fact) that everything that occurred before their own appearance was flat and static and that

*

Dakota means "allies" and includes the separate Council Fires. The Ojibwe—or Anishinaabe—were most often called *Chippewa* in the nineteenth century and still are today in some official documents. The Ojibwe, part of the Algonquian language group, came to the western Great Lakes from the east and across their northern shores. The names *Dakota* and *Anishinaabe* are some version of "us" that distinguishes them from "not us"— sort of like Catholics and non-Catholics.

the most important things that have ever happened were occurring in their own lifetimes.

Think how often people (maybe we ourselves) assert with a bit of a boast that things have speeded up and that change is happening faster and faster. This is not a statement of fact so much as one of cultural and historical blindness. A few drops of culturally aware history can open our eyes to the variety, complexity, and richness of the lives of the native people who greeted, welcomed, and fed white people when they (we) arrived in the Southwest, on the Pacific and Atlantic coasts, on the Great Lakes.[3]

No eye drops can make me see as an Indian sees or understand as an Indian understands. With a perspective sharpened by research and enhanced by imagination, however, I aim to look over the shoulders of the people I study. I know I can't see everything they saw or see or understand it as they did. And I won't tell the story by telling stories the way a Native American might, but I trust I can see enough to invite others to stand with me and see more than we saw before.[4]

When I look over the shoulders of the Dakota, Anishinaabe, and others native to this place, I see a world starkly different from my own. I see loss and hurt too painful to look at for long. I see the rage that comes from a dream desired, a way of life mangled, faces scarred by smallpox, land taken. I see alienation, languages wrenched away, honored images defiled. I see, too, resignation and demoralization, the despair that comes from having lost so much.[5]

If I keep looking, however, I see another past. We don't have to romanticize it as a time of perfect peace and harmony, of perpetual balance and an eternally right relationship with the earth, which it wasn't entirely, however attractive a consolation that might be in the face of the more bitter memories of the last three centuries. Instead, I see people leading meaningful, rich, and interesting lives connected to and aware of place and nature. Theirs was not the complexity of electronic technology but of religious belief, story making, dream work, and community building, of the power and influence of the subconscious mind, of subsistence patterns and political systems adapted to their particular environments. To offer one simple but revealing example: during the murderous forest fires of the early twentieth century in Minnesota's north woods, hundreds of Euro-American settlers perished. The Ojibwe of the Minnesota woodlands, however, did not. Understanding the nature of forest life, they knew how to survive its fires.[6]

I also see a people who have survived. Native American scholars and storytellers teach us that Native American culture and people did not, in fact, vanish. Millions of Indians died from European-introduced diseases.* White missionaries, politicians, and common citizens exerted enormous pressure to suppress native peoples and their ways, effectively dispossessing them of their land. Even so, Indian ways (and people) persist, as we learn from Indian storytellers and scholars—Ignatia Broker, Vine and Philip and Ella Deloria, Donald Fixico and Thomas Peacock, Brenda Child, Waziyatawin Angela Wilson and her father, Chris Mato Nunpa, and others. I see young people staying on reservations and adults returning; communities working hard to strengthen each other and the collective. I see much energy generated and being tapped into by recent court cases that upheld native treaty and property rights. When I look over their shoulders, I see a dynamic *then* with living connections to a *now* that looks something like this.[7]

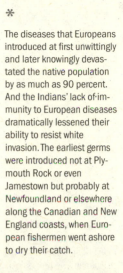

* The diseases that Europeans introduced at first unwittingly and later knowingly devastated the native population by as much as 90 percent. And the Indians' lack of immunity to European diseases dramatically lessened their ability to resist white invasion. The earliest germs were introduced not at Plymouth Rock or even Jamestown but probably at Newfoundland or elsewhere along the Canadian and New England coasts, when European fishermen went ashore to dry their catch.

Patrick DesJarlait, Woman and Blueberries, *1971*

WILD RICE, MAPLE SYRUP, AND CORN

The Legend of Nanaboozhoo

One evening Nanaboozhoo returned from hunting, but he had no game. As he came toward his fire, he saw a duck sitting on the edge of his kettle of boiling water. After the duck flew away, Nanaboozhoo looked into the kettle and found wild rice floating upon the water, but he did not know what it was. He ate his supper from the kettle, and it was the best soup he had ever tasted. Later, he followed in the direction the duck had taken and came to a lake full of *manoomin:* wild rice. He saw all kinds of ducks and geese and mud hens and all the other water birds eating the grain. After that, when Nanaboozhoo did not kill a deer, he knew where to find food to eat.[8]*

As wild rice grows in popularity outside of Native communities, it has attracted the attention of professional growers who are working to domesticate and industrialize the process. The lower price of this commercial rice attracts buyers who don't know the original version.

Native people have danced the rice in the Minnesota area since ancient times according to oral history and for nearly two thousand years according to radiocarbon dating. Not a true rice—more like wheat or rye—wild rice grows in water and is traditionally harvested by two people in a canoe. One guides the boat; the other bends the grass heads, knocking some kernels into the boat and some into the water, giving thanks for the harvest and assuring future growth. The rice is dried or roasted, then jigged—what some people called "dancing the rice," a method of separating the kernel from the hull (not unlike what Italians traditionally did with wine grapes). In the final stage, the harvester tosses the rice, letting the wind take the lighter chaff, and then gracefully catches the kernels in a wide, flattish basket. The Indian people carried some rice into their winter camps; they also buried supplies of food in bark barrels where they, but neither their enemies nor the animals, could find it later.[9]

Anishinaabe people in Minnesota still harvest wild rice in traditional ways and places. Rice remains a part of many Native American rituals, and rice helps grandparents tell stories of the ancestors to teach children right relationships. The work of ricing itself shares some of those lessons: it requires cooperation among the workers and in the community, it makes use of canoes and baskets, and it values knowledge of the traditional ways and an ability to plan for the year ahead.

Anishinaabe people see themselves in a special and reciprocal relationship with wild rice. The people and the rice have grown with and because of each other. They have sustained each other much as corn, squash, and beans do. Their intertwining over the years tells the story of both the tradition and the transformation of the Anishinaabe people from their earlier lives farther east on the Great Lakes, to their Minnesota-based lives, to their lives now.[10]

Indian people also have long memories of tapping maple trees and of different ways of doing it: the Dakota used carved sticks to carry the sap into wooden bowls; the Anishinaabe caught the dripping sap in birch-bark pails. With their different tools, Indian peoples collected sap, boiled it until it thickened, and made it into syrup or maple cakes, carrying out a process that Red Lake artist Patrick DesJarlait painted in *Maple Sugar Time* in 1946. The clothing of his subjects was specific to the middle of the twentieth century and the style of the painting reminiscent of cubism; DesJarlait painted this picture from life, not memory. But one critic wrote, "The picture conveys the feeling of sugaring, not just its appearance." Whenever white and Indian Minnesotans tap maples and make syrup, we carry on a long-practiced Indian way; I replicate another when I bake acorn squash with maple syrup.[11]

We also carry on long-practiced Indian foodways when we eat corn, potatoes, tomatoes, avocados, peppers, beans, pecans, cashews, and sweet potatoes. Native Americans were smart, productive farmers. How they raised corn, beans, and squash provides a good example of their skill. When grown together, these three plants nourish and assist each other and increase each other's nutritional value. Planted together in mounded up soil that holds moisture, the beans and squash climb the corn and with their ground foliage keep the weeds down.

Native people's diets varied, of course; as their locations changed, so did their foods. When Dakota people lived around Mille Lacs and Leech Lake, they ate more wild rice and traded for some corn. When they moved toward and onto prairieland and the Mississippi and Minnesota river bottoms, they grew more of their own corn and ate less rice.

All farming people follow annual cycles of the seasons, of the moon, even of their religions. German farmers traditionally planted below-ground vegetables during the waning moon and above ground during the waxing moon. Catholic farmers in Stearns County planted potatoes on the feast of the Holy Martyrs (March 11) well into the twentieth century. In these and other practices, Indians and Europeans farmed in some similar ways.

How was it, then, that Euro-Americans set their sights on teaching the Indians to be "farmers"? To many Anglo-Americans, farming meant fields, rows, and plows tended to by men. The Dakota and the Anishinaabe farmed by thanking the spirits for abundance, returning some wild rice seeds to the water, setting fires to keep down vegetation, growing plants to tangle in each other, and assigning farmwork to women (and hunting to men). In that fertile jumble, newcomers did not recognize the Indians' agricultural accomplishments.[12]*

The Reverend Samuel Pond praised his Dakota neighbors in the

1830s for their handiwork. Many had a fine craftsman's eye, he reported, and many of their things looked as if they were "from a cabinet maker's shop." He marveled, too, at the yarn women spun from basswood or from nettle bark. But he was sharply critical that the women "did much that is not considered appropriate work for civilized women," that they planted "without any regular rows," and that they didn't use plows. Anthropologist Ray DeMallie has argued, "Dakota religion lacked a structure that Pond could understand." Apparently, Pond also lacked a capacity to see the structure in Dakota agriculture.[13]

We can certainly criticize those Euro-Americans for their failure of imagination, their inability to see what was in front of them, and the damage they did by insisting on their own kind of farming, their own kind of civilization and religion. But the historian's central task is understanding—forgiving is neither our work nor our right; we seek what it was about their own cultural and religious education that limited their capacity for valuing what was different from themselves.

European settlers certainly recognized the wonders of American tobacco, corn, peppers, squash, potatoes, and tomatoes. In a short time, Europeans everywhere took up smoking, and Italians made tomatoes as central to their cuisine as the Irish made potatoes to theirs. The food transfers from the Americas made possible the very European population boom that resulted in the settling of the American continents. For their part of what Alfred Crosby has dubbed the "Columbian Exchange," Europeans introduced horses, pigs, sheep, goats, black pepper, bananas, coffee, peaches, wheat, citrus, and smallpox to the West.[14]*

*

Tobacco was among the transfers from the Americas to the Old World, where smoking caught on, of course, without attendant ritual.

DOLL, CRADLEBOARD, ARMBANDS, AND AMULET

The handwork that Pond so praised might have included dolls, cradleboards, quilled armbands, and amulets in the shape of a turtle—all of which were common among Dakota people and examples of which are housed at the Minnesota Historical Society, the Minneapolis Institute of Arts, and the Science Museum of Minnesota as well as at the Beltrami Museum in Italy, at the Bernisches Historisches Museum in Berne, Switzerland, at the Náprstek Museum in Prague, and in private collections as well as county and local history museums. The Dakota and Ojibwe took to the creation of functional objects a "craftsman's eye," as Pond called it, and an "artist's eye," as collectors certainly called it later. The Indian creators of these objects may well have considered it simply what they did. No line divided craft from art; none divided useful from beautiful, either. The Indian creators cared about how these objects looked and transformed them by using materials at hand.

The doll was made of reeds, transformed by twists and turns and bark strips into human shape, and decorated with bark pieces that look like feathers. The cradleboard allowed a mother to carry her baby from place to place or to stand it up against a tree or rock when not on the move, giving baby a ledge to stand on, a band to protect its head, and a view of the world. Leather thongs (with nail and wire added later) hold the cradleboard together. The rounded corners and smooth wood prevented slivers and kept the board from sticking into the mother's back; the gentle scallops across the top served an aesthetic purpose. The armbands are entirely for show—the rawhide strings decorated with yellow, red, and purple porcupine quills, dyed feathers, and twisted metal to encircle a man's upper arms, certainly to emphasize his muscles.

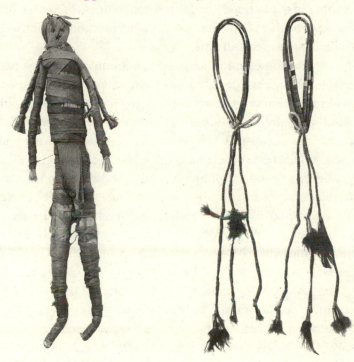

The small, turtle-shaped bag held a bit of a Dakota baby's umbilical cord. Ella Deloria talked about just such a bag in her book *Waterlily*, about a Dakota girl:

> She handed Waterlily her wooden playthings, the ring "teeth maker" and the little turtle with its entire back worked in colors to simulate the design on a real turtle. In a peculiar sense this was Waterlily's very own turtle, for was she herself not inside of it? Somewhere in the stuffing of down was the bit of withered navel that fell from her shortly after her birth. When she was old enough to wear an elaborately decorated gown, this turtle would be attached to the center back of her belt both as an ornament and as a talisman ensuring long life to her. Until then it was a toy.[15]

Indian people's objects, like their lives, preserve some traditional ways and incorporate new ones as it suits them. Their makers worked and reworked patterns that they knew and new ones that they imagined. The amulet—a traditional object—is decorated in a traditional style with dyed quills but bordered with beads that French fur traders introduced as late as the latter half of the eighteenth century. The beads and quills appear to belong together, so effectively have they been assembled. Both Dakota and Anishinaabe people incorporated beads rapidly and beautifully.[16]*

Louis Hennepin, while in Indian "custody," believed he was protected in order that other Europeans would come and bring goods.

When Indians were under pressure that threatened their very survival, they adjusted again. They transformed the objects of their everyday lives into gifts, into trade goods, into souvenirs for tourists. In this and other ways Native people have used their traditional skills to help their people survive then and now.[17]

We know that these and other objects belonged to Native people in Minnesota, though we don't know exactly how they passed out of Indian possession. Some were sold, others given as gifts, others appropriated, and some stolen. Many pieces live in private and public collections, some of them on display. Whites and Indians have different notions of what is appropriate to collect and display. Nineteenth- and twentieth-century collectors found Egyptian mummies, Indian remains, and the Elgin Marbles equally fascinating and fit subjects for study, perfectly legitimate to take and display. The Indians' or Greeks' objections to such practices held little sway for more than a century. The Greeks still have not persuaded the British Museum to return the marbles, but the Native American Graves Protection and Repatriation Act (NAGPRA), passed by the U.S. Congress in 1990, mandated and established processes for the return to native people of their "cultural items," defined by the legislation to include human remains, funerary or sacred objects, and "cultural patrimony." This legislation has resulted in the return to the tribes of some of their lost heritage and provoked conflicts between scientists who want to study human remains and Native Americans who want to bury them in protected (and secret) places. What should be displayed and how remain sources of differences and points of contention, some of it cultural.[18]

MINNESOTA WOMAN AND BROWN'S VALLEY MAN

"Minnesota Woman" wore a conch-shell necklace and a dagger made of elk horn. She died from drowning in glacial Lake Pelican, probably 10,000 years ago. Was she fishing? Floating on a raft? Daydreaming?

Physical evidence and native stories agree that people have lived in the upper Mississippi river basin for thousands of years. In 1931, a road-building crew in Otter Tail County unearthed the remains of a body that has come to be called "Minnesota Woman." In 1933, a man in western Minnesota digging gravel for his driveway unearthed another body, now called Brown's Valley Man. University of Minnesota archaeologist Albert Jenks dated those remains to about 8,000 years ago and identified the man as Paleo-Indian—a term meaning ancient, usually identified with the end of the last ice age (Clovis is another term for the period). Many scholars have hypothesized that Paleo-Indians came to the Americas from Asia across the Bering Strait. Indian stories and increasing archaeological evidence establish indigenous people here earlier; perhaps they even originated here.

Where Minnesota Woman or Brown's Valley Man came from originally—or whether they were fully native to this place—is subject to disagreement even among archaeologists. Both sets of remains, however, have been radio-carbon dated to about 8,000–10,000 BP (before present). The two tell various stories (different ones, no doubt, to Euro-American and Native American observers). One is about the existence of trade networks among native people. The shells buried with the woman could not have come from nearer than a thousand miles. She might have walked to the Gulf of Mexico and walked back with a cache of shells. More likely she traded with someone who had traded with another and another until the shells from afar found their way into her hands.

PLATFORM, BURIAL, AND EFFIGY MOUNDS

Mississippian people—descendants of Minnesota Woman and Brown's Valley Man and the ancestors of contemporary Indian peoples—built thousands of mounds, many along the Mississippi and Minnesota rivers, stretching from St. Louis to Winnipeg at least. The most elaborate were created in AD 900–1200 at Cahokia, in what is now Illinois. Unlike the Paleo-Indians, the Mississippians lived a more settled and permanent life, as indicated by the mounds and by their development of pottery. Cahokia, at its largest, was home to more than 15,000 people. Builders fashioned more than 120 mounds; the largest, Monks Mound, "covers 14 acres, rises 100 feet, and was topped by a massive 5,000 square-foot building another 50 feet high." Its construction required, by one estimate, the moving of 14 million baskets full of earth. The people also built what seem to have been markers for solar and lunar calendars (archaeologists have dubbed them "woodhenge") and two-mile-long fortresslike walls.[19]

On those flatlands near the Mississippi River, Cahokians built mounds that served as platforms for living quarters and governance; the height of any particular mound relative to others probably denoted status.

Cahokian farmers were knowledgeable enough and the land fertile enough to support a city population from what could be hunted, fished, and gathered, but, more importantly, from what could be grown. The sufficient production of food by some allowed others to become religious or civic leaders, artisans or astronomers. The population density allowed or provoked the development of a hierarchy large enough to manage the city, its suburbs, its defense, and a workforce willing to provide for the whole group.

Like Minnesota Woman, Cahokians took part in a complex trade network that brought them shells, copper, obsidian, and mica from hundreds of miles away. Their contribution to the network may well have been corn, of which some 700 species were grown by the time Europeans entered the middle of the continent in the seventeenth century. The trade reached even farther than that of Minnesota Woman, including turquoise from the Southwest and feathers from Mexico. Native people knew about other native people, interacted and traded with them, and sometimes fought with them.[20]

Sometime after 1300 the Cahokia site began to decline, and by 1400 it was abandoned for reasons still unexplained, though some attribute it to a Little Ice Age that made productive farming less so, as well as to failures of leadership and infighting. Today, the remnants of about eighty mounds (mostly platforms) remain. All of them are covered by grass and designated a World Heritage Site, under the protection of the National Parks Service and the Illinois Historic Preservation Agency. Lewis and Clark passed by them on the east bank of the Missouri River in 1805. With their attention keenly attuned to the wonders of the trans-Mississippi West, they missed the site of what once was the largest concentration of population north of the Mayans and Incas and of buildings north of the Rio Grande.

Mississippian era (AD 1000–1700) people built mounds near present-day Prairie du Chien (Wisconsin), Red Wing, St. Paul, and Mounds Park, nearly a hundred near Bloomington alone. More than ten thousand mounds have been located in Minnesota, and others certainly have been destroyed or remain hidden from common view. Many of them are located along bluffs, often on the east side of the river, and at other locations affording spectacular views. The Indian builders intended some of these mounds for burials, others for purposes still kept to themselves.

Many of the mounds are simple, roundish hillocks; others take the shape of animals and other figures. Snake shapes are easy to recognize from ground level, but the other effigies become evident from a vantage that the native people could have achieved only through imagination. Effigy Mounds National Monument, across the Mississippi River from

Prairie du Chien, includes nearly 120 mounds of various shapes and sizes. One, a bear, is the length of twenty six-foot people lying in a straight row toe to head; other mounds are half that size. One of the original seven clans of the Ojibwe was the bear clan, whose work includes watching for danger. Like the mounds at Cahokia, many of these effigies do not contain burials. Numerous people nonetheless consider them sacred space, where the connections among human, natural, and spirit world have been made manifest.[21]

Pilot Knob, across from Fort Snelling and the Minneapolis/St. Paul airport and next to Mendota, has been the object of conflict between developers on the one side, who imagine lovely condominiums on that hill, and preservationists on the other, who argue that Pilot Knob, like other burial places, was and remains a sacred site. The burials, they argue, have consecrated the ground; further, the tribes' use of the area for powwows and other ceremonies—including the signing of the Mendota Treaty of 1851—gives it historical significance.[22]

ARROWHEADS AND PIPESTONE

Talking about Indians as one group can also prevent us from taking account of the warfare that existed among various groups of native people. The Dakota and the Ojibwe may well have had a different notion of land ownership from that held by Euro-Americans, but each group had a sense of "our" land that led them to fight for and defend what they considered their own territory or the territory they wanted.[23]

A pair of mounds near Winnibigoshish tells the story of Indian rivalry and warfare. Around 1748 the Dakota and Ojibwe contested for ownership of land near Cut Lake. Dakota victors built a turtle-shaped mound to commemorate their triumph. The Anishinaabe, to note a later victory, encircled the turtle mound with a snake-shaped mound of their own.

Arrowheads in the hundreds of thousands and spearheads in the hundreds have turned up in archaeological excavations, farm fields, backyards, and boys' collections in Minnesota. Spears, in the hands of a skilled hunter, proved to be deadly weapons, especially when flung with the atlatl that spurred the spear's reach, speed, and force. A bow and good arrow did the job of a spear as effectively and from an even greater distance, thus adding stealth to the repertoire of Indian hunting skills.

Arrowheads ranged from small enough to kill a pigeon or a rabbit to substantial enough to penetrate buffalo hide or human skin. The points themselves tell about changes in the technology and culture of their makers. Minnesota archaeologist Daniel Higginbottom described thirty-seven different styles of stone points used over time by the peoples around the Upper Mississippi River. The thirty-eighth point was made not of stone but of pieces of trade goods. Until the repeating rifle was perfected, a skilled bowman could compete with a man armed with a gun. This skill served the bowman well in hunting and warfare. Guns, obtained from whites, added to the deadliness of the Indians' encounters, as did competition for white goods.[24]*

Indian people also had methods for negotiating peace with each other and pipes to smoke in ratification of peace agreements. Both oral traditions and archaeological finds indicate that native people have for more than a thousand years used pipes, often from stone quarried near present-day Pipestone, Minnesota. Petroglyphs—pictures etched in stone—there and at nearby Jeffers mark sacred territory from which members of many tribes gathered the stone they call the blood of their ancestors. It is also called pipestone or *Catlinite,* after artist George Catlin, who visited and painted pictures of the quarries and their Coteau des Prairies surroundings in 1835. As now codified in federal law, the right to quarry the stone is restricted to native peoples.

Indian people commonly used pipes, and among both the Dakota and the Anishinaabe the pipe marked important communal ceremonies as well as others with friends and enemies. Collectors have long recognized the beauty, carving skill, and significance of the pipe; many pipes, too, have ended up in historical collections. Although they do not generally fall under the provisions of NAGPRA, their display is considered sacrilegious by some and at least inappropriate by other Native Americans. Various objects, not in either category, remain in museum collections. In 1992 the Minneapolis Institute of Arts mounted an exhibit on Plains Indian life and planned to include several pipestone pipes from its collections. Similarly, the Minnesota Historical Society included "P for Pipestone" in its plan for *Minnesota A to Z,* an exhibit scheduled to open its new building and gallery space in 1992. In both cases, the idea was to honor native people by including these objects; in both cases, the institutions ultimately decided not to display the pipestone in response to objections from some in the American Indian community.

BARK LODGES AND HIDE TIPIS

Like native people across the two continents, the Dakota and the Anishinaabe proved adept at working with their environments to create living spaces that served their needs. In what we might call permanent camps (rarely permanent for long because of the tides of animals, but permanent enough to have known burial sites), the Dakota lived in large and square birch-bark lodges, set in close relationship with other

*
Estimated number of Americans who make fake Indian arrowheads: 5,000; Number of arrowheads they produce each year: 1,500,000.

similar lodges and a tipi or two. Anishinaabe women, too, built oval and smaller birch-bark lodges, bending long poles to make domed roofs. Both Dakota and Anishinaabe women knew to insulate against the cold by placing rolled-up rush mats in the walls; they pulled out the mats to let in summer breezes. Anishinaabe villages were often smaller than Dakota ones, as their bands and tribes were smaller.[25]

When they traveled, both Dakota and Anishinaabe people lived in tipis made of hides—the Dakota style was to sew them together; the Anishinaabe, to lay them over the poles. Dakota women decorated their tipis with paints and dyes, replicating their personal symbols. Portable and manageable, these lodgings suited their winter travel in following the herds; the tipis provided the warmth and comfort to tell stories and to ornament clothing, pouches, bags, and armbands with quills. The Europeans envied this comfort in comparing it to the chill of their own dwellings.

Native people always lived in clusters and played and worked in community. They hunted and prepared food together, worked with each other to construct their lodges and raise their children. The necessity of cooperation supported the culture of kinship and generosity that most Native Americans name as the central value of Indian life.

The British Library some years ago displayed two spectacular illuminated manuscripts, one from an Anglo-Saxon monastery and one from a Celtic monastery, both dating from the thirteenth century. A repeating, regular, and predictable pattern characterized the Anglo-Saxon illumination; spirals and circles in a spontaneous and free style, the Celtic illumination. Each demonstrated and reflected a different aesthetic and underlying worldview. What one illuminator might call order, the other could call rigid; what the one might call spontaneous, the other could label unruly. No wonder, I thought as I studied these two beautiful works, the English and the Irish warred for so long and with such catastrophic effect.

A life of circles and cycles made no sense to people of the straight line and forward movement. Jean Nicolet, a French explorer, made it as far west as Lake Michigan in 1634–35. Between 1654 and 1660, Pierre Radisson and Médard Chouart, sieur des Groseilliers, may have reached the Mississippi River, but they certainly saw and spent time on the west side of Lake Superior, then returned to Montreal and were arrested for illegal trading. Fathers Claude Allouez, Jacques Marquette, and Louis Hennepin traded in souls—not illegally but ineffectively—in the 1680s. Daniel Greysolon, sieur du Luth, and Robert Cavelier, sieur de La Salle, in the 1670s and 1690s planted their French flags and pinned their hopes on the new places they saw. Pierre Gaultier de Varennes, sieur de la Vérendrye, went to Lake Winnipeg and then to the Missouri River in the 1730s. These and other explorers and missionaries followed straight-line plans if not routes. They were looking for a passage from the Atlantic to the Pacific, for adventure, for fame and fortune, too.

The landscape and the Indian people they met forced these French-men out of their straight lines. They needed Indian guides to find their way, so they had to learn Indian languages. They had to (or had the good fortune to) travel by canoe. They ate the food that the country and the Indians provided. Father Hennepin reported wearing "shoes made after the Indian way." Europeans might attach their names to the land-scape and pretend to claim it for the mother country or the mother church, but they were the ones who had to adjust. Fur traders, too, had to bend themselves into a new shape to live with the Indian people. They could make money and control the trade only by using the means and processes determined by their native hosts. To carry on their trade they had to make themselves into kin and learn to negotiate in a world of re-ciprocal relations. Many more traders and missionaries learned to speak Indian languages than Indians learned French or English. And traders dressed more like Indians than Indians dressed like whites.[26]

The British, too, had an interest in the upper Great Lakes. Long in competition with the French (and Spanish), they had to learn French, the language of the fur trade, in order to make inroads. The trade prom-ised gains to both whites and Indians. Beads, copper kettles, blankets, guns, and alcohol proved desirable to many Indian people. Gaining con-trol of the fur trade, saving souls, and taking over the land proved desir-able to Euro-Americans. They had reason initially to cooperate with each other and eventually to oppose each other. When in the minority, the outsiders had to adjust. As their number increased, the outsiders seemed to forget their previous accommodations and they straightened again. No longer needing to get along, they sought to convert and trans-form the native people into versions of themselves—or at least propo-nents of a different set of values and way of living than they had before. By the 1850s, separation seemed the only answer.[27]*

Even by then, however, there were not two cultures but many. Dakota and Anishinaabe, Cree and Ho-Chunk people had some things in common. So did French and English and American. Yet people and lives are complex; they don't fit neatly into categories and boxes. Some fur traders became more Indian than white, some Indians saw some-thing in Christianity, some couples made relationships and children across cultural divides. Some just wanted people to get along; others wanted to fight to the death.

*

Some Indians had already been separating themselves from whites and moving west to avoid or escape contact. The League of Women Voters offers population figures of around 10,000 Dakota people in 1805 and 6,300 by 1846. Some of this de-cline in population is cer-tainly due to smallpox and other diseases that raged through Indian villages; some—like the Yankton and Yanktonai—decreased from 4,300 to 1,800, probably due to migration.

That the clash of cultures and the exercise of power caused desperate pain and loss is undeniable, but that Indian people and ways vanished is false. Testimony to the integrity and significance of Indian ways is their very survival despite disease, dispossession, and concerted attempts at eradication. The round of Native life continues. Sons and daughters who live away go home to remember and to practice the life in which people find meaning, their past, and their future in tapping the trees, drumming at powwows, and dancing the rice.

3

Campbell Country

FROM 1820 TO 1845, Scott and Margaret Campbell lived at the center of a regionally bounded world, anchored in and around Fort Snelling, at the confluence of the Mississippi and Minnesota (called St. Pierre's in the Campbells' time) rivers in what is now—but never was in their time—called Minnesota.[1]

Scott Campbell was born in about 1790 at Prairie du Chien. In the late eighteenth and early nineteenth centuries, virtually everyone with a stake in the western Great Lakes fur trade passed through or rendezvoused in this village. The Campbell family had something to do with most of them. His father, Archibald John (AJ) Campbell, was a Scottish-born, French-speaking trader who settled in Prairie du Chien without his first, Scottish-Irish wife but with two of his grown-up sons. By the late 1770s he married a Dakota woman named Ninse. They were two of the hundreds of European men and Native American women whose marriages forged kin—and trade—connections between the two groups.[2]

Indians had furs that Europeans wanted and Europeans offered in exchange numerous goods that Indians wanted: guns and alcohol, but in larger quantities blankets, kettles, beads, needles, bolts of cloth, silk handkerchiefs, steel awls, thread. It was a real trade—each had something the other wanted.

The kin connections formed the fur trade's basic organizing principle. A trader did not deal with a whole people, or even with a tribe, and only sometimes with a whole band, but his access to furs and his success in the trade depended on his ability to woo the influential members of a village. When it was to their advantage, native people wooed the traders, too, to gain primary access to the traders' goods and to control their flow and their benefits. A contract of marriage between a trader and a village woman signaled both the trader's and the village's acceptance and acknowledgment of the relationship. Likely following patterns that had been developing for several decades already, AJ Campbell probably paid a bride price and smoked a pipe with Ninse's father to seal the arrangements.[3]

Ninse no doubt consented to the marriage out of filial and community duty. It was also the case that native women who married European men often found their lives materially improved by the direct access to goods their marriages afforded them and their families. According to one scholar, such marriages meant that the wives "sacrificed considerable personal autonomy, being forced to adjust to the traders' patriarchal views on the ordering of home and family."[4]

The European-Native marriages were not only business arrangements, however. AJ and Ninse produced five children: Duncan, Scott, Colin, Nancy, and Margaret. Like hundreds of other mixed-blood offspring, these five partook of both cultures and belonged exclusively to neither.[5]

Scott knew the world of his father. He spoke English. He could read and write. He learned how to recognize and value a good pelt, how to drink, how to keep books. He knew, too, the French of the fur trade and, as the son of a trader, he was made useful in that trade.[*] He also knew his mother's world. He learned the words and ways of her people. He spoke Dakota as the native he was. He knew about the hunt—for goods and for food—about the ways of talking and doing among his mother's and—by relation—his people. He was called "half-breed" in his day.[6]

Life near Prairie du Chien revolved around the fur trade, but the local story took place in an international context in which France, Great Britain, and the United States vied for control of the western Great Lakes. The turmoil of the French and Indian War, the American Revolution, the Louisiana Purchase, and the War of 1812 all reverberated through the Great Lakes territory. Following the Louisiana Purchase, Thomas Jefferson sent Zebulon Pike and a band of U.S. Army men up the Mississippi River—beyond Prairie du Chien—to locate a site for an army post.

Pike agreed with Little Crow's Mdewakanton Dakota band at Kaposia—near present-day St. Paul—to buy a piece of land at the meeting point of the Mississippi River and what we now call the Minnesota River. Nothing happened—neither payment nor possession—until the conclusion of the War of 1812 jump-started the U.S. plan to construct a line of forts on the western frontier. The United States wanted a clear demarcation between American and European territory and sought to detach native people from the European, especially British, loyalties they had developed. In 1817, Stephen A. Long and a small party of army men returned and surveyed the site that Pike had located. Then, in 1819, Colonel Henry Leavenworth and his battery of army officers with their white wives and children and his enlisted men—without wives and

*

Samuel Pond reported that Campbell had been taken up by Meriwether Lewis during the Lewis and Clark expedition in 1804. Lewis, so the story goes, sent Campbell to school, probably in St. Louis, where he stayed until 1809, when Lewis died. It's possible but unlikely since the expedition passed so far west of the Mississippi River, nearer to the Missouri River—among Dakota certainly, but not his mother's Dakota band. If this had been the case, however, it would account for Scott's formal and schooled penmanship in the school-less world of Prairie du Chien at the turn of the nineteenth century.

children—arrived to build and occupy a fort. Originally called Fort St. Anthony, it was renamed Fort Snelling in 1824, after Josiah Snelling, its second commanding officer. Fort Snelling and its surroundings became what Prairie du Chien had been—the entry point into the lands upriver and west, the meeting and passing place of hundreds of people, with the trading post across the river at Mendota.[7]*

The fort and its surroundings attracted traders, squatters, liquor sellers, suppliers, missionaries, and dreamers. Scott Campbell, too. In 1819 he left Prairie du Chien and took a job with Major Lawrence Taliaferro, the newly appointed U.S. Indian agent assigned to the St. Peter's Agency. He served as the Indian agent's interpreter from 1819 to the mid-1840s.[8]

In the early 1820s, Scott Campbell married Margaret Menagre—not, as her name suggests, a Scottish-French woman, but the mixed-blood daughter of a Menominee mother and the French-Ojibwe trader Louis Menagre. They had ten children over the course of their thirty-year marriage.[9]

During those years, Scott and Margaret stood at the center of a world that included fur traders; native people; soldiers, their families, and various agents and personnel of the U.S. government at and around the fort; missionaries of several denominations; and various hangers-on, squatters, bootleggers, ne'er-do-wells, speculators, and illegal settlers. Margaret and Scott Campbell knew most of them and either participated in or observed most of the significant historical events that transpired in that place for over forty years. They witnessed the transformation of the fur trade, of native life, and of Euro-American life in the West. They lived and worked at the center of the overlapping and intersecting worlds of Indians, whites, mixed-blood people, old-timers, and newcomers that grew up around the fort.[10]

No doubt Scott had his closest dealings with Major Taliaferro, the first U.S. Indian agent for this region, who had arrived with the army people in 1819. He had an honorific military title (*major* being what Indian agents were often titled) but was a veteran of the War of 1812. His was a civilian position—a distinction that might have been lost on some observers but that was important to Taliaferro, whose agency was located slightly away from the fort, demonstrating both the independence of the two government presences and something of their conflict. Taliaferro's assignment included establishing an American government presence in the Northwest. The lingering loyalty of various native people to the British made the U.S. government see the necessity for a vital presence and for realigning those loyalties. Taliaferro's political connections and military experience—not any special talent for Indian relations—got him his appointment. His overriding charge was to keep the peace.[11]

Taliaferro had been raised in Virginia, and when he showed up in

1819 he knew English, perhaps a bit of French, but none of the native languages, a lack (mixed in with a little bit of hubris, nonetheless) he felt and even commented on. "If the Great Spirit had gifted me with your language," he said to a group of Ojibwe, "and that of the Sioux, no tears would be shed again in either nation." He knew even less about the people with whom he would be working. He was twenty-five years old when he arrived. He needed help. A language interpreter for sure, but an interpreter of cultures even more so. Who were these people among whom he would spend the next two decades of his life? He didn't know, but Scott Campbell did.[12]*

Taliaferro's responsibilities, as he saw them, included protecting Indians from each other, Dakota and Ojibwe, in particular, but others, too, who seemed ready to take after each other, to hunt in other's territories, to kill each other from time to time. In 1821 he lectured a group of Ojibwe: "I do not say you must be at peace but my advice to you is that the bloody war club be buried that both Nations may enjoy the same fire side." He used trade goods and other presents when he thought it would encourage peacekeeping. "My interpreter[,] being well versed in both Languages," Taliaferro reported, participated in most of these interactions. Campbell also served as Taliaferro's roving representative, to investigate some complaint or another or to carry messages, even to try to resolve some of the conflicts himself when possible.[13]

Campbell helped Taliaferro establish the agency's credibility with Campbell's relations. Drawing on the importance of kin ties to the native people, they could deal with their kin—Campbell—and through him with Taliaferro, a fact Taliaferro recognized. In 1838 he reported that for nearly two decades Campbell had been instrumental "in sustaining the credit of the government in the estimation of the Sioux."[14]

Taliaferro also wanted to protect the Indians from the traders—especially from their alcohol and firearms. He complained that proximity to whites was the most unsettling factor in Indian life and that most native troubles (except their ways between themselves) could be traced to whiskey. "But for the whites," Taliaferro remarked, "the Indians would do very well." The traders didn't like Taliaferro much better. An early biographer of one of the traders described the Indian agent as "splenetic, conceited, [and] opinionated" and charged that he "managed to keep up a standing quarrel with every trader."[15]

Campbell also helped Taliaferro get along with his Indian charges—by translating not what Taliaferro did say but what he should have said and by interpreting the Indians to Taliaferro. Because Taliaferro never became adept at the native languages or at understanding the differences among his charges, he probably never realized the liberties that Campbell took—or the troubles that Campbell saved him.[16]

*

Taliaferro did, in the course of his two decades in Indian country, learn some valuable lessons: "I warn all those who may come after me at this agency or elsewhere in connection with Indians to do all they can for those unfortunate and helpless people [that's not the wise part, this next part is] . . . but for the love of peace & honor *never promise—never promise* nay I say never promise an Indian—unless you are morally certain to perform in 10, or 20 minutes—put off not a day." Would that his advice been heeded.

Three generations of Mde-
wakanton Dakota men were
called by the name of Little
Crow. The third, also called
Ta-o-ya-te-du-ta, served as
the Dakota leader in the
1862 Dakota War. All three
generations (and earlier
ones of Dakota) lived in the
village of Kaposia, just
downriver from current-day
St. Paul.

†

The 1825 treaty brokered by
the U.S. government established boundary lines
between the Dakota and the
Ojibwe (in addition to other
territorial lines).

‡

Mary Riggs noted in the
1830s that military officers
usually had two or more
wives. She had heard of only
two officers who did not have
"an Indian woman, if not
half-Indian children."

§

Missionary Samuel Pond reported that Campbell was
the "general medium of
communication between
the Indians and all officers
and privates at the fort who
wished to converse with
them."

Campbell knew and understood the complexities and his place among them. Related through his mother to Little Crow's band at Kaposia and to the Menominee, he had skills and connections on which to draw.* That Taliaferro was, even his enemies admitted, both honest and incorruptible was due no doubt to his own temperament and inner life, but it's tempting to suggest that Campbell was perhaps a good teacher, too. Taliaferro so often used Campbell as his eyes and ears that Campbell must have also taught Taliaferro to see and hear better what he had little other training to understand.[17]

In 1825, in what white officials billed as an attempt to quiet Indian conflict but was more significantly an effort to lay the groundwork for the eventual transfer of land into U.S. hands, the government, through Taliaferro, convened treaty negotiations among several native groups. Campbell probably understood more about the proceedings than did virtually anyone else present. The provisions of the Treaty of the Sioux of 1825 (or the Treaty of Prairie du Chien) identified specific tribal areas for living and for hunting. Well over one hundred men from the Dakota, Winnebago, Chippewa, Ottawa, Pottawatomi, Sac, Fox, and Ioway signed this agreement. The witnesses included both Lawrence Taliaferro and S. Campbell, interpreter.[18]†

Scott and Margaret Campbell knew Taliaferro's Indian wife and daughter. They had a daughter of about the same age. Then they knew the white wife Taliaferro brought to the agency from Pennsylvania in 1828.‡ When Taliaferro finished his tour of duty at Fort Snelling in 1839 and returned to Pennsylvania, he left his daughter with a family of missionaries; although he may have provided money for her education, he had no further contact with her.[19]

The Campbells knew the military people at the fort as well, including Lieutenant Colonel Leavenworth and the other army people—and their families—who built and then staffed the fort. They knew Josiah and Mrs. Snelling, Lieutenant and Mrs. Bliss. They knew Joseph R. Brown, the one-time drummer boy who arrived at the fort when he was fifteen and who became such an important trader, town builder, and organizer. Scott spent many an evening with army men, playing cards and teaching them enough Dakota to get along (perhaps enough for them to engage with the Dakota women). Lieutenant Ogden and several of the men with Campbell made up a rudimentary dictionary.[20]§

Scott and Margaret Campbell also knew the slaves who had been brought to the fort by various army officers. When Taliaferro's father died, he bequeathed his slaves to his son. Taliaferro had no interest in returning to Virginia to take up his father's plantation life, so he had the slaves brought to him at Fort Snelling. He made various uses of them, hiring them out as servants to other officers and putting them to work around the agency. One of his slaves, Harriet Robinson, asked permission to marry one of Dr. Emerson's slaves, a man named Dred Scott. Taliaferro consented and—in contrast to the usual practice of white denial of slave marriage bonds—performed the wedding ceremony himself.[21]*

A new era in Campbell country began with the arrival of Stephen and Mary Riggs and Henry Sibley. In 1834, the Riggses, white Presbyterian missionaries, showed up at the fort. Like the Pond Brothers, Gideon and Samuel, who had founded a school on Lake Calhoun in the early 1830s, the Riggses wanted to educate the natives in the ways of God and of New England civilization. Although Stephen Riggs proposed to make his family "a garden enclosed" and forbade his children (unsuccessfully!) from learning Dakota, the Riggses and Ponds knew they needed to know the language so they could translate the scriptures and seek converts among the Dakota people. Campbell's not entirely dependable dictionary for the soldiers provided their early language lessons.[22]

The Riggses' aversion to their children learning Dakota stood in stark contrast to the Campbells' practice of learning as many languages as they could. Scott and Margaret Campbell had both grown up amid a babble of languages. All of their children spoke English and Dakota and French; some could speak Ojibwe as well as select words in a variety of other Indian languages. Other children who grew up around the fort also learned the local languages. Charlotte Ouisconsin Van Cleve, born in 1819 into an army family, reported that in her years at the fort (1819–27) she and her brother Malcolm spoke in Dakota, which was "as familiar to us as our mother tongue." The Riggs children defied their parents—in secret—and soon understood and spoke Dakota, but a new era had dawned nonetheless. Increasingly, the language of the fort and its environs would be the English of the army and settlers (rather than the French of the trade) and the life Euro-American.†

Henry Hastings Sibley played a major role in this transformation. He showed up at Fort Snelling in 1834 and declared the area a "terra incognita," a land unknown. What possessed Sibley to utter such a statement, when so clearly the land was known by so many for so long before he arrived, is not entirely possible to imagine, but then Sibley was a puzzling man. This twenty-four-year-old trader for the American Fur Company was raised in Detroit, spoke French, had ambitions, and became on his arrival at the fort a force to be reckoned with. He made sure that everyone knew him and noticed him. In 1835 he built a big limestone building that doubled as a trading house and his home. He might as well

*

Dred Scott was at Fort Snelling from 1836 to 1838. Based on his living there—in free territory—he brought his unsuccessful suit for his freedom in the *Dred Scott v. Sanford* case which so rocked the United States when the Supreme Court denied Scott's right even to bring a suit in its 1856 ruling.

†

In his reminiscences of his time as commanding officer at Fort Snelling, Colonel John Bliss noted that the only English speakers around were Selkirkers—immigrants from the Red River Selkirk settlement who squatted around the fort—and the army people connected to the fort. "I do not remember a single Indian, man or woman, who made the slightest attempt at learning our language, so we all picked up more or less of theirs."

have unfurled a banner—metaphorically, he did—announcing: "I'm here. Take note. Nothing will be the same." And it wasn't.[24]

The Hudson's Bay, North West, and Columbia fur trade companies, as well as dozens of independent or maverick traders, had stalked the woods from the 1730s to the 1830s. They competed fiercely—sometimes *fierce* proved too kindly a description of their dealings. The fur trade had gotten progressively more competitive as the number of traders increased, as the trade itself declined, and as the business organization of the traders professionalized. The number and quality of furs diminished dramatically by the 1830s, so that muskrat pelts were more plentiful and more often traded than beaver pelts. Inflation hit the fur market; so did the silk hat, replacing the once wildly popular beaver skin hat. These events did much to transform all of life around the Great Lakes.

Sibley arrived just in time to oversee the beginning of the end of the fur trade. He was a new breed of trader. Yes, making kin connections with the Indians was still important: he married an Indian wife and had an Indian daughter and even gained an Indian name, Wapeton houska (the Long Trader). But being a American Fur Company trader, he was also a businessman. He built that big "respectable" house, and when it was time he brought a "respectable" white wife to join him. He may have had a keen eye and much affection for the Dakota people he lived among, but in the later part of his life he remembered it as a "vast area over which roamed numerous bands of untamed savages, who claimed exclusive ownership, and which was the abode of beasts scarcely more fierce and dangerous than themselves." Was this the same place where Scott and Margaret Campbell and their children lived? It doesn't sound like it.[25]

In 1835, too, a new treaty was in the works. The 1825 Treaty of Prairie du Chien divided territory among Indians. Two treaties were negotiated and signed in 1837: one with the Mdewakanton for claims west of the Mississippi and south of the 1825 treaty line, the second with the Ojibwe for their claims east of the Mississippi and north of the 1825 treaty line. These two 1837 treaties set Indian removal into law and started the string of bad dealings that have characterized and poisoned Indian-white relations for the years since. As he had in 1825, Scott Campbell witnessed and interpreted at the 1837 treaty.

Taliaferro's era gave way to Sibley's, and with that the beginning of the end of Campbell's life as an interpreter. Taliaferro left Fort Snelling in despair and disgust, as well as with a clear idea that he had ultimately failed in his efforts to keep the traders' power in check. Campbell stayed on with Taliaferro's successor, Amos J. Bruce, for a time, but theirs was a much rockier relationship. By the end of Taliaferro's term Campbell was already drinking, and in 1843 Bruce dismissed Campbell.[26]

From 1819 to 1837, Scott and Margaret Campbell could be both Indian and white; they could have allegiances and loyalties to all their relations. They were part of a vibrant and tumultuous life that included good people, corrupt people, scoundrels, fair traders, and cheats; some of each were white, some Indian, some mixed bloods. For about twenty years Margaret and Scott Campbell could live in the middle of it all and be part of it all, too.

Scott died in 1850 in St. Paul. Margaret lived for another fifty years. She grew old in a country much changed from the one into which she had been born. In this new country she—and her children—would not be at the center but would have to choose sides—indeed, choose their race. But that's the story of another, later chapter.

4

Playing with the Future

PROLOGUE: Why a play? The name *Minnesota* conjured up multiple images in the 1840s and 1850s. To many Native Americans the name marked their elimination from the places they knew and the lives they lived. It tolled a death knell, too, for the traders, hunters, and voyageurs who could not reinvent themselves and for the tavern keepers, missionaries, and traders who made a living with the Indians. To Henry Sibley and Franklin Steele, *Minnesota* inspired a surge of anticipation and ambition (and for Sibley, perhaps, some twinge of regret). To John and Ann North, Harriet and Ard Godfrey, Sarah Sibley and Anna Ramsey, it brought visions of an ordered, clean, safe place to plant their families and their promised lands. But the future was not clearly laid out, the narrative not yet determined.

Minnesota did not exist in 1848. Between 1849 and 1858 it developed boundaries, a government structure, a constitution, a set of laws, elected officials. The people who lived in the territory—and even in the new state—had only a place in common. They played out their individual dramas on a common stage with serious—and unknown—consequences for the other actors. Yet they paid little attention to each other.

The dramas do not form a single narrative: there's not a single baton to hand off, but several. The future of the actors is unclear. The relationships among them are uncertain. In 1848 Minnesota did not exist, but by 1858 it did. The territory and then the state were legal constructs imposed on the land. The Minnesota that Congress recognized on March 3, 1849, was an aspiration, an idea. Minnesota was not discovered: it was made by many hands.

Henry H. Sibley
fur trader, speculator, entrepreneur, territorial delegate to Congress, first state governor, leader of white forces in the Dakota War, president of the Minnesota Historical Society (wrote under the pen name of Hal, a Dakotah)

ACT I

The curtain rises on Henry Sibley, Franklin Steele, and Joseph R. Brown walking up the outdoor staircase into Sibley's office on the second floor of his house in Mendota. Steele wears boots; Sibley and Brown, moccasins. All wear button trousers, hide coats, fur hats. They're oblivious to the dogs and men going in and out of the office. One table holds pelts and hides; another, papers and ledgers. There are bookshelves and a fireplace with a fire. The year is 1848.

Like the office, the stage is busy with activity: in the background a steamboat unloads passengers, mailbags, crates, and barrels; the women, men, and children wear all combinations of Indian and white clothing. Even the most traditionally dressed Indian wears clothing decorated with as many French and Italian beads as quill. Even the most traditionally dressed Yankee sports a bit of fur or hide. The clothing styles melt toward each other.

Downstairs (in the shadows) Sarah Steele Sibley superintends the arrival of her new piano. Her clothing is straight from Baltimore; no hair or hide decorations form any part of her style. Two women in their twenties and two men—one younger and one quite old but still fit—assist her.

Stage left: Four Dakota men sit on the ground around a small fire, talking quietly, looking into the distance.

Stage right: In a tavern, two white men huddle over a table covered with papers and ledgerlike books, bottles of ink, pens.

Stage far right: Other houses are going up. Lumber, nails, tools lie around. We hear sawing and pounding. In one house not quite finished, a woman feeds wood into her kitchen stove.

Water connects all the sets. Beyond the stage are more settlements, villages, missionary and trading outposts along the St. Peter's River. Those who don't live on the river reside along streams or on lakes. Water offers the easiest, most efficient mode of transportation for everyone.

The text in italics suggests what the various actors could be saying.

ACT I, SCENE 1:
HENRY SIBLEY'S HOUSE AT MENDOTA, JUNE 1848

A spotlight picks up the three men as they clomp up the outside staircase. They talk about the State of Wisconsin, just admitted to the Union. This clears the way for another attempt at establishing a Minisota Territory.* They've tried twice and failed—once for not enough white citizens, once because of bickering in Washington about who will name territorial appointees. Maybe they can try again.[1]

Maybe we're getting close. Besides, new settlers will pour in as soon as they can get clear title to the land from the Sioux, the Chippeway, and the Winnebago.† Only the U.S. government can marshal the resources to buy that Indian land. Until we're a territory, we won't get the federal attention to get

---

Franklin Steele
entrepreneur, businessman, land speculator, saw miller, laid out the town of St. Anthony, among the founders of the University of Minnesota (brother of Sarah Sibley)

Joseph R. Brown
came to Fort Snelling as a young boy in the army; fur trader, Indian agent, married three times (to Dakota/mixed-blood women); instrumental in the founding of Henderson and Brown's Valley; editor of *Minnesota Pioneer*, politician

Sarah Sibley
second wife of Henry H. Sibley, mother of nine children, hostess, historic preservationist

*

Minisota was the creation of Joseph R. Brown, and *Minnesota* became the official spelling at the 1848 Stillwater Convention.

†

These being the names whites most often applied to the Dakota, Ojibwe, and Ho-Chunk.

it done. We have access to the land between the St. Croix and Mississippi rivers, to pieces along the Mississippi and around Fort Snelling.

But that's not enough they agree, for different reasons. Brown wants more settlers and farmers. Steele has his eye on milling along the river and on the land around the Falls of St. Anthony. Sibley reminds them that with animals scarcer and scarcer, the fur trade hasn't supported this place for a long time and it's getting worse.

We need a different future. How will we negotiate the politics of state-making this time? The Union is polarizing over slavery. A few slaves have lived here because they belonged to military men at the fort, but the Northwest Ordinance outlawed it in the Northwest Territory. We don't have to worry about whether we're slave or free. But others do worry—all those southern senators. With the admission of Wisconsin, the Senate is balanced between slave states and free, but that's not going to last. There's too little land in the West suitable for slavery. Stephen Douglas and others in Washington have their own plans for us. Maybe we can work with them. They can figure out their national plans. We can take care of this place.[2]

If there are three men who can make this happen, they're the ones. No white man was better known around Mendota than Sibley, but Brown ran a close second. Of the three he'd been around the longest. He'd grown up with the place, having arrived at the fort in 1819 as a fifteen-year-old drummer boy. He forged family ties with the Dakota. He'd done a bit of trading, speculating, storekeeping—a little bit of a lot of things—been in the Wisconsin territorial legislature for two years, and been a justice of the peace.[3]

Steele admits he's a different kind of man. *I don't share your Indian loving. I want to build bridges, not to the past but to the west side of the Mississippi. I have a sawmill on the St. Croix. I want another at St. Anthony. I want a real bridge there, to get out onto the land. Timber milling and land—those are the future.*[4]

So, they conclude, *let's constitute ourselves and our friends as a territorial legislature, elect a delegate, and begin again the process of becoming a territory. Brown has the most legislative experience: he can call the meeting to order. We'll hold the convention in Stillwater,* says Steele. *Sibley, if you can shed your "Hal, A Dakotah" persona and remember your Detroit manners, you'll be an excellent delegate.*

Their plan doesn't work exactly, but Sibley is elected and seated in Congress as a delegate from the "Territory of Wisconsin" (the portion remaining after Wisconsin becomes a state). He arrives in Washington not as Mr. Buckskin but fashionably dressed. His sophistication surprises and reassures many of his colleagues and paves the way for the admission of Minnesota Territory on March 3, 1849, and the appointment of Alexander Ramsey as its first governor.[5]

ACT I, SCENE 2:

THE PARLOR OF THE SIBLEY HOUSE, MAY 1849

Twenty-six-year-old Sarah Sibley is fluttering around her house, directing her Irish servant, Catherine O'Brien. They are readying the house for Anna and Alexander Ramsey, coming to start their lives in Minnesota Territory. They will be staying with the Sibleys until their own house is ready a few months hence. Ramsey's appointment has more to do with his Whig Party loyalty than with experience, knowledge, or interest in this place. Sarah herself doesn't care much about these things, but for her husband's sake—and for their future—she wants to make a good impression (she, like her husband, is a civilized woman from the East) and to make her brother, Franklin Steele, proud of her.

Katie, Sarah instructs, *knives and glasses go to the right of the plate; forks and bread plate to the left; dust first, sweep second; make sure the embroidered cloth is straight on the piano; plump the pillows on the mahogany sofa. Show the Ramseys we haven't forgotten our manners.*

She talks as she works. *When I moved into this house, with my mother and sisters, I had a big job of making it a home. Henry had built a nice enough house, but he used it as a business office and storeroom rather than as a home. Men came and went at all hours. I think they spit wherever they wanted. The dogs roamed in and out at will.*

I don't intend to bend to the frontier, she announces. *If my brother Franklin can remain an "Eastern gentleman," I can remain a lady. I am keeping the dogs outside. The office work can go on upstairs, and those men don't need to track through my house. I will turn this hunting lodge into a home that speaks of our position. Besides, I'm hoping we'll be moving to St. Paul proper. If not right away, eventually. This place is too far away from society.*[6]

Sarah isn't the first woman bringing eastern sensibilities to the West. Dozens of white women aspire to "gracious Victorian family homes" on the frontier. Mrs. Josiah Snelling, the wife of the fort's earlier commander (1820–27), encouraged music and dance for the soldiers and neighbors. She opened a Sunday school for the soldiers as well as for the (white) children. Mrs. Eliza Taliaferro, after arriving at the Indian Agency in 1828, turned her husband's quarters into a genteel household welcoming guests, entertaining them at the piano, even playing duets with explorer Joseph Nicollet on his way into the wilderness. A good Virginia woman, she brought slaves to help her civilize her frontier home.[7]*

Mary Riggs, partner to her husband in missionary work, arrived in 1836 to run both school and household. She fears her Indian charges will never wash or knit or sew to her satisfaction, but she hopes they will eventually "imbibe a love of neatness and order."[8]

Harriet Bishop was recruited west in 1847 to open a school and exert

Alexander and Anna Ramsey arrived in Minnesota in 1849 so that he could assume office as the first governor of Minnesota Territory; he was also state governor, "trader" involved in the Traders' Papers deceptions at the 1851 treaty negotiations, a businessman

Josiah Snelling colonel in the U.S. Army, builder of Fort St. Anthony (later renamed Fort Snelling)

Lawrence and Eliza Taliaferro lived near Fort Snelling, where he was the U.S. Indian agent

Joseph Nicollet mapmaker and explorer in Minnesota

Stephen and Mary Riggs missionaries who arrived at Fort Snelling in 1836; worked with Dakota people for half a century; he was involved in the military trials following the Dakota War

Harriet Bishop early teacher in St. Paul

*

Among them was Harriet Robinson, who married Dred Scott, the slave of the army doctor at Fort Snelling.

a "civilizing force" on the new community of St. Paul. Even women such as Hester Crooks Boutwell, mixed-blood daughter of Ramsay Crooks and his Ojibwe wife at Leech Lake and wife of missionary William Boutwell, cultivate the "manners and dress . . . of an American [white] woman."[9]

William and Hester Crooks Boutwell
he was a missionary; she the mixed-blood (Ojibwe) daughter of Ramsay Crooks, an American Fur Company trader

A few of these women were Christian ministers. Arriving with their Bibles and pianos, good dishes and upholstered furnishings, they "worked hard to reestablish the kinds of homes familiar to them in the life they had forsaken when they followed the lure of the frontier." It was the duty of white, middle-class American women to civilize men and homes throughout the United States, even more so these men and this place. In the fur trade they had no interest. In the frontier they had no interest. "Civilization," conversion, a new, better society—these occupied them fully.[10]

ACT I, SCENE 3:
ST. PAUL TAVERN, LATE AUTUMN 1850

Charles Tracy and Henry Tilden
both farmers and settlers in the new territory, hired by the U.S. government to conduct an official census of two counties

Charles Tracy and Henry Tilden, huddling over their papers, compare notes. Tracy has counted the people in Ramsey County and Tilden those in Dakota County for the 1850 Minnesota Territorial Census.

The money isn't great, but it has been an interesting job, going house to house, talking to so many people. I have to tell you, though, Tilden confesses, *sometimes I just couldn't get to every household. My area stretched from the Mississippi to the Missouri rivers, but settlements in much of that area are scarce and far between. Sometimes I had to rely on neighbors—otherwise I would have been at this for months.*

I had an easier time of it, Tracy reports. *My area included both St. Paul and St. Anthony, so I had a lot of people to count, but not nearly so much space to cover as you.* Tilden continues, *I could list the Fort Snelling soldiers easily enough, but those French names in Dakota County defeated me. First, I couldn't understand people when they talked to me. Then I couldn't spell what they did say to me.* Bebo, *for example, is what I understood one man to say, but my wife, who knows a little French, says that it could be* Bebeau *or* Bibeau. *I asked him to write it down, but he signed his name with an X.*

You know, Tracy replies, *relatives of that man must live in Ramsey County, a whole big family of them from Canada, all with French names. Neither mother nor father, not even the older children, could write it. But I spelled their name as* Bibot. *I had fewer French names than you did; most of my people are Yankees from New York and New England, Pennsylvania, Ohio, and Michigan. Their names were easy.*

"Race" was the category on the forms that gave me real trouble, Tilden adds. *The options on the form are "white," "black," and "mulatto," but those are nearly useless here. And the instructions tell us to exclude Indians. What*

kind of census is this? There are more Indians around than whites or blacks or mulattos combined. You know as well as I do that a whole lot of people are part Indian and part white. I can't always tell, especially the women, especially when they're in American ladies' dresses. The Renvilles and Faribaults, for example—some are white, some full-blooded Indians, some mixes. I can't tell which, so I included them all.

Everyone knows Philander Prescott's wife, Mary, is a full-blood Dakota, so I didn't include her, but I did include the four children. And I didn't include Asa-Ya-Man-Ka-Wan—Old Bets, most whites call her—even though she's lived around here since 1788. In Little Six's village I listed the three mostly white families I met up with and then twenty-eight more in five mostly Indian villages, but there are hundreds of people I didn't list.*[11]

The two men continue comparing notes, recopying their field notes into big volumes in their best handwriting, making their facts and guesses look equally official, making the Indians disappear before any treaty removes them.

Census taking seems a matter of simple recording, but in its questions and categories, its ordering of people in particular ways, its inclusions and exclusions, the form itself and the questions it asks impose one kind of order, no matter the poor fit. The grid makes a place that doesn't look at all like Boston or Providence appear on paper to be like these places: head of household (white) with wife (if she's white) or widowed (if she's not) and children. The form doesn't ask which languages people speak or what band they belong to. It doesn't ask about grandparents. It asks first name and last. (Is *Little* a first and *Crow* a last name? What about Ta-o-ya-te-du-ta?) No wonder the census takers were inconsistent.

ACT I, SCENE 4:

THE KITCHEN OF ANN AND JOHN NORTH'S HOUSE ON NICOLLET ISLAND, ACROSS FROM THE VILLAGE OF ST. ANTHONY, JULY 1851

Ann tends the beans and potatoes in the garden outside her home. Mrs. Harriet Godfrey has come over to visit other friends on the island but stops to chat with Ann.

Wasn't that a grand Fourth of July party that Cyrus Northrop put on in St. Anthony? There must have been two hundred people there. Mr. Northrop is one of us, so he offered lemonade. Did you notice how many St. Paul people, though, brought liquor?† *The falls are so high with water these days: good thing the speaker stood farther away from them this year than he did last year. We could hear him this year. Didn't Mr. Atwater go into "quite an agony over the Union,"* Ann observes.[12]

A party was good for my spirits, Ann confides. *You know, my grandmother was here for nearly a year and has recently returned home. I so miss my parents and brothers. I knew when I married Mr. North that our marriage*

Philander Prescott
trader, sutler, worked with farmer Indians, married to a Dakota woman, killed on the first day of the Dakota War

*

Her Indian name was Keehai, and she was from the Lake Calhoun Band of Dakota.

Old Bets (Aza-ya-man-ka-wan [Berry Picker])
lived in St. Paul, converted to Christianity, appeared in many of the city's early photographs

Little Six
Mdewakanton activist in the Dakota War, fled to Canada, captured and executed in 1865

John and Ann North
New England reformers, settled in Minneapolis, then founded Northfield; he served as state legislator and helped found the University of Minnesota; she taught piano lessons and feverishly recruited other New Englanders to Minnesota; they finished their lives in California

Ard and Harriet Godfrey
their 1848 house in Minneapolis (moved several times) kept open by the Woman's Club of Minneapolis; she brought dandelions to Minnesota; he was a saw miller

Cyrus Northrop
businessman, second president of the University of Minnesota

†

"St. Paul people" would have been a code word for French and Catholic, few of whom shared the teetotaling sentiments of the Norths, Godfreys, and other Yankee prohibitionists.

would take me west; somehow I didn't think that I would be so lonesome or that Mr. North would be so occupied with his political, economic, and educational interests. Never mind: I have plenty to keep me busy here.

Your plants are doing especially well, Mrs. Godfrey notes. *I have an especially good crop of dandelions this year that will prove useful in salads, coffee, even a bit of medicine.*

She holds Ann's handbill offering piano lessons. The Godfreys have a piano but no one to play, so she's come to arrange lessons with Mrs. North for her daughter. She assures Ann that others, too, will cross from St. Anthony to Ann's house on Nicollet Island for lessons. It's simple when the river is frozen, treacherous when visitors must pick their way across on the logs in the channel. They try not to laugh at the memory of the Misses Libbey, Murphy, and Scofield venturing out to pay a call. Two of them ended up in the water. The ferryman found them dry blankets, but neither is likely to hazard the trip again soon.[13]

Harriet Godfrey and her husband, Ard, have lived in St. Anthony slightly longer than the Norths. Between their marriage in 1838 in Maine and their move to St. Anthony a decade later, Harriet gave birth to five children and lost two of them. Ard, a millwright, plied his skills in Maine, then in Savannah (leaving Harriet in Maine to tend their children), and collapsed into bankruptcy. He happily accepted Franklin Steele's offer of a partnership to build a dam and mill at St. Anthony.

Deciding this move would be permanent, Ard sold the family's holdings in Maine and, to soften the transition for Harriet, built for them a house replicating her childhood home. Unable to duplicate the Maine pine, he painted the exterior a yellow he hoped would approximate the color Harriet remembers. The family arrived on the first steamer in the spring of 1849.[14]

The Norths have gathered around them a large and vibrant Yankee social circle. Many newcomers stay with them until they settle in their own places. Various relatives have moved to or near St. Anthony. The Norths also entertain people passing through. The Swedish singer Frederika Bremer, in Minnesota for a concert, visited the Norths, played on Ann's piano, and joined them for a sightseeing trip to Minnehaha Falls.

Growing up around the Norths is a community of people, schools, church congregations, Sabbath schools, grocery stores, and a December Thanksgiving, neighbors who are kind and some who are "very queer—considerably deceitful." They write letters at least every Sunday and look forward to the arrival by steamboat—when the ice is out—of letters, newspapers, and more friends and relatives.[15]

Like Ann, Harriet welcomes newcomers and puts them up in her

Frederika Bremer
Swedish author (Finnish-born) who toured the United States in the 1840s to learn about American democracy, education, and feminism (when in Minnesota she visited John and Ann North)

house, cares for the sick, opens her home to meetings of the Masonic lodge, and upholds the standards of decorum she's been raised to.

Mr. North joins the two women; they exchange pleasantries. Mrs. Godfrey moves on, and Ann and John talk about the politics and his dealings with Franklin Steele that preoccupy him at the moment.

I like Steele well enough, and we both see the possibilities of developing St. Anthony. A magnificent place will stand here one day. It will nurture what is good and noble in people. It can also make us some money. At least Franklin and I agree about that; politics is another matter entirely.

As I see it, North tells his wife (not for the first time), *the voting population can be divided into the fur company, the mill company, the French, and our own group of American citizens. These groups disagree about a lot of things, and I fear that I will become Steele's enemy by fighting his milling interests and Sibley's enemy if I oppose his bid for reelection as territorial delegate to Congress. I don't see, however, that they will make Minnesota into the kind of place it could be.*[16]

North wonders aloud about the treaty work that Ramsey—as governor and superintendent of Indian Affairs—and Luke Lea—as Indian commissioner—are conducting with the Dakota. Several bands of Dakota have already ceded their land and agreed to move to reservations on the upper Minnesota River. The traders, by hook and crook, got the Indians at Traverse des Sioux to agree to pay their debts. They signed the treaty papers, then the traders' papers, and will begin collecting annuities and supplies every year. Out of sight, out of mind. The negotiations with the other bands have bogged down but should resume at Mendota before too long. The pressure of incoming settlers is just too strong to delay much longer.

Act I, Scene 5:
Mendota, August 1851

The spotlight moves to the group of men around the fire. Ta-o-ya-te-du-ta, Wa-kan-o-zhan, Wa-pa-sha, and Wa-koo-tay talk quietly, pausing occasionally, as is the Dakota way. They speak in Dakota. A few Dakota people do speak English; a few more speak French. Generally, though, whites and Indians communicate in Dakota, more and more often through translators. That fewer whites were learning Dakota was the surest sign of the passing of one era and the imminent triumph of another.

So what do we do tomorrow, these Dakota men ask. *We've put off the whites as long as we can. Lea and Ramsey are pushing hard for settlement. They offer money and land along the Minnesota River. The whites stalk our territory like hungry wolves, closer and more brazen in their trespass. Some*

Luke Lea
trader, Indian agent, signer of the Treaty of 1851, one of the traders who benefited from the 1851 "Traders' Papers"

Ta-o-ya-te-du-ta (Little Crow)
Dakota leader in the 1862 Dakota War

Wa-kan-o-zhan (Medicine Bottle)
Mdewakanton activist in the Dakota War, fled to Canada, captured and executed in 1865

Wa-pa-sha
Mdewakanton (several generations of men named Wa-pa-sha), after whom Wabasha is named; Wa-pasha III was a reluctant participant in the Dakota War

Wa-koo-tay
signer of the Treaty of 1851

white farmers already squat and set their animals to feed on Dakota land. The Sisseton and Wahpeton have signed away their land. The whites will surround us and cut off our hunting.

Our relatives among the traders and some of our brothers who have taken up farming urge us to sign. But our young soldiers threaten to kill the first setting a hand to this treaty. What choice do we have?

Wa-kan-o-zhan, called Medicine Bottle by the whites, wants nothing to do with the negotiations. Like Sleepy Eye—who walked out of the talks with the Sisseton and Wahpeton—Medicine Bottle foresees disaster. Wa-pa-sha reminds the group of the broken promises of the 1837 treaty the Dakota signed with the whites. They have paid some of the money but not all of it.

Let's demand the payments promised us before agreeing to more promises. These four men know that the whites—some of them "friends"— had recently tricked the Sisseton and Wahpeton into signing away much of their cash to the traders. And Stephen Riggs "pulled the blankets" of several men to get them to sign. No one—not even Riggs—translated the papers that took much of the payment to the traders. *At least we can keep that from happening to us,* Ta-o-ya-te-du-ta, known to whites as Little Crow, says. *And we can hold out for a larger reservation, with more woods.*[17]

What choice do we have? We can't keep the whites off our land for long. We don't have horses enough to know who has trespassed. And how will we feed our families? The game—big and little—has largely fled from our lands. Hunger stalks our villages.

Tomorrow, Little Crow declares finally, reluctantly but firmly: *I plan to sign. You each must decide what you will do. If you must kill me for signing, so be it.*

There was a moment when the land of Michigan, Wisconsin, and Minnesota might have become an Indian state. The moment passed. With settlers moving to Oregon and California, the territory in between— still underestimated—is being swept up in the manifest destiny of a United States spanning the continent. Land fever is on. The fate of the Indians is removal—one way or another. Alexander Ramsey and Luke Lea wait now at Mendota for the Mdewakanton and Wahpeton to sign treaties selling their land.

The 1851 treaties transferred the land and also bought 150 years of poisoned Indian-white relations in Minnesota. After the 1851 treaties, the Dakota pull up their lodge poles, roll up the hides that form their tipis. The Sisseton and Wahpeton—about 5,000 of them—pack up their belongings and undertake the journey to the reservation at the Upper Agency (Yellow Medicine). The Mdewakanton and Wahpekute—about 3,000—go to the Lower Agency (Redwood Falls). *Upper* and *lower* referred to their location on the Minnesota River.[18]*

Sleepy Eye
Sisseton Dakota, traveled with Agent Taliaferro to Washington, DC, to meet President James Monroe in 1824; signer of 1851 treaty

*

The treaties' ratification got caught up in national congressional politics, and a group of southern senators, thinking that such an action would make the treaties so unpalatable that the Indians would reject them, moved to make the reservations temporary rather than permanent. The Dakota were not offered the opportunity to revoke their agreements, so the treaties went forward.

Ramsey attempts to negotiate another treaty with the Ojibwe around Pembina in northwestern Minnesota but without success. In 1847 the United States negotiated for an area of Ojibwe land on which to settle the Ho-Chunk, exiled from Iowa. In 1854 and 1855, the Ojibwe will cede most of their land in exchange for annuities and land that will come to be Mille Lacs and the Cass, Sandy, and Leech Lake reservations. The United States will come into possession of other Ojibwe land in 1863, 1869, and 1889.

Even before the Dakota begin their move, whites race onto Dakota land. The population of Minnesota will increase from about 6,000 in 1850 to more than 150,000 in 1857—not counting the native people.[19]

The curtain falls.

ACT II

The curtain rises on a stage even busier than in Act I, but with a wider view including St. Paul and Mendota to St. Anthony and Nicollet Island, westward nearly to the Missouri River. Throughout this act, men (and a few women) come and go from a land office festooned with maps and flyers at the back of the stage. Their excited conversations bubble up throughout the act. A few Irish accents are heard as well as a few German, but the people mostly speak English and mostly about their dreams and plans.

I'm staying put, one says. *There's lots of opportunity in St. Anthony and now Minneapolis. Jobs everywhere. Not me,* says another. *I'm taking some land in western Hennepin County. You should see the soil out there; it will grow whatever we need. I know I've thought this before in other places, but this is the place, for sure.*

Stage left: Three men and one woman sit at a table talking quietly and looking at papers together.
Stage right: Little Crow sits in front of a frame house. A few frame houses and more tipis are in the background. Other Dakota men, women, and children talk, tend fires, play games.
Center stage: White men mill around and talk excitedly in a church sanctuary, where the chairs are arranged for a political meeting.

ACT II, SCENE 1:
HAZELWOOD, UPPER SIOUX, YELLOW MEDICINE AGENCY, 1856

Paul Mazakutemane and Simon Anawangmani, with Stephen and Mary Riggs, study plans for a church and boarding school they are about to build. They speak in Dakota.

With only a handful of Christians among the Dakota so far, a school housing twenty students will do. The students, they agree, *will cut their hair,*

*learn to read and write Dakota, hear the Good News, and take on other white
ways. It will be hard for these children,* Mazakutemane says, *because the
blanket Indians* oppose this path. But it will be harder for them if they don't
gain these skills.*

Dr. Riggs, Paul says, *you hold up the model of Cherokee and Choctaw, and
we want to become citizens and "Americans." Here at Hazelwood, we can
show our abilities and our seriousness of purpose. It is my honor to be elected
president of this Hazelwood Republic, and I look forward to our beginning
these buildings.*[20]

Mazakutemane and Anawangmani are among a small group of
Dakota who have made their peace with the forces of "civilization" and
tried to make a place for themselves in the America washing over their
territory. Mazakutemane was one of Dr. Thomas Williamson's first
pupils, and both he and Anawangmani are among the first Dakota converts to Christianity. They cut their hair and wear white men's clothing.
They have taken Christian names. They consider the Riggses their
friends. Later, during the Dakota War, they will protect the Riggses and
the Williamsons.†

The Riggses had worked in this frontier vineyard for fifteen years
before the conclusion of the 1851 treaty sessions, when all Dakota people
were moved to the reserves on the Minnesota River. This meant the
Riggses had to move, too. Their future does not lie with the white
people—though various missionaries trying to make Indian converts
have despaired and turned their attention to the white settlers. No,
where the Indians go, so go the Riggses. Daughter Mary has joined her
mother in teaching at the school; their son has returned to Hazelwood
after completing seminary.

The Riggses feared for "their" Indians—those they had converted—
after the treaty signings in 1851. Although many Dakota have adopted one
aspect or another of white culture, the more traditional Dakota deeply re-
sent the "farmer" Indians and pressure them to recant. Riggs proposed,
then, the founding of the Hazelwood Republic, on the upper reservation,
only about a mile from the Yellow Medicine Agency. The Hazelwood citizens grow corn and potatoes here in abundance, enough to sell.‡ In religion, education, agriculture, manners, and decorum, they do what they
understand is required of them to become "civilized." Their hopes for full
citizenship founder on the state's insistence that citizens speak English.
Many Hazelwoodians, after much work and study, can read and write in
their own language but not in English. But no matter what the Indians
do, they are not going to count in the new world.[21]

Act II, Scene 2:
Little Crow's house, Lower Sioux, Redwood Agency

Ta-o-ya-te-du-ta (Little Crow) sits cross-legged on the ground in front of a frame house, his house. Village activity swirls around him, but he is deep in thought. Women cook, boys play lacrosse, men tend fires and talk. Adults and children wear their hair long, dress in moccasins and blankets. Many wear an amalgam of Indian and white clothing. Little Crow wears hide leggings, beaded armbands, and feathers in his long hair. He uses an Indian pipe. He also owns a photo of himself in a black frock coat and white man's tie—and gloves that disguise his disfigured hand—garb that he put on at the urging of Alexander Ramsey.

Little Crow meditates on his people's future. He has recently returned from Washington, DC, where he was impressed by the white man's theater and entertainments and even more by the power and resources of the government and the number of people. He has distributed some annuities and knows how people have come to depend on them; their dependence endangers them. He knows the federal distributions will not feed his people adequately. Starvation has shown its face in remote parts of the reservation.

He has been pulled in two directions for several decades. He believes in the traditional life of his ancestors. He has three wives. He knows how to hunt and trap. He knows how to talk to his people and lead them, but there are fewer and fewer paths.

Fences are going up all around us. Missionary fervor burns hot, and more of my people are listening. Some to the religious words, some because they know that reading and writing our own language will be helpful. The annuities don't provide enough to feed us, and they don't show up on time anyway. The buffalo are being chased away, and hunting is poor around our reservations. Our people suffer.

At least if we're away from the whites and among ourselves, we can reestablish our more eastern village patterns in this westerly place. We can continue our spiritual practices, our ways of telling stories, of raising our children, of singing our songs, of honoring our ancestors. Hunting is outlawed, but we will hunt, and we will use buffalo hides and other skins for housing, clothing, utensils. We can adopt more white ways, like this frame house, when they suit us. What's the right balance?

Act II, Scene 3:
Congregational Church, March 1855

In the early 1850s, Minnesota's politicos divided primarily over local issues and patronage—who has the power to appoint whom to public positions. Ramsey (the first territorial governor) was a Whig appointee;

Willis Gorman
territorial governor, delegate
to state constitutional convention, served in state legislature, Union general

Willis Gorman (the second territorial governor), a Democratic appointee. By 1855, local issues have merged into national ones. The Whig Party has disintegrated, broken by differences over slavery, free labor, and immigration. The Know-Nothing (anti-immigrant and anti-Catholic, especially) and Free Soil (free land and no extension of slavery into the territories) parties have attracted members and energy. The disastrous Compromise of 1850 and the Kansas-Nebraska Act of 1854 finally killed off the Whigs and pushed other splinter parties to coalesce into a new party—the Republican Party. John North gavels into silence a meeting called by former governor Alexander Ramsey. (The announcement is tacked up on the walls.)

Our job today is to found a new political party—Republican it is called in Michigan, New York, Wisconsin, and Iowa. We'll be the fifth state to call this new party—and this new vision for America—into life. We will oppose slavery in the District of Columbia, and we'll fight its extension into any new state or territory. We favor prohibition of alcohol (to control those who imbibe, especially Catholics and immigrants and, in Minnesota, Indians). We want more and better education and believe the government should pay for it.

Henry Mower Rice
territorial governor,
U.S. Senator,
U.S. negotiator for
1851 Dakota treaty

Between 1855 and 1857, Democrats (including Sibley and Steele and Henry Mower Rice and former territorial governor Willis Gorman) and Republicans (including North and Ramsey) meet as a territorial legislature and then as a constitutional convention, both dominated by party fighting. One battle has to do with the shape of the state: Democrats prefer a state with a longer north side because it puts St. Paul right in the middle; Republicans prefer a state running from the Mississippi west to the Missouri—without the northern portion of the territory—because that shape favors agriculture. The proponents of the former prefer a St. Paul capital; the proponents of the latter, a more centrally located St. Peter.* The legislature awards the state prison to Stillwater to satisfy those along the St. Croix. Finally, in large part because of John North's efforts, the legislature locates the University of Minnesota in St. Anthony, balancing the distribution of economic booty.[22]

One colorful story of early
Minnesota tells of Joe
Rolette, who absconded
with the bill to make St.
Peter the capital and hid
out so that it could not be
signed into law. He re-
appeared after the legis-
lature adjourned, and St.
Paul's status remained safe.

A major economic downturn in 1857 causes enormous dislocation in the would-be state. The building of the railroad is derailed for a decade, and cash for investment is tight. Another partisan divide results in the meeting of two separate constitutional conventions and the writing of two constitutions. They are slightly different but not enough to cause lingering judicial problems. The constitution is ratified by the voters and accepted by the U.S. House and Senate, and Minnesota officially becomes a state on May 11, 1858. A bit of trouble on the frontier in 1857—a small group of disaffected Wahpekute searching for game kills a white family—lets whites know the Indian "problem" has not been solved, just displaced.[23]

The curtain falls.

ACT III

The curtain rises on Mendota. Fort Snelling, still in the background, is much smaller than before. The Sibley house, in the foreground, dominates the set. There are houses and buildings, shops and churches, white women dressed in the latest styles, men in boots and jackets, but barely an Indian in sight.

ACT III, SCENE 1:
MENDOTA, 1858

The lights come up on Governor and Mrs. Sibley, taking a walk near their home. Lace curtains cover the windows; flowers come up all around.

We can rearrange the house so you can govern from here, Sarah says to Henry. *Good, this place has been my office for over twenty years. Maybe later we can find a house in St. Paul, but not now. There's too much work to do.*

It hardly seems possible that not even a decade has passed since the Ramseys arrived and stayed with us. The changes in our family mirror the change around us. Like others, we have suffered losses—a son less than a year old—but we have four children growing strong. My mother, Sarah Sibley says, *seems to thrive in the Minnesota climate, as many said she would. My one sister has married and lives not so far away in St. Paul. Men continue to outnumber women two to one, and all of us live with danger, accidents, illness. Even so, the children exceed adult men and women combined. Losses, yes, but growth, too.*[*]

And just look at Mendota. The population has doubled and, more than that, has turned over almost entirely. Few of the people who were here in 1850 are still here now. The traders and voyageurs are mostly gone, many of them to new places, some just to new work. The hunters are gone and the builders, masons, millwrights, sawyers, and joiners have arrived and have more than enough work. That's the kind of labor we need now. This is no longer a rendezvous for white, Indian, French, Scottish, Canadian, and all sorts of mix. We need houses and shops, a respectable and responsible citizenry, courts, judges, laws, order. We are America now. Most of the Catholics are Irish, not French. Other churches are booming: Congregational, Baptist, Episcopal, Methodist.

We're also more American. The Indians were everywhere in those days— just up river and just down. Their men came to talk and to trade; their women brought cranberries and left with blankets and supplies. A few still live around Mendota and St. Paul—women like Old Bets, who seems to live nowhere and everywhere on the generosity of friends and strangers. Indians married to whites also remain—usually in white women's clothing, living the white way, at least in public. Even so, nearly all of our earlier neighbors were born in Minnesota or Canada; they were Catholic and predominantly French. Having the Indians and so many of these others gone changes the nature of the place.

*

Mendota was located in a Dakota County reconfigured smaller since 1850, but its population had increased twentyfold. Even more remarkable was the seventyfold increase in farmers. Census takers reported 400 people in 1850 and 8,437 people in 1858; 21 farmers at the earlier date and 1,449 in 1858.

Hypolite DuPuis
mixed blood, worked for
Henry Sibley and American
Fur Company and Joseph
Renville at Lac qui Parle

So many of our friends have moved away. Hypolite DuPuis left service as my clerk to become a bookkeeper in West Saint Paul. He's enriched himself with real estate. Alexander Faribault and his wife have made a success of the town of Faribault; he served in the territorial legislature.[24]

Franklin Steele has long since decamped to the far side of the Mississippi, across from St. Anthony; he buys up land there as fast as he can. John and Ann North claim Northfield as their home, occasionally coming to St. Paul to meet friends, attend the theater, go to church, have dinner at the Winslow House in St. Anthony. He comes to take his seat in the territorial legislature. Ann, and people like her, come to do their "trading"—not for furs but for the goods arriving by steamboat every day the river is free of ice. Alexander and Anna Ramsey live in St. Paul. Joseph R. Brown and his family have moved to Yellow Medicine Agency on the upper reservation.

Henry Sibley ruminates: *Politics have driven my friends and me apart. In the 1857 election I ran for governor—and won—against my friend and ally Ramsey. But my nemesis Henry Rice and a little-known compromise candidate, James Shields, are Minnesota's first senators.* (Perhaps he already knows he will serve only one term as governor.)

James Shields
U.S. Senator from Minnesota
(also at other times from
Missouri and Illinois)

After his term, Sibley will devote the remainder of his life to the university, to the Minnesota Historical Society, and to other work and institutions, striving to make the place he considers his into the place he imagines it could be.

5

One Mixed-Blood Family Looks for Its Place

PART I:

BEFORE 1862

DURING THE 1820S AND 1830S, when he interpreted for Indian Agent Lawrence Taliaferro, Scott Campbell and his wife and family lived across the river from Fort Snelling. The children—nine who survived to adulthood—learned to speak English, French, Dakota, and Menominee; several spoke Ojibwe. One eventually learned to read and write English. All were baptized by French-Catholic priests.

These Campbells lived close—physically and emotionally—both to Fort Snelling and to Little Crow's Dakota village at Kaposia. When the older Campbells were growing up, Indian people outnumbered whites; bark and hide dwellings outnumbered frame houses; traditional ways predominated new modes. Little Crow's meat may have been cooked in iron pots and trade beads rather than quills may have decorated his clothing; even so, he lived more like his ancestors than Sibley and Taliaferro lived like theirs. Until the 1830s, neither whites nor Indians felt a need to transform the other. The whites wanted the Indians to be Indian—to hunt, to trap, to connect with the people upcountry. Many Indians wanted what the whites offered—trade goods and weapons, especially. They wanted whites to buy their furs and connect them to markets and goods outcountry.*

The younger Campbell children came of age as the U.S. government took its first steps toward gaining possession of Indian land and the fur trade was in decline, after missionaries had begun trying to civilize and Christianize the Indians and mixed bloods and Taliaferro and Sibley had both married white women who brought pianos, antimacassars, fashionable dresses, and little desire to know much about their husbands' other wives and families.

In 1851—when the youngest of the Campbell children was ten years

*

Except, of course, the white missionaries, Stephen Riggs, the Pond brothers, Thomas Williamson, and others, who from the 1830s showed a messianic urge to convert the Indians to Christianity.

old—the Dakota signed the Treaties of Traverse des Sioux and of Mendota and, in exchange for the promise of funds and goods delivered annually (annuities), agreed to settle permanently on two reservations on the Minnesota River. The Wahpeton and Sisseton went to the land around the Upper Agency at Yellow Medicine River; the Mdewakanton and Wahpekute to the Lower Agency near the Redwood River.

These same treaties determined the fate of white people, too: their numbers would increase, their towns would multiply, their farms would flourish. Those who had known how to speak Indian would forget. Sibley and Ramsey and Jackson and Larpenteur*: these men would be in charge. Mills would replace trading posts; dams would invite more and more mills that would cut more and more wood and grind more and more wheat.

What about the Campbells? Where would they go? Where did they belong? They had been at home at the intersection of cultures; where would they stand as those cultures began pulling apart? They were not white like Taliaferro or Sibley; neither were they Indian like Little Crow and his son Big Thunder. They weren't Scottish-Irish or French or Menominee or Dakota but bound by kin ties to all of them. None had ever lived in a white-only or an Indian-only world.[1]

Nine of Scott's and Margaret's children survived to grapple with the question. They came up with many different answers.

Madeline	b. 1820	m. Olivier Rassicot (Roscoe)	d. 1899
Harriet	b. 1824	m. Benjamin D'Yonne (Young)	d. 1889
Antoine Joseph	b. 1826	m. Mary Ann Dalton	d. 1913
Matias Scott	b. 1827	m. "Sioux Indian Girl"	d. 1870
Paul (Hippolite)	b. 1829	m. Mary Rainville [Yuratwin]	d. ?
Baptiste	b. 1831	m. Rosalie Renville	d. 1862
Jack	b. 1832	m. "Sioux Indian Girl"	d. 1865
Margaret	b. 1837	m. Joseph Labathe	d. 1896
Marie	b. 1841	m. Fred LaChapelle	d. ?

Madeline before 1840 married a French-Canadian (white) blacksmith; they had ten children and lived at Read's Landing, near Wabasha. Harriet married a mixed-blood fur trader; they had five children and lived in Mendota. The transformation of their family names—Rassicot and D'Yonne—to Roscoe and Young by 1860 signaled that when forced to choose they leaned toward the "white" side (at least that part where other mixed bloods lived).[2]†

The oldest Campbell son, Antoine Joseph (usually called Joe), in 1845 married Mary Ann Dalton, a woman from Indiana who traveled in Yankee social circles. Henry Jackson, a leading St. Paul merchant, officiated

*

Henry Jackson: businessman, postmaster, and justice of the peace in St. Paul before moving to Mankato (after whom Jackson County is named)

Auguste Larpenteur: in trading business with Henry Jackson in St. Paul

†

Rassicot, Rusico, Rasico, Racicot are among the variations of Olivier's surname in the historical record. One could speculate that calling themselves "Roscoe" was simply easier. It would also have been the case that calling themselves Roscoe would have helped the family make a transition into a white world more easily than a French name, which in Minnesota in the nineteenth century almost certainly hinted at Indian ancestors.

at the wedding; the Larpenteurs, another prominent family, hosted the reception.* Joe worked as a clerk in St. Paul.[3]

In 1850, Joe settled his family in a house next door to his parents and their children who still lived at home. The next year, after Scott Campbell's death, Joe took over the care of his mother and younger siblings. After 1851, all of these Campbells moved with their Dakota kin to the Lower Agency. Joe's wife ran a boardinghouse at the agency, and they sent their two older daughters for a time to Catholic boarding school in St. Paul. Joe and two of his brothers got work at the agency trading post run by Nathan and Andrew Myrick.

Joe's two sisters stayed in eastern Minnesota. Joe's decision to move invites questions. Did he want to stay in St. Paul and go "white," as Madeline and Harriet seemed to be doing? His life certainly was pointing him in that direction. He had a job as a clerk in St. Paul. His marriage linked him to the white world. He learned to read and write English. When the family moved west, he sent his two older daughters away to be educated. Did he agree to go west because their Indian mother—though Menominee—wanted to be in a more Indian world? Did his brothers, who had neither wives nor jobs in 1851, see better prospects for themselves in the West, among Indian people, than among the whites? We don't know.[4]

Life in the west kept the Campbells and their Indian relatives in close association. The Inkpaduta-led uprising in 1857 and the 1858 treaty negotiations forged especially strong ties between Joe Campbell and his cousin, the younger Little Crow, who would play such a central role in the 1862 Dakota War.

In 1857, a small band of non-treaty Indians (meaning they lived off the reservation as renegades) led by a Wahpekute named Inkpaduta killed about thirty-five people in southwestern Minnesota and northern Iowa (the Spirit Lake Massacre, as the press called it then). After a small U.S. Army party failed to find Inkpaduta, the Indian agent at the Lower Sioux Agency sent out a party of 125—led by Little Crow and Joe Campbell (and including two other Campbell brothers)—to search. After a perhaps half-hearted chase and the killing of three of Inkpaduta's band, including his son, the Indian militia returned home, more angry at the Indian agent who had forced them into this service (and threatened to withhold annuities if they did not comply) than at the hapless if murderous Inkpaduta band.[5]

The next year Joe Campbell, as interpreter, and Little Crow, as spokesman, and a small group of Dakota (and mixed-blood) men traveled to Washington, DC. The government wanted more land. The Dakota

---

*

It was rumored that Mary Ann Dalton was herself a Cherokee mixed blood, but if she was she disguised her background even more successfully than did Madeline Roscoe or Harriet Young.

Dakota treaty party photographed in Washington, DC, 1858. This photo is especially striking for the formality of the dress: frock coat, white tie. Joseph Campbell (second from left) wore his hair short in a fashion of powerful political statement were he fully Indian, the "cut hairs" being the people who, in cutting their hair, demonstrated their willingness to take on white traits and civilization.

wanted to right some of the wrongs of the 1851 treaties. After a frustrating few months, the delegation returned home not only having failed to push back the crippling provisions of the treaties but having lost even more land.[6]

By the late 1850s, Joe's four younger brothers had all married Indian or mixed-blood women and lived mostly around the Lower Sioux Agency.

PART II:
SUMMER 1862

In the summer of 1862 the U.S. government was busy. In May, Congress passed the Homestead Act, which granted 160 acres to farmers who would improve the land and stay on it for five years. On July 1, the president signed into law the legislation that provided funding for a transcontinental railroad, and on July 2, the Morrill Act that funded land-grant colleges.

That same summer, French, Spanish, and British troops landed in Veracruz, Mexico, to collect on debts owed to them since the Mexican-American war, when Mexico's economy collapsed. The French eventually marched toward Mexico City. Did they have plans to help the Confederates fight the American Civil War? Abraham Lincoln had no forces available to reinforce the Mexican Army, so a poorly equipped but smart tactician, General Ignacio Zaragoza, and his forces had to (and did) hold off the French on their own.

Of course, the Civil War itself claimed most of the government's attention. The war efforts moved both politically and militarily. In July 1862, the Congress passed what would be the precursor to the Emancipation Proclamation, the Second Confiscation Act. It specified that persons who engaged in "rebellion or insurrection" or "give aid and comfort thereto" would be punished by imprisonment or a fine or "by the liberation of his slaves."[7]

This move was sparked, in part, by the North's military situation. These were dark days for the Union. In April, around 13,000 Union soldiers had died at Shiloh in Tennessee. In May, Union troops were defending the nation's capitol from Stonewall Jackson and his Confederate forces. Frustrated with General George McClellan's seeming refusal to act, Lincoln named Henry Halleck to lead the Union Army.

Few in Washington, therefore, were paying much attention to Indian affairs in the Northwest generally or Minnesota specifically, not even the attention that Congress had guaranteed to the Dakota in the form of annuities.

The summer of 1862 found the Dakota on the Upper and Lower Reservations hungry and in need of their money—and not confident that that money would ever arrive. The Indian people knew that the whites were engaged in war in the South. Traders, including the Myricks at the Lower Agency, had foodstuffs in storage but would not release them to the Dakota until the annuities arrived. When several of the Dakota pleaded, begged for food, Andrew Myrick is reported to have replied savagely, "If they're hungry let them eat grass or their own dung." Living in the shadow of a failed harvest in 1861, restrained from freely hunting buffalo (further hampered by a decreased buffalo population), and facing severe hunger in August 1862, the Dakota people had plenty of bitterness to chew.

In mid-August, five foolish, hungry, and brutal young men in a show of bravado killed a white family over a few stolen and broken eggs. The men fled to Little Crow's camp on the Lower Reservation. Little Crow and other Mdewakanton knew that whites would not allow such an act to go unpunished. They also knew that the whites were occupied with war in the South, so, some Dakota argued, if ever there would be a chance to expel the whites, this was it. Expulsion was not much of a possibility, Little Crow knew, but war was likely, and he accepted the sword of leadership.

The Sioux Uprising as it was called and the Dakota War as it is now called left dead five hundred to one thousand white settlers as well as an unknown but much smaller number of Indians. Governor Alexander Ramsey sent former governor Henry Sibley and a small army of mostly newly mustered soldiers to the field to quell the uprising. Within a month the war ended, and Little Crow and hundreds of Dakota fled westward, some to join relatives among the Lakota, some to Canada. Sibley took hundreds of Dakota men into custody and put them on trial in the field, finding over three hundred guilty of capital crimes. Through the intercession of Episcopal bishop Henry Whipple, President Lincoln reviewed the verdicts and commuted the sentences of all but thirty-six Dakota and three mixed-blood men, who were hanged in Mankato on December 26, 1862.[8]

The Dakota War ripped through Minnesota with a shocking ferocity. The Indians' slaughter—and their methods—stunned most whites. The outrage some Indians felt at their treatment by whites was now matched by the outrage of some whites at their treatment by Indian warriors. Jane Grey Swisshelm, for example, filled the columns of her *St. Cloud Visiter* for months with vicious calls for the extermination of all Indians.[9]

The war also ripped through the Campbell family. On the morning of August 18, Joe's mother, his wife and children, and other Campbell siblings and spouses were at home near the trading post. Joe and his brother Baptiste were at Myrick's post when the Indians attacked there. Joe and Baptiste slipped away from the killing at the trading post with the help of Indian relatives among the war party.

One of the Dakota men remembered later that the call had been to "Kill the whites, and kill all the cut-hairs who will not join us." Did the "whites" include Joe's wife? Was anyone in his family safe? It was too early to know. Among the other whites killed in that first wave were Dr. Philander Humphrey and his family, long disliked by many Dakota, and Philander Prescott, an old man with a fifty-year history in the fur trade and an Indian wife and mixed-blood children. Facing the armed raiders, Prescott reminded them of his longtime relations with the Dakota and his wife pleaded for them to pass him by. They shot him anyway. Mixed bloods weren't safe either. Louis Boucier, who immediately went to the side of his Indian relatives and reportedly killed several white settlers, was himself killed as he ran to join a group of Indians. The mixed bloods didn't know whether they were seen as friend or foe—or even whether they *were* friend or foe.[10]

On the next morning, Little Crow sent out orders for his Dakota relatives and others to come to his village to be safe. The Campbells were among the several hundred who responded. For six weeks they lived in tipis and dressed in Indian clothing.* Threatened if they tried to escape meant that they were captives, even if they were also kin.† The men had to decide whether to join up or not. Baptiste Campbell testified later that Indian warriors pressed many mixed bloods into service: "I had a wife and two children at Crow's village," Baptiste said. Little Crow "said I must kill all the White men I met . . . If I didn't . . . he would find a way to kill me." Another brother, Paul, whose wife and children were in the camp, also joined the Indian warriors. Jack, yet another brother, had joined the Union Army in 1861, a member of Brackett's Battalion. By one account he disappeared from his unit in Tennessee and went north to join Little Crow. The sisters in Wabasha and St. Paul must have followed the news accounts closely, not like their neighbors fearing attack but pining for word of their families. Did they fear for their lives too? White retaliation?[11]

Joe Campbell was pressed into service as well. Sibley and Little Crow needed an intermediary, and they turned to him. Neither trusted him completely, but he knew both languages and could read and write English. Joe, then, served as Little Crow's secretary—writing and carrying messages to Sibley. Sibley met with Campbell and sent messages back to Little Crow. The three together effected the freeing of captives at "Camp Release" that September, including Joe's wife and seven children, Baptiste's child, Scott and his wife and three children, and their mother.‡ Paul and his family fled the country with Little Crow, wandering in Dakota Territory and eventually landing in Canada with his aunt's Métis family. Jack slipped back to his battalion in the South.[12]

Joe and Baptiste were swept into the aftermath of the war in Minnesota. Sibley convened military trials in the field. Jumbled, sketchy trial notes make it clear that both brothers testified about their roles. Baptiste said he "went to the Big Woods on a war party." He was charged with "fir[ing] at a White woman." The military tribunals found more than three hundred men—including Baptiste Campbell—guilty and sentenced them to death. President Lincoln let stand thirty-nine convictions, including Baptiste's.[13]

On December 25, the eve of the public hangings in Mankato, the convicted men faced their fates quietly—except for the mixed bloods, who, one observer noted, "were the most of all affected, and their dejection of countenance was truly pitiful to behold." White missionaries worked the crowd that Christmas night, comforting, cajoling, working to convert. Stephen Riggs and others spoke passable Dakota, but not Father Ravoux,

*

Even Mary Ann Dalton Campbell dressed in Indian clothing; it made them safer, according to her daughter.

†

George Quinn, another mixed blood, went with "my people" against the whites. Joe Courselle, as much Indian and white as Quinn, declared that he did not trust the Dakota. Perhaps identity is as much about trust as about blood—and loyalty.

‡

"Camp Release" is the name of the place where the Dakota who surrendered to Sibley in 1862 were located (in Lac qui Parle County)

a French-Catholic priest. He called on Baptiste, a Catholic and a man of many languages, for translation.[14]

On December 26, 1862, Baptiste and the other convicts walked from a makeshift jail to a scaffold in the center of Mankato. They sang death songs on the way. White-style clothes made Baptiste and the other mixed bloods stand out among the Dakota. As their heads were covered, the men reached out to take each other's hand. The floor dropped from beneath them all at once. Hundreds of people—no doubt some Campbells among them—watched them fall to their deaths.[15]

There's no solid evidence of Jack's role in the war other than that he was missing from Brackett's Battalion for the duration. One army mate reported later that in 1863 Jack "denied having been north . . . but was well posted as to the outcome of the affair in Minnesota and knew that his brother Baptiste had joined the hostiles, been captured, tried and hanged . . . In his drunken condition he told me a good many things . . . that I did not believe then but found out afterwards were true." He said Jack swore revenge on all of Mankato for his brother's hanging.[16]

In what many Minnesotans considered the last gasp of the Dakota War, Jack Campbell showed up around Mankato in 1865 with a stash of money and wearing the clothing of a Mr. Jewett, who with his family had been murdered on his farm outside of town. After a trial only slightly less perfunctory than those accorded the prisoners of 1862, some Mankato townspeople lynched him outside the city jail.[17]

PART III:

IN THE WAKE OF THE WAR—
THE FIRST GENERATION

After 1862 the Dakota had few choices. They were exiled en masse and in misery, facing starvation. The men with commuted sentences went to prison in Davenport, Iowa; the others, with their families, went to Crow Creek on the Missouri River in Dakota Territory. Again, a few mixed bloods and whites, who'd made the Indian world their own, joined the Dakota. Stephen and Mary Riggs—missionaries who'd come to save them in the 1830s—stayed in Minnesota. Their son left with "his" people. He, then his son, and then his grandson were committed to civilizing and saving the people they still called savages.[18]

White people's memories of the conflict remained sharp; there was little sympathy, apart from that of Episcopal bishop Henry Whipple, for the Dakota. The mixed, complex, nuanced community in which the Campbells thrived had evaporated. Norwegians were not just Norwegians—they were non-Indians. Non-Indians were good. Indians were bad.* Jack's return with six "hostile Sioux" proved they still constituted a threat. Joe's work as a scout for the Sibley and Sully expeditions to chase the Dakota through the Dakotas in 1863–64 made him a white ally. Paul, another brother, had fled from Minnesota in September 1862 and gone to Canada with other, mostly Indian, refugees.[19]

Madeline Campbell Roscoe had eleven children before the end of the Dakota War. She continued to live, as she had for more than twenty years, at Read's Landing in Wabasha County, among other mixed bloods who had never moved west. She and her husband lived out the rest of the century where mixed bloods and whites had long lived side by side. So did her sisters Marie LaChapelle and Margaret Labathe and their families. All three were known locally as the daughters of Taliaferro's interpreter and as sisters of one of the "Indians" hanged at Mankato. Margaret Labathe's mixed-blood husband had served in the Union Army from 1863 to 1865. Other mixed-blood relatives—uncles, aunts, and cousins—lived nearby. The federal 1880 census identified Madeline as "white"; the 1895 state census as "I." Her obituaries called her an "old settler" without mention of her full heritage.[20]

Harriet Young had passed the Dakota War in St. Paul. Her mixed-blood husband served in the Union Army and after the war as a scout with Joe in the Dakota Territory. The 1870 federal census identified her race as "B"—for black. Before 1880, she and her husband and family moved to the Santee Reservation in Nebraska, where since 1866 the Dakota exiled from the state had been settled. When they moved there, most residents lived in tents and dressed in Indian clothing. Harriet had both an Indian and a white name—as no doubt all of the Campbells did. She used both in the formal Santee records.[21]

Harriet's mother, Margaret, stayed at the Lower Agency while her sons and son-in-law scouted for Sibley. Her son Paul urged her to join him in Canada. Instead, she, too, eventually settled at the Santee Reservation, where she died in 1892, at the age of ninety-three. She certainly had an Indian name. She did not use it in the official records.[22]

Joe Campbell, one-time secretary for Little Crow and Sibley, also stayed around the Lower Agency after the war with his wife and younger children. Perhaps they felt they belonged there among the whites more than they did among the Dakota. An 1865 *St. Peter Tribune* article reported that Joe's wife's "sympathies were entirely with the whites," among whom she counted herself. She died in the late 1860s, at which time Joe married Louise Frienier—a mixed blood like him. They, too, moved to the Santee Reservation, where Joe took up farming and lived for the next thirty years among the people he'd known all his life—Indian and mixed blood, some of them his immediate family, many

*

Before 1870 the race categories were not specified, though race was a category to be filled in by the enumerator. From 1870 the federal census offered as race categories only "white," "colored," "Chinese," and "mulatto." Indians didn't count at all.

his kin. He and Louise reported Indian names on the Santee census rolls. English was his first language; it had not been hers. He died at age eighty-seven, not at Santee but, ironically, in Minnesota in Camp Release Township, where he was visiting—and no doubt being cared for by—one of his daughters.[23]

PART IV:
IN THE WAKE OF THE WAR—
THE NEXT GENERATION

Scott and Margaret Campbell's two dozen grandchildren had to make other choices. Their difference in age, their parents' choices, and the war itself gave them diverse experiences from which to decide their lives. Madeline Roscoe's and Harriet Young's children were born in the fur-trading world of more integrated relations between Indians and whites. Margaret Labathe's and Marie LaChapelle's children, born in the changed Minnesota, came of age at a time of antagonism and fear.

Madeline's grown children mostly stayed in Wabasha. All four Roscoe daughters married whites—two were French-surnamed (Bibeau and DeRossier), two Anglo (Shaw and Pritchard). They stayed permanently in Wabasha. The Roscoes' three sons married white women. One couple stayed near Wabasha; another moved to Pipestone; the third, to Marshall County.[24]

When the Pipestone son died in 1911, his obituary identified him as the second son of Oliver Roscoe, a blacksmith, with no mention of his mother. Perhaps this was simple nineteenth-century patriarchy, but it also had the effect of erasing his mother's Indian heritage and that of all her children, the others also identified as white upon their deaths.[25]

*

Marie LaChapelle's son collected annuities, as did his sons but none of their wives, suggesting that the men of both generations married white women.

The children of the two youngest Campbell sisters—Marie LaChapelle and Margaret Labathe—mostly stayed in Minnesota.* Various Labathes counted themselves among the Christian and friendly Indians during the 1862 conflict and found some friendly quarter for themselves in white St. Paul. One Labathe son, like his Roscoe cousin, went to the explicitly Indian town of Sisseton (South Dakota), founded by Dakota from the Upper Agency after 1862. They had eluded attempts to send them to the Crow Creek Reservation.[26]

Harriet Young's sons—Joseph, Frank, and Benjamin—moved to Santee with their parents in the 1870s, and there they stayed. After their father died, their mother lived with Benjamin—the chief of police at Santee—and his family, in what the census called a "civilized" dwelling. In 1920, all three identified "Indian" as their mother tongue.

* * *

Joe Campbell's children were as divided as he. His sons Joseph and William moved with him to Santee. Both married full-blood Indian women. The census takers recorded English as their first language and listed them as half Indian, half white. They raised their children and knew their grandchildren among mixed- and full-blood people.[27]

Joe's daughter Celia, however, stayed in Minnesota and made a small industry of recording her family's history. Ignoring the fact that her uncle was hanged at Mankato, she wrote of her father as a savior of the whites and hero of the war. She did not acknowledge that her father or Baptiste were any part Indian or that Little Crow was a relative. Like her mother, she identified with the white captives. Celia's older sister, Emily, and both of her brothers at Santee had Dakota names; Celia no doubt did, too, but she did not refer to it. Her stepson described her as "almost white." The state and federal censuses of 1900, 1905, 1910, and later identified her as "white." She sought no complexity in her stories—or in herself.[28]*

In 1862, Celia was thirteen. She married Joseph Charon by 1870. After his death she married Francois Jette, who later called himself Frank Stay. Jette had been married to a Dakota woman who left him at the end of the 1862 war, saying it was too dangerous to be with a white man. Both Celia and Frank had children when they married; together they had another six. She lived until her death in 1935 at Stay's farmstead in Camp Release Township, not far from where she'd been held captive in 1862.[29]†

The Dakota War was the central event of Celia's life; she located herself on the side of the whites. In one account she declared herself "an American full-blooded." She never missed an Old Settlers picnic, and her house was a regular stop on county history tours. There she told stories of her heroic father and the dark days of the state's past. She never wrote about the executions or mentioned her uncle. In the obituary that she, no doubt, wrote at her father's death, she described him as a man who showed much courage "in encounters with the Indians" and reported that he "traced his heritage back to Sir Colin Campbell of Scotland." She did not mention that he had any Indian ancestry himself. One wonders what continuing relationships she had with her brothers at Santee. She didn't mention them either.[30]

Thus lived the Campbells, for fifty years before Minnesota had its name to beyond its fifty-year celebration of statehood in 1908. They began in the fur-trade world, profiting from overlapping, often cooperative relations, their kin ties binding them across racial divides. They lived through the fraying of those bonds. And as the world pulled into warring fac-

*

She and all of her siblings had been reported in the 1860 census as "m" for mulatto.

†

Celia Stay won second prize in a Minnesota Department of Tourism writing contest with a piece about her husband's experience of the war.

tions, they jumped to one side or the other. Some of the grandchildren of Scott and Margaret Campbell fit themselves into the postwar Minnesota of "whites"; others into the "Indian" worlds of Santee, Flandreau, or Sisseton. What we don't know is what their decisions cost them—economically, socially, culturally, emotionally. None of them got away free. All had to excise part of themselves and their pasts.

During those several generations, the Campbells were sometimes go-betweens, sometimes just between. They made friends, enemies, and marriages where they found them, in a many-cultured society. They made decisions about who they were, how they would live, and with whom. What they decided had something to do with race—but also with gender, opportunity, friendships, and duty. In the 1830s, Scott and Margaret Campbell lived in a place where the lives of whites, Indians, and mixed bloods intersected and overlapped. They could talk to everyone. Perhaps they felt themselves to be at the center of that place.[31]

By the end of the nineteenth century, Minnesota was disaggregated by race. The center became "white"—African American, Asian, German, Scandinavian, Yankee—with "reds" relegated to the margins or banished from the state. It became more and more difficult for mixed bloods to connect or jump from one group to the other. The Campbells may have done so within their families, but not much beyond.

The fur trade—and its particular kinship requirements—had drawn the Scottish-Irish Campbells toward French voyageurs and traders and both toward Dakota and other Indian people, into a shared and mixed world. The Dakota War—and the racial issues it both reflected and spawned—sent the Campbells into a centrifugal spin, throwing them to all sides—hostiles, friendlies, captives, condemned, praised, invisible, Indian, white.* Whoever cast the war as two sided never talked to them.

*
"Hostiles" and "friendlies" were the names applied by whites to the Indians who opposed or protected whites.

6

The War Touched Us All

PRESIDENT ABRAHAM LINCOLN'S CALL FOR TROOPS in April 1861 anticipated what presidents and warriors often dream of at the beginning of war: a brief skirmish and decisive victory. He asked for men for ninety days. By May he acknowledged bleaker prospects but still underestimated the work ahead, asking for three years. Men and a few women (most often in disguise) in Minnesota and elsewhere answered the call and enlisted. When enlistments couldn't offer up enough men, the government started to draft. By war's end, Minnesotans had mustered eleven infantry regiments (often in town-based groups, often with friends and relatives), three batteries of light artillery, three cavalry regiments (including one of mixed-blood volunteers), two companies of sharpshooters, and one regiment of mounted rangers—over 20,000 men in all.[1]

Young men they were, in their late teens and early twenties. Some recruits left professions—surveying, teaching, lawyering—but more were farmers, shop clerks, laborers. To some, the fantasy of heroic deeds and marching around with their friends—as well as escaping summer chores—was inducement enough to join. Others took their duty seriously and volunteered with purpose. They certainly all knew about death: of a parent, a neighbor, a child ("infancy" was one of the greatest causes of death in the state in the 1860s). Some knew about handling a gun from hunting. But how would they face killing a man, defending against a bayonet, watching a friend die? Some did better than others.

The First Minnesota soldiers fought at many of the Civil War's most important battles: Bull Run, Antietam, Fredericksburg, Gettysburg. At the Battle of Gettysburg in July 1863, General Winfield Scott Hancock needed time for reinforcements to arrive, so he called on Minnesota's First Regiment to charge the Confederate lines, in Corporal Alfred Carpenter's words, "at all hazards." Hancock and Carpenter and all the others knew that the Confederates could not be stopped but only delayed; they also knew that this would be a sacrificial mission for the First. It was. The regiment sustained nearly 85 percent injured or killed—140 wounded and 74 dead. As Carpenter recalled in a letter a short while after the battle—in which he was also wounded—"The Rebs were routed, and the bloody field was in our possession; but at what a cost! The ground was strewed with dead and dying, whose groans and prayers and cries for help and water rent the air."[2]

Organizing troops by place carried the advantage of strong ties already developed among the men but the disadvantage of their watching friends and relatives die. Patrick Henry Taylor, who left his job as a teacher in Little Falls to join the First, spent July 4, 1863, at Gettysburg helping bury the dead, including his brother Isaac.[3]

Estimates of those killed in the war vary, but we're not too far off remembering 200,000 killed in battle or of battle wounds and another 200,000 dead of disease (measles, diarrhea or dysentery, typhoid, malaria, smallpox, and tuberculosis). That was just on the Union side: nearly as many Confederates died, too. Defending freedom (or the union or free soil) on the one side and a way of life (or freedom of another sort) on the other may have been the overriding principles, but the daily work of war was surviving and killing. And marching and waiting—they did a lot of that.

Christopher Columbus Andrews—who entered the war as a private and finished as a brigadier general—wrote in his autobiography of his time in the Third Regiment Volunteer Infantry. In October 1861 he and twenty men made their way to Fort Snelling for swearing into the Third and within a few days marched out to start their lives as soldiers.

> On a beautiful day, Saturday November seventeenth, our regiment embarked at Fort Snelling . . . We landed at the foot of Eagle Street, St. Paul, marched up that street, all the way past throngs of spectators, to Third, down Third to Jackson, thence to the lower level, where we re-embarked on three steamboats . . . By Tuesday we were in camp, eight hundred of us, on a clover field five miles south of Louisville [KY].

Their main work for seven months was, it must have seemed to them, marching:

> December sixth and seventh we marched to Shepherdsville [KY]
>   April 27 . . . we marched toward Murfreesboro [TN]
>   June 11, the regiment marched to Pikeville [KY] across the Cumberland Mountains . . . The first day, twenty-four hours, I marched with my company forty miles.

On July 13, 1862, the men of the Third marched back to help defend Murfreesboro: "Up to this hour the only ground of discontent that had ever existed in our regiment had been that it had never had an opportunity to fight." But they fought that day. The Union officers (over Andrews's objections), fearing they were outmanned and outmaneuvered, voted to surrender.[4]

Madison Bowler, one of the men of the Third, gave his version of the surrender in a letter to his fiancée, Lizzie:

> I enlisted last fall through patriotic motives, with very little regard to my personal convenience or to position, and because I considered it my duty and privilege to do something for my country at an hour when my humble services were of some avail . . . I longed for the time to come when we should have the opportunity of trying our mettle on the field of battle, not that I felt particularly brave, but because that was what we enlisted for—*to fight*. That time came. We met the enemy and put him to flight in every encounter, when all at once our glorious war was turned into a shameful surrender by the unaccountable conduct of our officers.[5]

Bowler and the other enlisted men were taken to St. Louis, exchanged for Confederate prisoners (on condition they wouldn't bear arms against the Confederacy for the duration of their parole), and sent back to Minnesota, where they were put into service in the Dakota War in August 1862. Here, A. C. Smith of Meeker County takes up the story:

> [Following a march of about two miles] they formed in open line and ordered to advance which they did until they came within about two hundred yards of where the Indians had been seen, when the Indians opened fire on the company, which the company promptly returned.
>
> After fighting for some time, without any particular damage to either party . . . the captain ordered a charge . . . with fixed bayonets.
>
> This was probably the bravest act of the day—when we take into consideration that Captain Stout's company was mostly made up of business and commercial men and dapper-fingered clerks from Minneapolis and St. Paul, many of them hardly knowing enough about fire arms to load their own pieces.

These soldiers apparently could not fire too well, either. Smith told of a man they presumed to be Little Crow, who stepped up on a fence and shouted orders to his men. The captain called for his best sharpshooters to fire. They did and missed. In frustration, he called on the whole company to fire. It did and missed, too. Smith went on: "Whereupon Mr. Indian coolly stepped down from the fence, made a graceful bow, with a waive [*sic*] of the hand, as much as to say 'thank you gentlemen.' The whole affair was so bold and graceful that our men could hardly refrain from giving the old red-skin three rousing cheers." This was certainly the last lighthearted moment in the battle of Wood Lake, which left at least three Union soldiers dead and eighteen wounded, the Indian casualties unknown to the whites.[6]

In December 1862 Andrews rejoined the Third Minnesota, and in
January 1863 the company left Winona:

> Reveille was sounded at a quarter past three that stormy winter morn-
> ing. At daylight we marched out, going from La Crosse [WI] to Cairo
> [IL] by train, and by steamboat to Columbus, Kentucky.
>   At last the Third Minnesota was sent to the front. June fifth [1863] we
> embarked for Vicksburg [MS].
>   Our duty was to fell trees in the ravines and to dig rifle pits—contin-
> uous trenches—around the brow of the bluff and its spurs. We assem-
> bled and started out every morning at four a.m., marching a mile or
> more to the place of work.

With the Third taking part, Vicksburg fell on July 4, 1863, and 32,000
Confederates became prisoners of war. Six weeks later the Third participated in seizing and then holding Little Rock, Arkansas. The men of the
Third had suffered from measles at Murfreesboro; at Vicksburg many of
them took sick with malaria—poisoned, the Third Regiment's physician
reported, by poor water. After Little Rock, the men moved to Pine Bluff
(1864) on the Arkansas River, where nearly all of them sickened and at
least thirty died of malaria. Weeks passed before any quinine could be
procured even for the doctor, but Hans Mattson, one of the officers, secured a furlough for many of the men so that they could return to Minnesota to recover. By the summer of 1865, most of the men of the Third
were home for good.[7]

Much of the work of war is men's—the decision to go to war, to volunteer (or be drafted), to determine strategy and tactics, to follow orders.
Civil War folklore recounts tales of women who disguised themselves
as men to join up, but no more than a few entered the fighting. Even
Susan B. Anthony, whatever her beliefs about women getting the vote
and being accorded a fuller place in society, did not imagine that women
would take up arms in this most uncivil of wars. Fighting and dying
were men's work.

War creates enough work for everyone. Women didn't enlist and
march and fight and die, but they did follow the troops to do laundry,
make meals, and nurse the sick and wounded. Only rarely were they
lovesick and lonesome wives; more often they were hired immigrants
or African American women who needed the pay. One atypical woman
among the 20,000 northern nurses and hospital workers was Eliza
Garver from Dodge County, Minnesota. Dr. James and Mrs. Garver and
their children had moved from Ohio to Indiana, then to Minnesota in
1857. Believing when the war broke out that the soldiers needed their
help more than their children did, the couple went together to the front,
where he worked as a surgeon with the 136th Indiana Infantry and

she as his nurse. Their oldest son served as an assistant surgeon with another Indiana company. The Garvers' son lost his life; the parents remained in the South until the end of the war and their own illness sent them home.[8]

Most Minnesota women stayed home and picked up the reins—literally and figuratively—that the soldiers dropped. Hired men (when they could be had), partners, or older sons could carry on some of the work, but much fell to wives, mothers, sisters, daughters. In addition to the normal duties of making meals, clothing, bedding, gardens, and good children, women took on the care of animals and farms, tended the shops, ministered to the sick, and put out the newspapers. Some focused their efforts primarily on relatives and neighbors, limiting their work and benevolence to those they knew. All took on what in peacetime was considered "men's work."[9]

Women who hadn't done so before now had to learn how to manage a household and a budget, to make decisions. Lizzie Bowler, the wife of Madison Bowler of the Third Regiment, didn't entirely welcome her new role. She waved good-bye to Madison, "the one in whom all my happiness depends on this earth" in August 1861. When the Third returned to Minnesota after Murfreesboro, Madison and Lizzie married, and he continued on with his unit.[10]

Finding herself pregnant, Lizzie soon urged him to return: "I want you to make up your mind to come home by the middle of Sept not to make a visit but to stay."

Madison rejected her request: "I don't want to go home until the war is over . . . If I should go home now, I could not feel at home among the unpatriotic stay-at-homes."

Madison's absence forced Lizzie to handle the family's business as well as the birth of their daughter alone. On various business matters—should they buy Mr. Dodge's property or rent another piece, for example—Lizzie asked Madison's advice, which he gave, but he handed the decision to her: "I leave it entirely with you to do as you think best." Lizzie accommodated the demands of her war work but chafed at them, no matter how patriotic she felt.

Other Minnesota women assisted in the war effort in concrete and material ways, often through local aid societies. The U.S. Sanitary Commission (USSC), founded in New York early in the war by Unitarian minister Henry Whitney Bellows, aimed to provide supplies for soldiers and to consolidate local efforts. The commissioners depended heavily on women's contributions and fund-raising. Mary Livermore, codirector of the commission's northwestern branch in Chicago, reported receiving from Minnesota—and elsewhere—boxes of "beautifully made shirts, drawers, towels, socks, and handkerchiefs, with 'comfort-bags' containing combs, pins, needles, court-plaster, and black sewing-cotton, and with a quantity of carefully dried berries and peaches."[11]*

Livermore and the commissioners shared gender-role definitions that limited women's responsibilities in the USSC, but Livermore's work over the war years had the effect of radicalizing her. This woman who before the war turned a cold shoulder to the woman suffrage movement was an active suffragist by war's end. By stretching gender definitions about women's spheres, by allowing women leeway or pushing them to test their abilities, and by highlighting men's resistance to women's expanding roles, war work radicalized others as well.

In 1863 the Chicago office, having seriously depleted its funds in relieving the need among the soldiers at Vicksburg, wanted a new money-raising idea. Livermore and her codirector, Jane Hoge, organized a Sanitary Commission Fair, hoping to raise $25,000 by selling contributed items. "The gentlemen members of the Commission barely tolerated" so female a method, Livermore reported, but let the women go ahead. The fair raised $86,000, including $3,000 for the auction of the original copy of the Gettysburg Address that Livermore persuaded Lincoln to donate. The fair was so successful that others followed, and men took a much more active role.[12]†

In 1865, Governor and Brigadier General Stephen Miller, who also served as president of the Minnesota branch of the USSC, and Edward Eggleston, special agent for the Sanitary Commission Fair, appealed to Minnesotans not to fall behind other northwestern states in generosity, to contribute to a "Minnesota Department" at the 1865 fair to be held in Chicago. They requested wheat, butter, eggs, potatoes, "Indian curiosities of every kind," and fancywork from ladies' aid organizations. Miller and Eggleston called on the state's women to solicit and collect the contributions, promising, "A committee of Minnesota Ladies will take charge of the department in Chicago." The 1865 Chicago fair raised $325,000. By one estimate, women donated 25,000 quilts for auction at sanitary commission fairs. War work—materially and morally—was women's work after all.[13]

Of the men who went off to war, 2,500 did not come home and another 2,500 came home wounded. The number of men who returned with physical wounds or what novelist Gary Paulsen called "soldier's heart" and we now call "post-traumatic stress disorder" is incalculable. Moreover, because of the rapid population migration into the state after the war, the number of veterans from elsewhere who settled in Minnesota cannot be calculated. An incomplete list of veterans living in Windom in 1872, for example, included ten from Minnesota units, fif-

*

Minnesota's contributions lagged behind those from Iowa, Illinois, and Wisconsin, due in large part to the much smaller population of Minnesota but also due to the Dakota War and the relative immaturity of many of Minnesota's settlements. Between March 1864 and March 1865, for example, residents of Iowa sent 3,340 boxes to the Chicago office; Wisconsin, 3,165; Illinois, 3,918. Minnesota sent only 210.

†

Before the war's end, the various sanitary commission units had held thirty-four fairs and raised more than $4.4 million.

teen from Wisconsin, four each from Ohio, Vermont, and Iowa, plus a couple from New York and Illinois and one from Maine. They all brought crucifying memories of their war experience, but not all were incapacitated or crippled—physically or emotionally—by their experiences.[14]

Wartime letters from soldiers to family and friends at home rarely detailed the horrors of war or even the men's fears and sorrows. They did express loneliness. Perhaps some veterans whispered of other emotions to wives in darkened bedrooms, but few wrote of feelings in their autobiographies—sanitized accounts of brave deeds, sickness, and duty stoically borne. Officials believed the best medicine for returning vets was quick, smooth reintegration into regular society. Any "exemption from the ordinary rules of life" would corrode their morals and their will.

Neither do we know much about the effects of the war on women's lives. The deaths of so many men of marriageable age significantly decreased the marriage choices for a whole generation of women. If even half of Minnesota's war dead were already married when they enlisted or were drafted, that left more than 1,000 widows. Federal pensions for widows who could prove their husbands had suffered war-related deaths were appropriated in 1862. Requiring that women relinquish the pensions if they took another husband, they served to discourage remarriage. These two factors alone left an oddly configured society. What of the women whose men came home physically or psychically damaged? The winds of grief and pain (and their cousin emotion, anger) must have swirled through many homes and farms, towns and families, over the next fifty years. Did the wounded simply bury it?[15]

The need of some returning veterans for substantial care led Congress to fund—out of the proceeds of seized Confederate property—several Asylums (later called Homes) for Disabled Volunteer Soldiers. Fewer than half of the veterans admitted to the National Home in Milwaukee, Wisconsin, arrived with combat injuries; another 35 percent suffered some form of illness, ranging from blindness to syphilis. One veteran described his malady as shell shock, another as drug addiction. Over the years, alcoholism increasingly plagued the inmates (as cause or effect of institutionalization isn't clear). No more than five percent of veterans ended up in such asylums, but even that made for a total of more than 102,000 men treated there from 1866 to 1900. The last one closed in 1937.[16*]

Eliza Garver and her husband, James, came back from the war "broken in health," though they both lived another three decades. He practiced medicine for twenty years before applying for his Civil War pension. She opened and managed a hotel in Dodge County and became active in her Congregational church and in the Ladies' Aid in Dodge Center. Like many women across the country in the 1870s, Eliza participated in the campaigns against alcohol.[17]*

Not immediately but within a few years, veterans began forming local chapters of the Grand Army of the Republic (GAR), a self-help and benevolent association. Under the banner of "Fraternity, Charity, and Loyalty," the GAR, founded in 1866, helped veterans as well as war widows and orphans. It attended to pensions and memorials and provided company and companionship. No more than 40 percent of American veterans ever joined the GAR, but it proved especially popular among native-born white men, who built local halls, held regular meetings, and invited their women's auxiliaries to give picnics and parties.

In Meeker County, the Frank Daggett Post—named after a commander of two all-black, heavy-artillery regiments and the first grand commander of the Minnesota GAR—built its Litchfield hall to look like a fort. For many years after the war, veterans met in "encampments" with their soldier mates. As late as 1896, veterans met at a GAR National Encampment in St. Paul, living in tents, wearing their medals (both war medals and newly struck encampment medals) and what bits of their old uniforms had survived—hats mostly.[18]†

War did not stretch men's gender roles appreciably, though it did stretch women's. At war's end, many Americans were bent on reclaiming—reestablishing, perhaps even reinventing—a remembered social order. That meant imposing or restoring, sometimes strengthening, role definitions and boundaries. Women's role definitions snapped back into place in the blink of an eye. Some women—like Lizzie Bowler—seemed happy to relinquish the "man's work" that war had forced on them. But not all women. The last forty years of the nineteenth century saw women crafting public lives that, while still gender appropriate, provided avenues for them to develop and express their energies, talents, and opinions. The Women's Relief Corps (WRC), the auxiliary to the Grand Army of the Republic, shared the GAR's commitment to caring for veterans, widows, and orphans, served as the women's veterans association, and took as its goal "To cherish and emulate the deeds of our Army Nurses and of all loyal women who rendered loving service to our country in her hour of peril." The WRC knew what it was doing, too. It recognized that it "blazed trail" for other women's organizations by teaching its members discipline and parliamentary rules. As the veterans' relief work tapered off, WRC members turned their energy to teaching and defending patriotism, Americanization, "the spread of universal liberty and equal rights to all," and prohibition of alcohol.[19]‡

Robert Bruce, a barber in St. Paul since 1857—and one of the 250-plus African Americans in Minnesota—enlisted in the Eighteenth U.S. Colored Infantry. After the war, Bruce returned to his Irish wife and two children and to cutting hair. By 1900, Bruce, at age sixty-six, lived among hundreds of other veterans at the Minneapolis Soldiers' Home. Other African Americans came to Minnesota after and sometimes as a result of the war. C. C. Andrews, like many military officers, often employed black men (escaped slaves, usually) as servants, and they returned to Minnesota with him at the end of the war. While on duty in the South, Orin Densmore from Red Wing recruited African Americans to go to Minnesota to assist his labor-starved relatives and neighbors.[20]

The Civil War ended slavery but did not solve—indeed, made more complex—racial issues in the United States generally and in Minnesota particularly. The Civil War seemed to identify race and racial issues in America—ever since—as white and black. This was a new construction in a place where the English separated themselves by "race" from the French and considered the Irish to be lower than the French, where black and white Americans both occupied the category of Euro-Americans from the vantage point of Native Americans. Moreover, "Indian"—an amalgam of hundreds of distinct Native American cultural and linguistic groups—was a category still in the process of creation.[21]

Some white Minnesotans pushed the legislature to prohibit freed slaves from migrating to the state. Police officers and (reportedly) Irish immigrants—Catholic, non-Anglo, and frantically poor many of them—tried on more than one occasion to keep African Americans from stepping off the boats that brought them up the river to St. Paul, knowing or fearing that to many Minnesotans, Irish and blacks were little different. Some Minnesotans who had weathered the Dakota War resented the federal government's (however meager) attention to freed slaves in the face of its silent response to pleas for help in 1862.*

Neither were whites in the state exempt from the racism that was a part of white American culture in the mid-nineteenth century (and later). Jobs for black men and women became even more racially typed after the war. J. K. Hilyard had cleaned and repaired clothes; his sons became waiters and porters. Robert Bruce's son became a barber. As late as 1926, an Urban League history concluded that blacks had attempted "ineffectively and futilely to become a part of the industrial life of the community."

Despite this bleak and pained conclusion, some African Americans built churches, opened shops, and ran successful businesses; C. P. Wade was appointed postmaster; a few other black men accepted nomination to government offices. Women contributed to the Ladies' Union League, and men and women both supported the union's Benevolent League. Such particulars were testimony to the aspirations of African American people in the state—but also to their thwarted ambitions.[22]

* No matter that the white settlers should have held the government, not the black immigrants, accountable.

* * *

As a result of both the Civil and the Dakota wars, Minnesota's Indians occupied an even more precarious position after 1862. John Campbell and some other mixed bloods joined the Union Army for various reasons—to prove their patriotism, test their mettle, and get away from home—the same reasons other men volunteered. Campbell took up arms against the Confederates as a member of a German company of what later became Brackett's Battalion. "The Notorious John L. Campbell" proved a talented scout and "pressed his spirit of adventure to the limits." Other mixed bloods served just as ably and more responsibly, especially as scouts and, particularly after 1862, in the West, where with the troops of Henry Sibley (in 1863) and Alfred Sully (in 1863, '64, '65), they pursued Dakota people across Dakota and Montana territories.[23]

Ojibwe men made up a portion of the Ninth Minnesota Volunteers stationed in 1862 and 1863 in Tennessee, Mississippi, and Alabama. Captain Charles Beaulieu and twenty-five other Ojibwe soldiers served in Company G of the Ninth in southern Minnesota, including Mankato in 1862. The army had long exploited Indian rivalries by using one group against another. Was the army taking advantage of the traditional rivalry between Dakota and Ojibwe—cynically employing Indian to fight Indian—or simply deploying soldiers where they were needed?[24]

Not surprisingly, the Indians' war against the settlers proved more memorable to white Minnesotans than did their membership in the Union Army. After the war, most Indian soldiers—and other Indians— went or returned to traditional band villages or reservations at Grand Portage (designated 1845), Fond du Lac or Mille Lacs (1854 and 1855), Leech Lake (1850s–60s), White Earth or Nett Lake (1866), or Red Lake (1889). There they resumed the parts of traditional life they could, adjusting to outside demands when they couldn't. White insistence on Indian "civilization" increasingly took the form of sending the children to government-funded schools sometimes on the reservations but more and more often away—to boarding schools.[25]

The Dakota and Civil wars lingered in the state in multiple ways: in the people, in the virulently anti-Indian feelings of many settlers, in the legacy of Indian resentment, in the abiding veteran's organizations, the pensions, the encampments, the GAR halls, and the hospitals, in the memorials erected to make sure no one forgot. Together, though often in their separate ways, women and men—Indian, African American, Euro-American— richer and poorer, built new lives and communities from the ashes and opportunities of the war. The builders did not start on an even playing field; they did not leave the gate at the same time; they did not all run at the same speed. Some won, and some fell out of the race. Pioneering, like war, took people's limbs or lives; it bled them dry, made them heart-sick, imprisoned some and destroyed others. Like soldiers at the beginning of a war, however, most went to their pioneering with high hopes, only vague knowledge that some people would be lost, and confidence that it would not be them. Some pioneers surprised even themselves at how well they managed; others were surprised by how much harder it was than they'd imagined it could be.

7

Not Drawn to Scale

THE GROWTH OF FARMS, TOWNS, BUSINESSES, POPULATION, and railways dominated the fifteen years following the Civil and Dakota wars. Settlers from overseas had stayed away during the war, and internal migration slowed, but at war's end people cascaded into the state, enticed by peace and the free land offered under the 1862 Homestead Act.

Hans Mattson helped recruit a lot of those immigrants himself. As a nineteen-year-old Swedish immigrant, he arrived in New York in 1851. Traveling by rail, train, lake boat, canal, and wagon, Mattson ended up in Chicago, then finally came to Minnesota. Like many immigrants, Mattson served in the Union Army, then worked as a farmer, newspaper editor, land agent. By the late 1860s, Mattson found work as the director of the Minnesota Bureau of Immigration. It was his job to sell the state, one piece of land at a time. Far from considering immigrants to be drains on the economy, nineteenth-century boosters saw newcomers as the fuel for the engine of development, and land was one of the strongest allures.[1]

Mattson used words and ethnicity to sell. His *Land för emigranter utåt Lake Superior & Mississippi jernvagen mellan St. Paul och Duluth i staten Minnesota, Nordamerika* (in Swedish) and his *Land for emigranter ved Lake Superior & Mississippi jernveien mellem St. Paul og Duluth i staten Minnesota, Nord-Amerika* (in Norwegian) offered a land that, if not quite paved with gold, did hint of milk and honey. He worked in Sweden and Norway on behalf of the state of Minnesota and the St. Paul and Pacific Railroad, as well as for the land and immigration agent of the Lake Superior and Mississippi Railroad and later for the Northern Pacific. They had land to sell—lots of it.[2]

Guidebooks produced and distributed in English (or any one of a dozen other languages and circulated both in Europe and in major American cities) captured the images in words: "Thousands are coming annually to secure good farms for themselves and their families—farms that will, in a few short years, be in the midst of cultivated neighborhoods, with churches and school-houses arising at every hand, amid all the surroundings of civilization and progress" offered *The Minnesota Guide: A Hand Book of Information for the Travelers, Pleasure Seekers and Immigrants,* edited by John Fletcher Williams (later head of the Minnesota Historical Society). Williams told readers, for example, of Winona's "fine public schools," "several fine churches, and a number of costly and substantial business blocks and elegant private residences"—no doubt nearly true. "Winona," he went on, "will ere long be quite a railroad centre"—only a slight exaggeration (by about a decade). Settlers and businessmen were the main audiences for the maps and guides, but the authors sang the state's praises to hunters, too: "Minnesota offers extraordinary attractions for the tourist and sportsman," especially in the fall, when "the woods are full of game—deer[,] pheasants, pigeons, &c., and the lakes covered with geese[,] wild ducks[,] and game." He finished, "It is a sport fit for a prince, and costs but little." How could anyone resist?[3]

Mattson and Williams were ambitious for their state; in this they were not atypical nineteenth-century men. Individuals, villages, towns, counties, states—all were ambitious. Some places would rise and fall; others would rise and keep rising. Towns argued over who would have the county courthouse or poor farm; counties about the location of the prisons and the state mental institution, the state university and the capitol. Everyone who owned land wanted to make sure that their holdings were in the rise-and-keep-rising area. Land speculators were not a breed apart: they were what most any man (or woman) who could afford to be was.

This hunger and passion for growth created a ready market for maps in the nineteenth century. In 1850, just after Minnesota became a territory, Thomas Cowperthwait published a "Map of Minnesota Territory" that gave people some idea of the newly organized place. It shows county and township lines and a few numbered sections. It locates St. Paul, St. Anthony, Stillwater, and a few other Euro-American settlements; several trading posts; Fort Gaines and Fort Snelling. The map also identifies several Indian villages (only Black Dog, near Fort Snelling, by name), gives the "Southern Boundary of Chippewa Country," and denotes Assiniboine Country and the land of Menominees and Winnebagoes. The map pays special attention to transportation routes (St. Peter to Pembina), rivers and lakes, and the locations of ferries and of falls. Cowperthwait more often than not gave to waterways two names: Gull or Gayashk River, Minnesota or St. Peter's River; Rum or Isko de Wabo River; Arikara or Kettle Creek. He also identifies pre-1851 Native American locations.

After the Civil War, the hunger for land—and therefore for maps—accelerated, and mapmakers flourished by making what came to be called bird's-eye view maps. A cross between a flat surface map (like Cowperthwait's) and panoramic paintings (a centuries-old style for depicting towns), a bird's-eye view map looks down at a town from an oblique angle—like a plate tipped up at the back—and depicts individual buildings, streets and trees, wagons and horses, sometimes an idyllic landscape in the front. It makes for a strange perspective and for a violation of more than one rule of proportion and balance, but the mapmakers knew their market. Maps would sell better if people could point to a particular place and say, "that's mine."[4]

Before the Civil War, a few artists had drawn a few panoramic maps in the United States, but afterward itinerant artists traveled the United States and Canada making hundreds and selling thousands of these maps of American towns and cities. One of the most prolific of the itinerant panorama painters, and "the first to achieve success as a panoramic artist," was Albert Ruger, a stonemason born in Prussia. By the time he was twenty-one he had served in the Prussian Army and migrated to the United States. He enlisted with the Union Army in 1865, joining a company at Camp Chase near Columbus, Ohio, a camp that housed both new recruits and Confederate prisoners. While it was "one of the most ably administered camps in the North," it was severely overcrowded in late 1864–65, and prisoners in large numbers were dying of smallpox (499 deaths in February 1865 alone). Ruger spent a long enough time there to prepare an intensely detailed map of the camp—down to infantry exercising in the field, inmates in the prison yard, wagons, horses, canons, and trees sprinkled throughout. Long enough, too, to witness the agony that went on in camp.[5]*

*

Ruger must have picked up a pencil long before 1865, but one of his first (surviving) drawings depicts Camp Chase. There's no indication that the map was commissioned by the army, and, in fact, it was privately printed, so he probably drew it for money.

In 1866 Ruger joined this army of artists who traveled the United States drawing and hawking bird's-eye view maps and, as their most dedicated historian argues, "chronicl[ing] for us the swiftly changing appearance of the country's towns and cities" and offering to ambitious townspeople a handsome way to advertise their town's advantages. These maps and their artists gained commercial and popular success in the years between 1867 and 1890. Ruger drew eighteen maps of Minnesota towns between 1867 and 1870 and another of Minneapolis a decade later.[6]

Ruger's 1867 map of Lake City (at Lake Pepin on the Mississippi River) shows a town humming with activity and promise. A big paddle wheel and two smaller ones as well as a tugboat and barge, two canoes, several sailing ships, and a flock of birds rush across the foreground. He

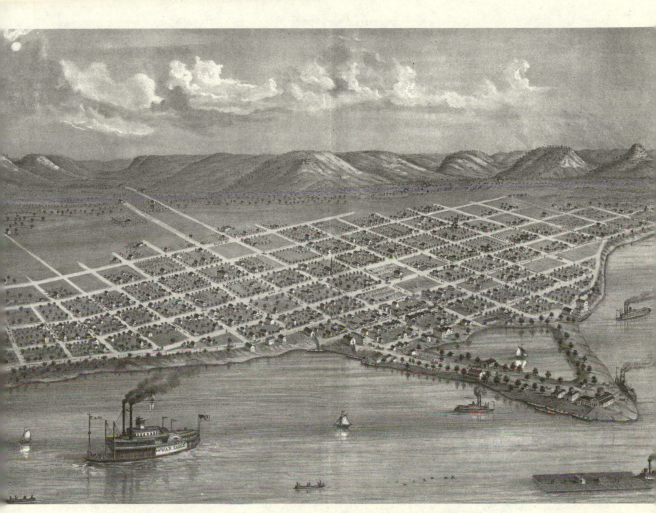

Bird's-eye view of Lake City, 1867

shows people, too, active and moving around: on foot, in wagons, on horseback, by water. Boats sit ready to be loaded with goods. The streets have names. They're wide and clean, and there are just enough trees to offer a little shade or decoration but not enough to impede the building of new houses or businesses. Even the few Indians who are identifiable have been put to "useful" work, paddling the two canoes—one of them is carrying a non-Indian couple; the other, three people, one of whom is holding a rifle. Telegraph lines and native canoes coexist peacefully in the Lake City of 1867.

Ruger drew his map of Faribault in 1869 from an especially steep angle in order, no doubt, to be able to include the Straight River and the Deaf and Dumb Institution (as it was called then) in the foreground, the Cannon River to the side, and the Milwaukee and St. Paul Railroad

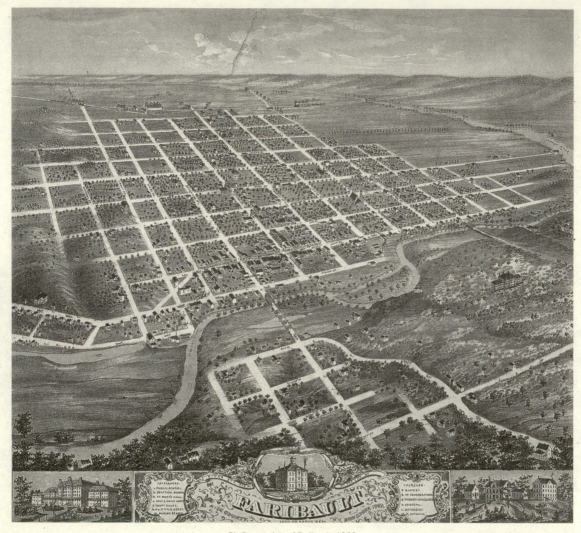

Bird's-eye view of Faribault, 1869

depot and two racing trains at the top. In addition, the map includes and
identifies six churches and the Shattuck, St. Mary's, and Parish schools.
Ruger's map shows the grid of the town, trees, houses, and businesses—
many of them with smoke pumping out of their stacks. Two trains—
steam blowing straight back to show their speed—head for the depot.[7]

   Cowperthwait's 1850 map took in the whole state; Ruger always
focused on a town and its environs. Cowperthwait showed rivers and
streams in careful detail and used dots and triangles to designate settlements. Ruger always included individual buildings, trees, and people.
Despite their differences, each map tells much about the place it depicts
and both look "objective," as if they are simply representing what was.

   But neither mapmaker simply recorded what he saw. As contemporary geographers remind (or warn) us: maps are always made for something and are good for something. They ask us to look at "projections"— the angle of vision. Every projection tells one thing and not another, is "good for one thing, but not another." Literary theorists, too, remind us that images in general—and maps in this case—"must be understood as a kind of language; instead of providing a transparent window on the world, images [present] a deceptive appearance of naturalness and transparence concealing an opaque, distorting, arbitrary mechanism of representation, a process of ideological mystification." We needn't follow the theorists too far down the path to "ideological mystification," but even a quick comparison of Cowperthwait's and Ruger's maps shows decidedly different points of view, conveyed by the selection of detail, the angle of vision, what's excluded, what's named, and so on.[8]

If Cowperthwait's map was good for showing transportation routes and a bit about the Indian/French and frontier past, Ruger's maps are good for showing industry and promise, order and religion, schools and courthouses. Cowperthwait's map is laid out, compass-like, facing north. Ruger's maps face west or northwest. They don't show fences or farmyards but instead open and presumably available land. The townscapes all have vacant lots, just ready to be taken up. They also show a Minnesota much changed from Cowperthwait's time and view.

Cowperthwait's map offers a history of the state in its double placenames; choosing neither one nor the other, he often included both. He identified Indian villages and trading posts. He let us know that French and Native people and Americans all had a history and a place in the Minnesota of 1850. Ruger's maps don't allow much history. Each river, each street, each place has one name only. No Indian territory and— except for those few Indians paddling the canoes at Lake City—nothing identifiably Native American takes a place in his bird's-eye views.*

By one account, the bird's-eye view maps turned into a near "mania" in the United States in the years after the war. Why, I wonder? Why not just use Cowperthwait-type maps? What "good" did the Ruger maps do in the postwar years? Maps—like the photographs in a later chapter— suggest not just what could be seen but a way of seeing, too. From their elevated vantage point, Ruger's maps remove themselves from whatever chaos, disorder, or reminders of the Civil War existed on the landscape. As his map of Camp Chase did not show—or even suggest—anything about the suffering of the men in the prison, his town maps do not show veterans with missing limbs, families with missing brothers or sons or fathers. From that distance, the maps don't show anything dark at all. All of his maps have big, puffy clouds on generally blue-sky days. It never rains in his places; buildings don't burn, ships don't sink, people

*See two canoes in lower left corner of Lake City map, page 75.

don't struggle. Did Ruger and other survivors of the Civil War need to be reminded of the country's glorious future? Did they need to stand at some distance and see an orderly and promising world?

He didn't tell us, but the maps tell us that there was a passion for the bird's-eye view that began around 1867 and cooled by the 1890s. No doubt many towns by then had too many details, but many smaller towns that could have been mapped remained unmapped. Perhaps, however, by the 1890s people didn't need so much distance, at least not as much distance as they'd needed in the late 1860s and early 1870s.

When we look at the bird's-eye view maps of this period, then, we see two versions of postwar America: the ambitious and enthusiastic energy for growth and a hint of the lingering pain of war. If we drop down to ground level and look at other "images," we see other stories.

If Albert Ruger had visited Geneva Township in Freeborn County, he would have seen much of the same ambition and growth he chronicled for other places. The township's historian reports that 230 people lived there in 1860, including Milton Morey, who moved from Austin (thirty miles away), and thirty-seven other farmers; ten laborers, merchants, manufacturers, and blacksmiths; four women teachers (Mrs. Clark, Mrs. King, Miss Lucy Thomas, and Miss Charlotte Dalton) and one woman doctor (Mrs. Elizabeth Stacy);* a postmaster, one minister and one priest, a tanner and shoemaker, a carpenter, and "Two Swedes, named Lohyed and Matison [who] put up a store." Elmer Eggleston from Ohio arrived in Geneva with "a grip sack" and an umbrella and high hopes. Other settlers came from Iowa, Illinois, Missouri, New York, Vermont, Canada, Sweden, and Germany. Michael Fenton, an Irish brick maker, lived in eight states (including three years of army service in Florida and a stint in the Mexican war, during which he was wounded) before settling in Geneva Township with his wife and three children.

Within the next decade or two, the two Swedes and the hotel and saloon keepers sold out and moved on. All three businesses changed hands several times, in fact. Milton Morey—one of the farmers—lost his cabin to fire, gave up, and "took his family in an ox team and turned his face towards civilization [home to Austin]" before trying his luck in Yankton, Dakota Territory. Others moved on to Steele, Faribault, Kittson, or elsewhere, "carried off by the western fever," the township historian reported, "which was epidemic." The Irish brick maker and his wife had three more children. They lost five of them, then he died, and she remained with her one son and his family, their "fever" cooled.[9]

Geneva wasn't exceptional in the mobility of its population. Mary and George Carpenter moved from Rochester, Minnesota, to Marshall, Minnesota, and back again repeatedly in the 1870s. The Christie fam-

*
In the conventions of the time, women who carried the title of Mrs. and then their own first names were most often widows, whereas the women who were Mrs. without a first name were living with husbands; "Miss," of course, meant not married.

ily moved from Scotland to Ireland to Wisconsin to near Mankato, Minnesota. Three Christies went south for army duty in the Civil War. Later, two of them and their sister went to Wisconsin for school, after which one went to Washington, DC, another to Turkey. In this era, many Americans had many kinds of "fever" that took them from one place to another, to another, to another. Whether as a result of Mattson's recruitment or Ruger's maps or the strongest inducement of all—land—immigrants crossed oceans and continents to make their way to Minnesota. Not just Germans, Swedes, Norwegians, and Danes, Belgians, Swiss, and Luxembergers, but Hungarians and Ruthenians, Romanians and Greeks, Turks, Armenians, Icelanders, Finns, Bohemians, Czechs, Poles, Slovaks, Ukrainians, Middle Easterners, Latvians and Estonians and Chinese.[10]

Dreams might sometimes foretell the future, but sometimes they blinded people, too. One day in 1867, Gertrude Braat came home from school in Amsterdam to find her mother and their family servant packing up the household goods. Her parents and a group of about thirty friends had plans to move to Silver Creek Township, Wright County, Minnesota. These were not country people or farmers, but urban families. Gertrude's own father was an architect; another in their party was a clothing designer; others were businessmen or small merchants. Only the doctor had practical skills that would be immediately useful in their new life. Nor were they leaving behind a peasant house and barn. Theirs was a big Amsterdam house with high ceilings, a library, and many fine things. One grandfather had been mayor of the town of Gouda; the other, a manufacturer of cod-liver oil. Her grandmother took pride in setting a beautiful table, and her great-aunt served tea in delicate china cups. Her grandfather could trace his ancestors back three hundred years and had an elegantly drawn family tree to show the connections. Gertrude found her mother crying as she packed, not so much because they were leaving as that she had to leave behind so many of her fine things (including the portraits of the ancestors). It wouldn't be the only thing Mrs. Braat would cry about.[11]

Gertrude's father had bought—sight unseen—a house and two barns. He certainly knew that he wasn't moving to a place like the one he was leaving behind, but even he was dumbstruck to find that he'd purchased a roofless log house and two log stables.*†

The men and the women and the children, nonetheless, turned to farming and adapted to their new lives. The Dutch women knew how to plan meals, how to oversee servants making them, how to lay a table with fine china—but not how to make meals or take care of a household

*

This was likely a farmstead abandoned in 1862 during the Dakota War, when so many white settlers simply fled, never to return. About Indians Gertrude wrote, "We had heard of Indians before coming to America and had seen many pictures of them with their bright shawls and feathers, and their bows and arrows . . . It never occurred to us they would harm anyone." Their personal experiences with Indians proved friendly enough, but local stories made them mistrust their judgment.

†

When Mr. Braat built his house he insisted on lumber—no logs for his house; neither would they have dirt floors—only wood floors, even if some of the hired men spit their tobacco on them.

themselves. They quickly learned how to pack lunches—with their china no less—for the men working outdoors. One by one those china cups—and the dreams they represented—broke and were discarded to be replaced by more durable and practical, if uglier, thick white cups. The men, too, adapted. When Gertrude's father was assigned to plant corn, without understanding but having watched other men sow wheat, he flung the seed as he'd seen them do. Later attempts to replant the corn in straight rows failed, and the Dutch settlers reaped no corn crop that first year.

One by one the Dutch families gave up and moved to town, some back to Holland. Gertrude's family stayed, however, and "the emptiness that made a place for bitter woe crept through our hearts." The Braats eventually made a living in Minnesota, but it took a long time. They earned their first cash in their third year, gathering and selling cranberries and ginseng. In their fifth year, the Braats and other Minnesota farmers faced a plague of biblical proportions when Rocky Mountain locusts (grasshoppers) descended on the crops, clotheslines, and chicken yards of at least one-third of the state. Like thousands of their neighbors, the Braats stood helplessly by, watching the grasshoppers' first astonishing appearance in 1873 and then their repeated appearances until 1878. There was little beyond guarding the clothes on the line that they could do to defend any of what they had. Sometimes the grasshoppers were so bad that Gertrude's family hung their wash indoors. They lost crops and vegetables; the more grasshoppers the chickens ate, the worse the chickens tasted. The grasshoppers ate everything except the cranberries and, as Meridel Le Sueur later remarked, the mortgage.[12]*

*
Meridel LeSueur: daughter of socialist crusaders Marion Wharton and Alfred LeSueur, author, historian (*North Star Country* [1945]), blacklisted during McCarthy era

Farmers—even skilled and experienced and well equipped—struggled through the 1870s. The grasshoppers afflicted at least one-third of the state's farms. The 1873 panic and depression affected farms and towns. As people increasingly tied their livelihood to the national economy and regional and national markets, they became more and more vulnerable to rises and falls in that national economy. One of those precipitous falls happened in 1873 (another in 1893). Prices for farm products dropped, transportation costs increased, brand-new railroads went under; businesses not on firm ground slipped away. Residents of Duluth who were banking on their role as middlemen in the international grain and corn trade were hit hard. So were factory workers and people whose work depended on market demands and the availability of cash (dressmakers, implement dealers, shopkeepers, day laborers).

To be connected to national and regional markets, Minnesotans needed transportation. The Red River oxcart trains squeaked their way diagonally across the state from Pembina to St. Paul, carrying carts full of fur pelts coming south, other goods on their return. But most settlers could not transport everything by animal power—too expensive, too slow, perhaps too bone-rattlingly uncomfortable to ride (and too far to walk)—so every farmer, hamlet, and small town dreamt about railroads roaring nearby.

Many of Ruger's maps captured these railroad aspirations. The depots figure prominently with the churches and schools as features pointed out in the map legend. One of the characteristic elements of Ruger's maps, in fact, was two trains racing toward the depot, one coming in from the right, one from the left (sometimes on the same track and sometimes long before any such trains or depots actually figured on the landscape).

Town builders and boosters competed with each other to get the railroad to come to their communities. In April 1869, a group of citizens in Austin met with the representative of the Southern Minnesota Railroad to see what mutually advantageous deal they could work out. There were cheaper routes, the SMR representative explained: perhaps the good people of Austin would help offset those costs by giving the railroad the right of way through town, by offering property for a depot, and by issuing bonds to underwrite the expenses of building a depot. What choice did the town have, the people asked each other. "If we secure this road it will make Austin a junction," the Austin *Democrat* argued. If not, many people feared, "it will kill the town." The town did all it could but, because of the "greediness of the railroad company," failed to secure the SMR line through Austin.[13]*

Dreams were built mile by mile or dashed when land sales dipped or collapsed as they did in 1873, bankrupting several aspiring companies. The railroads that promised (and later delivered) so much did struggle through the 1870s, but the lines grew and extended inexorably, from about six hundred miles of track in 1868 to nineteen hundred miles four years later. At the same time, improvements in milling and wheat seed increased the profitability of wheat farming, if the farmers could get their grain to market.

Ruger's maps feature the railroads but largely ignore the farmers. This might have been just what farmers feared in the post–Civil War years. Farmers, increasingly dependent on the railways, felt ever more invisible and undervalued, as if they were losing their place in society. With all of the enthusiasm—one might say a "mania" that more than rivaled that for bird's-eye view maps—for railroads, as well as with what

*

Even so, such was the growth of railroads in the late nineteenth century that Austin became a stop on the Milwaukee and the Illinois Central lines, both major midwestern routes, and eventually boasted of having "railroad facilities second to none in the State."

*

To help farmers get started
and to push settlement onto
the prairies and plains, the
federal government allotted
160 acres of land to farmers
who paid the filing fee, improved the land, and lived on
it for five years. To support
the building of railroads (before there were enough settlers to create a demand),
the federal government gave
to the land-grant railroad
lines every odd-numbered
section (640 acres) for
twelve miles on both sides
of the right of way. Relatively
more Minnesotans got their
land from the railroad than
from the government under
a homestead claim.

must have seemed to be government support that more than surpassed their own benefit from homestead land in Minnesota, some farmers felt especially victimized by—and thus rageful at—the railways.* But to what end? What else could they do but live with the rates set by the railroads? They could and did begin to organize themselves into various associations. The farmers' first expression of protest came in the form of the Patrons of Husbandry. Founded by Minnesotan Oliver H. Kelley, the first Minnesota Grange was organized in 1869; 538 others had organized five years later. Increasingly, farmers felt they needed to fend for themselves.[14]

The 1870s were hard years to fend alone, farmers learned. African Americans learned, too, as the window that had slid open a few inches after the Civil War—with the passage of the Thirteenth, Fourteenth, and Fifteenth amendments—slammed shut with the end of Reconstruction in 1876 and the increasing desire of (white) Americans to stress their unity rather than their disunity. Ojibwe people, too, found their lives growing more and more difficult in the 1870s–1890s, combating cruel poverty, confined to reservations that offered little and were under constant pressure and danger of disintegration, their children sent away to white boarding schools that received government funding only if they followed "civilizing" rules—cutting the children's hair, forbidding them from speaking in their native tongue, straining their ties to family and community. In the years after the Civil War, a few Dakota people made their way back to Minnesota (and eventually received small allocations of land, including Prairie Island), but most lived at Santee in Nebraska or gave up annuities and were trying to make a go in such places as Flandrau, Dakota Territory.

Even Ruger himself has a story to tell—beyond the ones he tells in his maps. Thousands of Americans (native-born and immigrant) traveled around the United States to chase work. Ruger himself spent time in at least twenty-four states and two Canadian provinces. Peddlers, knife sharpeners, patent medicine sellers, actors, opera singers, circus performers, milliners, coverlet weavers, hired girls, farmhands, railroad workers, tinsmiths, portrait painters, photographers, teachers, even preachers moved from place to place for work. Most of the women who traveled were either widowed or unmarried; some of the men had wives and children in one place or another. Ruger had a wife in Ohio who seems to have stayed there whatever his travels. And there were drifters, people disconnected from family and friends, from community and church, from politics and place, who moved as the winds and impulse took them. These people, too, were part of the population of Minnesota and of the United States in the years after the war.[15]

Ruger's bird's-eye view maps don't speak to us of all that was Minnesota in the postwar years, but they do speak of people's hopes and aspirations and, by implication perhaps, about their fears and pain, too. They're pictures worth pondering.

Baseball flourished in Minnesota in the 1870s and proved a wonderful diversion if nothing else. A few baseball clubs had played in the late 1850s, but after the Civil War city teams began competing against each other. The North Star Club from St. Paul was the real powerhouse, beating the Fort Snelling team 38–14, the Hastings team 49–16, the Minneapolis team 56–26. Henry Sibley accepted the presidency of a St. Paul round-robin tournament that must have established some records for all-time-high scoring: Vermillion defeated the St. Cloud Arctics 100–44; when the North Stars were up fifty runs on the Arctics, the game was called; then St. Paul beat Vermillion by only 43–35. Trophies and prizes were awarded. These and other games entertained especially the "lady viewers," as one newspaper reported, in most of the towns in the state.[1]

8

Making a Living, Making a Life

MINNESOTA BURST WITH THE ENERGY of nearly 800,000 people in the 1880s. Most of them lived on farms or in small villages. Most of them were white. About one-quarter had arrived in Minnesota from another state (mostly New York); of the immigrants from other countries over 30 percent had come from Germany by 1880, 30 percent from Norway, 19 percent from Sweden, and 19 percent from Great Britain and Ireland.* They all arrived with hope and high expectations. If not streets paved with gold, opportunities and land and promise would do almost as well. There was no Civil War to dim those hopes, nor a Dakota War. The depression and the grasshoppers and the cinch bugs and the killing frosts that had devastated the economy in the 1870s had passed away.[1]

Instead, these hopeful settlers spent the 1880s getting on with their lives, recovering from wounds and losses, getting back to work. One person who can carry the baton of the state story in this era is Mary Gillett, a seamstress who lived in Red Wing, Goodhue County, for a few years in the 1880s.

Goodhue County shows evidence of longtime Native American presence. Set against the backdrop of (and on top of) Indians mounds (4,000 of them, by one estimate), Goodhue County and Red Wing city have an extraordinary beauty. The mounds on Prairie Island alone number over two hundred. They contained Indian remains, objects, evidence of complex human life. Red Wing—named after a Dakota man whose translated name was closer to "Wing of Scarlet"—was home in the late eighteenth century to Dakota Indian people involved in the fur trade. Joseph W. Hancock in 1849 was among the first Euro-Americans to take a bead on the Red Wing area as fertile ground, he hoped, for his missionary zeal. After the first white settlers arrived in 1851 (even before the Dakota had ceded the land in the 1851 treaties of Mendota and Traverse des Sioux), Hancock, like many of the region's missionaries, was more converted himself by his attempts to preach to the Dakota than he was successful

* As is evident in these census figures, the largest single group of immigrants came from Germany, the next from Norway, the next from Sweden, the next from Great Britain and Ireland. When, however, we add together Norwegian and Swedish (and Danes) and call them "Scandinavians," the largest single group is the Scandinavians.

at converting Dakota to his brand of Christianity. In the process he became a fluent speaker of Dakota. The local Indian people contended, too, with disease and were less able to resist its effects, cholera especially.[2]

When Mary Gillett moved to Red Wing, she would not have met or known many—or any—Indians, all of them having been displaced or moved before 1883, when Mary took a job as a seamstress. In 1880, the Red Wing city population stood at just under 6,000; about 40 percent were foreign-born (in comparison to 34 percent statewide); countywide, 75 percent of the immigrants were from Sweden or Norway.[3]

In 1860, fewer than 4,000 women held paying jobs in Minnesota, but then women poured into paid employment of one kind or another. Their numbers increased by nearly 200 percent by 1870, another 140 by 1880, and 150 by 1890. The jobs women held in those years ranged from domestic service to ironers in laundries, from bookbinders to candy rollers. The highest paid were the vampers in shoe factories ($8.50 per week), cigar bunch rollers ($8.00), shoe and boot stitchers ($7.75), and fur finishers ($7.35). Domestic workers got paid the least ($2.79 per week, sometimes with and sometimes without a room). At least a few women worked as prostitutes (*demi-monde* was the state census term), but the Bureau of Labor Statistics did not offer figures for their average income. By comparison, teachers in Minnesota in 1880 earned, on average, $8.50 per week, and virtually everywhere schools paid men teachers more than they paid women.[4]*

Though it certainly revolutionized people's lives, worldview, sense of time, and ways of making a living, industrialization did not occur as a "revolution." There was no defining "shot heard 'round the world" that opened it, nor a peace treaty that ended it. Instead, industrialization was a process of gradual speeding up and "rationalization," specialization, and mechanization of production that changed the relationship of producer to product and between producer and consumer (more distant and impersonal in both cases). It made its first and most evident impact in the United States on the textile industry. The spinning jenny and power looms had speeded up production so that by 1824 the Merrimack Mills in Lowell, Massachusetts, employed women and girls to do at least seven distinct jobs—including doffer, speeder, dresser, spinner, weaver (at different levels of pay, depending on skill)—and men and boys to do ten other jobs—including stripper, grinder, second-hand carder, overseer (also at different levels of pay, all of them higher than the highest-paid woman).[5]

Manufacturing of all kinds, but especially milling, was rapidly overtaking agriculture as the state's economic base.† Minnesota's many waterways made the state an ideal place for assorted milling ventures.

*

In 1880, of the 5,100 teachers in the state, 3,300 were female and 1,800 male. Also in 1880, Minnesota reported having 3,700 seamstresses, dressmakers, and milliners.

†

In 1880, agriculture accounted for only 40 percent of the state's economic base. While Ignatius Donnelly was organizing farmers, urban laborers were also organizing. The first Knights of Labor chapters were founded in Minneapolis in 1878 and in St. Paul in the early 1880s. The St. Paul Trades and Labor Assembly was founded in 1882. Some of the state's most active labor organizations would await the opening of the mines on the Iron Range; the first shipments of iron ore occurred in 1884.

Early on, individuals had mills for their private or local use, but in 1839 the first commercial mill was built at Marine on the St. Croix River. Later, the Pillsbury family moved into Minnesota, and while John served as governor, his brother Charles started large-scale flour milling. In 1883, the Pillsbury Company opened the largest mill in the world. William Washburn (a former Minnesota senator and brother of Cadwallader Washburn, governor of Wisconsin), John Crosby, and William Dunwoody formed Washburn, Crosby and Company.[6]

These men, especially the Pillsburys, developed and applied revolutionary new methods such as the use of middlings purifiers and porcelain rollers to make and sell "Gold Medal Flour" worldwide. By 1884, Minnesota millers were providing one-fifth of the country's export of wheat. The Minneapolis Millers Association cooperated to control prices by taking charge of both storage and the grading of wheat. (The farmers campaigned against all three of these practices.)

Another important kind of miller worked with wood. Minnesota had plenty of trees ready to be turned into logs or timber. A huge need existed for both. Houses and barns, sheds and elevators—all required millions of board feet of timber. Then there were windows, doors, furniture, and shingles for roofs; until the flour sack came into use those flour millers needed barrels, millions of them; the railroads needed rail ties, billions of those. Then there were crates and boxes, farm equipment, and railroad cars—for a time, wood even fueled the trains themselves. Some Minnesotans might have had access to trees or timber for these purposes, but settlers in the more arid and less wooded lands to the west did not.

In the 1880s, industrialization had not yet significantly transformed the mining of iron ore. The Cornish (some of them directly from England and others by way of Michigan) were among the first wave of miners to move onto the Iron Range. Cornish men had been taking minerals out of the ground for generations, and they didn't need power tools or mechanization to do it. "As late as 1855," one historian of the mines wrote, "Cornish miners were descending into mines by ladderway and locating lodes of ore with divining rods." The climbs themselves could take more than an hour when a shaft took men down 1,600 feet. These men worked in family or community groups most often and for a contract, not wages. The major changes in mining occurred after World War I, when machines started to replace mules and men.[7]

Red Wing's location on the Mississippi River, "picturesque in the extreme," provided easy access to shipping—by river and train both—so that it grew up early and fast as a commercial center. It became a shipping point for wheat—and therefore a holding spot with elevators and warehouses—as well as a manufacturing town. Lumber, sash, and doors—the Red Wing Manufacturing Company—and furniture—Red Wing Furniture Company—were among the first industries. The factories were close to the river to collect logs that came downriver and close to the Chicago, Milwaukee and St. Paul Railroad to send its products out. The clay nearby was excellent for the making of stoneware, which "proved to be a success from the start." At the main shop of the Red Wing Stoneware Company, three rail lines entered—the Milwaukee and Chicago, the Minneapolis and St. Louis, and the Duluth, Red Wing and Southern—and carried its pottery, by the 1890s, to at least twenty states. The Red Wing Shoe Company did not open its doors until 1905 but was predated by the Trout Brook Tannery as well as several manufacturers of shoes and boots. These industries made Red Wing a magnet for people in search of work—especially the young and single, especially immigrants.[8]*

Perhaps because sewing, mending, knitting, and quilting had long been "women's work," women found employment in both the cloth and clothing industries. And, when respectable women needed work, they could become seamstresses or dressmakers without appreciable loss of status. Women needed the help of professional sewers, too. "Sewing was," writes material culture historian Marguerite Connolly, "a never-ending, time-consuming task for virtually every woman: farm and city dweller, young and old, rich and poor." Industrialization in the textile mills had made supplies of cloth more readily and widely and plentifully available. The increasing American attention to "style"—another product of industrialization—encouraged the proliferation of clothing, too, among those who could afford it. Connolly catalogs the things that nineteenth-century women made: "all or most of her own and her children's garments, including underclothing, plus some garments for her husband [men's ready-to-wear was more easily available to buy]. In addition, each household had to be supplied with an assortment of linen, including sheets, pillowcases, tablecloths, and towels for bathing and kitchen use, as well as household furnishings such as curtains and throw pillows. All were stitched, hemmed, and mended by the women of the house and her daughters." No wonder the demand for sewing help increased the number of seamstresses and dressmakers throughout the second half of the century, though even "such assistance did not remove the burden entirely from [women's] lives, even for the wealthy."[9]†

Among seamstresses who did not work in factories but in small one- or two- or three-person shops, "industrialization" took the form—such as it was—of sewing machines. Sewing machines almost certainly speeded up Mary Gillett's work in the seamstress shop in Red Wing, though her

*

The other towns that developed early and strong industrial and manufacturing establishments included Winona, Wabasha, Faribault, Rochester, Minneapolis, and St. Paul.

†

Between the 1830s and the early 1870s, every state legislature—including Minnesota's—granted to married women the rights to their own property (including wages). Fifteen states, including Minnesota, continued to hold the view that "when wives entered the world of business and commerce they still needed special care and protection." Single women and widows, legislatures agreed, did not need the same protection.

shop was so small that she still would have had relationships both with her customers as well as with the whole garment or item that she made.[10]

Miss A. M. Gillett—her family called her Mary—had been born in New York in 1861. After the Civil War her family moved to Wisconsin, then to Frankford, Mower County, Minnesota. By 1883 her three brothers were working on the farm with their parents, and her younger brother and sister were attending school. Mary, the second oldest in the family, had moved to Red Wing, where she took work as a seamstress. Mary Gillett was one of eight women in Red Wing in 1880 who earned her living in this way. Eleven others worked in town as dressmakers. Of these nineteen, eight were American-born, six from Norway, five from Sweden. Eleven were single girls or women who still lived with parents and/or siblings, two were widows, and five lived in boardinghouses.[11]*

*
As late as 1900, of the 84,000 Minnesota women who held paid employment, 42,000 worked in domestic service, 14,000 as seamstresses, dressmakers, milliners.

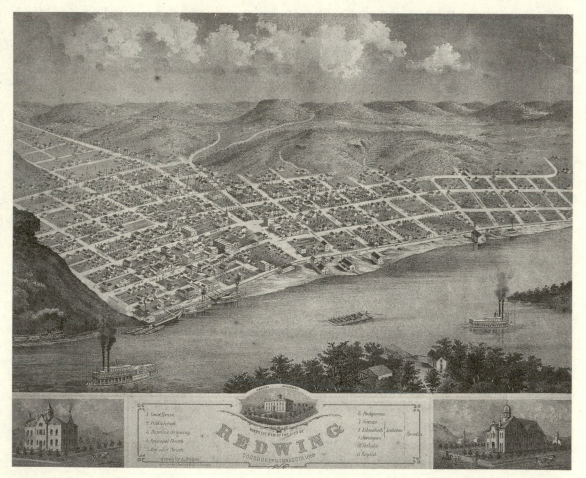

Bird's-eye view of Red Wing, 1868

Perhaps Mary went to Red Wing looking for marriage prospects, perhaps she was a superb and gifted seamstress, perhaps her family needed her to earn some money (perhaps all of the above). The census records and city directories don't tell us that kind of information, but they do help us know something of her life.[12]

Mary lived in a boardinghouse at 110 Third Street in Red Wing, Minnesota. She worked a few blocks away at 409 Third Street. If she walked directly to work, she would have passed through a busy and varied part of town:

111 Third Street, a Prussian cigar maker and his son and apprentice;
218 Third Street, the grocer;
221 Third Street, a carriage maker;
307 Third Street, a saloon;
314 Third Street, the barber;
316 Third Street, a photographer;
319 Third Street, the blacksmith;
320 Third Street, the lawyer, collection agent, and real estate dealer.

At the corner of Third and Bush, Mary could mail letters to her family, look over the furniture made in a small workshop right on her street, and browse the Red Wing shoes made and sold in her town. In her own 400 block of Third Street, Mary could buy candy, stop at a drugstore,

Mary's view walking toward work, Third Street, Red Wing, 1890

make a deposit at the bank, watch the butcher at work. She might have been less interested in the farm implement dealer's or the gunsmith's offerings, but she almost certainly frequented Sam Lee's laundry at 421 Third Street.* If she took a long way to work, she walked past the Red Wing Wagon Company, two other grocers, a dentist, the livery, the marble manufacturer, the printer's shop, fifteen churches, the schools, the meeting place of the GAR. If she finished work after dark she would have walked home along gas-lighted streets; if she spent the evening at home her activities were also lighted by gas.[13]

It's not possible to know for sure if Mary attended church and, if she did, which one. But the Reverend Hancock's history of Goodhue County suggests something of the local sentiment about church attendance. "Everybody goes," he wrote, "it is the proper thing to do, and you have to go to church." She wouldn't have attended the Swedish Evangelical Lutheran (services in Swedish), and perhaps not the Catholic Christ Church. As a "Yankee," however, she could have been attracted to the Methodist, the First Presbyterian, or the Episcopal church. Each of them had strong New England roots. They offered clubs and social groups as well as parish aid, a guild, a library, and a reading room.

If she had gone to Red Wing a decade earlier, Mary might have attended Hamline University. It had opened its doors to women and men (and boys and girls) and graduated its first students—Elizabeth and Emily Sorin—in 1859. Oberlin College in Ohio had been admitting both women and men for over twenty years, but few other colleges followed suit. Instead, Vassar, Smith, Wellesley, and Mills colleges opened especially for women. By the late 1860s Hamline closed; it reopened in 1873 in St. Paul.

Or she might have joined one of the women's organizations that grew up in the late nineteenth century: the Daughters of Rebekah or the Pythian Sisters. If she stayed as late as 1887, she might have joined the newly formed chapter of the Women's Christian Temperance Union, perhaps even a woman's suffrage organization. Women did not yet have the vote in Red Wing or Minnesota. In the 1890s, various proposals—the vote in municipal elections, the vote on matters that had to do with liquor, one that extended the vote to taxpayers—all failed.[14]

In Red Wing, Mary saw the benefits of urbanization as well as the raw materials, the process, and the products of industrialization all around her. As a river town, Red Wing was a depot for the transportation of farm products out of Minnesota and of manufactured goods in. It was possible for her to get back and forth to see her family in Mower County as well as to take an occasional adventure to St. Paul or Minneapolis.

*

Messrs Wah Sam and Chang Sam, who had run a laundry in Red Wing in 1880, had been replaced by the young Quong Long, who stayed a few years before moving on to his own Chinese laundry in St. Paul by 1889. (At least in St. Paul he might have made friends with other Chinese, of whom as late as 1895 there were only 116 in the whole of the state, fifty-one in the Twin Cities. If he had stayed a few years he might well have come within the circle and even eaten at the Chinese restaurant run by the Moy family in St. Paul.)

Mary's life intersected with many different immigrants in her work and in her boardinghouse. Increasingly in the 1880s and later, single men and women—rather than families—made the trip to the United States. Many of the men became farmers or farm laborers or helped build the railroads. Women in large numbers went to work as domestics, or as dressmakers or milliners (hat makers) or lace makers, even as shop girls as they improved their English. At least until marriage—when some women by choice, others by convention went home to take care of husbands and families.[15]

In her neighborhood were many single women her age: Etta Ladd, also a seamstress, from Maine; Olive Toflen, a Swedish dressmaker; Mathilda Wolfkugel, a twenty-three-year-old teacher from France; Hattie Shebrinski, a Polish servant for a big Red Wing family; Catherine Collins, an Irish American woman who made hair switches; and Anna Macauley, who managed the Western Union telegraph office. If she had left Frankford for better marriage prospects, she would have had many men around her age to choose among: James Boyle, an Irish American cooper; Henry Hunstable, who hailed from Virginia and worked for the Red Wing Shoe Company; Ole Oleson, a teamster from Norway; the Swiss American bartender Chris Schneider; Charles or John Bird, both potters at Red Wing Pottery; or perhaps William Stout, a teacher from Pennsylvania.[16]

Perhaps she knew—and was even attracted to—James Fogg, a waiter in a Red Wing hotel and the son of a seamstress mother and barber father. James and his father had been born in Tennessee, his mother in Alabama, and all of them were "mulattos," according to the census category.* By the 1880s, James Fogg lived in one of the most interesting households in town: it included his five-year-old adopted sister, Cecelia (the white daughter of an unmarried German mother); Cecelia and Cornelia Roos, twenty-six-year-old Swedish twins (one a servant and the other a boarder); and Joseph Parker—a forty-three-year-old black laborer born in Kentucky.[17]†

If Mary read the paper—she certainly would have been literate: 96 percent of Minnesotans were in the 1880s—she might have followed the state's politics (though she herself could not vote, she could be politically active in other ways). Lucius Hubbard's election in 1881 as governor (one bead in a long rosary of Republican state governors) probably surprised no one, but the defeat of William Windom in his bid for a third term in the Senate (he had also been a five-term congressman and a member of the cabinet of two different presidents) did. Politics was more often than not bruising, enough that in 1882 reformer Ignatius Donnelly gave up for a time and went home to write. The Republicans had a lock on Minnesota's political life, and in the early 1880s there was

*

His mother's ethnicity is not clear: *mulatto* was a term most often used to describe a person of mixed Caucasian and African American parenthood, but his mother "says her mother was an Indian," as James reported, so perhaps she was. It's hard to know whether being Indian or black in Red Wing would have been more difficult (or more acceptable to neighbors).

†

The Densmore family was heavily invested in timber in Goodhue County. Knowing the shortage of labor in Red Wing during the Civil War, Benjamin Densmore had hired freed slaves to go to Red Wing. Many of those freed slaves stayed after the war years. Frances Densmore—Benjamin's daughter—made the collection of Indian music her life's work.

little political will yet to mount the kind of reform politics that Donnelly—and other farmers and laborers, especially—favored. The economic prosperity of the 1880s encouraged people to let politics slide for a time or, more likely, allowed them to get on with their lives. This would change later in the 1880s and especially with the economic depression that swept the nation in 1893. Then farmers and working people turned their attention more fully back to politics and to the increasingly evident disparities in wealth and economic philosophies that were made so much more intense—and evident—in hard economic times.[18]

She might also have read about the tornado that swept through Rochester in 1883, after which the Sisters of St. Francis of the Congregation of Our Lady offered to build and finance a hospital if Dr. William Worrall Mayo—a longtime physician for the Chicago and Northwestern Railroad and for the Union Army in Minnesota and a volunteer surgeon at the state hospitals at Rochester and St. Peter—would run it. He agreed if his son, William Mayo, Jr. (called Dr. Will to distinguish him from his more proper father), who finished medical school at the University of Michigan in 1883, would join, too.[19]*

She could also have read about Dr. Martha Ripley, who opened a medical practice in Minnesota in 1883. One of only a few women students in her Boston University class, Ripley was older than her classmates (forty), married, and the mother of three daughters. When her husband suffered a disabling injury about the time she finished medical training, they moved to Minneapolis to be near his relatives. Like most other female doctors of her time, she concentrated on women and children. But she defied social convention in her care of unmarried mothers. That hospitals routinely turned away unmarried mothers offended Dr. Ripley's medical and feminist principles. In 1886 she opened a home for pregnant, unmarried women that eventually grew into Maternity Hospital in Minneapolis. She served as superintendent of the hospital for more than twenty-five years and took an active role in the state's woman suffrage association.[20]

A third Minnesotan, Charles Eastman, was in 1883 on the path to becoming a doctor. Ohiyesa—his Dakota name—had been four years old during the Dakota War. Relatives who believed his father would be hanged at Mankato spirited him away to grow up Dakota and safe in Canada. His father—Many Lightnings—was not dead but imprisoned, and in those post–Dakota War years he converted to Christianity, decided that "life on a government reservation meant physical and moral degradation," and took up the white path. He claimed a homestead, renounced government assistance, and changed his name to Jacob Eastman.† In 1876 he tracked down his son in Canada, brought him

*

Dr. William Worrall Mayo is not much revered among many Dakota people. He was part of a long tradition of doctors who used cadavers to perfect his medical techniques, but he offended Dakota people deeply when he dug up the bodies of men hanged at Mankato in 1862 and practiced on them.

†

Jacob Eastman took his wife's maiden name, Eastman, as his new name. His wife was the daughter of Seth Eastman, the army artist who painted extraordinary pictures of Dakota life around the fort. Seth Eastman served at Fort Snelling twice. During his first term, a brief one in 1830, he married Stands-Like-A-Spirit. He returned to the fort from 1841 to 1848 with a new and white wife, Mary Eastman.

back to Minnesota, renamed him, and cut his hair. As the adult Ohiyesa remembered, "all my old ideas were to give place to new ones, and my life was to be entirely different from that of the past." He attended the Santee Normal School, then Dartmouth, a college that though originally founded for Indian boys didn't have more than a few Indian students when Charles was there. He was certainly the only Indian in his 1889 graduating class at the medical school of Boston University—Martha Ripley's alma mater.[21]

Dr. Eastman began his practice at the Pine Ridge Reservation in Dakota Territory, finding that he—like most Dakota people—didn't fit into the "new" Minnesota. In the early 1860s about 7,000 Dakota lived in Minnesota; in 1866, only 374. By 1870 there were 176 "friendlies" at Traverse des Sioux who lived under the protection of Episcopal bishop Henry Whipple and a few others elsewhere in the state. The Ojibwe who hadn't gone to war in the 1860s retained some of their land in the northern and northeastern part of the state in 1883. Whites and Indians both lived within the boundaries of Minnesota, but they had little else in common. The Ojibwe ceded to the U.S. government nearly 2 million acres of land in exchange for cash, annuities, and the promise of schools, houses, and a string of reservations at Red Lake, Leech Lake, Fond du Lac, Net Lake, Gull Lake, White Oak Point, Mille Lacs, Otter Tail, Cass Lake, Lake Winnibigoshish, Bois Forte, Grand Portage, and White Earth. If whites saw a bright future, most Indians saw only more bleak prospects and located their best days behind them. The Nelson and Dawes acts (1887 and 1889) aimed to concentrate Ojibwe on reservations and reallocated Indian land from bands to individuals. The ostensible purpose of these laws was to teach Indians the joys of individual property ownership; the effect was to deprive them of it.[22]

Mary might, too, have read the obituaries of two prominent early Minnesotans who died in 1883: Stephen R. Riggs and Harriet Bishop. Stephen and Mary Riggs and their several children had arrived in 1837 fired by religious fervor and firm determination to convert the Indians. If Mary looked between the lines, she might also have judged that the Indians had had more success in "converting" Riggs. He learned to speak Dakota and helped translate the scriptures. Several of his children turned into dedicated Dakota-speaking missionaries (and one daughter into a missionary who took her calling to China). He became a scholar of Dakota life, legends, and language. His "Mythology of the Dakotas" appeared in *The American Antiquarian* that year.[23]

It was with the hope of improving other people's lives—and the actuality of improving her own—that Harriet Bishop had made her way to St. Paul in 1847 with missionary fervor, a "calm, undefinable joy," and all the uprightness and superiority that her New England upbringing had inspired. She opened first a day school and then a Sunday school of seven "scholars," three whites and four "halfbreeds." For over thirty-five years she made her living among such scholars. There's no indication that her forty years in Minnesota dimmed her sense of superiority; if anything, her experiences, especially relating to the Dakota War, confirmed all her ideas of white superiority. Riggs and Bishop, however, had had a lifetime of associations with Indian people; most new Minnesotans in 1883 and after 1883 had none.[24]*

John Ireland captured more than one headline in the 1880s. Born in Kilkenny, Ireland, in 1840, John settled in St. Paul with his family by 1855. There he captured the notice of Joseph Cretin, the Catholic bishop of St. Paul, who sent Ireland to seminary in France. Following ordination, Ireland served a two-year term as an army chaplain in the Civil War, then settled into St. Paul, where he dominated Catholic life for the next half century, as bishop and then archbishop.[25]

Father Ireland championed three causes: temperance, Irish colonization, and Americanization. He developed a vision of turning his Irish compatriots into American patriots. He resisted parochial schools, fearing they hindered assimilation. He feared, too, that alcohol harmed the members of his Irish flock and kept them from the American mainstream. He had founded and nearly single-handedly run the Catholic Colonization Bureau, which settled Irish Catholic farmers in Irish-named places in western Minnesota—Avoca, Tara, Dublin, Clontarf, Adrian, Iona, Connemara—but folded in 1883. Too many Irish people, having faced such crippling crop failures at home, wanted neither farm life nor rural isolation.[26]

While German emigrants, Catholic and Protestant, had little passion to assimilate to American ways, Ireland believed success in the new place demanded a full-hearted commitment to the new place.† That he left Ireland as a child and that he'd attended school in France served perhaps to loosen his Irish ties; his first pastorate among Union soldiers must have heightened his American loyalty as well. In any case, Ireland championed Americanization. He wanted Irish-Catholics to become American as quickly as possible. On this matter he and his German colleagues disagreed. While, according to one historian of American Catholicism, "The Germans expressly used their schools to fend off assimilation," John Ireland feared that separate parochial schools "delayed the integration of immigrant children into the American mainstream." He pushed and argued and campaigned, then, for public schools (where Catholic schools were leased by the local authority and nuns were hired to teach). Becoming good Catholic Americans was the goal.[27]

In 1883, Mary and some of her friends might well have traveled by train to St. Paul to the grand opening of the Northern Pacific's line from Minneapolis to the Pacific, where they would have seen and heard from Minnesota's great train baron himself, James J. Hill. He presided over the opening of the NP, but his own railroad was the Great Northern. In the 1870s many railroad investors—including Jay Cooke, the leading banker and investor in Duluth—lost both their fortunes and their dreams. Others, including James J. Hill and Norman Kittson,* wagered everything to buy the bankrupt St. Paul and Pacific, which by 1881 made them a profit of about $13 million.* An immigrant from Ontario, Hill was one of the men who actually fit a "rags to riches" plotline. His success drew on his strengths (ambition, willingness to work hard, attention to detail) and made virtues out of his weaknesses (an inability to delegate, absorption in details, willingness to sacrifice personal life to workplace demands). For some of those years Jim and Mary Hill and their growing family (ten children eventually) lived in Lowertown in St. Paul. In 1891 they moved to their palatial Summit Avenue house. That $1 million mansion, with its multiple bedrooms, music room, and art gallery, its finely carved, wood-paneled entry hall and upsweeping central stairway, dominated the St. Paul skyline as clearly as Hill's empire dominated the economy.[28]

Hill's life and fortune interwove with the lives and fortunes of countless other Minnesotans—especially men—in the second half of the nineteenth century. Thousands of men built, repaired, drove for, conducted, loaded cars for, sold tickets for, cleaned, and otherwise worked on the railroad. Many of these employees were Irish (Chinese further west); some were homegrown, including a number of African Americans. The railroad offered relatively good paying work for black men, particularly where discrimination was commonplace, which it was in Minnesota.

Even so, St. Paul and Minneapolis became home in the 1880s to a growing middle-class population of black lawyers, doctors, ministers, charity workers, barbers. Fredrick McGhee was one of them. Born in 1861 in Mississippi, McGhee first practiced law in Tennessee and then established what quickly became a thriving practice in Minnesota. He worked for white clients but concentrated on civil rights cases when he could. (In the wake of the Civil War, the U.S. Congress passed several civil rights laws which the Supreme Court declared one by one to be unconstitutional; the last of their decisions, issued in 1883, held that the federal government had no authority to regulate public accommodations).†

McGhee played as active a role in state politics as white Republicans allowed. Named a presidential elector in 1892, he was denied the seat; elected to the national Republican convention in 1893, he was refused

---

✻

Norman Kittson: American Fur Company, ran Red River cart business, with James J. Hill founded the Red River Transportation Line (for barges and boats)

---

†

In 1896 in *Plessey v. Ferguson,* the court declared separate (and unequal) facilities as constitutional. It was another fifty years before Congress again acted to establish civil rights in the United States.

admission. Thwarted there, he looked for other ways. He directed the legal division of the Afro-American Council. He hosted Booker T. Washington's Minnesota visits. Perhaps most importantly, McGhee helped found the Niagara Movement, the forerunner of the National Association for the Advancement of Colored People (NAACP). His involvement in the St. Peter Claver Catholic Church in St. Paul forged a long friendship and alliance with Bishop Ireland, both of them dedicated to the extension of civil rights to African Americans, to the Irish, to Catholics. [29]

The railroad shaped Mary's and other people's lives in multiple ways. Perhaps most subtly, it changed people's relationship to time. When mail took weeks to get from one place to another, people contented themselves with the wait. When the trains started to carry the mail and delivery time decreased from weeks to days, it seemed that people's impatience did not decrease, but increased. The railroad also had the effect of making people more conscious of time and of the "accuracy" of clocks. The tax records of the late nineteenth century show an increasing number of watches among people's taxable property. Clocks did not set the schedule for farmwork—the cows in need of milking or the pigs in need of food or the corn that needed to go in as soon after the last killing frost as possible (but how did you know for sure?) did. Clocks did set the schedule, however, for trains. Before the train, what did it matter if someone in St. Paul called it 10:00 and someone in Hutchinson called it 10:10? Standardization mattered only when the trains wanted to collect and deposit passengers and freight predictably—and when they wanted to avoid each other on shared railroad lines. In 1878 Carleton College's observatory in Northfield started to "distribute" time to the railroads. Via telegraph lines, the observatory emitted time signals for three minutes every day, from 11:57 until "the last stroke of the third minute being understood to mark the time of twelve exactly." The time was also transmitted to St. Paul, nearly forty miles directly north of the observatory. Thus, every person who kept time synchronized with the railroad. On November 18, 1883, the railroads adopted a standard time system, and most Americans followed suit. [30]*

The railroad speeded up the time it took Mary to get to and from Austin to see her parents. It increasingly took over from the steamboats the delivery of goods that Mary could buy from or at least admire in the shops. The cash the railroad injected into the local economy, even that of the wages paid and spent in the town, helped other people make money, too—money that helped keep Mary and her sister seamstresses in business. The railroad also brought to town the ready-made clothing and household items that both relieved women's sewing work and would eventually drive seamstresses out of work. The home sewing

*

Not until 1918 did the federal government adopt the standard time zone system.

machine, invented in 1851, seemed to increase the work for seamstresses; ready-made clothing decreased it.[31]

While Mary was at work in Red Wing, her brothers and father continued to farm in Mower County. If they were like many other Minnesota farmers in the 1880s, they had ambitions to get ahead. By the 1880s her parents had already moved from New York to Wisconsin to Minnesota in efforts to improve their lot in life. Farm acreage more than doubled in Minnesota from 1870 to 1880 (from 6.5 million acres to 13.4 million), and so did the number of farms (from 47,000 to 92,000). Farmers turned more and more of their land over to wheat—a cash crop.

The farmers who survived depression, falling prices, and grasshopper plagues in the 1870s faced in the 1880s an agricultural world that, by comparison, didn't look half bad, though it was decidedly more competitive, especially when bonanza farmers—owners of farms of over 3,000 acres, though several of them were over 20,000 acres—in the Red River Valley introduced large amounts of capital, specialization, the latest machinery, and hired workers and managers: wheat growing on a grand scale. Profits could be increased, they wagered, through economies of scale and the principles of industrialization. If Minnesota was going to compete successfully against not only Nebraska but also the expanding wheat fields of Poland and Russia in the internationalizing world of farm production, it could not continue to use old values or outdated methods.[32]

Walking down that street in Red Wing from her boardinghouse to her workplace or wandering through town or on a trip to St. Paul, Mary would likely have seen men with crippled hands or absent limbs, some the victims of industrial accidents—increasingly common with the addition of machines and the speeding up of work—some war veterans. The residents of every village and small town and bigger town must have become accustomed to the sight of these men. At the end of the Civil War, the U.S. surgeon general ordered that all soldiers be furnished with artificial limbs at no cost.

Farmwork took its toll, too, in the loss of fingers and toes and other injuries. Factories and the railroads posed daily dangers to workers' bodies. Until the automatic coupler controlled the coming together of two railroad cars, trainmen risked limbs and life trying to coax together railroad cars that weighed tons and didn't respond to gentle treatment. In response to so many damaged bodies, and to the government's support for artificial limbs, enterprising manufacturers put enough of the state's wood to work that Minnesota for fifty years became a center for the production of wooden arms and legs. Although they underwent improvements in the post–Civil War years, they remained crude, if nonetheless helpful, devices.[33]*

Among the big men in the lumber industry—excluding the mythical Paul Bunyan—were Henry H. Sibley, who already in 1837 was buying land from the Ojibwe; Charles and John Pillsbury, who avidly bought up white pine around Duluth in 1882; and Thomas B. Walker, who concentrated his interests around Crookston under the name of the Red River Lumber Company that was, until the Weyerhaeuser Company moved into Minnesota, the largest timber enterprise in the state.

Among the "little" men—though few men who were physically small could withstand the rigors of life in the woods—was Lyman Warren Ayer. A descendant of Lyman Warren—an American Fur Company trader at La Pointe, Wisconsin—and of Frederick Ayer—a Presbyterian missionary who opened a school at La Pointe—Lyman Warren Ayer was a "cruiser." Cruisers walked the woods to find good stands of trees and made recommendations about which parcels timber companies ought to buy. Ayer was unusually well suited for the job: he had been born near Pine City—in the north woods—and, like his parents, he spoke Ojibwe. Agnes Larson reported, "He had never worn a white man's shoe until he enlisted for the Civil War." He knew the woods as well as anyone, and the company that hired him was lucky. One of the most faithful of the "little" men was Frank Magel, who started sweeping floors for the Hubbard Milling Company in Mankato on August 6, 1883, when he was ten years old. He retired on March 2, 1946—sixty-three years later.[34]

Mary, if she was lucky, slept under a blanket from the Faribault Woolen Mills. Faribault had started out producing cloth, then switched to clothing, but specialized in blankets. During World War I, Faribault produced hundreds of thousands of blankets for the U.S. Army; the company has set itself on a profitable course ever since.

The accumulation of wealth by some in Minnesota generated a culture of benevolence in the state. The leisure time afforded to wives by the money their husbands made gave them time to do volunteer work, to look around and see what good needed to be done, what hospitals and orphanages and asylums and schools needed. Already in the 1880s, women were organizing themselves—some for the vote, some for prohibition, some for Tuesday musicales, some for their own education. As Mary Hill ran a big household and raised her ten children, she played an active role in John Ireland's Catholic church and in the philanthropic affairs of her days.†

Factory and lumber and mill laborers might have preferred to get higher wages, but the owners and their spouses—and their companies—used their wealth to benefit the state and started a tradition of Min-

*

In 1890 there were twelve artificial limb manufacturers in Pennsylvania, nine in New York, and nine in Minneapolis.

†

Some say she directed that the Hill house on Summit Avenue have a porch on the second floor from which she could see her beloved St. Paul Cathedral.

nesota benevolence. Dr. William Mayo taught his sons that it was wrong to make money from the sickness and injuries of others, so they funneled profits into the Mayo Foundation. William Dunwoody contributed the funds to found the institute that still bears his name and trains students in industrial arts and trades. He and others founded the Minneapolis Institute of Arts. The Pillsburys, Washburns, and Crosbys supported the University of Minnesota and the Minnesota Historical Society. Subsequent generations of various wealthy families and companies have contributed to the well-being of Minnesota and surrounding states: Bush, Blandin, Northwest Area, and McKnight are only a few of the names that currently identify these foundations.

It's not possible to know how long Mary stayed in Red Wing. By the late 1880s there is no such person in the Red Wing city directories. Perhaps she moved away; most likely she disappeared into a married name.

The Minnesota story in 1883 includes Mary and all of these people, and nearly 800,000 others. Together they made the state—a state of immigrants and Yankees, of German and Irish Catholics, of Protestants and Jews, of millers and farmers, of the hopeful and the despairing, of the generous and the greedy, of the conventional and unconventional. Theirs is not the story of every place but the story of a place with water and trees, farmland and mills, a plentitude of workers, smart entrepreneurs, ambitious immigrants—a place in the process of being defined by these people and their lives.

9

The Fairbrothers' Christmas

IN 1898 EDWARD AND MINNIE FAIRBROTHER celebrated Christmas
with their two-year-old son, Eddie, and one-year-old daughter, Edith, at
home in St. Paul. They decorated simply—a balsam tree strung with popcorn and cranberry necklaces, oranges, and a few presents. Edward gave
Minnie a broom and a dustpan; she hemmed handkerchiefs for him.
They gave dolls, dollhouse furniture, bowling pins, and a pull-wagon to
their children. That year and for the next dozen, Edward took a picture
of their Christmas tableau.

The oranges catch my attention. A few to a dozen appear almost
every year in Edward's photos. They're not apples, potatoes, eggs, or
onions, which were raised locally—but oranges. They look like hard,
dark cannonballs. But if we could pull them out of the picture, we could
rub their bumpy, slightly oiled skins and release their sharp, sweet smell.
In 1898, no oranges grew within 1,500 miles of the Fairbrothers' living
room. So where did these come from and why?

Answering that question takes us on a chase from China and India
to Valencia and Brazil. Crusaders and Columbus play starring roles;
John and Ann North (whom we met in St. Anthony in the 1840s), supporting ones. The storyline includes subplots about the railroad, commercial
agriculture, the birth of advertising, Americanization, the invention of
the traditional Christmas, and the relationship of Minnesota to many
places through this fruit.

To put it another way: the answer to the question is the tale of a
Canadian immigrant buying a Brazilian orange grown in California,
picked by Chinese workers, carried by newly invented refrigerated cars
on newly laid rail lines (made from northern Minnesota iron and
wooden ties), sold by a German grocer, to celebrate an Anglo-American-
Dutch-based holiday. All this had consequences for international trade,
government policy, and national and international migration patterns.

The little pile of oranges in an 1898 St. Paul drawing room tells a big story.

No oranges grew in the Americas before 1492. The delicious fruit originated in China and then spread to India and the Middle East. The Moors carried oranges across northern Africa and into Spain. French crusaders took seeds home with them. Portuguese explorers got oranges directly from India, and missionaries brought them home from China. Columbus, Ponce de Leon, and by law all Spanish sailors carried orange seeds on their journeys to help fight scurvy. By 1800, oranges had spread to southern France, Italy, Spain, Portugal, South and Central America, the Caribbean, and Florida and graced every mission yard in what would become California.[1]

An enterprising entrepreneur, William Wolfskill, started the first commercial grove there in 1841. The gold-crazed seekers flooding into California in the late 1840s and early 1850s ate oranges happily. More than one prospector found a greater fortune in oranges than in gold. From 1860 to 1880, Spain was the largest producer of oranges in the world; as late as 1880, most oranges in the United States came from southern Europe. By 1920, however, the United States dominated the world market in citrus.[2]

John and Ann North played a role in changing all this. These one-time Minnesotans had long been dreamers. They moved in the 1840s from upstate New York to what later became Minnesota Territory, staying long enough to help found St. Anthony, the University of Minnesota,

Fairbrothers' Christmas tree, 1898

the state's Republican Party, and Northfield, the town bearing their name. Both were enthusiastic community builders, and wherever they went, others followed. In 1862 the Norths went to Nevada by way of New York, Panama, and California, where they first saw orange trees. Their next political appointment took them to Tennessee. Ann hated living in the South, and after John stepped between a lynch mob and its victim, they decided it was time to move again.

Always town builders, the irrepressibly idealistic Norths had visions of oranges dancing in their heads. In 1869 they founded a California orange-growing colony in the place that would become Riverside. Joined by friends from New York, Michigan, Minnesota, Iowa, and Washington, DC, the colonists set out to make "a better St. Anthony" on the West Coast. They bought 4,000 acres to plant their dream of a temperate and communitarian colony in California. Mrs. Eliza Tibbetts brought to the colony several Bahia orange seedlings acquired from her friend and DC neighbor, the head of the Washington Botanical Garden, who had received them from a missionary in Brazil. Of the four trees the Tibbettses nursed, one died and one fell victim to a hungry cow. But two survived. In 1878 they bore four oranges; in 1880, one full box. By 1907, these trees and their descendants, the *New York Times* reported, produced 10 million oranges.[3]

The most common early oranges were small, a little sour (some called them "bitter oranges"), pithy, and seedy, with thin skins. They came into fruit from late spring into fall. The fecundity of oranges made them plentiful where they grew. Their fragility and the difficulty of transport kept them rare elsewhere. The Norths' Washington navel oranges, by contrast, were sweet and seedless; their thick skins make them easy to peel and slightly more hardy to ship. They come into fruit from November through February or March—perfectly timed for Christmas.[4]

The Norths had other dreams to chase, and they didn't stay long enough to make their fortune in oranges—it took six years from planting to production. But Riverside became an orange heartland, and oranges fueled the reorganization of the southern California economy from wheat to fruit.[5]

Both Republican and Democratic leaders in the nineteenth century knew that government had to work with business, especially in terms of railroads and tariff policy. The government made two significant contributions to the development of the fruit-growing industry—and to virtually all other industry in the United States. First, Congress imposed a series of duties on foreign-produced goods—sugar, for example, and fruit—that aimed to raise revenues and protect domestic production. Second, through the distribution of public lands, Congress supported the growth and expansion of the railroads. The railroad generally and the transcontinental Union Pacific (completed in 1869) particularly changed travel patterns, then national and even global patterns of food production, marketing, distribution, and consumption.[6]

In 1877, the first train car of oranges left California bound for the East. By the 1880s, the oranges traveled in ice; by 1900, in air-cooled if not air-conditioned freight cars. Encouraged by the promise of train transport, gentlemen farmers planted a million seedless orange trees by 1889. By 1900, 5.5 million trees bore fruit. In 1903, growers had 66,000 acres in oranges; in 1915, there were 170,000.[7]

The Southern Pacific and the Union Pacific railways got oranges out of California and to Kansas City, Omaha, St. Louis, and Chicago. Minnesota sat too far north for a stop on the main transcontinental route, but it had been busy for over a decade building its own railroads. In 1865 Minnesota had twenty-two miles of working track. The Civil War's end unleashed extraordinary growth, however, and by 1872 the state boasted of nearly 2,000 miles of track, on which Jay Cooke had earned a fortune. The Panic of 1873 seriously realigned the ownership of multiple railway lines—including Cooke's—but derailed their expansion only temporarily. James J. Hill and Henry Villard made huge fortunes owning, building, and expanding the Great Northern and the Northern Pacific lines especially. These went a long way toward connecting Minnesota with major domestic and foreign markets.[8]*

Railroads connected isolated places to everywhere. No wonder so many nineteenth-century railroad depots were such imposing and central buildings. Much like cathedrals in medieval European cities, railroad depots were the portals to other worlds. The railroads invited people to go or, if they couldn't actually go, to dream of going. They opened bigger horizons.

Edward Fairbrother was from a family with big dreams. His English-born parents migrated to Ontario; Edward migrated to Minnesota. He wrote ahead and secured a job that he held for all of his working life as a clerk for the Northern Pacific Railroad. Edward's position entitled him to free travel, a benefit he used to visit his parents almost every year. He lived originally within walking distance to his work in St. Paul, but as train connections improved, he moved his family to White Bear. Sure, the commute was twenty-five minutes by train, but it didn't cost him anything but time and he had the best of both worlds with his "country" house. He also used his railroad passes just for fun. His son, Eddie, remembered trips to Duluth to cool off on hot summer days.

Clerking for the railroad, Fairbrother sat at the nexus of the movement of people and goods. At least ten lines ran into and out of St. Paul and Minneapolis in the 1890s, and each offered multiple choices of times and destinations.

*

Henry Villard bought the bankrupt Northern Pacific during the depression of 1873–78, finished its construction, and then sold it at a substantial profit.

Thousands of people climbed off the trains just outside his office: some were traveling salesmen or businesspeople; others were newcomers loaded with possessions and dreams. And Fairbrother, no doubt, watched people climb onto the train—people passing through, visitors, migrant workers home between jobs, more businessmen, and people giving up, taking their baggage and their dreams elsewhere.

From his window he could watch railway workers unload boxes, barrels, and cases of Swiss, Edam, and Gjetost as well as New York and Wisconsin cream cheeses, Crosse and Blackwell's Pickled Little Onions from England, cigars from Key West, barbed wire, glass, cloth from India, and fruit from Florida, Georgia, Colorado, Cuba, and California. He also saw Minnesota products go out—wheat and lumber especially.[9]

From his perch, he could gauge good times and bad, probably. Those same trains that linked people to the national and international economy also made people increasingly vulnerable to economic swings and forces far beyond their control. The economic panic in 1873 and its subsequent depression followed by a more severe panic in 1893 and depression delivered severe blows to farmers in Minnesota and throughout the Midwest and South. Minnesota farmers complained that millers kept the prices down (because they could get wheat from growers farther and farther away) and railroads kept rates up (because they had no competitors and could charge whatever they could get). The farmers and others felt powerless in the face of these big corporations.

Some people inside and outside of Minnesota, including Minnesota's one-time lieutenant governor and congressional representative Ignatius Donnelly, saw a solution in organization and electoral politics. They formed the Farmers' Alliance and then the People's Party, which trumpeted the value of the farmers and workers who "produced" and railed against the monopolies, the trusts, and the wealthy, who only "consumed." "If any will not work," the 1896 Populist platform declared, "neither shall he eat." Donnelly, the author of at least the preamble to this program, wrote "They propose to sacrifice our homes, lives, and children on the altar of mammon; to destroy the multitude in order to secure corruption funds from the millionaires."[10]

Other farmers saw more immediate and effective solutions in organizing cooperatives like creameries and grain elevators for the production and sale of their produce, as well as credit unions, oil companies, and electrical cooperatives to manage their expenses. One of the most successful was the dairy cooperative called, since 1922, Land O'Lakes.[11]

Edward Fairbrother was eventually able to buy oranges in St. Paul because the same pressures that hurt Minnesota farmers were hurting California citrus growers, and they, too, responded by forming themselves into cooperatives to pack and ship their produce. When most

Minnesota farmers were protesting against industrialization, the California growers "embraced corporate managerial capitalism" and created the California Fruit Growers Exchange (CFGE).[12]

The exchange so streamlined picking and packing that orange shipments increased by almost 600 percent between 1894 and 1914, while the nation's population grew by only 60 percent. The CFGE hired G. Howard Powell, a brilliant pomologist, and Don Francisco, a marketing genius, to figure out how to increase the "fruit-eating habit" of Americans. They achieved their goal by stressing the health benefits of oranges, by directing their ads at mothers, by changing the CFGE name to "Sunkist," by commissioning shipping labels that disguised the unhealthy work of orange picking by offering Tuscan-colored landscapes. On crates that arrived in wintry and snowy places, these labels suggested warmth, health, a version of the American dream. By 1910 the "orange special," a train that ran directly and swiftly to the Midwest, carried $40,000 worth of oranges.[13]

Sunkist also hired people who worked, as Everett Brown did, to make sure that Minnesota grocers stocked and featured California oranges. Brown almost certainly represented Sunkist to Andrew Schoch, who ran one of St. Paul's largest grocery stores, located just a few blocks from where the Fairbrothers lived.

The German-born and -raised Schoch went into the fruit and vegetable business and with sons and daughter built and ran Andrew Schoch Grocery in St. Paul for over half a century.* While at first the store depended primarily on local products, it expanded its range as the railroads carried more goods. The Schochs—no doubt at Mr. Everett Brown's urging—stocked Washington navel oranges.[14]

It was Sunkist's good fortune that the orange harvest coincided with Christmas. Many Christian Christmas practices derive from pre-Christian midwinter rites. The attention paid to the poor and to children at Christmastime reenacts the topsy-turvy world of long nights and short days. Candles especially recall the solstice celebrations of the return of light. Few "traditional" Christmas rituals actually have much to do with the birth of Christ, which largely explains why Puritans in colonial America and many devout Christians into the nineteenth century played down the day. As historian Stephen Nissenbaum has argued, "Christmas has always been an extremely difficult holiday to Christianize."[15]

In the nineteenth century, however, the holiday was Anglicized and Americanized. Clement Moore's *A Visit from Saint Nicholas* (1822), illustrated by Thomas Nast, and Charles Dickens's *A Christmas Carol* (1843) did much to define the look and rituals of Christmas. Queen Victoria and Prince Albert helped set the style when, in the 1840s, they decorated

*

Charles became a partner, Isabel a cashier, Phillip assistant secretary, Edward superintendent of the garage, Paul a clerk in the grocery, and Louis manager of the fruit department.

Windsor Castle with Christmas trees and loaded the branches with presents for their children. The British interest in traditional music encouraged the singing of carols. The adoption of penny postage (the sender paid, not the receiver) encouraged the creation of holiday cards. Washington Irving and other New York Knickerbockers (Dutch-Americans) adapted St. Nicholas/Sinterklaas traditions into American customs, hanging stockings rather than putting out shoes and moving their celebrations from St. Nicholas to Christmas Day. As children became the center of family attention, Christmas became an occasion for offering gifts to them, too. The exchange of presents between adults came much later.[16]

Christmas stockings appear in Moore's Christmas household but not much before. Elizabeth Cady Stanton remembered that sometime before 1830 she tied her stocking to a broomstick suspended between two chairs near the fireplace, which may have had something to do with the Dutch custom of Sinterklaas exchanging treats or switches for animal feed left by children in wooden shoes near the fireplace.

However, there was no nineteenth-century tradition of dropping an orange into a Christmas stocking. Various midwesterners report receiving an orange for Christmas—not in a stocking but as their gift for the year. One woman cherished the orange peel, which she tucked among her clothes to catch its fragrance. But oranges as a staple of Christmas celebrations seems to occur only very late in the nineteenth century and into the beginning of the twentieth.

James J. Hill sent hundreds of boxes of Minnesota-grown apples as Christmas offerings to friends and associates along his railroad line. Easily available, apples were part of the local landscape and sometimes a part of Christmas, too. But oranges—oranges were special, from a different and exotic place. Perhaps the enticement was natural, but Sunkist's passion to expand its market couldn't have hurt.

The Fairbrothers' Christmas included many of the rituals already "traditional" to Christmas at the turn of the nineteenth century: tree, gifts, focus on children, Santa. Nothing in their Christmas photos is especially religious: no crèche, no baby Jesus, no Christian symbols or decorations, not even a star on the tree. But oranges sit front and center year after year.

The story of how those oranges got under the Fairbrothers' Christmas tree is one of industrialization, national and international marketing, the combining of cultures, the power of advertising, the genius of marketing—the meeting of traditional customs and modern capitalism. It's a national story and international story played out, too, in Minnesota.

10

Becoming Better and Becoming American

BETWEEN ITS TWENTY-FIFTH BIRTHDAY in 1883 and its fiftieth in 1908, Minnesota changed in ways big and small. In 1883, the Swedish-born Christina Nilsson had been in the United States for seven years. She'd worked in Worthington as a house servant and then taken a waitressing job before moving to Minneapolis, where she met and married another Swedish immigrant, Swan Turnblad. By 1908 they ran and had made a small fortune publishing the *Svenska Amerikanska Posten*, a Swedish-language newspaper with a circulation of 40,000 (she did most of the writing while he managed the printing). They were building the grand house on Park Avenue in Minneapolis that in time became the American Swedish Institute but was now to be their home.

After forty years of Yankee governors, Minnesota voters in the 1890s elected Knute Nelson, the state's first foreign-born governor. In 1904, they elected John Johnson, a second-generation Swedish American, the first governor born in the state. Minnesota's population had grown by another million people between the mid-1880s and the mid-1910s. The urban population had nearly doubled, and the number of wage earners had quadrupled (which also meant the number of farmers was decreasing). All three Minnesota iron ranges—Vermilion, Mesabi, and Cuyuna—had been discovered and developed. Millions of tons of earth were being moved to uncover the ore and iron ore that left daily from Duluth and Two Harbors bound for

Wedding portrait of Chinese immigrant James Mar and Polish American Julia Zyzner from Silver Lake

the U.S. Steel plant in Pittsburgh. The Aerial Lift Bridge in Duluth was completed and so was Chester and Clara Congdon's Lake Superior mansion, Glensheen. Frederick Weyerhaeuser had built a timber industry out of Minnesota trees and was already looking for new stands to harvest.

Only four Minnesota soldiers lost their lives in combat in the Spanish-American war, but hundreds had died in fires that swept through Hinckley, Virginia, Chisholm, and other towns in the trees. In 1898, Olof Ohman unearthed (or himself chiseled) a tablet claiming that Vikings had been through the Kensington area five hundred years earlier. Still believed by some to be authentic, the Kensington runestone was more likely Ohman's attempt to make fools out of the uppity townspeople who had long condescended to their rural neighbors.[1]

In 1883, Minnesota's higher education system consisted largely of ministerial and teacher training academies and colleges; private schools were largely organized around ethnic group and denomination and gender. The state normal schools—not really colleges, in that students did not need a high school diploma in order to attend—at Mankato and Winona, a little later in St. Cloud, specialized in teacher training. In that year both Hamline and Carleton had larger student bodies than did the University of Minnesota.* St. Olaf's student newspaper appeared in both English and Norwegian until 1925, and its ministry candidates were taught in Norwegian. William Carleton and Charles Macalester and Hugh Derham made major donations that assisted in the founding and development of Carleton and Macalester colleges and the College of St. Catherine. All the state's private and public colleges benefited from the contributions of wealthy donors, especially James J. Hill. The North Central Association of Colleges and the American Association of University Professors each emerged in this period—the first to establish standards for the colleges and the second to protect faculty members' freedom of speech.[2]

Clearly, colleges were trying to figure out what they should do and be during these years. Educating people to be leaders was certainly one part. Should both women and men be educated? Carleton—in the Congregational tradition—admitted women from the start. St. Thomas did not do so for a hundred years, and Saint John's still does not. The colleges of St. Teresa, St. Scholastica, St. Catherine, and Saint Benedict admitted only women.

One of the issues that convulsed many of these campuses was the role of athletics. Gustavus Adolphus trustees dropped intercollegiate football between 1905 and 1917 and found that enrollment also dropped. Carleton and Hamline built gymnasiums, and the state's colleges formed the Minnesota Intercollegiate Athletic Conference (MIAC) in 1920. Bernie

*
Enrollments in 1883:
University of Minnesota, 278;
Hamline, 327;
Carleton, 321.

Bierman's football powerhouse did not fire up until the 1930s, winning national championships in 1934, 1936, 1940, and 1941, but intercollegiate athletics were an important part of university life.

The graduate school at the University of Minnesota remained small until historian Guy Stanton Ford was hired first as dean in 1913 and then as president. In Ford's first five years as dean, graduate enrollment grew from 160 to 460. In 1903, St. Olaf hired as music and choir director Melius Christiansen, who built a world-renowned music program.

In 1908, another kind of college was formed: Tyovaen Opista, the Work People's College. Originally founded as the Finnish People's College and Theological Seminary (Suomalained Kansas Opisto ja Teologinen Seminaari), it aimed to educate Finns to be ministers and liberals. It failed in Minneapolis but resurrected itself outside of Duluth and revised its mission away from religion and toward both Darwinism and Marxism.[3]

The push for more education and better schools was part of a larger movement for people to improve themselves, their communities, their state, their nation, and their world. Idealism fueled many, and prosperity helped. People had time to see problems that needed to be fixed and the time, as well as the impulse, to set about making changes. They also had the confidence to believe they knew what the answer was.

A group of Plymouth Congregational Church members in Minneapolis organized to teach newsboys and eventually expanded their work to found the Pillsbury House for the education of immigrants. Besides English language classes, it offered and taught child care and ran an employment bureau. A group of African American, middle-class, native-born women opened the Phyllis Wheatley House to focus on the needs of African Americans in Minnesota. Such settlement houses, as they were called, worked privately and depended on the benevolence of generous patrons. Westminster Presbyterian Church developed a school for Chinese immigrants and established "mission" churches for Swedes in the Cedar-Riverside neighborhood of Minneapolis. The B'nai B'rith helped resettle Jewish immigrant refugees in Minnesota.[4]

Minnesotans had long been forming clubs and organizations. Old Settlers' Associations and Territorial Pioneers as well as the GAR had been holding meetings and picnics for decades. Farmers had formed cooperatives, and coopers joined forces to protect their jobs when the flour milling industry moved from barrels to sacks. Even so, Minnesotans took to organizations in a bigger and more enthusiastic way in the last years of the nineteenth and the first years of the twentieth centuries. Safety in numbers motivated some; fearing cracks in society or seeking ways to cope with modernization moved others. The passion for organizing showed itself especially among middle-class women, men and women laborers, and political reformers.[5]*

Mary Dillon Foster's 1924 *Who's Who Among Minnesota Women* details the lives of thousands of Minnesota women who formed or joined clubs as varied as the Mozart Club of Owatonna and the Thursday Afternoon Musicale Society (later the Schubert Club) in St. Paul, the Minnesota Federation of Colored Women's Clubs, the Madonna Del' Assunta Society, the Political Equality Society, the Women's City Club of St. Paul, the Order of Hermann Sisters of New Ulm, the Women's Auxiliary to the National Association of Railway Postal Clerks, the Guild of Catholic Women, the St. Paul Needlework Guild, the Campfire Girls, the Hebrew Benevolent Society, and the PTA.[6]

Women's study groups considered municipal government, urban sanitary problems, the plight of poor and working women, state politics, labor concerns. Businesswomen's organizations offered mutual support. The Oxboro Health Community League organized to support a Sunday school and to build a church. Other women organized to help people with tuberculosis, to found hospitals, to improve local schools, to clean up city streets, to get spittoons removed from public buildings, and to provide "rest rooms" for women in town for the day. Some women belonged to local branches of national associations: the Young Women's Christian Association, the Women's Christian Temperance Union, various missionary societies, the National Woman Suffrage Association.

During the generation before the woman suffrage amendment to the Constitution was ratified in 1920, women found their strength in numbers and exercised as much political and social and communal clout as they could muster. Reading the meeting minutes of these various women's organizations and charting the huge amount of work they did in those years, one can feel women's ambition straining against the limits imposed by societal gender roles, by conventions about "ladylike" behavior, by a mythology that told women their highest calling was at home. A few of these club women were single, but most were married with children, and many of those children were grown. Virtually all of them were middle-class women whose families had the luxury of a single breadwinner. What were they to do with their energy and time and passion?[7]†

Minnesota saw an explosion of organizing and organizations among working-class people in those same years. The Knights of Labor grew from its first local in 1878 to more than ninety by 1890. This group provided the opportunity for working-class women to develop their own voices. Eva McDonald Valesh, a Knights organizer in Minnesota, worked on William Jennings Bryan's 1896 presidential campaign and afterward

*

Native-born and urban women in this period had declining fertility and fewer children. The large population of single women in cities, especially, provided a workforce for many of these clubs and organizations.

†

Kate Donnelly advised and counseled her husband on his politics; her practicality might have made her the better candidate for office, had she been eligible to stand for election.

went to work for the Women's Trade Union League. Julia B. Nelson of Red Wing was active in both suffrage and temperance organizations and ran, on the Populist ticket, for Red Wing Superintendent of Schools.[8]

The first strike on the Iron Range was not union inspired but grew out of local ethnic and religious organizations. In 1892, Slovenian and Italian workers refused to work on Corpus Christi Day—a holy day, but more importantly a day they considered unlucky. In response, the Soudan mine owners temporarily laid off over three hundred workers and requisitioned the state militia. The Minnesota Federation of Labor that succeeded the Knights—and the Corpus Christi Day strikers— adopted a more modern labor union structure to fight the speeding up of production, falling wages, and stricter hours that increasingly characterized industrial labor by the turn of the century. Sometimes political action was the method, as in the Workmen's Compensation Act of 1913, but the strike remained and became even more fully the mode for exerting collective action.[9]*

As long as mines were locally owned and run, sociologist Paul H. Landis found, labor and management relations remained relatively cooperative. Both sides knew they needed each other, and they built on this common need. When mining ownership moved off the range, to Duluth or places farther east, local workers organized.[10]

In 1887 Weyerhaeuser workers struck for a ten-hour day (which they got in 1892). Labor organizations materialized among many working groups: bicycle repairers to fix prices; plasterers for wage increase; woodworkers for eight-hour day; and nurses (but hospital board members responded to the strike threat by warning "there will be no difficulty in filling the vacancies")—and these were the news reports covering only a week in early January 1900. In 1902 Minneapolis truckers and in 1903 Washburn Crosby mill workers walked out in pursuit of an eight-hour day. In 1905 the socialist Industrial Workers of the World and the Western Federation of Miners sent organizers to northern Minnesota. By 1907, the WFM had established fourteen locals. Miners in 1907 struck for an eight-hour day. Dockworkers at Duluth and Two Harbors walked out in a show of solidarity. Local merchants withheld credit from the strikers, and the owners fired many of them—Finns, especially. The organizers mined a deep vein of anger and resentment among timber workers and miners.[11]

Two major strikes rocked the range, one in 1907 and one in 1916. These were bitter, angry strikes. The strikers accused the owners of kidnapping organizers. Owners hired not only strikebreakers but also spies to report on the workers and private policemen to protect their investments. In 1916, the miners walked out over pay, the use of contract labor,

*

In 1900 one-half of the state's manufacturing workers held jobs in the flour, grist, and lumber milling industries.

and the eight-hour day (again). In 1916 the Teamsters and machinists struck and in 1917 the Minneapolis streetcar workers struck over the right to organize; both were met by a private army of Citizens Alliance members. The CA organized to defeat the unions and to keep Minneapolis union free.[12]

In 1918, led by Myrtle Cain, the women telephone operators of the International Brotherhood of Electrical Workers walked out of their jobs at the telephone company in Minneapolis, shutting down telephone talk in the city. The strikers' ladylike singing on the picket lines disguised a determined labor force willing to adopt whatever means necessary to win their demands for higher wages—cutting telephone lines, intimidating strikebreakers, damaging telephone company property. After twelve weeks, the government—in the interests of the war effort—stepped in and declared the strike over. The women put down their picket signs and picked up their headphones, no richer but more class conscious and determined.[13]*

*

Myrtle Cain was elected to the state legislature in 1923. She and Mabeth Hurd Paige must have disagreed about virtually everything during their short time together in the legislature. Their class proved a much more significant difference between them than their gender could bridge—at least politically.

Women and laborers mostly had to work outside of the mainline political system. Many reformers saw that they needed to engage the government if they hoped to bring about the changes they wanted, but until the turn of the century the system was not open to much reform. The American political scene changed dramatically, however, when Theodore Roosevelt assumed the presidency in 1901 (after William McKinley's assassination) and was elected on his own in 1904. He wanted to make a difference, a big difference, and he believed the federal government could be better than it had been before. The Progressive Era, as the years between 1901 and 1916 are often called, was both cause and effect of the national reform movements that showed themselves in dozens of ways, from urban reform to World War I itself.

Minnesota Progressives used the government apparatus with success during those years. They spent some of their energy fixing the government itself. Recall gave voters a way, between elections, to remove officials from public office. The direct election of senators—the Seventeenth Amendment, ratified in 1913—removed one layer of batting between the voters and their elected officials by giving to the electorate, rather than to the state legislature, the right to elect U.S. senators.[14]

Reformers pushed through the Minnesota legislature thirty-five bills protecting children. One act gave to the State Board of Control the responsibility of superintending adoptions, maternity hospitals, foster homes, state institutions for dependent children, all blind children, and the juvenile court system. Controls were put on child labor, standards set for school attendance, and methods for enforcement instituted.

Another of the reforms central to progressivism in Minnesota—and most other states—was woman suffrage. Some women had been campaigning for the vote since the 1830s, an earlier reform era during which women had found that their lack of voting rights curtailed their ability to bring about desired reforms, especially the abolition of slavery. In favor of the vote for black men that was added to the Constitution as the Fifteenth Amendment, women had been persuaded to wait. They waited for more than fifty years, and then the push for votes for women began again.[15]

Some proponents of woman suffrage always argued that women were entitled to the vote and deserved the vote. Some advocates—perhaps bowing to the pressure of the opposition's argument that the vote would desex women and roughen them—adopted the argument that women would be *better* able to fulfill their roles as wives and mothers if they could vote. The first (in fact, the only) inroad to woman suffrage in Minnesota prior to the passage of the Nineteenth Amendment had been won on this ground—that as the mothers of children women had to be able to play a role in the governance of their education. Powerful opponents of woman suffrage were the brewery and bar owners, who feared that women would vote overwhelmingly for prohibition if given the opportunity. Finally, fear propelled some people into the woman suffrage camp—if not to expand the rights of women, then to curtail the rights of immigrants. At the beginning of the twentieth century, male immigrants who had taken the first step toward citizenship but were not yet citizens were eligible to vote. If woman suffrage could extend the vote to women but limit the vote to "citizens," the amendment would result in an increase in white, native-born, middle-class votes and a decrease of what many considered "undesirable" voters—recent immigrants in particular.

Even the socialists in the state turned toward traditional politics, and the voters of Crookston and Two Harbors and Minneapolis elected socialist mayors. The largest of the leftist political organizations in this period, the Nonpartisan League, also made political inroads in the state. The NPL began as a North Dakota organization and spread—in historian Robert Morlan's words—like prairie fire across the upper Midwest. It had the passion of desperation and aimed to break the stronghold that Minneapolis grain merchants, millers, and railroads had over farmers. If they could advance their cause politically, all the better; if not, they would use what weapons they had.[16]

The Progressive Era was remarkable for the enthusiasm of people to do, make, expand, grow, improve, develop, and beautify. Farmers, prohibitionists, suffragists, city and child and women's labor reformers all believed in themselves and in their ability to bring about change, perhaps even to control their surroundings. All looked right with the world. Reform raced along for fifteen years on a flatbed created by a coalition of progressive-minded people, held together by the cement of prosperity and the isolationism afforded by world peace. Somehow, the Federated Women's Clubs and the Nonpartisan League, the National Association for the Advancement of Colored People, the Croatian Benefit Society and the Sons of Norway all flourished in this context.

World War I, however, cracked this coalition. If the Progressive Era saw people wanting to make the world better, World War I made people afraid and punctured the dreams of change. The war added the toxins of fear and hyperloyalty to that fix-it mentality of progressivism and fostered a climate of suspicion: of anyone who spoke in a different voice or accent or the language of dissent or pacifism—in short, anyone who didn't fit into a particular (and particularly narrow) definition of what constituted "American."

The Minnesota Commission of Public Safety was the most powerful product of this mixture. In 1917 the state legislature created the MCPS to protect the state from its domestic enemies. Officially, the MCPS would be made up of a home guard of 1,000, motor corps of 2,500 (useful in emergencies), and police officers without uniform numbering 600, "of much assistance in securing evidence of disloyalty," Governor Joseph Burnquist explained, in addition to controlling the liquor traffic and dance, billiards, and pool halls. "The Commission," Burnquist went on, "very early took steps to rid the state of certain anarchistic agitators by requesting cities and villages . . . to define such persons as vagrants and providing for their suitable punishment." The greatest danger, he warned, would come from within: all citizens needed to be especially vigilant.[17]

The MCPS pressed the towns and villages to deny meeting spaces to Nonpartisan League gatherings and jailed the 1916 Socialist Party candidate for governor for encouraging draft resistance. With the implicit backing of the MCPS, local mobs tarred and feathered NPL members, beat up pacifists, ran dissenters out of town, and turned their suspicion and fury on aliens—especially those who had not become Americans.* Other state and even local legislation—and then vigilante actions—followed suit. "It is high time Douglas county was acquainting itself with the propaganda of bolshevism," the Alexandria newspaper editorialized. "It is the vilest and filthiest doctrine conceived by any human being and any man who will endorse such a dirty creed brands himself unfit for decent human association."[18]

The *Pine County Pioneer*—and Pine County officials—took no less severe a line in criticizing Representative Ernest Lundeen, a Minneapo-

*

Local newspapers carried hundreds of reports of anti-war demonstrations broken up, pacifists harassed, political gatherings disrupted.

lis congressman who, having refused to "resign in as graceful a manner as possible," had been court-martialed by his Veterans of Foreign Wars post because of "his attitude on the war question in Congress" and because he "has made an ass of himself by his attitudes on various public issues." The Pine County War Board declared that no Nonpartisan League recruiters would be allowed into the county and that any meetings, solicitations for new members, or attempts to start a newspaper would be considered unpatriotic acts. The newspaper reported, too, on people suspended from their jobs for various kinds of sedition and disloyalty. A Bemidji candy shop that was suspected of being pro-German "was painted a brilliant yellow and a sign posted asking [!] him to move in 30 days." In southeastern Minnesota's Houston County, following a school board meeting that dropped German from the curriculum, the townspeople burned German textbooks while singing the "Star Spangled Banner." In St. Peter, Gustave Krueger was severely beaten by his neighbors for refusing to buy a Liberty Bond. In Sandstone, another man who refused the war bond solicitor, saying things "that can't be tolerated," was arrested for seditious utterances. Mrs. Martha Ranta and eight others charged with spreading seditious ideas among pupils and Finn residents in Virginia were acquitted, but a statewide move was afoot to ban all "alien" teachers from Minnesota schools. Charles Lindbergh, Sr., who openly opposed the war, was burned in effigy in Willow River. In Moose Lake, Nels Rutledge was tarred and feathered for his sedition, and he wasn't the only victim of such treatment in the interest of the good of the country.[19]

Millions of immigrants had poured into the United States in the thirty years before World War I. Fewer and fewer of them came from northern and western Europe; more and more of them from southern and eastern Europe. More and more of them were darker skinned and Catholic or Jewish; more and more, too, it seemed did not take the necessary steps to become citizens or, more importantly, to become "American." Various Progressive reformers had "helped" immigrants by teaching them "our" ways and Americanizing them. Americans of older immigrant groups seemed increasingly worried about who "we" were and about what it meant to be American. The immigration laws were loose (the Chinese were the only national group excluded from free entry into the United States), and nativists waved the flag of American loyalty and fear. They probably would not have called it "fear" but rather "protection" or "concern for the well-being of the United States," though their behavior bore the hallmarks of people afraid.[20]*

The Commission of Public Safety also required that all immigrants who were not citizens declare themselves, their current addresses and

*

The Republicans had a greater likelihood of weakening the Nonpartisan League as well as more leftist groups by attacking their patriotism than by answering their charges. Between 1917 and 1918, the Republicans had cause to worry: NPL membership grew from 30,000 to 50,000 members.

occupations and property holdings, as well as why they had not become citizens. What a variety of people the registration recorded: in just one day at the North East Neighborhood House, people of nineteen different nationalities registered. Many who delayed citizenship were simply preoccupied or hadn't gotten around to it. George Ashenbrenner, for example, was born in Beurn, Germany, in 1874. In 1898 he arrived in New York, and eventually he settled in New Ulm, Minnesota. Between 1900 and 1918, he and his wife had eight children: Rosa, Elsie, Joseph, Carlein, Ignatz, Franceska, and Floyd. He took out his first citizenship papers in 1918, when he was forty-four and just after the state began requiring all "aliens" to register. Slightly misunderstanding, he answered the unasked question of why he had waited so long simply, "Neglected." Carl Bach, a seventy-one-year-old bookbinder born in Lingen, "Preusen," had come to the United States in 1868 and within a month taken out his first citizenship papers. In 1918, however, he wasn't yet a citizen and said, in answer to the same question, "I don't no." Margaret Bakken was nineteen when she emigrated from Eidsvold, Norway. She was a nurse in 1918 but not a citizen and hadn't even taken out her first papers. Why not? "Overlooked." Mrs. Annie R. Boulten lived in Moose Lake in 1918, having been brought to the United States from Canada when she was just a year old. She also had never applied for citizenship: "I left that to my husband and he neglected to do so."[21]

Other Minnesota immigrants did not apply because they did not intend to stay. John Carlson, a twenty-four-year-old carpenter in Minneapolis, had "not decided whether he will stay here or go back to Sweden." George Andrechuk had left his wife in Russia and had been working in lumbering camps since 1914. He had registered for the draft but not for citizenship: "Expect to go back to Russia," he reported. Stories of neglect or indecision fill the registration forms.

Women had been sympathetic proponents of the commission's business, too, helping to burn books, to report sedition, to campaign against the NPL. The Women's Bureau of the commission collected information about women workers that demonstrated the difficulty, even for citizens, of being accepted as "American" in this period. The bureau listed hundreds of women born in the United States but recorded their nationality as Irish or Norwegian or German. It wasn't clear what it took to become "American" in the eyes of the MCPS.[22]

Congressman Lindbergh was one of those who believed the United States should not enter the war. He, like many reformers, feared that turning attention Europeward would distract Americans from needed reform. He also feared that the United States was being pulled into the war, not as Woodrow Wilson claimed, to make the world safe for democracy, but to make the economy better for owners. He may well have believed that he and other reformers were on the verge of making some progress. He had been advocating reform and found a congenial home in the Nonpartisan League. In 1918 he ran for governor on the NPL ticket in a bitter, contentious campaign that he lost.

Immigrants were one focus of the loyalty campaign waged by the Minnesota Commission of Public Safety. NPL members were another. All over the state, political activists associated with the NPL were subjected to both physical and verbal harassment. The NPL was denied meeting places. Members were tarred and feathered. Some were beaten, some driven out of town. All of these actions occurred under the guise of upholding the war effort. The police powers of the state were sometimes brought to bear against the NPL, rarely to protect the rights of NPLers to speak or to convene.

Many Americans continued to believe that World War I was a battle to make the world safe for democracy. Two communities in Minnesota, in particular, saw in that rhetoric a language in which to couch their own appeals for justice and reform. *The Appeal,* a black-owned and -run newspaper, argued again and again that the same efforts to assist the Belgians and other Europeans ought to be applied to improving the circumstances of blacks at home. *The Tomahawk,* the Indian-run newspaper on the White Earth Reservation, made a similar case—repeatedly, but without noticeable consequences. *The Tomahawk* on January 17, 1918, ran a letter from Andrew Bellecourt, an Ojibwe soldier in France, and on January 24 printed an editorial: "We Indians will fight for Uncle Sam as loyally as any American citizen, but along with this, we do demand recognition as self-respecting individuals and entitled to all the rights of citizenship."[23]

Over 100,000 Minnesota men joined the military, and about 1,500 lost their lives. The war's greater impact on the state had to do with the flu epidemic that plagued much of the world in 1918. Minnesota newspapers started reporting occasional occurrences of the flu, then a full-fledged epidemic. As more and more men were called to duty, more and more of them contracted the illness. By the middle of 1918, the state prohibited political meetings not any longer out of fear of disloyalty but with certainty of the flu's deadly effect. Between 1918 and 1920, as many as 12,000 Minnesotans died of the flu. The world was increasingly a dangerous place—outsiders, aliens, war, even friends could bring peril. It must have been deeply troubling.

When Christina and Swan Turnblad moved into their Park Avenue mansion in 1908, they entertained in the grand rooms of their main floor but lived mostly on the top floor, in what were designed originally as servants' quarters. Like many Minnesotans of the Progressive Era, they aimed to improve themselves, to become better, to become "American." Like many Americans, however, they didn't seem entirely comfortable with all that that meant.

The 1920s proved to be quite different in feeling, tone, activities, and focus from the preceding twenty years. Reform, progress, improvement—they slipped below the horizon of Minnesotans' attention. Too disruptive, too angry, too hateful, too much.

11

PART I:
THE PICTURES

IN THE NINETEENTH CENTURY, Mathew Brady, Julia Margaret Cameron, Edward Curtis, and other pioneering photographers slipped their heads under black cloth to see the world in a new way. Mathew Brady took chilling photographs of the crushed men and broken landscapes of the Civil War. An India-born English woman, fortuitously named Cameron, specialized in portraits intimate enough to convince viewers a camera could steal a person's soul. Edward Curtis took monumental and nostalgic photos in the West. The technology imposed limits on what could be photographed and how. Glass plates made developing exposures a fragile and expensive undertaking.[1]

By the 1920s, however, the technology had zoomed ahead, and hundreds of men and some women made a business of professional photography: over one hundred in Minneapolis and St. Paul, seventeen in Duluth, four on the Iron Range. Even the village of Albany had its own portrait and commercial photographer.

From 1904 to 1946, Henry Briol took pictures of weddings, funerals, prize bulls, strings of fish, barns, fraternal and school groups, first--communion classes, firemen, and picnics in and around Albany. The Stuntebeck Ford Authorized Sales and Service and other businesses hired him to take formal photos of their operations. He captured the drama of a fire in Freeport, a tornado in Melrose, a touring car stuck in a ditch.[2]

In the early part of his career, Briol took what had already become a typical midwestern style of photo: long shots that showed off the barn and house, the possessions, sometimes even the animals, and of course the families. Long after the convention faded elsewhere, Briol continued to capture these images of success. In 1910 he pictured a family in front of the farmhouse; in 1920, in front of the house and gas station.

Family in front of farmhouse, 1910

Family with house and gas station, 1920

Clifford Peel worked primarily in Minneapolis. His photos portray a Minnesota different from the one shown by Briol, a few years his junior. Born in Iowa to Swedish immigrant parents and raised in Pipestone, Peel went to photography school in Illinois in the 1910s and then joined the U.S. Signal Corps. After the United States entered World War I, he was shipped to England to develop photographs taken behind enemy lines. He processed thousands of pictures that General John Pershing consulted to develop the Allies' strategy and tactics. After the war, Peel returned briefly to Pipestone, took a job in Brainerd for a short time, then fled to Minneapolis and the studio of Charles Hibbard, the city's premier commercial photographer. After Hibbard's death in 1924, Peel and another Hibbard photographer, Walter Norton, went into business on their own.[3]

Peel and Norton took pictures of businesses, new and big buildings, businessmen, sports teams, settlement houses, jazz bands, the Minneapolis Symphony, movie theaters, inventions, and a series of the Foshay Tower under construction. As commercial photographers, they took more work photos and fewer family groups.

In addition to Briol, Peel, and other professionals who made Minnesota pictures for a living, amateurs made pictures for a million different reasons. The readily available Kodak Brownie wasn't point-shoot-and-enjoy but almost. Flexible film replaced glass plates, and rolls of film could be turned over to someone else for developing. So, in the 1920s, the pleasures of photography were available to anyone who could afford the time and the one-dollar Brownie.

Both professionals and amateurs found people delightfully photographable. A few pictures—like Briol's—showed houses big and people small. More often, however, they focused on people—working, playing, showing off their cars, politicking, making music, dancing, dating, marrying, drinking (illegally).

The photos suggest the variety of work people did, the forces shaping the workplace, and the changes reshaping and reinventing it. Pictures of farmwork show men tending to their cattle; couples feeding their chickens; men, women, and children using horses to plant potatoes; farmers using a truck to pitch hay. Inmates at the Minnesota Reformatory for Women at Shakopee worked in the fields and barns, raising some of their own food. John Bergeron rolled logs with skill, grace even; loading a flatbed car with pulpwood required brute strength and cranes. Harvest hands by the hundreds rode the rails to and from work, catching some photographers' attention.

Photos show other changes, too: Henry Walseth added a soda fountain to his store in Ihlen (a modern idea in the 1920s). Some Indians took up farming. The work of sorting and delivering mail was routinized. Butter making—long a woman's task and a source of independent income for many—moved into dairies that by the 1920s were increasingly factory-like, with the employees (still mostly women) in uniforms and hats. Building houses or barns or businesses, no longer the work of friends and neighbors, occupied many hired laborers: bricklayers, joiners, framers, electricians, plumbers, and painters.

One photographer captured a female painter at work, but many jobs remained gender and race typed, as the photos document. The dining-car workers for the Northern Pacific were black men; the cooks and managers, white. Postal workers and junior high school faculty were white men; butter packers, white women. Black women and white women—middle-class, at least—joined volunteer organizations to improve the lot of themselves or others.

Bands and sports entertained many Minnesotans as both participants and spectators in the 1920s. They were not only or even primarily school bands or teams but organized by workplace or town: the Donaldson Department Store Kiltie Band, the White Earth Town Band, the Washburn Crosby Gold Medal Flour Band, the Brainerd Ladies' Band, the St. Cloud Reformatory Band, the Pike Lake Auto Club Harmonica champions; the (integrated) Garfield baseball team, the girls' football team at Gustavus Adolphus College (pads, helmets, uniforms, and all); the Danish Young People's Home soccer team and the Munsingwear women's basketball team. The employees of the Andrew Schoch Grocery in St. Paul dressed and paraded every year for the city's Winter Carnival.

Nothing says 1920s with more fanfare and promise than motor vehicles of all kinds: trucks, tractors, threshing machines; fire trucks, homecoming parade floats; cars for show, parade, and politics. Henry DeGrood and his wife posed with their six children in front of their first touring car; probably the eight of them could not fit in all at once. Lorna Dunn showed off her stylish hat, coat, and shoes, pointing to her equally stylish 1924 Lincoln. Motorcycles most often were the playthings of men such as those at Guy Webb's shop or Mr. E. S. Moody, who took his family out for an afternoon drive in his sidecar.

Many photographers in the 1920s featured houses and buildings. In a photo that looks more like the 1880s than the 1920s, a couple sits outside an unfinished log cabin in Beltrami County. The battered bucket sitting on top of the well at the front of the photo hints at hard use; the stack of lumber, of buildings to come. Summer birch-bark houses at Red Lake declare Ojibwe persistence and the survival of a seasonally organized life. In seasonally organized leisure, tourists escaped to cabins or tents. None had indoor plumbing, electricity, or the variety of conveniences increasingly available in town.

Still, not everyone in town had as many bathrooms as the Watkins mansion in Winona. Paul Watkins, the son of the founder of the Watkins Product company—which specialized originally in patent medicines, then turned to pepper, cinnamon, and vanilla—had a photographer follow the building of his house and had photos taken of each room, including the six bathrooms—one for him, one for his wife, one for his daughter, one for his son, and two for guests—each modern, with tiled tub and shower. Was this what Thorstein Veblen meant by "conspicuous consumption"?

Proximity to the woods made lumber a common and cheap—if hazardous—building material in Cloquet and other northern locales. Cloquet grew into a timbering town boasting wide roads, gutters, paved sidewalks, and houses of wood, as befitted its economy and location. The great fire of 1918 roared through those houses, and the photographer at Olson's Studio took a shot of the wreckage. He returned five years later to that exact spot and captured the resurrected town.

Photos of defeat or failure (without redemption) rarely made it into the historical record in the 1920s. It was so much more satisfying to show that "we made it" than that "we didn't." Moreover, the "moment" for picture taking is rarely so pronounced at the end of a subject's life as at its beginning. An abandoned, windowless building in Shotley near Red Lake tells of hopes unfulfilled. Its design—the storefront facade, the windowless side—anticipates other buildings lining up with it to make a Main Street. Shotley was, for a time, a trading outpost, but too few people showed up and stayed. The once hopeful owner moved on. Later, the building slid off its foundation.

In the 1910s and 1920s, the Oliver Mining Company built and rented houses to workers in Coleraine, Taconite, and other range towns. When the company discovered a particularly rich vein of iron ore under Hibbing, it jacked up the houses, set them on wheels, and transported them to a new Hibbing. The houses ranged in size from four to twelve rooms, each equipped with bath, washbasin, toilet, hot and cold water, laundry tubs, and electric or gas lights. Who got which house was determined by the job held rather than by the number of children or even the ability to pay. Even so, the superintendents' and workers' houses in Hibbing stood closer in proximity, style, and class than did the steel workers' tenements in Pittsburgh with Andrew Carnegie's mansion in Manhattan. Many a Pittsburgh tenement housed sixty-four people in a few rooms; Carnegie's sixty-four rooms housed only a few people. Iron Range workers and managers never experienced quite so wide a difference in their accommodations.[4]*

Chester Congdon, a lawyer for the Oliver Mining Company until 1905, did not live on the range but in Duluth on the shore, in what was perhaps not a mansion by Carnegie or Vanderbilt standards but certainly was by Minnesota ones.

The mining company commissioned photos of its gigantic open-pit mines, for sure, but also of its houses, of employees' gardens, of the Hibbing move, of water fountains and safety equipment at the mines, of company-run hospitals, of its longtime employees and pensioners, of the parks it provided, of its rest home in Ishpeming, Michigan—for "wives of employees who are in poor health, due to family cares."[5]

The photos show that no clear line demarcated where urban America stopped and rural America began. Chickens pecked around a yard in St. Paul, in the shadow of houses and the German Evangelical Lutheran Church. People living in the Bohemian Flats of Minneapolis kept gardens, chickens, and probably a few other farm animals—no matter if city ordinances outlawed them. Tony and Anteonetta Sanchelli and their neighbors in Swede Hollow could grow some of their own food and look up at the same St. Paul Cathedral that Mary Hill looked at from the balcony of her house on Summit Avenue.†

†

After her death, the family turned the house over to the St. Paul Archdiocese; the house passed from private use to public by 1925—perhaps representing the Catholic church's success (and integration into American society) as the house itself had James J. Hill's.

New houses and new suburbs tried to draw lines more distinctly. No chickens pecked around the house at 4614 Edgebrook Place in Edina. Its family identified more closely with the city some miles distant than it did with the farms just a few hundred yards away. It had city water and sewer and a tuck-under garage to house the car that the man of the house almost certainly drove to his office to make the money he and his wife used to buy (probably on time) new furnishings, a vacuum cleaner, a washing machine, a refrigerator, and a radio. Pets would have been their only animals and flowers their only garden produce.

More and more people in the 1920s moved, too, into apartment buildings—no pets or flower gardens allowed—for single people, newly marrieds, transients, and others who wanted independence or privacy or had nowhere else to go. The Great War had pretty much ended the custom of living at home until marriage. Soldiers returning from the war; women whose soldiers didn't return; clerks and secretaries and nurses and teachers; artists, social workers, and bankers; misfits who couldn't survive in a smaller place—all could find affordable space in the apartments (and emotional space in the towns).

The single people who had long dominated central city life—young men, often seasonal workers who came to the city between jobs to spend money, renew friendships, escape the strictures of contract labor—rarely lived in such apartments. They settled instead into flophouses or transients hotels.

Earlier buildings persisted into the 1920s, including the library in North Mankato, its facade resembling in miniature the church face of a bygone era. The decade's photographers put most of their effort into photographing the new and modern buildings going up all over the state, none more modern or inspiring than the Foshay Tower—Minneapolis's first "skyscraper," the tallest building west of Chicago—completed in 1928. Then, of course, there was Charles A. Lindbergh, Jr., son of the Minnesota senator who had opposed U.S. entry into World War I, who flew his nonstop flight from New York to Paris in 1927. He didn't start the flying craze, but he fueled its takeoff. In Minneapolis and St. Paul, the parks system ran the first airport (after reclaiming land that earlier developers had hoped to turn into an Indianapolis-like speedway).[6]

Henri Verbrugghen rehearsing with the Minneapolis Symphony Orchestra, 1929

Aster Theater, 1929

Potato planters, Princeton, 1920

John Bergeron rolling logs, 1920

Harvest hands en route to South Dakota, 1920

Henry Walseth and daughter Hannah in Walseth's store, Ihlen, 1924

Ojibwe men with farm team in field, 1920

Sorting of mail, St. Paul Post Office, 1925

Woman painter, Minneapolis, 1920

Northern Pacific dining car crew, 1930

Roosevelt Junior High School faculty, 1920

Federation of Negro Women, 1920

Women painting furniture, Lake of the Isles Congregational Church

Town band at June 14 celebration, White Earth Indian Reservation, 1920

St. Cloud Reformatory band, 1920

Harmonica champs, St. Louis County Farm Bureau Recreational Institute, 1927

Greeley School baseball team, 1925

Girls' football players at Gustavus Adolphus College, St. Peter, 1920

Soccer team, Danish Young People's Home, 1925

Automobile for Theodore Christianson's gubernatorial campaign, 1928

Henry DeGrood family with touring car, 1925

Lorna Dunn with Lincoln sedan, 1924

Motorcyclists in front of Guy Webb's shop, Minneapolis, 1925

Log cabin, Roosevelt, 1925

Ojibwe summer homes along Red Lake, 1925

Roleff family camping at Gooseberry River, 1922

Paul Watkins bathroom

Ghost town of Shotley near Red Lake, 1925

Rust Iron Mine, Hibbing, 1925

Cloquet after 1918 fire

Cloquet, 1923

Home of Oliver Mining Company general superintendent, Hibbing, 1912

HOUSES.
Coleraine, Minnesota. 1920.
Oliver Iron Mining Co., Architects and Owners.
C. F. Haglin and Sons Co., General Contractors.

Oliver Mining Company houses, Coleraine, 1920

Chickens in St. Paul yard, 1920

4614 Edgebrook Place, Edina, 1925

Lynnwood Apartment Building, Minneapolis, 1925

PART II:
THE STORIES

The photos of the 1920s included here provide a many-angled view of Minnesota: farm and town people of many occupations and hobbies, housed in everything from tents to mansions, showing the state and its people, their aspirations and some of their dashed hopes. Together, such a range of photos tells us our attempts to characterize a place and time dissolve into overgeneralization. The images remind us how easily a person, family, or decade slips into the categorical noose we slide around them. One of the great values of photos is their insistent particularity.

Photos seem to be objective records of reality, but they're not. Taking a photo is an act different from simply looking at something: A photo freezes a moment and preserves it. It gives life to one way of looking. Every photo is "made," and each tells a story or several stories. Sometimes the photographer tells a story intentionally and consciously; sometimes he or she simply takes a snapshot that touches or amuses. When we look at photos, then, we must not just look at what the picture shows at first glance but ask what story it tells and why.

The number of 1920s photographs showing people in groups other than families and in settings other than home (or yard) is striking. Such photos suggest two sets of questions (at least). The first set has to do with families: Why are so many people pictured with others of their own age and circumstance and, compared with the 1890s and 1910s, less often with their families? The photos can't tell us that families were in decline, but they do say that individuals met the world as individuals rather than as members of families—in the workplace, at the university, in clubs and organizations, on teams.

The pictures tempt us to ask, too, why the St. Cloud Reformatory had its own band, why the Munsingwear factory had its own basketball team. If the band was a way to keep inmates occupied, perhaps cooperative, was that also the motive of Munsingwear, Washburn Crosby, or Donaldson when laborers elsewhere were organizing for higher wages? What about all those other bands? Was the town band at White Earth evidence of Indian "civilization" or a way to integrate white and native men?

The photos also show women away from home and in groups with other women—making music in Brainerd, playing football at Gustavus, painting chairs for charity, and registering voters. Black women, too, met and worked together. Women got the vote by amendment to the Constitution in 1920; that and the more powerful forces hinted at in 1920s photos, including the house at 4614 Edgebrook Place in Edina and the apartments in town, were reshaping women's lives.

The photographers of these images may not have been conscious that they were showing changes in family life or women's roles, but even the most casual picture takers consider focus, angle, and background. Professionals make their life's work attending to such details. Zooming in or out, holding a camera at one angle rather than another—these choices capture different images of the same scene. The photographer must decide which is "best." But best for what?

Mathew Brady in the 1860s carefully arranged his Civil War battlefield shots. He moved himself and his camera and, if necessary, the bodies to emphasize war as terrible, senseless loss. Dorothea Lange in the 1930s posed and reposed that Oklahoma mother and her children until she captured the woman's nobility and the heavy hand of undeserved want. In my own vacation photos, I position the camera to cut off the parking lot on the one side and the irritating hordes of people on the other, to depict the beach as I would have liked for it to have been. Brady's photos taught generations of people how to "remember" the Civil War. Lange's woman became the face of the Great Depression. My beach photograph eventually replaces my own memory that includes the cars and the people.

If we remember that photos tell stories, we can ask whose story they tell and why. James Stewart photographed the Washburn Crosby elevator in Minneapolis in 1919. His photo shows the building to good effect, but even more effective is its perspective. At dead center in the distance is the Municipal Building's clock tower. This could not be accidental. It's too perfect, too indicative of how the milling companies wished to see themselves and be seen—as the city's foundation.

The Oliver Mining Company certainly tells a story with its photos of the houses, drinking fountains, gardens, picnics, and Ishpeming Rest Home. Perhaps the company simply wanted a record for itself. That explanation might be persuasive if the state's mining industry were not so embroiled in turmoil in the 1910s and 1920s.

The Iron Range witnessed several especially bitter—and unsuccessful—strikes in the first two decades of the twentieth century. Workers resented the undistributed power and wealth, the bad working conditions of mining, and some tried to organize to improve their lot. Owners and managers—and many Minnesotans outside the range—feared what they saw as the radical leanings of the labor unions. Would labor organization—particularly when backed or fomented by the Industrial Workers of the World—lead to class chaos? Did laborers threaten the company's well-being or profits?

Governor John Lind at the turn of the century had resisted the company's urging to call out state troops to control the strikes, and progres-

Washburn Crosby elevator, Minneapolis, 1919

sive politicians in Minnesota and elsewhere had for years worried about the unbridled excesses of corporations. So worried, in fact, that they had pushed, with some success, for state and federal limitations on the ability of corporations—including mines—to maximize profits by exploiting workers. Courts were upholding the constitutionality of laws that set working hours and conditions.[7]

The mining companies had defeated the strikers; the Great War had pushed back some of the reforming impulse; in the 1920s business and corporations were in ascendancy. The "business of America is business" philosophy of presidents Warren G. Harding and Calvin Coolidge certainly gave the mining and other corporations some respite. But photos demonstrating how alert the mining company was to worker health and well-being certainly did not hurt in its campaign to deflect regulation. Such photos show the mining company to good effect—helpful, humane, concerned about not only its workers but the workers' families as well. It provided good housing—not tenements or slums—in decent towns with parks and other amenities. The company photographers did not make up any of this; the photos are accurate. They just tell their stories from a particular point of view.

The workers individually and the unions collectively did not have access to resources to tell other stories, their stories—gardens ripped up when the company moved to Hibbing or men with black lung disease or the companies pitting miners against each other. Without photos from their perspective, the mining pictures demand careful interrogation.

PART III:

THE PHOTOGRAPHERS

All photographers are visible in their photos. The ones more attentive to what they see through the viewfinder may not make the mistake that some did in recording their own shadows. But photographers are always present in the choice of subject, the angle, the background, the details. Briol's and Peel's photos, then, tell us about the worlds they inhabited and, perhaps, even their views about those worlds.

Briol lived and worked in Stearns County—a predominantly German American area. As late as 1917, many churches, schools, stores, businesses, and families conducted their lives in German. The war frightened the state into forming the Minnesota Commission of Public Safety that rooted out disloyalty even where it did not exist. The commission turned much of its energy on German Americans, questioning the loyalty of people whose families had been in the state for upwards of fifty years and who themselves had never even been to Germany. The commission identified the speaking of German as disloyal and frightened the language underground.

The amendment for Prohibition fell heavily on these same people, for whom beer was both a drink and a tradition. Prohibitionists, usually white, middle class, upwardly mobile, and urban, sought to control ethnic, working-class drinkers. Attacking drinking was a way to loosen the ties of ethnic tradition. More than one German American hid a still somewhere on his property (even the monks at Saint John's Abbey are rumored to have kept one in their woods). But the effect of a ban on drinking was the portrayal of German people as outsiders, as different.

Norton and Peel photographer, 1930

Briol lived in the midst of this and more. The forces of rural life had long pulled people toward self-sufficiency, family, rootedness, tradition—a Jeffersonian definition of what made America America. Those forces had weakened in the nineteenth century. Populists cared about free silver and rural cooperatives, of course, but their central concern was that rural people and Jeffersonian ideals had been pushed from center stage and replaced by the values of money, speed, urbanization, and industrialization.

In the 1890s, historian Frederick Jackson Turner, having studied patterns of settlement and found that no part of the United States had a population under two persons per square mile, declared the American frontier closed. One path, then, for American growth and development had ended, he concluded. New paths to new places would have to be found, with the traditional one now closed and America's geographic boundaries filled in. The U.S. Census Bureau in 1920 announced that a majority of Americans lived in urban places. That the definition of *urban* was incorporated places of 2,500 or more—a village today—and that many states, including Minnesota, did not meet this threshold as demonstrated by village population in 1920, did not keep the bureau, the newspapers, and others from trumpeting the fact that the United States had become an urban nation.[8]

These two announcements signaled a dramatic reorientation of American life and values. It did not happen all at once or immediately in 1920: Minnesota did not become urban by the census definition until 1950. Nonetheless, this new force exerted a stronger and stronger pull from the rural toward an urban and industrial culture of specialization, individuation, efficiency, and consumption. The new ways were in ascendancy and the traditional ways in decline—whether one lived in New York, Minneapolis, Mankato, Slayton, or Ross.

These two forces pulled against each other and explain, in part, why the 1920s were such a turbulent time. Urban and rural forces and people saw themselves fighting for the definition and direction of America. The outcome may already have been set, but the battle was fierce.

However much exhilaration and liberation the 1920s offered to apartment dwellers, new voters, and car buyers, they frightened the Ku Klux Klan into resurgence even in Minnesota. The klan stirred up enough hatred and misplaced self-righteousness to lead otherwise upstanding Duluth townspeople to lynch three black circus hands for rapes they did not commit. First they trapped a frightened—and probably sexually active, though not with the accused—young woman into charges resulting in the murders. The perpetrators imagined they did an upright and moral thing.

Sinclair Lewis railed against the stultification of Main Street and the shallowness of the Babbitts of the 1920s as fiercely as evangelical preachers including Sister Aimee Semple McPherson and Reverend William Bell Riley in St. Paul railed against the sins of the modern. Movies glorified and sexualized the milieu. Cars offered many temptations; disillusionments of war inspired others. Prohibition promised salvation for many; its widespread disregard offered testimony that the road to heaven was bumpy. Jazz, an art form that sang the talents and worldview of African Americans, offered its own pleasures, as did the stylized but liberated Charleston, in which women danced without being led by a man.

Briol's photos sing the praises of rural life and defend its German American residents. They offer a record of upright citizenship and emphasize the old-fashioned entertainments of picnics, family reunions, parades. But they give lie to any strict demarcation of rural and urban. They delight in the car going into the ditch; they delight in the horses pulling it out. They relish the motorcycles and the men skilled enough to keep them running. These people were neither traitors nor hicks but upstanding, hard-working, stable, responsible, sturdy citizens who also knew how to have fun, to take advantage of the modern when it suited.

Peel had come from a farm town, but he left it in his early teens. Given his war experience, he didn't have to bother with questions of loyalty and patriotism. His photos tell instead of thriving businesses, powerful businessmen, children cared for by charitable organizations, people dancing and playing, clean and orderly work environments—of a Minneapolis that worked. He featured urban advantages: the University of Minnesota; Young-Quinlan, Dayton's, and Powers department stores; movie and vaudeville theaters; the Minneapolis Symphony, nightclubs, and roller rinks.[9]

Perhaps each man, like the Oliver Mining Company photographers, simply took the pictures he was paid to take. That explanation might be convincing if the photos did not also explain with sympathy and care what seems to have been the central conflict of the 1920s.

Together the photos of Briol and Peel show a Minnesota in which rural people were neither isolated nor shielded from new ideas. Urban people did not throw out all of the old. Some differences separated people—rural/urban, male/female, adult/child, white/other, ethnic/native born. All of the lines had cracks, and none was final. They show a Minnesota not easily categorized but not totally foreign, either. It's a Minnesota of puzzles that also makes sense. It was not one thing—then or now.

CODA

Henry Briol left two images that may have been mistakes or proofs wait-ing for cropping in the darkroom. They let us peek into the process of photography; they suggest that Briol knew just how much construction a photo required and that he wanted us to know that he knew.

Take his photo of siblings—spiffed up and outfitted in clothing be-yond their Sunday best. On each side of Briol's photograph we see the edges of a decorative background screen. On the far left we see the par-tial profile of a woman—the mother of these children, perhaps, her hands on her hips. Disapproving? Paying close attention? The children look serious; only the two older girls, at each end, allow a bit of a smile.

In a second shot, Briol again let the camera view outside the edge of the backdrop. In so doing, he told us to look again at the figures—hardly the hard-drinking hombres a first glance at the photo suggests. These are guys posed at a studio. Even the photographer can't take them seri-ously; the photo is a kind of joke.

Both images remind us that a photo is a story about reality, con-structed and told by its creator.

Formal portrait of brothers and sisters, 1900

Three men drinking at a table, 1900

12

Hanging on for Dear Life

EVEN IN GOOD ECONOMIC TIMES, many Minnesotans made only enough to get by, and the 1920s were not good times. Magdalene and Peter Court, for example, married in 1924 and in 1928 rented a farm in St. Augusta Township about twelve miles south of St. Cloud in Stearns County. They worked that farm for nearly forty years. They raised corn, some small grains, a few animals, chickens, lots of garden vegetables, raspberries, a few fruit trees, and five children. Cash? They never had any to speak of. Pete reportedly made a little extra by selling homebrew to his German-speaking friends. He worked off some of their local taxes by repairing roads for a few days a year. They bartered eggs for coffee and such at the nearby Luxemburg store and traded potatoes for a radio. They got along well enough, Mrs. Court remembered, pretty much like their neighbors.[1]

> Out of bed between 5:00 and 5:30 and sometimes earlier if work had to be hurried. First were cows to be milked then the milk had to be separated with a separator. Which had quite a few parts to be washed when the separator was done. This was done after breakfast which had to be prepared first. Children were taken care of and sent to school. Then day's work began.
>
> A noon meal had to be prepared and sometimes if it was hard work the men were doing, a lunch was required around 9:30 A.M. Spring time the afternoons were spent in cleaning up the yards and planting the gardens while the men were out in the fields doing the crop planting. Then lunch around 4 o'clock and work till 7:00 P.M. When it was supper time. After that the cows had to be milked again and fed. This was done day after day. So in the evening a person was glad to relax.[2]

Legions of men, for another example, worked in the woods, on threshing crews, laying railroad track. Doing these seasonal, transient, and essential jobs, the most determined worker could put together perhaps eight months of work a year. In between jobs they often returned to friends, cheap accommodations, and employment bureaus, where they awaited the next assignment. They lived in flophouses in cities and small towns, usually close to a railroad station. Used to being outdoors, they often spent their days standing around outside, playing cards, sleeping in the parks. They looked just like the "unworthy" poor that they weren't. As a group they got the reputation for drinking, and some certainly did. However, local Minneapolis ordinance limited bars to the same Gateway area where most of the transient workers lived, so anyone (from college students to the wealthy to traveling businessmen to casual partiers) who wanted to buy a drink showed up in the Gateway—giving the sober workers a bad name.* Like the Courts, many workingmen might well say they got along well enough.† No cushions were in place to soften their fall when the hard times came, and they did come.[3]

That many people faced and endured crippling, debilitating, and soul-numbing poverty tells one plot line. That government programs invented new ways of helping people constitutes another. That those programs constructed a social, cultural, and physical infrastructure that touched and, in fact, improved the lives of nearly every Minnesotan is a dominant one. That through all of it some people carried on as "normal" is yet another. Minnesota's Depression stories started in the 1920s, and their effects shade even into the present.

The agricultural boom of the 1910s had driven up both wheat prices and speculation. People lived on the future. The slow, steady, quiet rain of economic trouble, however, soaked the Minnesota ground in the 1920s. Wheat that had sold for $3 a bushel in 1920 went for under $2 two years later, then under $1, then $.40 by the middle 1930s.

The urban as well as the rural economy in the state and the nation showed signs of trouble in the 1920s. Following World War I (as a result of repayments of war debts and tariffs collected), the United States had a disproportionate share of the world's gold and a few Americans controlled a disproportionate share of the nation's wealth. Debts, both international and personal, left the global and the national economy unstable enough that when the stock market dropped, then dropped again, then collapsed in October 1929, the national economy was plunged into what historians and others call the "Great Depression," the period between 1929 and the beginning of World War II in which businesses failed, banks foreclosed where they could and failed when they couldn't (taking their deposits with them), factories slowed or stopped, mines went quiet and men took to the rails, John Steinbeck's Joads—and others—loaded up their worldly possessions and went in search of work and salvation. Unemployment—around three percent nationally in the 1920s—reached 25 percent, and desperation reached higher than that.

*

The State Planning Board rejected the idea of some that "the transient group has brought their insecurity upon themselves and [therefore] should be left to their own devices," arguing instead that "transients are actually necessary."

†

Jay Gorney and Yip Harburg would memorialize these people with their 1931 song, "Brother, Can You Spare a Dime," sung and recorded by Bing Crosby in 1932. It begins:
*They used to tell me I was building a dream, and so I followed the mob, When there was earth to plow, or guns to bear, I was always there right on the job.
They used to tell me I was building a dream, with peace and glory ahead, Why should I be standing in line, just waiting for bread?*

In some farm areas, drought compounded the effects of the economic depression. So, for example, even when corn prices were relatively high, farmers in drought areas could not benefit.[4]

What had been trickles of trouble turned into flash floods and lifted people like the Courts, the transient workers, and millions of others off their moorings. People, hanging on as best as they could, watched as their jobs, houses, and dreams floated away. Some families lost their grip on each other and drifted apart. Some people themselves slipped under the water and did not come up.

A minority of farmers owned their farms in 1930—over 20 percent rented and another 50 percent lived on mortgaged property. When the economy collapsed, rural people didn't lack for work—there was always work to do on a farm—but they did lack for a crop that could bring in some profit. When it cost more to raise a pig or to produce milk than could be recovered in the sale, what good did it do to have lots of milk and lots of pork? To force prices up—and to draw public attention to their plight—farmers killed piglets and dumped milk. What else could they do? Then drought strangled the life out of many fields and dust seeped through the tightest window, filled ditches, made people's mouths dry and their eyes itch. Farmers had to share what did grow with grasshoppers who ate "everything but the mortgage." Many farmers did have enough to feed themselves—their own milk and butter and eggs and garden food, fruit, honey, berries. They could butcher their own chickens, can beef, and cure pork in salt.[5]

People in town didn't even have that. The economic catastrophes that intensified dramatically in the 1930s took a serious toll on people who presumed they stood on more solid footing: teachers, telephone operators, bank tellers, accountants, office clerks, bookkeepers, stenographers, barbers, nurses, teachers, bankers, middle-level managers, supervisors, bosses. Already in 1931, over 60,000 people in Minnesota who had previously held work no longer did.[*][†] Vonnie Kuchinski and Callum DeVillier were just two of the thousands of people who came of age as the Depression took hold. Vonnie, seventeen years old in 1930, worked as a stenographer and lived at home in Minneapolis with her parents and three brothers. Callum, age twenty-three in 1930, worked in a restaurant, probably washing dishes, and lodged with the Kuchinskis. By late 1932 neither of them had a job. They counted themselves among the thousands of unemployed in Minnesota who needed money and couldn't see work that could get them any.[6]

By 1932 General Mills had laid off half of its employees. Over 70 percent of workers on the Iron Range lost their jobs—not just miners but all of those who worked in jobs that the miners' patronage supported.

*

In Minneapolis, the ranks of the employed decreased by 30 percent from 1928 to 1932. In January 1931, at least 35,000 were unemployed.

†

Between January and December 1930, national unemployment rose from 4 to 7 million, then by 1933 to 14 million. Elizabeth Faue argues that applications for relief in Minneapolis jumped from 214 in the 1920s to 10,000 in 1932. Moreover, the kinds of people who found themselves among the 10,000 (more often married and more often younger) were different from those who had been among the 214 (older, single, sick).

Even Wilbur B. Foshay—builder of that extraordinary Minneapolis office tower that represented the hyped hopes of the 1920s—saw his fortune and dreams crumble following the stock market crash and found himself first unemployed, then in jail for mail fraud.* At one time or another as many as 25 to 30 percent of Minnesotans were without work completely; others lived with reduced hours and wages; others got pushed completely out of the job market. Minnesota reported 103,000 wage earners in 1930 and 80,000 in 1940. Where did those 23,000 workers go?[7]

Already in January 1931, 35,000 workers in Minneapolis were unemployed. In November 1932, the Union Mission was taking care of 1,800 men every night. Hobos and others at loose ends knocked on doors looking for a handout. Sometimes people just up and left for a job—or the hope of a job—elsewhere.[8]

Sometimes the economic difficulties fell differently on women than on men, such as when the Minneapolis City Council in 1932 imposed six-months' unpaid leave on female employees whose husbands had jobs of any kind. Women "hobos" as such did not exist, but women without work and place seemed to disappear, despite their numbers. In 1930, some female workers were put up in the Minneapolis jail, not as prisoners, but as homeless and without resources. Between 1932 and 1933, over 10,000 other women turned to the Seventh Street Club (a respectable name for a private relief agency). Women might have preferred being known as hobos and subjected only to the judgments inflicted on hobos. Instead, women additionally faced the likelihood, if they were single, of being thought sexually suspect.[9]

Black hobos probably would have been happy, too, to be regarded only as hobos. Railroads laid off steady workers; so did meatpacking plants. Domestic service offered fewer and fewer jobs for black men or women. Their options were even more limited and their circle of support more circumscribed (if sometimes a bit more sympathetic) than those white workers could claim.[10]

In any case, only ironic Americans were humming the Harry Warren and Al Dubin 1933 hit, "We're in the Money."[11]†

Hundreds of banks simply closed down. Others, in order to stay open, foreclosed on loans. What else could they do? Sometimes the out-of-work banker might become a milkman or the teacher would find a seasonal job in a cannery. But most people couldn't find replacement work. A relative or friend might help for a time, but who knew when their job might give way? A broad swath of people suffered enormously, and virtually everyone in the country lived under the cloud of national and local distress. These conditions resulted in widespread and public

*

Foshay engaged in shady, then illegal business practices that got him convicted and sent to Leavenworth Prison in 1932, where he stayed for three years.

†

The opening several lines are: *We're in the money, we're in the money*
We've got a lot of what it takes to get along
We're in the money, that sky is sunny,
Old Man Depression you are through, you done us wrong.

poverty. Few Minnesotans—or other Americans—knew how to think about, let alone what to do about so many people in need.

The American poor relief system had long operated—and in most places still did—out of township- and county-run boards that recognized two kinds of needy: the worthy and the unworthy. The "worthy" (widows, orphans, the sick and maimed), in need through no fault of their own, received what was called outdoor relief (to distinguish it from the indoor relief of the poor farm): small—often miserly—gifts of cash, loads of wood, baskets of food, a doctor's visit, or placement in a county poorhouse or poor farm. The "unworthy" (everyone else in need) received even less, or nothing, because they were presumed to have caused their own difficulties by drinking too much, working too little, or otherwise behaving irresponsibly.[12]

This system reflected deeply held beliefs about the roots of poverty, about gender, and about America. Namely, that in America, by dint of hard work and strong will, a man could determine his own fate. If he failed to make something of himself, he had no claim on public assistance (or sympathy) because he had only himself to blame. This idea proved remarkably resistant to evidence that the men most likely to succeed in America were those whose fathers had succeeded. The belief that men controlled their own destiny belied how little control people actually had. Luck, good friends, connections, good health, a winning personality, white skin, a Y chromosome, even good looks all helped people get ahead. Of course, most people who got ahead worked hard, but thousands, indeed, hundreds of thousands of Americans who worked just as hard or harder never got ahead. America expected women to work hard, too, but never promised them that this was their path to success. Purity and then marrying up was the way—the only way, really. Women in "trouble," as out-of-wedlock pregnancies were euphemistically called, could expect neither help nor sympathy.[13]*

This system showed many cracks by the end of the nineteenth century. The crash and Depression broke them open and showed the faults in the system. Too many needy people had no family to rely on; too many counties were paying to send the needy to the next county seat; too few townships had enough funds to care even for the "worthy" poor. Jacob Riis and other photographers were chronicling the depth and breadth of American poverty;† Progressive politicians had begun rethinking the government's responsibilities to its citizens; private charities and a raft of women's volunteer organizations had turned their attention to the poor. Even so, most Americans—including the poor themselves—still didn't believe in no-fault poverty, so to ask for aid was humiliating. The problems became more and more apparent, but the solutions didn't. Believing in self-help and sharing

*
One report offered a variety of reasons why people might have ended up on the public rolls, including "individual improvidence" and "individual incompetence," but asserted that 64 percent were in need because of unemployment; another 20 percent due to "military causes" (mentally or physically unfit as a result of war service or living on pensions); and no percentage attributed to improvidence or incompetence.

†
Jacob Riis: a New York photographer who specialized in showing how poor people—especially immigrants and children—lived in industrial America

the idea that asking for help was humiliating, few people turned initially to the government for assistance.[14]*

One group of unemployed in Minneapolis in 1932, led by Reverend George Mecklenburg of the Wesley Methodist Church, formed the "Organized Unemployed, Inc." to avoid asking for public assistance. Its members would keep their dignity by helping themselves, which they did by issuing scrip and working out a barter/trade arrangement that included businesses and professional people, even movie theaters.[15]

Similarly, the Farm Women's Co-operative formed in 1933 to market products from their own orchards and gardens—especially pickles, jellies, jams, and chili sauces—that they would sell under the name of "Farm Home Products." They agreed to common recipes and a share of profits. As the *Minneapolis Tribune* reported, "This work is expected to prove a boon to many Minnesota families who have found it difficult to get along on the small prices they have obtained for their grain crops in recent years."[16]

A few people did demand assistance. About 700 protestors picketed the Minneapolis City Hall in July 1932, demanding "$5 million for city relief, an $8 [a] day grant to unemployed workers, and a slum clearance program." Four months later, the voters of Minneapolis responded to those demands by electing A. G. Bainbridge as mayor. He had run on a platform that called for police officers (rather than social workers) to investigate relief cases. Only the unworthy—communists, probably, many thought—would ask for such help.[17]

A group of World War I veterans demanded government help but still not relief. They only wanted a service bonus due to them in 1945 to be allocated in 1932 when they needed it. This "Bonus Army" marched on Washington in the summer of 1932 to lobby their legislators. They set up "Hoovervilles" (tented communities) and picketed the Capitol. When Congress declined the demands and the marchers refused to go home peaceably, President Herbert Hoover called out the U.S. Army. He didn't intend it, but the soldiers burned the camps and scattered the protestors. The protestors were not demanding help, however: this payment was legislated in 1921 and belonged to them but hadn't yet been paid out. Their actions did not reject Americans' attitudes about need and the needy or change notions of the role of government. Hoover didn't pay much attention to them as "needy," instead defining them as troublemakers and possible communists.[18]

And Hoover was more sympathetic to the needy than many others in government specifically or society generally. During World War I he had helped organize relief for war victims in Belgium. In 1927 he'd done a masterful job as head of relief efforts for the great Mississippi River

*

Edward Pickett, about to graduate from the University of Minnesota in June 1933, echoed these beliefs, even in the hardest days of the Depression: "Around school, it's pretty much a fellow's ability and willing[ness] to work that gets him ahead. I've an idea it's the same in the business world. If I have the stuff and am willing to give it, I'll get somewhere, depression or not."

flood. As president from 1929 to 1933, he acted and pushed Congress to act. Congress appropriated a loan of $300 million for state and local governments to fund government construction. Congress also authorized the distribution of government-held wheat and other commodities. State and local work projects testified to the government's inexperience with helping people in need. The construction projects were not intended as relief. The work bore no relationship to the workers' skills; the pay came more often in the form of goods rather than cash. And it all came steeped in traditional attitudes about the poor (Were these people worthy? Were they taking advantage of the public's generosity? Would they misspend cash contributions? Were they of strong moral fiber?). Hoover, like many of his contemporaries, believed in altruism and charity. He did not believe in federal government programs.[19]

Even for these efforts, conservatives reviled Hoover's soft-heartedness. Some even voted for the patrician Franklin Roosevelt, thinking that he would adopt more conservative relief practices than Hoover had. What was the right role of government? Citizens, the needy, politicians didn't agree. In the same year that Minneapolis voters elected the conservative Bainbridge as mayor, the state's voters went in large numbers for Franklin Roosevelt.

"March 4, 1933 was a day which I still remember very well," Mrs. Court wrote fifty years later. "It was the inauguration of President Franklin Delano Roosevelt." Few people outside of New York, where FDR had served as governor, anticipated either Roosevelt's activism or his attitudes about relief. Steeped in a tradition of noblesse oblige and educated by his own polio, Roosevelt abandoned traditional American relief ideas and practices in the face of the desperate need gripping so many Americans. He—and his Brain Trust staff—inaugurated an alphabet soup of agencies, organizations, projects, and schemes that defined the problem of poverty and unemployment as systemic rather than individual, collective rather than personal. As Mrs. Court also remembered, "Shortly after the inauguration all the banks were closed and no checks could be transferred. But the speech Roosevelt gave had many words of hope for the people and help came in many ways. Some of which included distribution of surplus foods like grapefruit, apples, canned beef roast. Also the works program administration or W.P.A. which was most welcome in the area and the opening of C.C.C. camps for young men."[20]

Many others criticized Roosevelt for his activism, but it only spurred him to pursue more energetically what he saw as his and the government's duty.[*]

Good thing, too, some might argue, because more and more people

*

Many of the programs of the First New Deal, as many historians call the years from 1933 to 1935, were haphazardly invented and put together under intense pressure to do something. Many of them were flawed, therefore; the programs that had the longest-lasting effects, Social Security, for example, were products of the Second New Deal, 1936–41.

in need were organizing—not just to help themselves but to target flaws in the system. The Farmers Holiday Association moved to stop farm foreclosures or to defeat foreclosure sales by making bids of a penny or two and keeping all other bids out and bidders silent (either by appealing to farmer solidarity or, sometimes, by threats). Other farmers marched on the State Capitol to show their circumstances.[21]

Laborers—despite the often strong and strong-armed efforts of employers to resist them—formed unions to defend against layoffs and pay cuts. In 1933 workers took over the Austin Hormel meatpacking plant to demand higher wages. The local sheriff called on Governor Floyd Olson "to dispatch militia." When journalists appealed to the working-class Olson to break the strike, he called them "blood-thirsty swivel-chair warriors." In 1934 the truckers' union shut down Minneapolis to all but food and coal trucks in order to pressure higher wages—these were desperate depression times. Armed with baseball bats, fists, and guns, pickets and anti-unionists fought each other, leaving dozens wounded and, eventually, several dead. Photos of Citizens Alliance army members and strikers taking baseball bats to each other told a story of a system that had collapsed. When Minneapolis police fired on the striking workers, killing two and injuring over sixty, it seemed that war had begun.[22]

A 1935–36 strike at Strutwear Knitting also provoked violence before the company eventually gave in and negotiated a pay raise. Most of the Strutwear workers were women, and most were not union members. The strike was called, however, when eight men were fired—for incompetence ostensibly, but for being active union people as the workers understood it.* Women and men both walked out and stayed out for eight months, until the company acceded to the strikers' demands in April 1936.[23]†

When timber workers walked out on Weyerhaeuser in 1937, the Farmer-Labor (and communist) governor Elmer Benson ordered that state relief funds be used for the strikers and called in state police to keep order.‡ The Leaf Lake Community Party in Otter Tail County deposed the township board because of its treatment of people in need. The Workers' Alliance of nearby Fergus Falls protested the "hardship and suffering" that township relief practices imposed, typified among other things with township officials still "deporting" needy people to other counties and treating the homegrown poor astringently. Albert Lea in 1937 was "on the verge of civil war" between the striking workers at the American Gas Machine Company and a group of local citizens (and the sheriff). Mabeth Hurd Paige, a Republican state legislator from 1922 to 1944, feared that communism loomed dangerously close. Dur-

*

Olson called out the National Guard to try to keep the peace (and to force a settlement).

†

By refusing to transport factory equipment, the truckers' union had prevented an attempt by the Strutwear Company to close down its Minneapolis operations and send its equipment to another plant in Missouri.

‡

The company recognized the union and agreed to a pay raise.

ing the truckers' strike, she feared that the city, *her* city, had become "the center of industrial warfare." Was the world falling apart? A nightmare, she called it: "This was not mere radicalism—this was anarchy."[24]

In fact, the Depression and the New Deal resulted in the opposite of anarchy at the state and federal levels. The Minnesota Farmer-Labor Party emerged early in the twentieth century as a party of protest. It achieved what the Populists and Knights of Labor had aspired to for fifty years, building a successful political coalition between farmers and laborers that could get people elected. The first significant victory for the Farmer-Labor party came in 1922 when Minnesota voters elected Henrik Shipstead, a Minneapolis dentist, to the U.S. Senate (he was reelected twice more on the Farmer-Labor ticket and a fourth time as a Republican). In that same year F-Ler Knud Wefald was elected to Congress (he was reelected once), and in 1924 three more F-Lers, Charles Lindbergh, Sr., Magnus Johnson, and Ole J. Kvale were all elected to national office. Minnesota chose the Farmer-Laborite Floyd B. Olson for governor in 1930 and reelected him in 1932 and again in 1934 with a platform that many Minnesotans considered communist in its call for the public ownership of utilities, old-age pensions, unemployment insurance, and an income tax.[25]*

*

Olson died of a brain tumor before the 1936 election.

Olson, an immigrants' son from north Minneapolis, explicitly identified himself as a radical and put himself in a Jeffersonian tradition of radicalism. The Farmer-Labor program was less radical, he argued, than the Declaration of Independence. Besides, he didn't advocate the overthrow of any government, but he did believe that the American government no longer functioned "in the interests of the common happiness of the people." So "his" government was going to. In 1933 he declared a moratorium on farm foreclosures. At the 1934 Farmer-Labor convention he spoke forcefully: "I am not satisfied with tinkering. I am not satisfied with patching. I am not satisfied with hanging a laurel wreath upon burglars and thieves and pirates" (no wonder Mrs. Paige was frightened). Olson sought to protect the workers rather than defend the system: "He aimed to put the power of government on the side of the needy and the angry and the protesting." Elmer Benson succeeded to the governor's office in 1936 after Olson's death and, elected in his own right a few months later, spoke and acted even more forcefully. Hailing from a farm near Appleton, Benson frightened Representative Paige even more, especially when he led a "mob" into the state's House and Senate chambers to demand more assistance for workers.[26]

The people who brought the most radical changes (and who, thereby, helped stave off the anarchy that seemed to be threatening on the horizon) worked at the federal level, included many in Franklin Roosevelt's cabinet (and in his own household), and showed their radicalism by completely rethinking what the central government ought to do and could do. In the course of Roosevelt's first two terms in office, his Brain Trust and the Congress instituted somewhere in the neighborhood of fifty agencies that came to be identified by a spaghetti of initials: the AAA to support farm prices, the FDIC to insure bank deposits, the SEC to standardize and safeguard the sale of securities, the FCA and HOLC to provide low-cost farm and home loans, the TVA to build dams and other forms of flood control, the NLRB to outlaw unfair labor practices, the NRA to set rules for fair practices, and the SSA to establish an old-age pension system.

The WPA, the CCC, and the REA provide the best examples of the strengths and weaknesses of New Deal programs. Each one of them labored under often hastily established and inefficiently run organizations, paid low wages, was more or less successful depending on location and the individuals involved, wasn't free of favors and inequities. Even so, much of the work completed under these programs wouldn't have been done otherwise and provided societal improvements from which contemporary Minnesotans (and Americans) benefit.

Harry Hopkins played a key role in the development of the federal works projects. Born in Sioux City, Iowa, and graduated from Grinnell College, Hopkins did settlement house and child welfare work in New York City. During World War I he directed relief efforts for the Red Cross in New Orleans. Early in the 1930s, Governor Franklin Roosevelt appointed him to head up New York State's temporary relief work programs. Within days of Roosevelt's inauguration as president in early March 1933, Hopkins contacted Frances Perkins, the just-appointed secretary of labor, with the germ of an idea about putting people to work. She took the idea to FDR, who appointed Hopkins head of the Federal Emergency Relief Administration (FERA) in May 1933.[27]

Hopkins's training and his experience in social work taught him that the single most significant cause of poverty was unemployment. He proposed not to improve the poor, not to change their habits or characters, not even to protect society from them, but to find them work to do.* From 1933 to 1938 he headed first FERA, then the Civilian Works Agency (CWA), then the Works Progress Administration (WPA), all of which asked and tried to answer one central question: how can we put people to work that is useful to the community but doesn't compete with private industry? Tracing the rise and fall of work relief programs is like watching an agile mind at work: *Let's try this; whoops, too much direct relief; let's try that. What about this organization of responsibilities? Isn't a regional*

*

The Temporary Emergency Relief Administration that Hopkins directed in New York tried out in 1932–33 on a small scale what the Federal Art Project would later do on a much bigger scale—providing funds for artists.

*approach better than a local one? Don't urban and rural people need different
kinds of help? What about women and men? Welders and actors?*[28]

In March 1935 Congress approved $5 billion for work relief projects
under the umbrella of the WPA and FDR allocated $1.4 billion for imme-
diate expenditure on jobs.* "Almost overnight," historian Jerome Tweton
reports, "the WPA transformed Otter Tail County into a beehive of activity."
In that western county alone, the number of WPA workers ran between
500 and 750. In September 1935, about 4,500 people statewide had WPA
work; three months later, in December, 56,612. The number of WPA employees varied from month to month and fluctuated depending on what
many administrators found to be a maddeningly unpredictable set of
rules and requirements; nonetheless, between 35,000 and 62,000 Minnesotans held WPA jobs at any given time between 1936 and 1941. On
February 28, 1937, for example, about 6,000 were at work in and around
Duluth; 1,200 in Stearns County; 12,000 in Hennepin and 8,000 in
Ramsey counties; and 23,000 more elsewhere in the state.[29]†

Pete Court was one of those WPA workers in Stearns County. He and
his neighbors took turns building roads: "Many roads were built and
every week a different man could work with his team of horses which
was a means for extra income which was very welcome." He needed
gloves for this winter work but hadn't a penny to buy any. The local
store let him charge for a pair that he paid off with his first WPA check.[30]

Some unidentifiable number of federal workers no doubt deserved
the leaning-on-a-shovel reputation that got popularly affixed to WPA
hirees, and some of the workers may not have had the skills they
claimed or needed for their jobs. Even so, federally funded workers in
Minnesota built and repaired thousands of miles of roads and 732 new
buildings (schools, libraries, town auditoriums, bus shelters). The Willmar Auditorium, for example, included a stage, auditorium, and
kitchen; meeting, projection, and band rooms; dressing rooms and
showers. WPA workers built airport runways, band shells, city parks and
swimming pools, tennis courts, ice skating rinks and warming houses;
they planned and built and maintained water mains, storm sewers, lev-
ees, and embankments. They painted the indoors and outdoors of public buildings, cleaned streets, and repaired public statues.[31]

This work signaled some change in attitudes—certainly among the
people who accepted WPA work and, no doubt, among many in the wider
American population as well. Not all, of course—hence the long and
sturdy stereotype of the WPA shovel leaner—but the work itself testified
then and continues to demonstrate how much was actually accom-
plished with government relief funds.

In addition to the outdoor work, even more federal relief work went

*

WPA (with its own alphabet of
stepchildren: the FAP, FTP,
CWA, PWA, FWP, etc., and its
cousin the CCC).

†

Of these 50,000 in 1937,
one-fifth were women. The
total unemployed in the
state is difficult to determine. By one report, Min-
neapolis unemployment
averaged over the year
about 20,000 in 1930,
38,000 in 1931, 58,000
in 1932; in St. Paul, 6,000
in 1930, 17,000 in 1931,
23,000 in 1932.

on indoors. Nationwide, WPA workers repaired nearly 1.5 million library books, made almost 4 million items of clothing, served over 3.5 million school lunches, and repaired 10,000 pairs of shoes and 16,000 pieces of furniture. WPA people designed and drove bookmobiles and helped establish the habit of publicly funded libraries. Others indexed and catalogued over 15 million public documents. Still others modernized police records, transcribed 175,000 pages of text into Braille, and created more than 25,000 Braille maps. Scientists carried out medical, engineering, sociological, and dental research. Historians conducted oral interviews, surveyed historic properties, catalogued county records, and indexed newspapers. Others ran children's health camps, nursery schools, clinics, and handicrafts projects, including Indian handicrafts. Writers (and would-be writers) put together *Minnesota: A State Guide* (1938), a volume of over six hundred pages that includes thirty-five road and canoe trips (any one of which would still be worth taking), and a separate guide to northeastern Minnesota, *WPA Guide to the Arrowhead* (1941), plus books on Bohemian Flats and Kittson County. The Workers' Education Division produced other kinds of research and writing, too, including "Women Wage Earners and Wage Differentials" by Leonard Vogland, which carefully documents white and black women's employment, unemployment, and pay patterns. WPA and Federal Music Project workers organized child and adult bands, orchestras, and choirs—including the Twin Cities Jubilee Singers—and hand-copied sheet music. Teachers offered lessons in music appreciation and on musical instruments, foreign languages, citizenship, housekeeping, painting and drawing, crafts, tap and folk dancing, and labor history. University researchers studied mosquito breeding and poultry husbandry; they improved methods for sterilizing and testing surgical gloves; they traced population trends in Minnesota, the course of civil liberties in the United States, and the problems of "rural aged persons."[32]

The WPA transformed the Walker Art Gallery from a sleepy and quiet place into a thriving community art center. Thomas B. Walker made most of his money in the lumber business in the late nineteenth century and invested in art. Hudson River School paintings as well as jade sculptures especially appealed to him. He displayed his holdings in his home and, in 1879, opened it to public view. In 1927 his collection moved into a grand Moorish-style building on Minneapolis's Hennepin Avenue. The stock market crash—and its effect on the Walker Foundation's assets—effectively shut down the new gallery, and by the middle of the 1930s it was open only a few hours a week, run by a tiny staff, and visited by just a handful of people. It wasn't the intention of the WPA to save the Walker, but its effect was to transform it by reinventing it.

The WPA took as one of its projects the creation of art centers that had a strong commitment to their communities and the forging of better connections between artists and the public. Centers were created in Duluth and St. Paul. The largest and most long lasting was the Walker Art Center, which Daniel Defenbacher transformed from a crypt for art into a vibrant community center. He set the Walker on a path to draw people to its doors, to teach and entertain, to amuse and engage. The Walker employed as many as sixty-five artists, and during its first year (1940) provided art classes for more than 3,000 students. Evelyn Raymond worked on her sculptures in the entryway, where people watched her, often for hours at a time. Professional and amateur artists, adults and children exhibited. As artist Syd Fossum said, "People . . . wouldn't go to museums, but they went to these WP art centers." The WPA enlivened the Walker, and the Walker enlivened art in Minnesota.[33]

The Federal Art Project (FAP) enlivened artists, too, and helped create a genre of American and Minnesota art that was new and distinctive and recognizably local in settings, at least, and in themes where possible. Under the auspices of the New Deal programs, Minnesota artists created over 1,500 drawings, paintings, and etchings and over sixty murals.* Strongly influenced in style, color, and idea by the Mexican artist and political radical Diego Rivera, mural painters all over the United States and in Minnesota decorated public spaces with depictions of heroic-sized and -physiqued men and women workers. One depicted men doing mine work of a kind that was increasingly unavailable on the range and elsewhere but showed workers with dignity and authority. Others, at the Gillette Children's Hospital and Sister Kenny Institute, presented fairy tales and wall-sized depictions of children at play. Patrick DesJarlait painted stylized scenes of wild ricing and berry picking. The FAP supported work by budding and established Minnesota artists George Morrison, Dewey Albinson, Mac LeSueur, Evelyn Raymond, Miriam Ibling, John Socha, Cameron Booth, and Syd Fossum.[34]

The federally funded artists drew often on inspiration from their surroundings, as had the Ashcan School painters of the 1910s and the "American Scene" painters of the 1920s. Thus, among other contributions, this body of artwork provides a visual record of Minnesota in the 1930s. Moreover, the FAP work brought artists together and federal support for their work kept artists at home. In the 1920s, artists who hoped to prove themselves went to Europe (if they could afford it) or at least to New York. In the 1930s, American artists largely stayed in America and Minnesota artists stayed in Minnesota, thus creating homegrown, home-inspired American art. Some identify in the 1930s a significant break

*
Minnesota artists—especially the muralists—were supported by the Treasury Relief Art Project as well as the Federal Art Project. The Historical Section of the Farm Security Administration hired photographers who traveled the country documenting the lives of people in the 1930s. John Vachon, for example, took extraordinary photos in Minnesota, many of which are accessible on the Library of Congress website.

Clara Mairs, Clara and Clem, *1930*

with European traditions and in Minnesota art a real explosion of local talent.[35]*

Clem Haupers, the regional Federal Art Project director and himself a fine Minnesota artist, saw in the project the opportunity not only to support needy artists and to provide artworks for the state but also to fuel interest in and appreciation for art among the general public, to educate people in the arts and crafts, and to spread art beyond urban areas. He made a deliberate effort to introduce "awareness of the visual sense into areas that didn't have it." Minnesota's strong heritage of art, of state and private support of the arts, of strong artist in the schools programs certainly can trace its roots to the FAP and the WPA.[36]

State governments had been creating state parks for over fifty years by the time of the Depression; the New Deal supported the work of making parks accessible. The Minnesota legislature established Minnehaha, Camp Release, and Itasca state parks between 1885 and 1891 and the Minnesota State Park System in 1923. These efforts—as well as those in the state's cities and towns—to create parkland reflected a larger American interest in preserving individualism and virtue (of a kind that contact with nature supported and strengthened) as well as a desire to preserve pockets of nature at the moment that Frederick Jackson Turner

*

The FAP operated on national director Holger Cahill's principle that "it is not the solitary genius but a sound general movement which maintains art as a vital, functioning part of any cultural scheme."

declared the American frontier to be closed. The two interests created some tension over the purpose of parks: was land to be set aside and protected from development or built up to accommodate visitors? New Deal park programs adopted the developmental, rather than preservationist, approach.[37]*

The Emergency Conservation Work Program (popularly and then in 1937 officially called the CCC, for Civilian Conservation Corps) had two goals in mind: the employment of young, single men and the creation and development of parkland.

Most of the men the CCC had in mind were white and urban, and most of the CCC workers in Minnesota—like most Minnesotans—were, in fact, white. But not all: the CCC Indian Division employed young men who were neither white nor urban. Unlike the CCC, the Indian Division aimed to keep young men at home and put them to work on their own reservations. Over 2,500 Ojibwe and Dakota men strung telephone lines and built ricing camps, housing, and roads; practiced fire prevention and fire-fighting; and improved trails and stands of trees—which meant that over 2,500 families benefited from the infusion of money into the reservation. Their improvements, too, aimed to serve their home populations immediately and directly.[38]†

Most white—and eventually African American and Mexican American—CCC men, however, worked on creating or improving park- and forestland for visitors and outsiders. President Roosevelt's National Resources Board recommended that no person should be more than forty miles from a state park. Minnesota's parkland should be increased, the board therefore recommended, from 40,000 to over 100,000 acres, and it allocated $85 million to the state to acquire the land and create the parks. The CCC went to work to improve this land, make these parks accessible, and upgrade older parks.[39]

Men in Minnesota's widely scattered seventy-four Civilian Conservation Corps—including eventually separate (that is, segregated) African American camps—planted tens of thousands of trees and cut others to make trails and firebreaks; they laid sewer lines and strung telephone wires. At Lake Bronson in Kittson County they built a bathhouse and beach; at Beaver Creek Valley in Houston County, an entrance road and picnic grounds. In Lyon County the WPA built parking lots, bridges, and buildings for crafts, for eating, for group camping. In cooperation with the WPA, CCC men did archaeological work in Chippewa County and built a reproduction of Thomas Williamson's mission site. In short, they did whatever projects local park people determined needed to be done (and could get approved).[40]‡

The Minnesota State Legislature authorized preservation of the area

*

Dewey Albinson, who had visited and painted at Grand Portage Indian Reservation in the 1920s, was on the side of preservation and decried the damage that the state parks had done to the wilderness areas along Lake Superior, especially at the Grand Portage site.

†

Total statewide CCC expenditure: $85 million; on Indians, almost $4 million.

‡

One of the African American CCC men in Minnesota was Gordon Parks; he was also the only African American photographer for the Farm Service Administration.

around Gooseberry Falls in 1933. Two different teams of CCC workers set up tent camps in 1934 and went to work, eventually putting up twenty-seven buildings, including "10 army-style barracks, an infirmary, mess hall, latrine, officers' quarters and various service and administrative buildings [and] an education building" they called "Gooseberry Falls University." They also created picnic and camping areas with tables, fireplaces, and parking lots. The CCC camps closed in 1941, but the buildings continued to serve park visitors until the new Visitors' Center building opened in 1996.[41]

CCC work is identifiable in its distinctive WPA stone- and timberwork style. The CCC didn't invent but specialized in "rustic style" buildings constructed of locally available materials used as naturally as possible (stones left rough rather than smoothed; logs rather than finished timber) and intended to blend into their environments. The buildings' natural look belies the care and fine craftsmanship of their construction.

Some of the best examples of the rustic style were built at Gooseberry Falls, due in part to the park's proximity to Duluth.* Duluth was blessed with talented and able Italian stonemasons, who created spectacular stone facades and detailing on public buildings and even many modest private homes. Their work gives to Duluth a distinctive look. Some especially thoughtful CCC administrator had the foresight to bring two of those stonemasons—John Berini and Joe Cattaneo—to superintend the work at Gooseberry Falls.

Berini and Cattaneo were not young and single—the main criteria for CCC workers—(though they were white, which was in most places the third criterion), so they were not regular CCC workers but skilled workers paid for their experience and abilities. Guiseppe Cattaneo della Volta had migrated to the United States in 1914, having served two years in an artillery unit of the Italian Army. He served as a Musician Class 1 in the U.S. Army; he became a citizen in 1919. His wife and older son joined him in 1920—six years after he'd arrived—and a younger son was born in Duluth in 1923. By 1930 the Cattaneos owned their own house on Fourth Street West in Duluth, worth $2,500. John Berini and his wife owned their own house in Duluth, too, and lived with their two sons only a few blocks from the Cattaneos.† Joe's and John's experience and their artisan's eye is evident at Gooseberry Falls in the selection and placement of the different colors of granite—some quarried in Duluth, some of it from nearby East Beaver Bay.[42]‡

The workers remembered the long hours, the healthiness of working outdoors, the "three hots and a flop" that the work guaranteed, and the real aid provided to them and their families. The CCC legislation required that 90 percent of the workers' pay be sent directly to their

* These and others in the state parks system have been added to the National Register of Historic Places.

† The ships' passenger list for 1937 shows Guiseppe Cattaneo della Volta a "well to do" man returning to the United States from Genoa. Perhaps he went home for his fiftieth birthday. He died in Duluth in 1944 at age fifty-eight.

‡ The buildings were designed by Edward Barber of the Minnesota Central Design Office of the National Park Service. George C. Lindquist, an architect, worked at Gooseberry Falls and designed some of the buildings and oversaw the implementation of plans.

families. So, it was estimated, each wage assisted four others in addition to the worker. The CCC parks and improvements testify to the significant contributions of these men—and these programs—to the welfare of the state into the present.[43]

The wages and room and board offered to these young men and the money sent to their families no doubt proved welcome. But the wages for both CCC and WPA workers were low, even in comparison to what private employers were paying at the time. Jobs programs kept most minority men and women out (or segregated). Programs were cancelled without warning, wages cut for no clearly understood reasons, layoffs common. When Minneapolis WPA workers on a sewing project struck against low wages and long hours in 1939, police broke up a fight between workers and anti-strikers (reportedly supported by the coalition of Minneapolis business owners called the Citizens Alliance) and arrested the strikers. CCC men rarely returned home better trained or equipped to take up local jobs (though many of them ended up in the U.S. Army in the 1940s). It is easy to romanticize the life of the CCC soldiers, and many veterans do tell wonderful tales of their work, but any visit to the north woods except in deep winter will remind us at the very least of what it might have been like to be working among the mosquitoes, black flies, and gnats that alone can make woods life unbearable.

The single most popular program among farm people was the Rural Electrification Authority, which went forward "with missionary zeal in stimulating rural electrification." At the REA's inception, fewer than ten percent of Minnesota farms had electricity. Not having electricity can be imagined by people who have it, but few of us would imagine the work that came from kerosene lamps, wood stoves, and hand pumps.

The Courts and their neighbors lit their house in the early mornings and evenings with kerosene lamps, "which had to be filled and the chimneys cleaned quite often, almost every other day." Mrs. Court also cooked three meals and two "lunches" a day on her wood-burning stove; "Also there was canning to be done when the vegetables were ready." She carried water from a pump to do her washing and then had to heat the water on the wood-burning stove. This held true for washing dishes as well as washing clothes (and children). To heat all of that water, Pete in the winter "made wood," as they called it. He cut the wood with a saw and an ax and loaded it onto a sled to drag it nearer the house, where he cut it into "fire wood size pieces" and stacked it so it could dry and be ready to be used the following fall. Electrification didn't change making wood but did decrease and then eliminate the need for quite so much of it. Washing clothes took a lot of wood, a lot of water, and a lot of work. Mrs. Court described it like this:

> In the early days washing clothes was done by hand on a wash board and sometimes wooden tubs. First the clothes were soaked in luke warm water than rinsed out of that and put in hot water, that is the colored clothes. Whites clothes were put in a wash boiler on the stove in water and boiled. This was done for about 15 to 20 minutes and then rinsed in 2 changes of water then another change of water with bluing added. Then it was ready for the lines. This was only done when the weather was nice.

Tuesday was ironing, which she did with irons she heated on the stove and that "cooled off very quickly." Mrs. Court admitted that she skimped on the wash in those days.

Some farms used small windmills, for water pumps especially, and gas-powered machines. In the 1930s, gas washing machines became available. "But," Mrs. Court remembered, "not much money was available so I had my first power washing machine when my husband made wood and we traded that for the machine." In the 1930s Mrs. Court bought day-old chicks and kept them in an upstairs room in the house. In the night she put them in boxes, but in the day she kept them warm with hot water jugs. She noted, "For quite a few years we had a kerosene brooder stove for heat but there was always a worry about fire breaking out." All of this trouble, though, could produce up to 500 chickens and roosters ready to butcher and sell; "This was a big amount of work every fall until the last one was cleaned." In 1937 radios came into the area, but electricity still hadn't made it to Stearns County, so the Courts ran a line to a wind charger and sometimes a car battery, "and when that ran out the car would not start." No wonder rural people looked forward to the coming of the REA.[44]

In the first year of the program, government workers strung nearly 1,500 miles of lines and electrified almost 5,000 farms. It was, nonetheless, more of a life improvement than a work relief project. It took more than a decade just to get lines strung and a pole and light to each farm—a big step—and it took many farm people another decade and their own funds to get electricity into the barn (usually first) and then the house. Even conservative anti–New Dealers found little to criticize in a program that brought electric power into the houses and barns of thousands of farmers.[45]*

That economic disasters raged didn't mean that everything changed. Some things stayed remarkably the same. For some, changes weren't apparent because either their wealth or their longtime poverty left them

*

Originally part of the Emergency Recovery Authority in 1935, it became its own separate agency in 1936.

unaffected. Alice O'Brien was one of the lucky ones, and during the Depression years she spent time raising money for the Women's City Club in St. Paul and for Children's Hospital. There was money to be had, and she was able to build the club, which later became the Minnesota Museum of Art.[46]

Some sought an escape, any escape. Others, like most of us, simply held contradictory ideas and experiences in their heads and lives at the same time. Newspapers in Minneapolis, St. Paul, and Duluth as well as in Fergus, Redwood, and International Falls throughout the 1930s carried ads for stylish new clothes and washing machines, cars and radios. The bridge columns continued to offer advice, and kids went to school and had birthday parties and graduated, and Minnesotans (and Americans) continued to see movies and to dance. At the Roxy, the Palace, the Park, the State, the Gopher, the Time, the Paradise, and the Wonderland movie theaters, people sat transfixed by *All Quiet on the Western Front* (1930), *I Am a Fugitive from a Chain Gang* (1932), *Mutiny on the Bounty* (1935), *Mr. Deeds Goes to Town* (1936), *Lost Horizon* (1937), *Stagecoach* and *Wizard of Oz* (1939). Only the occasional movie included anything about economic troubles. *The Fugitive* certainly spoke to loss of faith in the system, and King Vidor's *Daily Bread* aimed to change people's minds more than to entertain them. But more movies simply took the times as the background or ignored it entirely and played out their plots. In *It Happened One Night,* the recently fired newspaperman Clark Gable met up with the runaway (and rich) Claudette Colbert. The two found romance, despite their class and personality differences, taking the bus, sharing (modestly, of course) a motel room, and trading witty repartee. And what Depression survivor wouldn't have identified with Scarlett O'Hara, who triumphed over one defeat after another by her own will (however devious and manipulative she might have been) and her pledge "As God is my witness I will never be hungry again" in *Gone with the Wind* (1939)?

Fred Astaire and Ginger Rogers traded wisecracks, but they never had to triumph over very serious problems, nor did they have to hitchhike anywhere. They flew to Rio, sailed the Atlantic, sashayed around Paris, London, and San Francisco, and—between 1934 and 1939—danced their way through nine films, including *Gay Divorcée* (1934), *Top Hat* (1935), *Swingtime* (1936), *Shall We Dance* (1937), and *Carefree* (1938). They stepped lightly and deftly across elegant rooms, wearing even more elegant clothes. They smiled as if it weren't the Depression; as if 14 million people weren't unemployed; as if John Steinbeck's Joads in *The Grapes of Wrath* weren't on their last leg. In their 1936 film *Follow the Fleet,* he sang and they danced to a wonderful Irving Berlin tune that warned, "There may be trouble ahead" and then advised, "Let's face the music and dance."

A number of Minnesotans had long faced their troubles by dancing, and they didn't stop during the Depression. The crash pushed many ballrooms and nightclubs over the edge and hurt the music and entertainment industry generally. The repeal of Prohibition in December 1933 helped bring them back and actually rescued many from their shady 1920s incarnations. So, people kept dancing. The Hegges, a farm family in Otter Tail County who lived on $20 a month plus their own food, for example, went dancing regularly at the White Eagle Lodge just outside Fergus Falls. Yes, they had four kids and a farm to support but, Mrs. Hegges reported, "still we could have fun."[47]

Dakota people marked the opening of a mission at Redwood Falls with a dance. Ojibwe people held powwows at Red Lake, Nett Lake, Prairie Island, Cass Lake—even a Consolidated Chippewa Powwow at the Nicollet Hotel in Minneapolis in 1934. Whites and Indians, African Americans and others danced to the tunes of the Nicollet or the Prom ballroom dance bands. At other ballrooms, dancers moved to the music of Leonard's Dance Band from New Prague, or Rudy Clemenson and his Gold Coast Orchestra, Red Clark and his Jockeys, El Herbert and his Swing City Band, Les Beigel and his Dixie Land Band, and Alma Milch and her Queens of Syncopation.[48]

They may have played some of their own tunes, but more likely they played the music that Tommy Dorsey, Duke Ellington, Benny Goodman, Louis Armstrong, and Artie Shaw's orchestras were making popular on road tours and records. Like other parts of the economy, the music industry collapsed in 1929, but with the increase in phonographs and records as well as the radio broadcasts of dance band performances, the music industry rapidly recovered and then expanded even more quickly.

In addition to the ubiquitous dance bands, the 1930s boasted some of the best songwriters and singers in American history. Folk, country, bluegrass, and jazz musicians caught the Depression in their music. Woody Guthrie wrote and performed a raft of Depression-era and -themed songs: "Dust Bowl Blues," for example. A. P. Carter wrote and the Carter Family sang "No Depression in Heaven." Roy Acuff in 1939 recorded "When our old age pension check comes to our door / We won't have to dread the poor house anymore." Revealing something about the lives of people who were poor long before the Depression and faced problems more devastating even than poverty, some of the singers and songwriters paid little attention to the Depression at all. Huddie Ledbetter, best known as "Leadbelly," sang songs that grew out of his southern sharecropper culture. Billie Holiday's recording of "Strange

Fruit" by Abel Meeropol reminded listeners of the lynchings that were scarring America throughout the 1930s, while the Southern Democrats kept a legislative lock on a federal antilynching law.

Some musicians stayed away from Depression songs and told instead of love and loss, loneliness and romance. Vernon Duke's "Autumn in New York" (1934), "Goody, Goody" by Johnny Mercer and Matt Malneck (1935), Dorothy Fields and Jerome Kern's very funny and smart "A Fine Romance" (1936), Cole Porter's "In the Still of the Night" (1937), Hoagy Carmichael's "Nearness of You" (1937), "Where or When" by Lorenz Hart and Richard Rogers (1937), Ruth Lowe's "I'll Never Smile Again," (1939), and "Summertime" by George Gershwin, DuBose Heyward, and Dorothy Heyward from *Porgy and Bess* (1935) were among the chart toppers. No matter that these songs came from New York and Hollywood; Minnesotans heard them on the radio and juke boxes, hummed them, tapped their toes to them, and, as the decade passed, bought the records or the sheet music and danced to them.

In the woman suffrage, consumerist, short-skirted, Harlem Renaissance, *Great Gatsby,* Prohibition days of the 1920s, young people (and older ones, too) had already experimented with various dances—like the Charleston—that challenged the traditional middle-class life. The steps were not dictated by convention, nor did a caller direct the dancers. Nor, even, did the man take the lead. Neither the controlled dance of the upper class nor the raucous and sweaty dances of the country, the Charleston and its offshoots were the loose, expansive, sexy dances of the working classes, African Americans especially, brought north from Charleston, South Carolina, and taken up by the white middle classes. The Lindy Hop of the late 1920s—named after Charles Lindbergh, of course, and celebrating his 1927 trans-Atlantic flight—called for some of his aeronautical abandon. He was the spinner, she the spun. Couples all over Minnesota danced their way through the 1930s (and later), doing the Lindy—and its variations, the jitterbug and swing—in addition to the polka and the schottische, the two-step, and other homegrown dance styles.[49]

While all the other dances might have been simply fun or distractions from life's other cares, the desperation of some Americans also showed itself on the dance floor. Flagpole sitting, dishwashing, even Lindbergh's nonstop flight had captivated people as contests of endurance in the 1920s.* Marathon dancing in the 1930s, however, gave endurance an entirely new meaning. The rules of marathon dances varied but usually provided ten minutes every hour for bathroom breaks, even catnaps, and allowed sleeping as long as one half of the couple

*

My favorite endurance contest was the woman in Pennsylvania who washed dishes for thirty-one straight hours.

could hold the other up. Screaming at your partner (or at the other dancers), slapping, arguing, or other "unsportsmanlike" behavior would get a couple disqualified. Otherwise, all they had to do was stay upright longer than the others. The sponsors offered a cash prize, sometimes a chiropodist or nurse, and seating so an audience could watch people pushed to their limits.[50]

Vonnie Kuchinski and Callum DeVillier, who found themselves among the thousands of unemployed looking for work and not finding it in the 1930s, entered a dance marathon on December 28, 1932. Five months and six days later—on June 2, 1933—they captured both the world record in marathon dancing and a cash prize. The world record is recorded; the amount of the prize isn't. Not as fatally desperate as the marathon dancers in Harold McCoy's 1935 novel *They Shoot Horses, Don't They?*,* Kuchinski and DeVillier show what some Minnesotans faced, what some people would do to avoid being called "poor," what steps people would take to help themselves, and what limited choices they had.[51]†

Minnesota's Depression story is as diverse as federal programs, the music and movies of the 1930s, the myriad ways people coped or didn't with what they faced. Every person and every family had its own Depression story. Individuals and families hold their own stories still—in ancestral accounts, in ways of saving, even in habits of mind about the right role of government.

*

In 1969, Sydney Pollack directed and Jane Fonda starred in a movie version of this novel. So desperate were the dancers and so willing to push themselves that doctors' and women's groups campaigned to have them stopped by law. The state of New York outlawed marathon dancing that lasted more than eight hours in 1933.

†

Callum DeVillier's Lakewood Cemetery tombstone, which was designed by him, shows a dancing couple (ballroom style, not marathon) and bears the inscription: "World Champion Marathon Dancer, 3780 Continuous Hours."

13

We Never Had Enough Sugar

WAR HAS A VORACIOUS APPETITE—it chews up people and places. It consumes people's dreams and traditions, as well as their fiancés, friends, spouses, sons, and daughters. It makes heroes and martyrs of ordinary men (and women) while devouring their youth and maiming their bodies and spirits. More than 300,000 Minnesotans left for military service in World War II. Some returned to Minnesota; others made new lives elsewhere. About 8,000 of them did not come back at all.[1]

World War II needed more people to make weapons than to carry them: it also had a prodigious appetite for civilians. By one account, U.S. factories turned out one ship and 240 airplanes a day. The Chaska *Weekly Valley Herald* reported in 1943 that the Puget Sound Naval Yard needed workers, especially men with mechanical aptitude. Hundreds of other employers—in California, Florida, New Jersey, even London, Iceland, Burma, and Australia—induced thousands of Minnesotans to leave the state to do their duty elsewhere, to open new doors, to make new friends, and often to make a lot more money. One of those workers, Mabell Draxton, went to Virginia with her husband, and both got shipbuilding work. Out of her first paycheck, Mabell bought herself a fountain pen. "Oh, I felt rich," she remembered. Draxton, like thousands of other Minnesotans, started a new life during the war and did not return to the state.[2]*

*

Women's Army Corps veteran Jeanne Bearmon remembered, "I was patriotic. It was also adventure. It was an opportunity to experience people and places I would not have otherwise gotten to know."

Most Minnesotans did their war duty without ever leaving the state. The U.S. Selective Service exempted men under age twenty-one (later eighteen) and over thirty-five years, married men with children (usually), the flatfooted and sickly, the odd and homosexual (when the draft boards knew or suspected), and all women. The military discriminated in regard to gender but not on the basis of ethnicity, at least as to draftability. Race mattered when it came to job assignments. The military confined African American soldiers, for example, to an even narrower range of jobs than they had as civilians. Local draft boards also exempted men in essential occupations—a definition that varied over time and from draft board to draft board, but kept at home or delayed the induction of a broad range of men from miners to meatpackers to farm laborers.

Employers and draft boards sometimes disagreed about what constituted "essential"; on occasion, they played strategic games with each other. When Cargill's grain traders were not exempted, Cargill put them "in Charge of Procurement and Distribution of Grain." This worked for a while before the draft board called up those procurers and distributors, too.[3]

When that didn't keep enough grain traders home, Cargill cracked not the glass ceiling but the glass door that had kept women out. Many employers who before the war had not considered hiring women did so when forced by the enlistment of so many of their male employees. Many women—out of necessity—had long been doing whatever "men's work" they could (men's work paying more than women's work). Prewar widows and wives of ne'er-do-wells or of men who were sickly or underpaid or seasonally employed had long taken whatever work they could get in a gender-typed workplace. The demands of war opened the door to jobs that women's needs had not been able to budge. In fact, it threw open the doors, and women went to work making ships and cars and Scotch tape, delivering mail, managing offices, driving streetcars—and making more money than they had been making or could have made if they held a "woman's" job. The war may have bent some of the traditional gender conventions, but not of all the jobs, and not for all women, and certainly not permanently.[4]

Some women went down into the mines, though these places did not throw open their doors. Neither did women often knock—the social conventions were too strong, the work too hard. Labor organizers on Minnesota's iron ranges continued to work for better wages and conditions for miners, but the war's demands for iron ore kept the work steady and the National War Labor Board kept wages stable. Besides, in World War II, as in World War I, the social pressure for silent loyalty kept many reformers mute.[5]

War also consumes huge quantities of "stuff": war materiel from steel and food to rubber and socks, tin and gasoline, and thousands of other products, many of which were raised, processed, invented, designed, and/or manufactured in Minnesota. The increased wartime demand for food—the average GI ate 25 percent more than his counterpart at home, and the production of foodstuffs internationally was severely interrupted by the war—had a special impact on Minnesota's food-production industries, sugar especially.[6]

In 1941, before the United States officially joined the Allied war effort, the Lend-Lease Act passed by Congress offered assistance to any nation fighting aggression (which effectively meant any nation but Germany and Japan) and pushed for the rapid expansion of meat production. The government called on the nation's meatpackers to provide 4 million, then 8 million, then 15 million cans of tinned meat weekly for shipment abroad. The John Morrell and Company plant in Sioux Falls—drawing much of its meat supply from southwestern Minnesota farms—specialized in *tushonka,* or canned pork with onions and spices, for the Russians. Hormel speeded up its production of Spam, another version of canned pork that had both a domestic and a foreign market. Once the United States officially entered the war, all American meatpackers increased their output of fresh as well as packaged meats and meat products: hams, sausages, stew, whole chickens, hash.[7]

In response to the staggering loss of so much of the Pacific Fleet at Pearl Harbor in December 1941 and the need for as many ships as could be built, the government also called for as much iron ore as the northern Minnesota miners could extract. During the war years, the Iron Range provided more than 85 percent of the country's iron ore total.[8]

Minnesota Mining and Manufacturing—as 3M originally was called—provided many useful products for the military. "Wetordry" strips of abrasive, when applied to airplane wings, cockpit floors, and ambulance running boards, kept people from slipping in rain or heat or cold. 3M's Scotch tape, developed a decade before the war, and masking tape only five years before that, became indispensable immediately. Electricians, engineers, repairmen, and thousands of other military men put to use 3M's other specialty "abrasives" (sandpaper, that is).[9]

Sometimes demand meant that businesses and others simply did more of what they'd already been doing; more often it meant going in new directions. In addition to a predictable expansion in its milling, grain brokering, storage elevator, and railroad businesses, Cargill, for example, developed entirely new enterprises in soybeans (a new crop with new uses), dog food (a new byproduct), and shipbuilding (a new venture but not a long shot for a company that had been shipping millions of tons of grain worldwide for decades). Cargill received a $10 million contract from the U.S. Navy to build six auxiliary oil and gas carriers (AOGS), and from its new shipbuilding yard at Savage (on the Minnesota River) launched the first of eighteen AOGS in 1943.* The number of Cargill shipbuilders at Savage increased from zero in 1941 to 2,067 in 1944—all essential workers.[10]

Another 3M product combined adhesive and abrasive to make a reflective coating for the backs of cars and trucks, for the undersides of airplanes, for the edges of wings, for road signs, for curved railings.

*

So important was iron ore, in fact, that the Office of Defense Transportation turned over to the iron ore industry virtually all Great Lakes shipping in 1942. Cargill—used to moving much of its grain and flour by water—had to find alternatives.

These, as well as their derivatives—yellow and white paint that didn't wash off for marking the edges and middles of roads—made driving safer at home as well as at the warfront, requiring less light at night. Various 3M wartime inventions and discoveries became some of the company's most important postwar products: magnetic sound-recording tape, filter facemasks for medical people, and the Scotch brand sandblast stencils, which made red stop signs possible.[11]

The flour milling industry had long depended on mechanics and inventors who kept the machines in working order and improved the milling processes—from the steel rollers to the flour sacks and filling machines. During the war years, General Mills' Mechanical Division produced precision war instruments including gun sights and torpedoes. Its most unconventional work was a project to turn pigeons into guided missiles (never put into operation).[12]

Other Minnesota businesses—in addition to their core work—made various contributions to the war effort. Honeywell assigned its designers to make posters to remind people, "Don't Relax. War is not yet won!" as well as that missing work or arriving late "will help [Japanese General Hideki] TOGO win the war." The Pillsbury Company used its publicity arm to urge "good nutritional practices" and the reduction of waste. General Mills sponsored radio programs like *The Lone Ranger* to keep morale up, *Lonely Women* to sympathize with those whose sweethearts, husbands, sons, and brothers were gone, and *Thus We Live,* featuring stories about Red Cross workers. General Mills fictional figurehead Betty Crocker put out pamphlets and cookbooks like *Your Share,* which helped home chefs cook wartime meals. That company, which had already introduced Wheaties, followed up with Kix ready-to-eat breakfast cereal; Pillsbury developed Cheerioats (later known as Cheerios) in 1941 to help busy mothers save time without skimping on nutrition.[13]

In 1939 the U.S. War Department contracted with Professor Ancel Keys, head of the Laboratory of Physiological Hygiene in the University of Minnesota's School of Public Health, to develop a nutritionally sound packet of food that paratroopers could fit into their pockets and thus carry with them at all times. These K rations (after Keys) initially included biscuits, sausage, and sweetened chocolate. The full K rations eventually expanded to include cigarettes, toilet paper, powdered coffee, sugar tablets or granulated sugar, a fruit bar, a chocolate bar, a wooden spoon, a can opener, matches, and chewing gum. The fixings varied depending on whether the K ration was intended for breakfast, dinner, or supper, but the contents always included protein, a wooden spoon, and sugar (granulated, cube, or candy).[14]*

Most sugar in the United States before the war came from a carefully

*

The amount of sugar that reached market grew from 250,000 tons in 1800 to 3.8 million tons in 1880 to 16 million in 1920 to 30 million in 1945. By the beginning of the twenty-first century, American sugar growers produced 30 million tons by themselves; the rest of the world, another 40 million tons. In 1924 Minnesota beet growers harvested 235,000 tons and in 2003 nearly 10 million tons, making the state the largest beet producer in the United States.

calibrated balance of foreign and domestic sources. The Philippines and Hawaii and Cuba exported sugarcane; farmers in the American South also cultivated sugarcane. A few Americans—including some in Minnesota—had for a long time raised small crops of sugar beets. In the 1920s, a sugar beet industry began to develop around Chaska and East Grand Forks. The Sugar Acts of the 1930s limited the acreage Americans could devote to sugar beets to protect the revenue received from tariffs on imported sugar. Nevertheless, the limits on sugar beets were going up all the time because Americans had a sweet tooth. Sugar, "a luxury in 1750," had become a "virtual necessity by 1850" and part of a daily American diet by the time of World War II according to sugar historian Sydney W. Mintz. On the eve of the war in 1941, Americans ate 104 pounds of sugar per person per year, a 300 percent increase in sugar consumption since 1900. Americans' love affair with sugar—and then the war's intense demand for it—turned sugar beets into very big business.[15]

In developing K rations, Ancel Keys certainly knew the minimal nutritional value of sugar, but he also understood the relaxation that a few cigarettes gave to some as well as the energy burst and pleasure afforded by a candy bar. K rations were designed not to turn soldiers into healthy eaters but to keep them good fighters. If cigarettes and candy bars helped achieve that goal, so much the better. Those cigarettes and candy bars became trade goods, even gifts. The Hershey bars—handed over by liberating soldiers to children in newly liberated war zones—became an iconic representation of American generosity and largesse, perhaps even the promise of a better postwar world. K rations also had the advantage of being slow to spoil and, because they were flat and of uniform shape, easy to pack and transport.

Just this alone—a piece of sweetened chocolate as part of millions of daily allotments of food—intensified the wartime demand for sugar. So, too, did the military's need for sugar to make the alcohol necessary for manufacturing smokeless ammunition. The war cut off shipments of sugar from Hawaii and Cuba; the government's need for all shipping vessels further diminished imports. The demand for sugar beets exploded. In 1920, Minnesota growers harvested about 250,000 tons of sugar beets; in 1940, about 325,000; by 1942, domestic sugar beets accounted for the "largest single source of sugar for American consumers." The limits evaporated: "Plant Sugar Beets to the Full" was the word from Washington. By 1954, American growers harvested more than 815,000 tons of sugar beets.[16]

The supplies, nonetheless, could not satisfy the sweet tooth of both the war machine and the civilian population, so civilians had to cut back. Sugar was among the first products rationed in 1942 and one of the products most in demand on the black market (along with tires and gasoline). Civilians were generally allowed half a pound of sugar per week (70 percent their normal use), and institutions and industrial users were cut to 50 percent. From its prewar high of 104 pounds of sugar per person, the American per capita consumption declined to a wartime low of 74 pounds. Only in the 1950s did the supply recover sufficiently for the average consumption of sugar to top 100 pounds per person again.[17]

Labor had long been a problem in sugar beet fields and factories. As demand for sugar increased in America—which it did, even during the Great Depression—so did the number of farmers willing to abandon other crops—potatoes in the Red River Valley, for instance—for sugar beets. Besides, American Crystal Sugar Company, like other sugar processors, offered to buy a farmer's crop before it went into the ground. To stay within government limits—and supply the sugar beet processing plants at Chaska and East Grand Forks—the company determined the volume of beets it needed, and that controlled the market. Farmers who did not have a contract with the company needn't bother to grow sugar beets because the costs of transportation and the fragility of the turnip-like beets made it impossible to ship them even short distances. That certainty of sale and price must have proved an intoxicating brew for farmers battered by the uncertainty of Depression-era agriculture. Those who could get a contract did.

Growers who had fewer than about twenty acres in sugar beets usually could handle them on their own or with a bit of help from neighbors or passersby. For more than twenty acres, however, a farmer needed help intermittently for half a year. During the "campaign"—in sugar beet language, the planting, cultivating, and harvesting or "lifting"—the work was more than any one family could do. This recipe required migrant workers. More than one midwestern farm boy followed the wheat harvest in the 1930s, when jobs were scarce at home and when their own farms choked from dust. But these weren't the migrant workers who ended up "lifting" sugar beets in the fall.[18]

The sugar beet industry had long depended on itinerant workers— or turned would-be year-round employees into temps—because of the seasonal nature of the work. The Canadian-born James Booth got his first job sweeping floors in the Michigan salt factory where his father had lost an arm. Then he advanced to apprentice cooper (barrel maker). In the 1910s he left the salt business and got a job as a cooper for a sugar beet factory in Marine City, Michigan. Like others in the factory, Booth's work wasn't year-round, so he turned into a "sugar tramp"—his term— who worked seasonally and temporarily in sugar beet factories in Ohio, Iowa, Wyoming, and Washington. In the early 1920s he got full-time and full-year work as an assistant master mechanic for the Minnesota Beet Sugar factory in Chaska, Minnesota; then he moved in 1925 to its new factory in East Grand Forks, where he stayed until the American Crystal Sugar Company opened yet another new plant, in Moorhead in 1946.[19]*

World War I resulted in a dip in European immigration to the United States and led Congress to open the door more widely to Mexicans—primarily as temporary laborers. In the 1920s the Minnesota Sugar Company sent agents to Mexico and Texas as well as to Kansas City to recruit both field and factory workers, offering to bear the cost of transportation to and from the valley. The company tried to teach the growers a few Spanish phrases as well as some practices (sending Christmas cards and small gifts during the off-season, for example) to gain loyalty; it also sought to establish minimum standards for the housing provided to workers.† The Mexican workers largely traveled, lived, and worked in family groups. Some sugar beet growers did build relationships with their workers so that the same families returned year after year to work the same farms. Most workers, however, took what they could find and put together as many different seasonal jobs as they could because work in sugar beet fields or factories occupied them for only a few months a year.[20]

As demand for sugar increased, so did the number of Mexicans in Minnesota. Already in 1920, the majority of the 237 Mexicans in the state were sugar beet workers, though a few worked for the railroad, in St. Paul's meatpacking plants, and as day laborers. Raymond and Concepcion Cruz, who had been in the United States for two years by 1920, worked at the sugar factory in Chaska.[21]

By 1928, the rapidly expanding sugar beet industry in the Red River Valley employed more than 7,000 Mexican workers. Unlike the Canadian James Booth, whose sugar beet life followed an upward trajectory, most Mexican workers stayed in a cycle of similar, and similarly low-paying, jobs alternating with periods of unemployment. The life stories of Mexican Minnesotans tell not of migrants cycling from Mexico to Minnesota to Mexico, but of people like Tom and Petra Cruz, beet workers in Martin County in 1930, moving again and again to find work and community. The Cruzes married in 1914; their eight children were born in four different states: Juanita and Frank in Kansas, Raymond and Victoria in Colorado, Mary in Nebraska, and Francis, Alice, and Phyllis in Minnesota. Similarly, their neighbors worked in Colorado, Wyoming, Iowa, Texas, and Michigan before settling in Minnesota. Small communities of Mexican families, couples, children, in-laws, and cousins clustered wherever there was work for them and wherever others could assist them should work be hard to come by. By 1940, Mexican-born

---

* Like millions of others in 1918, Booth was struck down in the flu epidemic. His flu turned to pneumonia, and it took him six months to recover.

† These were low standards, for sure—usually a one-room shack without electricity or running water, a situation made only slightly more palatable by the fact that not all of the growers had electricity or running water in their own homes either. Even so, the accommodations for migrant workers were substandard.

workers—despite Depression-era pressure to hire the Minnesota-born—did 75 percent of the work in the sugar beet fields.[22]

Mexicans did not flock to Minnesota because they had a lot of choice. Instead they endured what historian Antonia Castañeda calls "coerced displacement," a result of the 1910 Mexican revolution, which haunted and hurt the Mexican economy for decades. Even in the worst of the Depression years, sugar beet work was not attractive to white—or Mexican—farm laborers who could do anything else.[23]

The war changed the sugar beet economy again. Classified ads in the Crookston and East Grand Forks newspapers during the war years offered board, wages, and draft deferment to potential farm workers. In some places draftees were routinely deferred at least until the end of the harvest season. Most important, wages for sugar beet workers rose nearly 40 percent during the war years. The recruiting offices in the southwest reopened, and Minnesota sugar beet factories, packing-houses, and railroads all began again to look for Mexican people who would work in Minnesota.

These World War II workers from Mexico were workers of a different kind—*braceros,* whose work circumstances were defined in a 1942 agreement (revised in April 1943) between the United States and Mexico "For the Temporary Migration of Mexican Agricultural Workers to the United States." Braceros were mostly single and male agricultural laborers who would "not be engaged in any military service" or "displace other workers, or [be used] for the purpose of reducing rates of pay previously established."* The number of braceros in the United States increased dramatically from just over 4,000 in 1942 to 62,000 in 1944, then decreased to fewer than 20,000 in 1947. Of those who came in 1943, 350 Mexicans went to work in the sugar beet fields and 1,000 in canning factories. In 1944, 1945, and 1946, the numbers quadrupled. In 1947, an agreement between the United States and British governments put Jamaican and Bahamian workers in the fields.[24]

The wartime labor shortage inspired desperate measures. In 1944 the U.S. government started sending Italian and German prisoners of war to the United States to work. Minnesota had twenty-one POW camps; the prisoners cut trees in northern Minnesota, packed corn, peas, and beans in Le Sueur, and worked in the sugar beet fields.[25]

The real answer to the problem of too few workers seemed to be mechanization, and various improvements in tractors made their use for sugar beet work more practical. Between 1910 and 1940, tractors became smaller (an advantage for getting around in a field), more dependable, less expensive. The replacement of steel wheels with rubber tires made the ride more comfortable, and enclosed motors made them safer. The

*

The bracero program lasted from 1942 to 1967. The largest number of braceros in any one year was 445,197 in 1956. In 1967, the number had declined to 7,703.

transition from steam to internal combustion engines made them lighter and more maneuverable. From 1925 especially, more and more farmers put their horses to pasture and invested in a John Deere or an International Harvester or one of the dozens of other tractor models on the market. In 1929, farmers bought 116,000 tractors; in 1932, only 25,000. During the lean years, even those who owned tractors often parked them to use horses instead. They could feed their horses more cheaply than they could their tractors.[26]*

* Farm people had long been fixing and taking care of machines: cars, tractors, binders, cultivators, windmills. They'd had to become adept at fixing or at making do. It's not farfetched to imagine that these skills served the United States well when these farm boys went off to the service in the 1940s.

Even while the war's consumption of steel strained the production of tractors, the intense labor shortage made their use a necessity. New cars could hardly be bought for love or money, but more than 200,000 tractors were sold annually between 1941 and 1945. By 1944, tractor usage replaced about 850,000 workers in the United States.[27]

No matter how many machines were put in the fields, sugar production could not keep up with the increased war demand, let alone Americans' craving for sugar. Sugar workers were deemed essential and deferred or exempted from the draft, and sugar was one of the first commodities rationed when the United States entered World War II. Gasoline, tires, shoes, meat, and dozens of other commodities followed. Even products that weren't rationed—socks, for example—were often hard to get. Tom Reichert of Albany remembered his mother slipping an old light bulb into threadbare socks to darn them yet again. The putrid tellow--green pack of socks she was able to find and buy embarrassed her teenage boys, but they had no other choice. Unfortunately, Tom recalled, those socks never seemed to wear out. Work shirts did, however, and more than one farmer plowed in what had been a dress shirt.[28]

In East Grand Forks, sugar rationing was front-page news for months, starting in April 1942 when wholesalers, retailers, industrial users of sugar, and families were required to register for their sugar rations. The East Grand Forks *Weekly Record* informed residents of the schedule and procedure for registering: a delegate from each family must show up at the local high school with detailed information about the age, size, and occupation of each family member. The state director of rationing was to give final details in a May 1 statewide radio broadcast. The newspaper over the next four years carried reports from the University of Minnesota Extension agents about how to make cakes and sweets with less sugar. Women who canned and preserved food—all were encouraged to do so—faced particular challenges and sometimes, upon special application, could get an extra portion of sugar for making jams and jellies.

The ever-helpful Extension Service nutritionist Inez Hobart reminded people that they shouldn't use sugar anyway. It had too many calories, was bad for the teeth, had little nutritional value. Most popular magazines offered recipes for menus using less sugar. The Catholic *St. Anthony Messenger* and the *Farmer Magazine* as well as *Ladies' Home Journal* and *Good Housekeeping* published recipes for honey cake, butterscotch sugarless cake, pies made with honey and molasses.

Rationing did not worry everyone equally. Arlene Frazier Boggs remembered that "rationing affected me none" because her family "didn't eat that much sugar." Her children, though, outgrew their shoes faster than the shoe coupons allowed replacement, so she traded her sugar coupons for someone else's shoe coupons. Doris Shea Strand remembered rationing meat, shoes, and butter and that people often bartered with family and friends. "You just roll with the punches," she concluded; "On the sugar bit, my two sisters were both married in 1946 . . . Even then my mother had to take the sugar coupons to the Hasty Tasty Bakery to let them bake a wedding cake for the girls." Another woman, Lucinda Holst, had plenty to eat during the war. She kept a big garden, and she picked "Pails of green beans. And cucumbers. Carrots by the bushels. We weren't suffering that way." Her only suffering was lack of sugar, but she used syrup, "a good substitute," when she could.[29]

Food occupied the attention of soldiers, cooks, homemakers, and scientists. Ancel Keys, developer of K rations, turned his research attention to the hungry. Keys requested funding from the U.S. Department of War to study the effects of starvation. He argued that, at the end of the war, hungry people—particularly the millions in central Europe—would be vulnerable to Communists and Fascists. The Allies needed to know the best and fastest way to rehabilitate people.

In a study funded in part by the military, in part by the University of Minnesota's athletic department, the National Dairy Council, and the Sugar Research Foundation, Keys embarked on what came to be known as his starvation experiment. The terms of the experiment required that volunteers live for six months on half their normal caloric intake. That would, Keys argued, result in about a 25 percent decrease in a man's weight, enough to "effect meaningful, measurable changes, both biological and psychological, in the test subjects." Then the real experiment would begin—to find the best way to help a man recover from such hunger. Over the second six months of the study, Keys and his assistants would employ different ways of returning volunteers to their original body weights. They would measure the effects of hunger and the best means of rehabilitation. "This data," Keys was confident, "would be an invaluable contribution to the massive relief effort that was certain to follow the end of the war."[30]

For volunteers, he turned to the pool of conscientious objectors.

Some accepted military but noncombatant appointments as medics or orderlies or secretaries. However, 12,000 of them refused military service of any kind but volunteered during the war for alternative service—firefighting, mental hospital work, and medical experiments. Two hundred of these religiously motivated pacifists and idealists applied for inclusion in his experiment, hoping their suffering would help others. Keys accepted forty volunteers, who arrived for a year on the campus of the University of Minnesota. They lived and worked in a space in the athletic facilities and had the freedom to come and go, to date, take classes, do whatever they wanted so long as they ate only what the experiment provided.

Thirty-eight volunteers made it through the year. The men lost weight and, almost immediately, any interest in sex. They were afforded free tuition at the University of Minnesota for the duration, and one volunteer, Max Kampelman, worked on his undergraduate degree in political science, met Professor Hubert Humphrey, and went on to law school. He eventually joined the Humphrey political circle and served as Senator Humphrey's legal counsel. Most of the subjects, however, found that they quickly lost the ability to concentrate on anything other than food. Without enough, they daydreamed about food; they dreamed about food. Sometimes they dreamed about being surrounded by piles and piles of food; sometimes they had nightmares about ruining the experiment by taking a bite. The temptation to "cheat"—and at least one man did sneak off to eat—prompted Keys to require that the men go out only with a buddy, never alone. That so many of these men, in the face of what turned out to be real torture, did not cheat is remarkable testimony to their pacifist convictions.

The end of the war did not cause much of a ripple among the volunteers, and Keys was nowhere near to findings that could assist in addressing the "starvation on an epic scale" that indeed existed. His final report, *The Biology of Human Starvation,* was published by the University of Minnesota Press in 1950.[31]

His most useful finding led Keys to help transform the habits of people who ate too much. He discovered that his subjects had healthier hearts than the population at large. Pursuing this idea, his later research showed the damaging physical effects of saturated fats and elevated cholesterol on the heart and prompted him to declare war on Americans' suicidal eating habits. He and his wife, Margaret, wrote a cookbook—*Eat Well and Stay Well*—of Mediterranean-style recipes (paella and gazpacho, for example) published in 1959. Its emphasis on olive oil, nonsaturated fats, and fresh vegetables did not transform the American diet overnight, but it did get Keys onto the cover of *Time Magazine* in 1961. And it did help Americans begin to understand the language of cholesterol and make changes in their diets. Keys himself lived to age one hundred.[32]

Not all the hungers were physical in these years, as African American photographer, novelist, and moviemaker Gordon Parks's memoir—*A Hungry Heart*—details. His "choice of weapons" in the war for racial equality at home was the camera. A one-time busboy at the Minneapolis Club and the Lowry Hotel in St. Paul, a dining car waiter, and a fashion photographer, he was, as one review called him, "a one--man wrecking crew of racial barriers." In addition to his work for the Farm Security Administration as a photographer, during the war years he served in the Office of War Information and then became a photographer for *Life* and *Vogue* magazines, a movie director (*The Learning Tree* [1971], based on his own autobiographical novel, and *Shaft* [1971]), a musician and composer, and a writer. As he remembered in *A Choice of Weapons*, "I did a lot of thinking about the white man, and about his brutality—realizing it was nudging me into a hatred of him. I lay aching until dawn, reassembling all the scalding experiences one by one." He may have hungered for sugar or meat, but, like many African Americans—and Native Americans and others who contributed to the war effort for freedom without earning that just reward—he hungered more achingly and angrily for the civil rights that went so long denied.[33]

The people who were sugar-deprived or who had to darn their stockings again and again or who had to make do in hundreds of small and big ways bore their suffering with patriotic stoicism. The suffering of those who lost family members to the war cut far more deeply. The suffering of nurses was indelibly incised. The suffering of the soldiers—from the sights they saw at Pearl Harbor, Bataan, Normandy, Anzio, and in Burma, from their killing, from seeing their friends die, from witnessing the survivors of and the mountains of bodies of those who did not survive concentration camps—was incalculable.

World War II created in the United States a new world—a world of broken and quiet men sent home from the war's many fronts, a world of women happy or bitter about being sent home from work to make way for those men, a world of grieving parents, spouses, friends, and children, a world of more tractors and fewer migrant workers, a world of people who knew the effects of and lived in the shadow of the atomic bomb, a world leaving wartime alliances and enemies behind for a newly aligned Cold War, a world of people who, like Parks, were "becoming more sensitive to any situation that revealed a white man's attitude toward me."[34]

American society also realigned. The exodus of so many workers and soldiers from the state and of so many from its farms radically altered the nation and Minnesota. Before the war, a majority of Minnesotans lived on farms or in small towns; after the war, a majority lived in bigger towns and cities. Many never went home to the farms. They needed new lives and new places to live.[35]

No wonder overeating became a problem in the United States. No wonder so many went quiet in the 1950s, turned inward and homeward. No wonder they found appealing the abundance of food and goods and products that came to define America in the 1950s.

14

Style Comes to Staples

LIKE HUNDREDS OF OTHER SMALL TOWNS in Minnesota, Staples, in Todd County, limped out of the 1940s battered by war, then depression, then another war. The town and people of Staples had weathered nearly two decades of hard years. Located on the main Northern Pacific Railroad line from St. Paul to Seattle, Staples originally had oriented itself to rail and timber. The land around it was never prime farmland but good enough to yield a living. The town was much like many midwestern towns—main street, at least two good cafes, and a meat market, as well as food and appliance stores, Phil Anderson's Our Own Hardware, Carlson Furniture, and Huff Furniture Store and Funeral Parlor. Nothing too fancy. No one would accuse Staples of being "modern" in 1940. But by 1960, Staples was home to modern furniture, cars, televisions, highchairs. Staples wasn't New York or Minneapolis, but it was a lot closer to those places than it had been. This is the story of the 1950s—how modernism came to Staples.[1]

Tight times and the more important business of war had accustomed people to worn carpets, walls that long since needed a new coat of paint, a davenport past its ability to give rest. Besides, that old furniture was homey, a refuge from a dangerous world; the heavy draperies kept winter cold out and summer cool in; antimacassars kept sofa arms clean. Photos of relatives long gone vied for space with pictures of radiantly dutiful and uniformed men and snapshots of young women frolicking with girlfriends in California or wearing Red Cross hats and handing out doughnuts and coffee to soldiers.[2]

Todd County men who went away to war included the eager and the reluctant alike. The men who didn't come home to Todd County included Benedict Nalawaja, a coast artillery corpsman whose fate remained a mystery; Ralph Kliem, an infantryman who was buried in Belgium; Niels Chievitz, who was buried in Arlington National Cemetery; air corpsman Chester Tucker, the son of a barber, who was lost; Phillip

Rydeen, buried at Fort Snelling; Robert Wiebesick, a private first class in the army, buried in Hawaii; Kenneth Tonsager, another private first class who was killed, earned a Purple Heart, and was buried in the Philippines.[3]

Women who joined the service from Todd County are harder to identify after the war. Magdalene Balcom, for example, joined the Quartermaster Corps of the Women's Army Corps; Inez Campbell left her job as a sewing machine operator and a year of college to enlist in the Women's Army Corps in April 1944. Did they come back? Perhaps with new names, but no one of those names moved back to Todd County in the postwar years. They may have been among the people who accounted for Todd County's decline in population from 27,000 to 25,000 in the ten years between 1940 and 1950.[4]

Veterans developed a reputation for being reluctant to talk about their experiences. Some must have suffered, without being able to name, post-traumatic stress disorder (PTSD) or were tortured by the mix of emotions that always trails soldiers—relief, remorse, survivor's guilt, the exhilarating intensity of war life and friendships. Besides, they were men, and didn't men have a responsibility to not crack or whine, cry or complain? It wasn't men's only role, but a dominant one.[5]

Women who'd gone away to war work and come back, even those who'd taken over "men's work" in Staples, must also have had to mute some of their feelings. Yes, they could talk about having been lonely, but about reveling in the pleasure of being away, on their own, out from under family supervision and the neighbors' eyes? Not likely. How many of them settled down to lives with fiancés they no longer knew or husbands they didn't recognize? How could they complain about giving up their jobs to returning soldiers who so clearly needed (and deserved) them more? Wasn't that another version of their patriotic duty? It was certainly a happy time for many, but it must have been excruciatingly painful for others.

The postwar years brought new fears: of the Soviet Bear, the "loss" of China, the Berlin Wall, the Korean War, mutually assured destruction when the Soviet Union tested its own atomic bomb in 1949. Wisconsin's U.S. senator Joseph McCarthy's accusations of communists in government service magnified the terror.

A rise in church membership in the late 1940s and into the 1950s reflected gratitude but also, perhaps, those fears and a need for comfort. The baby boom surely expressed a pent-up ache for family and home, for intimacy and connection. All of these factors turned people toward home and family, toward safety, comfort, security, and home decorating.

Yes, home and safety and security, that was all true. So was exuberance and pent-up desire. All those cakes that hadn't been baked because there hadn't been enough sugar; all that abstinence from meat—didn't those sacrifices deserve a reward? Frugality had been the watchword all over America in the 1930s and the 1940s. It wouldn't be the attitude of the 1950s. The war had been fought and won in the name of democracy. "Grand Expectations" is the term contemporary American historian James Patterson uses to describe the theme of the 1950s. Buoyed by the prosperity of the 1940s and the 1950s, people who had not previously dreamed of a grand life began to.[6]

Not all Americans, of course. One-third of Minnesota's rural people still awaited electricity; poor people in Minnesota and the nation awaited the American Dream (or no longer cared about it, if they ever did); African Americans' service to the war effort had not demolished many barriers to equality (and the consequences of the GI Bill for decades furthered the economic divide between whites and blacks). Native Americans, no matter their contribution to the war effort, continued to be plagued by the "civilization" supposed to have saved them. Mexican Americans, despite their enthusiastic enlistment and service, also continued to be concentrated in jobs and neighborhoods, whether or not they wanted to be.

These and other people were ignored, rejected, or excluded from full participation in the revolution heralded by the 1950 Oldsmobile that rocketed across America and by the delivery vans full of swivel chairs, turquoise bathroom fixtures, melamine dishes, television sets, and new ideas that began arriving in small towns—including Staples—all over the United States. Small towns—once "island communities" and isolated one from the other—had gotten connected by railroads, highways, and radio. Other trucks showed up with diapers, strollers, swing sets, tricycles, highchairs, toys, dolls, train sets, cowboy and Indian costumes—mountains of kid's stuff. The kids may not have needed it as much as the parents did. Nothing was too good—or apparently too much—for their kids. Isn't that how we show them love? Isn't that what we fought the war for—to make sure our kids have everything they need?[7]

Patriotism proved a strong glue, and the shared suffering, rationing, and making do of the war years lured Americans out of more local connections into a national identity. The war turned Irish-Catholics in St. Paul, Poles in Todd County, Norwegians in Chisago, Swedish-Lutherans in Austin, Croatians and Finns on the Iron Range into "Americans." In the 1950s, that shared identity was enhanced and reinforced by Lucy and Desi, by Elvis Presley, by Kraft Macaroni and Cheese, and by that new 1950 Oldsmobile.

American manufacturers, desperate to make sure they survived the transition from war to peace, had put designers to work even before the end of the war dreaming up products that would catch the attention of postwar consumers. Some furniture designers and manufacturers anticipated that returning soldiers would crave comfort and the safety of the familiar, so at war's end they speeded up production of traditionally styled furniture. American colonial living room suites—with their maple color, turned spindle backs, figured upholstery, and pleated skirts—in name at least conjured up images of heroes of another time.[8]

Other manufacturers, however, had only been waiting for their chance to unleash upon America the revolution that was called "modernism." To people such as the European architects Marcel Breuer, Ludwig Mies van der Rohe, and Le Corbusier, Americans Frank Lloyd Wright and Louis Sullivan, as well as Minneapolis architects William Purcell, George Elmslie, and Lisl and Winston Close, modernism had a very specific aesthetic, cultural, even democratic definition. The 1905 Cass Gilbert–designed Minnesota State Capitol building in the Beaux-Arts style represented all that the modernists hated (backward looking, monumental, overly decorated, and pretentious). Louis Sullivan's bank in Owatonna in 1906 and Frank Lloyd Wright's 1912 house for the Francis Little family in Minnetonka—both in the Prairie Style—were very close to what the modernists loved: strong horizontal lines, room to breathe, open spaces, and honest materials—wood, tile, steel, leather, concrete. The Bauhaus modernists wanted to go further—to transform people's tastes from Victorian overstuffed, ornamented, pretentious copies of what rich people bought to good-quality and well-designed and affordable things for the masses. This wasn't the kind of democracy World War II had been fought for, but it was, the designers believed, profoundly democratic. Some version of this modernism affected American design for the rest of the century and found a place even in the living rooms of Staples, Minnesota.[9]

Modernism proved to be the light at the end of the depression and war tunnel. Modernism would direct people to look forward and not back, would redirect people's attention from the privations and limitations of the past. Get rid of that overstuffed chair that belonged to the man who wouldn't be coming home; throw away the scuffed table and ratty rug that told of making do for so long. Do something, get something, buy something new; be new. As early as 1949, Yungbauer Furniture Manufacturers in St. Paul turned out what could certainly be called modern furniture: blond and modular tables and crisp and sleek casual sofas.[10]

At the end of the war, a few adventuresome buyers in Staples might have ordered furniture from Yungbauer Manufacturers, but more of them likely shopped in town at Carlson Furniture or at Phil Anderson's Our Own Hardware or at the Huff Furniture Store and Funeral Parlor.* These Staples businesses, not certain what their customers would go for, made mostly utilitarian arguments for their goods. Huff's offered good deals on mattresses and box springs. Anderson's advertised beautiful ranges that could "make tastier meals in less time" and had a special "vitamin-saver simmer set." Carlson's advertised platform rockers that were also beautiful and useful.[11]

Then something happened. Out of a confluence of prosperity, new babies, televisions, and manufacturers who, according to historian Shelley Nickles, "modified modernism from the avant-garde to the average," modernism as a mass phenomenon, as popular culture was born. The modernist philosophy—that speed is good, style is good, change is good, new is good, and more is better—caught on in most of the United States. Not simply an urban phenomenon or a coastal one, it engaged people even in towns as small and as close to the end of the earth as Staples, Minnesota.[12]†

Television helped. A lot. Televisions themselves symbolized the new; they also piped into every owner's living spaces an avalanche of new ideas, images, language, and definition of self. One of the ideas that took stronger and stronger hold was the notion that everyone deserved a refrigerator, a good stove, a new house, their own house, their own car, their own television. These were toys and pleasures not just for the rich but for all Americans.[13]

The Valter family in Minneapolis bought a molded plastic dining room set; state senator J. A. Josefson's family in Minneota ate at a blond dining room set from 1951 through 1958; Gene and Dorothy Sylvestre hired a local architect and helped build their own modern house and, in the spirit of the 1950s, furnished it with, among other things, a butterfly chair. Lisl Close designed furniture out of plywood and rope for a client's home on the St. Croix River. Somehow, in the 1950s, nurses and bank managers, electricians and teachers, clerks and homemakers in the Twin Cities and Rochester but also in International Falls, Jasper, and Staples accepted, indeed embraced, a new aesthetic, but it wasn't quite what the Bauhaus had had in mind.[14]

This is the way of democracy: it goes its own way. Breuer wanted high culture for the masses. What happened instead was that mass-produced came to mean mass—and eventually pop—culture. The process started with refrigerators, but it spawned cars that looked like rockets, chairs that looked like butterflies, coffee tables that looked like amoebas, lamps that looked like artichokes, and houses that looked like each other.

The modernists had aimed for universal and permanent principles

*

The combined furniture/funeral operation was common all over the Midwest well into the middle of the century. The overlap of the woodworking for furniture and coffins made sense. Besides, the wagon that was big enough to deliver furniture could certainly carry a coffin to the cemetery. These commercial marriages broke down as furniture came to be objects of style and fashion, even for the citizens of Staples.

†

It is still a powerful force but one now with many competing voices. The environmental movement of the 1960s—small is beautiful, reuse, recycle, and return—are all later inventions. The VW Beetle, introduced in 1938, was the first real counter to the big move-ment. For most of the 1950s, however, the philosophy went largely unchallenged.

of design. They reached a mass audience, for sure, but permanence did not characterize the consumer goods of the 1950s. Ads promised that consumers were "buying a lifetime of beauty and comfort." But furniture, like cars, became stylish enough to go out of style before long. One General Motors official is reported to have said that he wanted car owners to stay thrilled with the sleek styling of their cars for the year it took the company to introduce another. *Planned obsolescence* was the term for the corporate strategy to get people to buy what they didn't need before what they had wore out. It proved enormously successful.[15]

Citizens of Staples and New York alike took up the same styles, fads, frivolity, and fun: Kellogg's Sugar Frosted Flakes, Kraft Cheez Whiz, Holiday Inns, Disneyland, Eveready AA batteries, Certs breath mints, Sports Illustrated, Barbie, Play-Doh, and Davy Crockett hats. The new products encouraged greater informality and promised convenience and efficiency: cake mixes, panty hose, disposable sanitary napkins, credit cards, Bic pens, Jiffy Pop, and a sour cream/french onion soup recipe for a dip that, with chips, was perfect for impromptu and casual entertaining.[16]

It wasn't too long before even Staples's stores joined the chorus of advertisers to sing the "modern" praises of their offerings. Phil Anderson's Our Own Hardware had long sold dinette sets, but in 1954 the ads described its "Tru Chrome" sets as "modern" and the Staples furniture suppliers competed for buyers. These sets were formed out of tubular steel—like the Breuer chair—but with "Lamex" (also called "the Wonder Plastic") seats with "locked in color" that could repel all spills and smears.* "Chromecraft" dinettes—sold at Huff Furniture—were constructed out of tubular steel, too and other brands of plastic chair covers. Then Anderson offered the sets in decorator colors that would "add sparkle to your home." Then Huff's offered dinettes in new styles and sizes. Anderson offered them in new colors, as well as styles and sizes. The variations among them were smaller than the ads might have wanted buyers to realize.[17]

*

Something about the "x" seemed in the 1950s to be a code for modern: Xerox, Deluxe, Permalux.

Neither furniture stores nor designers imagined that consumers would throw out all of their old furniture, so Anderson, Carlson, and Huff continued to offer sofas and chairs in several styles. The stores and the increasingly popular "ladies" magazines—*Good Housekeeping, Ladies' Home Journal, McCall's*—encouraged people to mix and match, to put a modern table with an Early American sofa, a new lamp with a Provincial chair. The range of styles was broadening; so were the choices of finishes and materials: fabrics, vinyl and plastic, blond and genuine walnut veneer, platinum mahogany, and "modern limed oak." Dishes in many new designs appeared about the same time. An International Falls ad described a set of dishes as "utterly modern, strikingly original, yet poised and restrained." Able to blend with any style furniture or silver-ware, these dishes also had a "touch of perkiness."[18]

During the war the manufacture of televisions in the United States had been suspended, but sales ballooned quickly after the war. In 1947, Americans owned 40 million radios and 44,000 television sets. In early April 1950, Americans owned 5.3 million sets; by the time the first *I Love Lucy* program was televised in October 1951, Americans owned 13 million sets. In 1957 that number had increased to 41 million, and by 1960 the ownership of televisions surpassed that of radios.[19]

The first really new furniture that won wide acceptance were those things that accommodated the new television sets. The Staples merchants offered swivel chairs that could turn from television to conversation and back to television without requiring the sitter to get up. Long prized as a footrest, the hassock got a new lease on life as a casual TV stool, especially when neighbors (without television sets) turned up to watch the coronation of Queen Elizabeth, the Republican national convention, the Friday night fights from Madison Square Garden.

More and more people invested in recliners—man-sized they were often called, emphasizing the house-as-castle idea, the resting-place-after-a-hard-day-at-work idea that so shaped men's and women's roles in the 1950s—with built in footrests, just right for relaxing into television watching. Metal trays could accommodate eating while watching (and TV dinners after 1954). Moreover, in the 1950s, most televisions resembled furniture more than appliances—big, boxy, enclosed in wood (or veneer), set on sofalike legs (and later on chairlike legs of metal). The televisions didn't accommodate the other furniture; the other furniture was designed to accommodate the televisions.[20]

Advertisers did a brilliant job of selling products by selling concepts. They described TVs, refrigerators, and bedroom sets as forward-looking, modern, completely new, revolutionary, breathtakingly ahead of their time.* In addition, postwar advertisements in Minnesota newspapers emphasized power: "powerful" stoves, dishwashers, freezers, mixers, coffeemakers, and, of course, cars! The idea of cars as powerful is so much a part of American culture that it's difficult to remember that it was not simply a fact but a concept invented and sold to consumers: power steering, power brakes, power seats, and push-button transmission; "frisky powerglide" in the 1956 Chevy, "top-thrust and take off" in the Pontiac, and "deep chested power" in the Plymouth.[21]

Why this emphasis on power? People who *are* powerful don't need to buy power. People who don't have it (or feel they don't or wish they did) are the ones in the market for it, not intentionally and not con-

*

All of these phrases appeared in ads in *Staples World,* the weekly newspaper in Staples, Minnesota, between 1950 and 1956. The ads were obviously provided by the manufacturers, because virtually the same ads and sometimes the exact ones appeared in the papers in Staples, Rochester, Jasper, International Falls, St. Paul, and New York City and Los Angeles.

sciously, no doubt, but susceptible to its charms and allure. Who would those people have been in the 1950s? Returning soldiers? Women forced home? Employees of big corporations or factory workers? People who felt the shadow of the atomic bomb and the Cold War? People who worried about the communist menace? No wonder people wanted a powerful car.* Besides, people who grew up with little and then, in the booming economy of the 1950s, found that they had something bought cars and refrigerators and bedroom suites. The Depression, World War II, and the Cold War each contributed to the expansion of buying in the 1950s.[22]

Since the 1920s, at least, one aspect of American consumerism has been the identification of things with ideas and identity, so an object increasingly carried the weight not only of performing its function—being a shoe, for example—but also of identifying the values and aspirations, indeed even the "self" of the wearer. The Mall of America, in Bloomington, the second-largest shopping mall in the world, in 2005 ran an advertising campaign that made this point explicitly: "MOA: more ways to be yourself." But the 1950s ads used the values and the image to sell the objects: the 1956 Dodge promised "the Look of Success." Carlson offered sofas that said "young at heart" and a bedroom dresser that "says so eloquently that our married life grows richer each year."[23]†

The rocket fuel that propelled many of these changes was the Serviceman's Readjustment Act of 1944—the GI Bill, as it was commonly called. As a result of this government program and the shortage of homes, modernism pulled into Coon Rapids in the 1950s on the beds of trucks piled high with sacks of concrete, boxes of nails, stacks of cedar shakes, spools of wire, and miles of copper piping. The GI Bill provided funding for the education of returning veterans, for medical care, and for low-interest mortgages on new homes. Between 1944 and 1949, the government underwrote nearly $50 billion in loans to returning servicemen.[24]

The demand for new housing far outran the supply, and individual contractors could not keep up. They needed a new way; a few of them—William Levitt in New Jersey and New York and Orrin Thompson in Minnesota—understood that if production of consumer goods could be speeded up—and made more affordable—by mass production, why not houses? A lot of houses built to the same design, in close proximity to each other, could go up quickly, cheaply, and profitably.[25]

Orrin Thompson's plan for building communities of quality and affordable houses took him out of the cities and even beyond the first ring of suburbs to Coon Rapids, Cottage Grove, and Apple Valley. The village of Coon Rapids—about half an hour north of Minneapolis and St. Paul—on the Mississippi River had been a stopover for the Red River

*

Elaine Tyler May makes much of "containment" as a philosophy of home life and women's sexuality as well as of the Cold War. Many men must have felt unable to control their wives as they did these other threats around them—no matter how they tried. (That's the problem with control, isn't it?)

†

Vice President Richard Nixon and Soviet Premier Nikita Khrushchev both understood the transcendent meaning of material goods when they debated in Moscow in 1959 about the merits of their respective political and economic systems by arguing about kitchen appliances.

carts on their trek in the early nineteenth century between Pembina and St. Paul. In the early twentieth century, Northern States Power had built a dam at Coon Rapids. The residents incorporated as a village in 1952.

Between 1950 and 1960, the state's population increased by 17 percent, from 2.8 million to 3.2 million. In those same years, Anoka County's population increased from 36,000 to 86,000 (150 percent) and new households increased by 30 percent. Coon Rapids turned itself from a village into an incorporated city in 1959 as 2,000 new people moved in between 1958 and 1960. The people may have moved out to Coon Rapids and Anoka, but the jobs didn't. The men of these households were coughed up every morning to climb into their cars and head into Minneapolis or St. Paul or someplace else for work. Children, though, would go to school nearby. The absence of sidewalks didn't encourage walking, but that was why mom had a car, too.

In the mid- to late 1950s, Orrin Thompson built more than 2,000 homes in Thompson Park in Coon Rapids. In the 1960s he also built Thompson Heights and Riverview Development, also in Coon Rapids. His homes boasted picture windows, cedar shake siding, three bedrooms, one bath, a living/dining room combination, and kitchen. Each house had its own front lawn, small backyard, and driveway (no garage) and looked much like the houses on either side. These houses were arrayed on streets named Ilex, Juniper, Kumquat, Larch, Magnolia, Norway, and Olive, though only the occasional real tree found a home on the landscape. Thompson's idea of a community did not include shops or stores, only houses. The community did hint, however, of California and its "easygoing lifestyle," so reminiscent of the west and southwest in those ranch houses.[26]

It's easy to disparage their sameness, but similarly styled houses were nothing new—Americans had long called them brownstones or row houses in city settings. For the Coon Rapids buyer, these houses had many advantages that those city homes didn't: space, of course, and privacy and affordability. Moreover, they had the advantage of being new and as good as Thompson could build while still keeping them affordable.

Couples could—and certainly did—bring family furniture into these new homes—a sofa from her mother, a chair from his grandfather, lamps that were leftover from somewhere—but these homes invited new and modern furniture. The photos of the display house feature the sectional sofa, two Scandinavian-style step tables (with a light, perhaps limed oak finish), and fashionable table lamps. The pattern of the curtains is a staple of 1950s design. The white walls and the bright room are just the right setting for the Scandinavian look as well as for the new colors that promised to liven up the living room. To assist people in furnishing their own houses, the developers made suggestions and the furniture stores increasingly offered suites, entire sets of living room furnishings that included sofa, chairs, tables, lamps, sometimes even matching TV trays and just the right serving bowls and dishes. Couples could purchase these new things close to home, or they could climb into their cars and explore.

Modernism in Coon Rapids meant new houses, new furniture, new appliances. It also meant new ways of life centered on the car. Already in 1957, Coon Rapids was too big to take a walk across. Children could not usually walk from the Northdale Addition to school. Families did not walk to church or to buy groceries. Cars in the early 1950s had been designed for men; by the late 1950s, Ford and other automakers were offering cars for women and cars for men. The Ford Fairlane station wagon was "femengineered" so that women could get themselves and their children where they needed to go. The Ford Thunderbird had men in its sights. He could drive his car to work; she could have the family car.

The kids? They, too, would be raised by new and modern standards, described by Dr. Benjamin Spock. Give children more attention, give them what they want, organize the household around them—wasn't that what the postwar years were about anyway? So much the better to have a doctor's affirmation of these practices. Spock's advice book sold a million copies months after it appeared in 1946. Like the house and the car, this book put women at the center of the family life with the children, but the postwar years did hint at the change in gender roles that was knocking at the door. Men were supposed to be parents; they were to spend time with their children, even if it was only cooking on the barbeque in the backyard or taking the wife and kids for a ride.[27]

On the weekend they could go shopping together—perhaps even at Southdale, just southwest of Minneapolis in the slightly older suburb of Edina. American shopping malls had been around since the opening of Country Club Plaza in Kansas City in 1923. Dayton's had a better idea, certainly a better one for Minnesota and, it turned out, a popular one in hot as well as cold climates: an enclosed, indoor mall. Designed by Victor Gruen and Associates in 1952, Southdale Mall opened its doors in 1956. It housed Dayton's, of course, and seventy-one other stores on two floors around a central courtyard with long sightlines, open staircases, lots of light (artificial, not sunlight), surrounded by 5,200 parking spaces. No one walked to Southdale.[28]

In the early Southdale years, the new Interstate and Defense Highways were still in the planning stages, so getting to Edina from Coon

Rapids would have been a long and tedious drive. In 1919, Captain Dwight D. Eisenhower had taken part in a cross-country automobile trip that took sixty-two days because the army vehicles averaged about five miles an hour. When he was elected president in 1952, Eisenhower set as one of his goals a streamlining of the American road system. Congress passed the Federal Aid Highway Act in 1956. It provided funds to build about 42,000 miles of "limited access" four-lane (at least) roads, ostensibly for defense (but more often used to get to and from shopping, relatives, vacations, jobs). An eight-mile stretch from Owatonna to Medford was in 1958 the first bit of interstate—on I-35—completed in the state.[29]

Minnesota acted quickly to build because the state had a well-developed state highway department and system, widespread popular support, and the belief that freeways would lead directly to progress. Nine years after those first eight miles, another 352 miles were added to the state's interstate highway system.[30]

It was the "limited access" that distinguished these roads from other highways (of which there were many by the mid-1950s; a drive across the country in 1956 would not have taken sixty-two days). It meant that cars could enter or leave the system at only specified and designated places, usually no less than two miles apart (sometimes a little closer in cities) and often with much longer stretches between entrances and exits. This idea of the 1950s—speed, efficiency, streamlined, forward leaning—was wonderful for the people on the highways but sometimes a little (or a lot) less wonderful for the neighborhoods the highways serrated or the towns they bypassed.[31]

St. Mark's Catholic Parish in St. Paul, for example, was split by Interstate 94. After the building of the freeway in 1961, parishioners who had previously been able to walk to church (and school) had to walk miles instead, and most didn't. They changed to other schools and parishes. That same stretch of freeway had an even more dramatic effect on the Rondo neighborhood. Rondo was home to many African Americans in the 1950s. Many black middle-class people lived there, as well as many who aspired to the middle-class but hadn't yet achieved it. It certainly was home to urban poverty, too, and to what city and road planners, no doubt, called urban blight.[32]

Some urban planners in the 1950s and 1960s tried to eradicate urban poverty by tearing down the buildings in which the urban poor lived. In Minneapolis, for example, city and federal authorities invoked eminent domain to clear out blocks and blocks of low-income housing, businesses, bars, rooming houses, pawnshops, and transient hotels, replacing them eventually with parking lots (other plans had been dreamed but never materialized). The decision to cut through Rondo certainly had racial motives; it also had economic motives. It seemed a way to do at least two things at once: to make way for the freeway, yes, but also to "improve" the neighborhood.[33]

The St. Anthony–Rondo freeway clearances eliminated 433 households: 121 white and 312 "non-white," almost entirely African American. A study of those who were displaced followed up on 328 of the households and found that 10 percent of the whites and 85 percent of the African Americans moved to another "non-white" neighborhood. The freeway clearances had the effect of increasing the density of the black population and of further reducing the neighborhoods in which whites and blacks both lived. Some Rondo residents had no interest in leaving a black community and mourned its destruction in the interests of faster traffic. Some of the residents who looked for housing elsewhere met discrimination and redlined neighborhoods closed to them. Some did not try to move, usually out of fear of discrimination.[34]

The 1940s opened the path for more egalitarian gender, social, and racial roles and relations. The 1950s shoveled the path clearer, but only for some. The GI bill–funded suburbs further divided Minnesotans by class; the interstate highways divided people by race. The emphasis on home and homemaking pushed women off the career path. The Civil Rights tide had not turned in the late 1940s and early 1950s, but it was on its way. The *Brown v. Topeka Board of Education* case was moving through the federal courts system, and in 1954 the Supreme Court would strike down the "separate, but equal" decision of the 1896 *Plessey v. Ferguson* case. Prejudice and discrimination against Jewish, Native American, African American, and Mexican American Minnesotans did not diminish suddenly in 1948 or 1954 or 1964, but Minneapolis mayor Hubert Humphrey in 1948 put the state's and the nation's Democrats on alert for changes that were to come. Not soon enough and still not enough, but rumbles of change were on the horizon.[35]

The consumerism of the 1920s had sent novelist F. Scott Fitzgerald out of the state and away from the "stuff" he felt strangled his creativity. Many artists have fled Minnesota specifically and the Midwest generally to find something better, bigger, more charged and electric elsewhere. In the 1950s, too, artists had to decide where they could work. By decade's end, Robert Zimmerman knew Minnesota was not the place for him and fled to New York, where he reinvented himself as Bob Dylan. The potter Warren MacKenzie, by contrast, fled only to his studio in Stillwater. That was far enough away to allow him to stand against the tide of plastics and disposables that rolled across the United States after the war. Like the modernists, he wanted people to be able to surround themselves with well-designed things but not mass-produced things. After studying and, with his first wife, Alixandra Kolesky MacKenzie, living with the English potter Peter Leach and working in the tradition of the Japanese potter Shoji Hamada, he and Alix settled into their Stillwater place and stayed. "There is something about living in Minnesota, or living in the Midwest," MacKenzie said in 2002. "My pots are really most at home in the Midwest . . . [this area is] sympathetic to hand pottery. And it doesn't have to be fancy hand pottery, such as you're likely to find in the big galleries in New York or San Francisco and so on, the latest thing. They want pots they can use in their home." That's what they did and he continued to do after her death: make everyday pots at reasonable prices, always with a whiff of the Leach/Hamada style in them.[36]

The 1950s were for many people domestic years—making their homes, raising children, earning enough money to buy furniture and cars, settling into a post-Depression and postwar life. The Minneapolis Lakers played professional basketball from 1947 to 1960, when they moved to Los Angeles (more fans, more money, bigger arena). Met Stadium was built in 1956; the Twins played their first game there in 1961.

In the 1950s, a landslide of modern ideas, images, language, and things swept into Minnesota—on the hoods of cars, on the television airwaves, in delivery trucks of stuff. All of these new things had the effect, in part, of democratizing America, as Breuer and other designers had hoped. It also took America down the road toward a more common— some might say homogenous—culture and brought Americans into the same time period. With televisions, people in New York and Staples got their news at the same time. In 1957 they all heard about the Soviets' launching of Sputnik and Dwight Eisenhower's use of federal troops to desegregate the public schools in Little Rock, Arkansas, and the death of Joe McCarthy. They also got other kinds of "news": Elvis Presley's debut on the Ed Sullivan Show; Lucy, Ricky and little Ricky's move from their New York apartment to their Connecticut house. People who watched television had limited choices, at most three networks of programs. This sameness—as well as the sameness, then, of the advertising on the three networks—encouraged a kind of homogenization among viewers.[37]

Moreover, the same cars and refrigerators, television sets and card tables showed up in all of these—and other—places at virtually the same time. Car makers in the mid-1950s made a fetish of ceremonially unveiling the new year's model everywhere all at once. Stoves came in new models, too; so did lamps and chairs. In the nineteenth century, new things, new ideas, even new news came slowly up the river or across country by wagon, wire, or rail, up to Pembina, out from Duluth. Slowly. New Yorkers might think of Minnesota as a backwater and people in Edina might consider Staples the end of the world, but modernism and mass production and mass consumption—and televisions—joined people in time and across space. This was how Staples and International Falls and Jasper—even Minnesota itself, considered by many outsiders to be the middle of nowhere—became part of everywhere in the 1950s.

15

"The House That Hubert Built"

THAT IS WHAT *Time Magazine* called the political world that Hubert H. Humphrey designed, built, and ran for nearly thirty years. During that time, Minnesota fielded three presidential nominees, two vice presidents, several cabinet members, one Supreme Court justice, and one chief justice of the Supreme Court.

So many rooms in the house that Hubert built, but his own was the biggest. It had to be—big enough to contain the man's dreams, energy, ambition. Everyone who knew him talked about how much Humphrey talked, how fast and how effectively. A "torrential talker," *Time* called him. Joseph Ball, his opponent in the 1948 Senate race, lamented that Humphrey "could talk a bird off a tree"; someone actually did count and found that he talked three times faster than Ball. Humphrey made a point of remembering people's names and enough details of their lives to ask about their kids or jobs. Fifteen thousand of his close friends received Christmas cards regularly. He entered a room like the wind and commanded the attention of a tornado.[1]

Trained first in pharmacy, then in political science, Humphrey developed ideas about how a political party could and should work. But first he had to create one.

Historian Paul Kleppner, capturing something of the moral intensity that party designations invoked in the late nineteenth century, described parties as "political churches." Using that language, Minnesota had two major churches: Reformers (both of the Yankee and the Norwegian kind) belonged to the Republican congregation while Catholics (Irish and German) and German Lutherans belonged to the church of the Democrats. The Republican Party lived for a time on its laurels as the anti-slavery party and, as the Democrats legitimately complained even up to 1896, the Republicans used the rhetoric of the Civil War—"waving the bloody shirt" it was called—to keep the public ever mindful of the moral rectitude of the Republicans versus the Civil War–causing Democrats.[2]

The Republican Party dominated political life in post–Civil War Minnesota, but the party's increasingly pro-business orientation marginalized some small-town and rural Minnesotans and ushered them out of the fold. Where could they go, though? They had been Republicans long enough that they were certainly imbued with the rhetoric of Republicans good/Democrats bad. The ethnic and religious composition of the Democratic Party kept some people from jumping there. How could a good Norwegian join an Irish Catholic "church"? Most of them couldn't. Some people, then, looked to a third party.[3]

Ignatius Donnelly, for example. The Republican lieutenant governor, then Republican congressman, then Republican state senator found himself increasingly out of step with the Republicans, so he ran for Congress in 1884 as a Democrat. He lost. Four years later, he reinvented himself as an Independent candidate for the state senate and won. Then he found a home in the newly rising People's (or Populist) Party. He played an active role in the party's founding and employed his practiced pen to write the prologue to the 1892 People's Party Platform, which joined a reforming passion with economic demands: a graduated income tax, an eight-hour workday, liberal pensions for Civil War veterans, immigration reforms, and opposition to "any subsidy or national aid to any private corporation for any purpose."* This was a church that Donnelly could attend and certainly one where he could preach.[4]

In a state where the Republicans aligned themselves, increasingly, with old stock and Yankee Americans and those with money and the Democrats continued to offer haven for "undesirable" immigrants, political reformers and laborers and WASP-ish immigrants and even some would-be communists followed Donnelly's lead, moving from there into the Nonpartisan League and then into the more electorally successful Farmer-Labor Party. A local party, focused on local issues and able to win local elections, the FL Party emerged as Minnesota's second party—outdistancing in popularity the state's Democratic Party.

Four Farmer-Labor senators and three governors served between 1923 and 1939.† The most important FLer might have been Senator Henrik Shipstead, who served in the U.S. Senate from 1923 to 1947, but was instead the charismatic and visionary (for good or ill!) Floyd B. Olson, elected governor in 1930.[5]

Olson could talk to Republicans and Democrats, and his charming demeanor softened some of his sharper opinions. After he died of a brain tumor in 1936, the party self-destructed in a bitter 1938 struggle over whom to endorse for governor. The more radical—Communist, by his own identification—Elmer Benson won the nomination but lost the governorship to the young Harold Stassen, ushering in another sixteen

*

The platform also called for the restriction of "undesirable" immigrants, which in the late nineteenth century did not mean Norwegians or Swedes or even Germans (especially if they were not Catholic) but did mean Slavs, Southern Europeans, Italians, Croatians, Slovenians, Poles—almost all Catholic or Orthodox—and Jews. The People's Party, then, formed itself as a pro-American, pro-labor, anti-business, anti-Catholic reform party.

†

Henrik Shipstead, Magnus Johnson, Elmer Benson, and Ernest Lundeen. Shipstead held office for so long—from 1923 to 1947—that he outlasted the reinvention of the FL Party under Elmer Benson. The FL also controlled the governorship from 1931 to 1939: Floyd B. Olson, Hjalmar Petersen, and Elmer Benson.

years of Republican governors. Benson had lots of principles but no charm, no ability to build coalitions or make compromises. The Farmer-Labor Party did not die with him, but it ceased to be the kind of force it had promised to become under Governor Olson.

The Democrats were even weaker than the FLers, winning only an occasional statewide office, but they were buoyed by Minnesota's vote for Democrat Franklin Roosevelt in 1932, 1936, and 1940. In 1944, members of both parties knew that neither would be singularly able to defeat the Republicans, so they formed the Democratic-Farmer-Labor Party.

The DFL, like the FL, was home to real, live, committed communists and "fellow travelers." They didn't deny it—there was no need to until after the end of World War II and the birth of the Cold War. But when the USSR—ally against Germany—again became the enemy of the United States, so did American communists and socialists. Panic about the "fall of China" and the Soviet race to develop its own atomic bomb meant that in 1948 no party hoping to be viable could harbor communists. That year, the Democratic wing of the DFL—led by Humphrey—evicted its communist members from the party.[6]

Humphrey's masterminding of the ouster of the communists left a wake of ill feeling among the state's leftists and revealed his intense ambition. He was ambitious for himself and for his dreams; his idealism matched that of many Minnesotans and probably inspired it in others. He was a New Deal liberal who believed that New Deal liberalism would transform the world. This idealism was an intrinsic part of Humphrey; so was his loyalty. He didn't remember names just because politicians should remember names but because people deserved it. If you did him a good deed or a bad one, he didn't forget it. This combination of ambition, idealism, and loyalty made him a formidable politician—and it eventually destroyed him.

Humphrey the Democrat ran unsuccessfully for the mayorship of Minneapolis in 1943. Humphrey the DFLer, however, won the job in 1945 and again in 1947.

Humphrey served a largely white population in Minneapolis. Even so, he early made civil rights one of his central issues. As mayor he successfully pushed through a Fair Employment Practices ordinance, the first in the nation, and established a Mayor's Council on Human Relations. In the spring of 1948 Humphrey wrote to the secretary of defense urging an end to discrimination in the armed services, and that summer he stepped into the national spotlight on this issue.[7]

Already a candidate for the Senate in Minnesota, he attended the Democratic National Convention and took part in debates over the content of the platform. With the encouragement and support of his friends

Orville Freeman (also a Minnesota delegate) and Eugenie Anderson (the National Committeewoman for Minnesota), Humphrey rose in the full convention to file a minority civil rights plank, forcing the delegates to decide between the party's longtime weakness on the issue (in deference to its southern membership) and his own stronger call for civil rights. He swayed the delegates with his powerful call: "The time has arrived in America for the Democratic Party to get out of the shadow of states' rights and to walk forthrightly into the bright sunshine of human rights."

When Humphrey's plank barely won, northern liberals cheered and marched, the most astute among them realizing that he had tampered with, perhaps even picked, the South's lock on the Democratic Party. Southern Democrats walked out of the convention, formed their own splinter group—the Dixiecrats—and nominated Strom Thurmond for president. The party was never the same again.[8]*

In that year, 1948, the state and the nation were on the verge of cataclysmic change—change that exploded between the time of Humphrey's entrance on the national stage and his presidential defeat in 1968, change that put a hurricane behind the sails of a charismatic man.

One change in Minnesota was demographic. By the calculations of the U.S. Census Bureau, the United States had become "urban" in 1920, meaning that more people lived in cities than outside them. Minnesota, however, did not become urban by that definition until 1950. Time in the armed services, war work, changing values and opportunities, and memories of grinding poverty and grueling labor during the years of the Depression shifted people away from farms and into town.

Two other changes were of an economic and ideological nature. Minnesota's postwar prosperity and the reality of good, clean jobs did much to invite change. The GI Bill encouraged men who would not previously have attended colleges and trade schools to continue their education. Colleges across Minnesota took in all the students they could, and more students arrived. Quonset huts and former war-work buildings became dormitories; supply closets turned into rooms for teachers; gymnasiums into classrooms. Affordable and pleasant living in new homes in new suburbs, the 1950s feeling of plenty that followed the 1940s restraint, the spread of the automobile, and the promise of so many new children—all of these engendered optimism, hope, plus the belief that improving people's lives was government work and good work, too. Wasn't this what World War II was about? And wasn't it also the basis of America's position in the Cold War? Prosperity and idealism often spawn change.[9]

Other changes came sweeping through the state in the years of Humphrey's political career. Eight books published in those years fore-

*

Elected to the Senate, Humphrey met a cold reception when he joined his Democratic—and Dixiecrat—Senate colleagues in Washington in 1948, the same year Lyndon Johnson from Texas entered the Senate. Humphrey and Johnson formed an alliance and a competition of ambitions that ultimately resulted in Johnson's election to the presidency with Humphrey as his running mate in 1964 as well as in Humphrey's defeat in the 1968 presidential election.

told the direction of the change. Grace Metalious's popular 1956 novel *Peyton Place* depicted shocking sexual escapades in a sedate New England suburban community (demonstrating what Alfred Kinsey was writing about in *Sexual Behavior in the Human Male* and *Sexual Behavior in the Human Female*). In *The Singing Wilderness,* also published in 1956, Minnesota naturalist Sigurd Olson recounted his spiritual encounter with the wilderness while on a canoe trip in northern Minnesota. In 1962 Rachel Carson published her explosive and pathbreaking environmental work *Silent Spring,* which quietly, pointedly, effectively enumerated the dangers of pesticides and insecticides. At least as compellingly, Michael Harrington in 1962 articulated the suffocating poverty of *The Other America.* Betty Friedan's *Feminine Mystique* appeared in 1963, offering a less racy but more incisive look at the lives of postwar, usually suburban, women than had *Peyton Place.* "The problem that has no name," she called the disquiet and depression that seemed to plague many American women who should, they and others believed, have been happy and content. Why weren't they?

In 1963, James Baldwin published his brilliantly angry and prescient *Fire Next Time,* about problems that had names: racism and the alienation that simmered among African Americans. In 1965, Ralph Nader enumerated the dangers of the automobile and the intractability of car manufacturers in his *Unsafe at Any Speed.* For Catholics, the publication of the *Documents of the Second Vatican Council* (1965) and the council itself rocked the church to its foundations.

All these works—including Olson's but not the council documents—made it to the *New York Times* bestseller lists, and a remarkable number of Americans bought and even read them. Their popularity in Minnesota specifically and in the United States more generally tells something about the homogenization of culture that had been such a powerful force since the late nineteenth century but intensified explicitly in the 1950s. These books and the issues they highlight—the sexual revolution, the environmental movement, feminism, the war on poverty, the civil rights movement, and the wilderness protection movement—articulated an agenda that demanded attention and realigned politics and power in Minnesota and the United States in the 1960s and beyond.[10]*†

A young, Catholic president following the heroic but grandfatherly Dwight D. Eisenhower heralded a new world. *Brown v. Topeka Board of Education* had given hope and encouragement to a civil rights movement that pushed ever more for voting rights, then equal rights (and met increasing resistance). The baby boom accounted for big population increases in the state. Between 1960 and 1968, for example, Minneapo-

*

The only issue that did not have its storyteller in this period was the Vietnam War, though we have to look back only a few years to 1955 to find Graham Greene's *The Quiet American.*

†

Lady Chatterley's Lover was not yet available in the United States, but it would be very soon. So would Masters and Johnson's *Human Sexual Response* (1966) and Alex Comfort's *Joy of Sex* (1972).

lis alone grew by 13 percent, virtually the entire increase due to the higher number of births—not to migration.

The same ingredients that ignited the fires of the 1960s elsewhere in the United States sparked them in Minnesota: youth, turning from the past, prosperity, the liberating and inspiring effects of the war and its ideology. Minnesota had, in addition, a tradition of peoples trying to make things "better," both for good and ill. Those Yankee reformers in the 1830s–50s who believed that everything could be changed and got a whole lot of changes made, including the abolition of slavery and the founding of a state, a university, and a land open to settlers (and cleared in large part of Indians who seemed impervious to change). Then German farmers who wanted to make things better by making their land and their families productive, and Scandinavian people who had political dreams, too. Progressive reformers who had tried so hard to fix so much. Yes, they'd all floundered and even failed, but Humphrey's brand of idealism did prove startlingly appealing in the early 1960s.

In 1960, the median age in Minnesota was twenty-eight years (a number disguising how young the state's population actually was because long life expectancy pulled the median upward). A youth culture was emerging—rock and roll, the Beatles. In the 1950s, Bob Zimmerman, later Dylan, had fled Minnesota. In the 1960s, the First Avenue club in Minneapolis turned into a popular venue for real rock and the Cedar-Riverside neighborhood near the University of Minnesota spawned folk music and clubs.

Humphrey faced this new world with enthusiasm but not by himself. He never liked being alone—personally or politically. His house, therefore, had lots of room for lots of other ambitious and idealistic and loyal people. They included Orville Freeman, Arthur Naftalin, Donald Fraser, Miles Lord, Eugenie Anderson, Geri Joseph, and Walter Mondale. These people managed each other's campaigns; they worked on each other's staffs; they attended the state and national conventions together. They advised and supported each other. They all traced their roots to the Populists of the nineteenth century and the Progressives of the twentieth, even if they denied any Communist roots. They made political plans and dreamed liberal dreams of more civil rights, better schools, good jobs, fair labor practices, medical care for the old and the poor, courts that worked, clean air and wilderness, businesses attending to the needs of the people, and governments doing that, too. That was their dream, a dream that compelled enough Minnesotans—and Americans—to elect these friends of Humphrey to public office to play significant roles on the public stage for the next forty years.

Freeman chaired the state DFL in 1948 after Benson's departure, then was elected governor three times (1954–60), after which he served as secretary of agriculture under Presidents John F. Kennedy and Lyndon B. Johnson. Naftalin, another of Humphrey's inner circle, earned master's and doctoral degrees in political science at the University of Minnesota, where he taught except during the six years (1960–66) he was mayor of Minneapolis.[11]

Mondale, never as gregarious or mellifluous as his friend and mentor Humphrey, had many talents, including a knack for being in the right place at the right time. After serving in the military, he finished his undergraduate work and then his law degree at the University of Minnesota and worked in Humphrey's 1948 Senate campaign—with Orville Freeman and Miles Lord. Mondale in the 1950s worked on and then managed Freeman's campaigns for governor. When Miles Lord was appointed a U.S. attorney in 1960, Governor Freeman selected Mondale to serve the remainder of Lord's term as attorney general. In 1964, Mondale was appointed to finish Humphrey's Senate term when Humphrey was elected vice president.

Mondale, at thirty-four young as attorneys general go, stepped into the national spotlight in 1962. In June of that year he received a routine request from the State of Florida to file an *amicus* brief in support of a state's right "to determine their own rules of criminal procedure." The case involved a man named Clarence Gideon, who in a pencil-written letter to the Supreme Court argued that he had been denied legal counsel and was therefore being held in prison unconstitutionally. In August, Mondale replied, but not as the Florida attorney general anticipated. Mondale agreed that states' rights should be protected from federal encroachment, but he believed even more strongly that it was both "fair and feasible" for states to supply counsel to destitute defendants. "I would welcome," he concluded, "the courts' imposition of a requirement of appointment of counsel in all state felony prosecutions."

Encouraged by University of Minnesota law professor Yale Kamisar, Mondale pursued the issue further and sent copies of his correspondence to the Massachusetts attorney general, who in turn handed it to the chief of the Division of Civil Rights and Civil Liberties for the state, who wrote a brief in support of Gideon. The Massachusetts attorney general, Kamisar, and Mondale persuaded twenty-one other states to join their brief against Florida. The Supreme Court in *Gideon v. Wainwright* unanimously agreed that Gideon had a right to counsel (at public expense if need be), arguing that, in Justice Hugo Black's words, "Lawyers in criminal courts are necessities, not luxuries." The large number of attorneys general weighing in on Gideon's side made a big impression on the court. Mondale had made his first mark.[12]

Several others in Humphrey's circle also came of age making important political contributions. Don Fraser, another University of Minnesota Law School graduate, worked as an office boy in Humphrey's 1948 campaign. He was elected in 1954 to the state senate, where he served for eight years; then voters sent him to the U.S. Congress for sixteen years. After a bruising defeat in the 1978 DFL contest for the Senate nomination, Fraser was elected mayor of Minneapolis and served for fourteen years.

All of the movements foretold in those books had their expression in Minnesota—none of them so ultimately divisive as the environmental and wilderness movements. Another member of Humphrey's circle, Miles Lord, chose the judiciary as his vocation. Lord won election as Minnesota's attorney general in 1954 and again in 1958. He resigned in 1960 to accept appointment as a U.S. attorney in Minnesota. In 1966 President Lyndon Johnson appointed him a federal district judge. Lord's motto—"if you're going to be a judge, judge"—placed him in the center of two crucial environmental cases in Minnesota.[13]

In 1955, when much of the best and easiest-to-remove iron ore had been dug from the Iron Range, the Reserve Mining Company at Silver Bay began taking a lower grade of ore that required processing to remove the ore from the "tailings"—the soil and rock surrounding it. Reserve Mining captured the ore and dumped the tailings into Lake Superior. As Minnesota Public Radio reporter Stephanie Hemphill counted it, "They dumped enough to fill a railroad car every two minutes. They did this around the clock, for twenty-five years." By 1964, Walter Sve had to go seven miles out from shore to fish in clean water. Residents as far away as Duluth started drinking bottled water, afraid of the city water that came from the lake. At the same time, Reserve Mining provided a good living for about three thousand workers and their families, and the town of Silver Bay flourished. As long as the complaint was primarily aesthetic, it didn't win many converts, but when the Environmental Protection Agency discovered asbestos-like fibers in the water, the battle was on.[14]

Nearly a year into the court case, after a particularly testy exchange between the judge and the officers of Reserve Mining, Judge Lord ordered the company to stop dumping, effective immediately. The company appealed and was allowed another three years to find an alternative method of dumping. Lord's action—which many businesspeople considered rash and punitive and which many environmentalists cheered—established government, not industry, as the entity setting pollution standards. Lord could not have done more if he'd been in the Senate. In 1976, finding that Lord had "assumed the mantle of the advocate," the Eighth Circuit removed him from the case.[15]

Lord also presided over a case at the heart of Minnesota's political life in the 1960s. By 1910, more than a million acres of forestland (about two percent of Minnesota's area) had been designated Superior National Forest, and the area expanded several times before the publication of Sigurd Olson's 1956 book, which outlined his concerns about the loss of wilderness. Olson's wasn't the first voice, but he joined a growing chorus of people worried about the speed at which logging and mining, as well as motor-propelled recreation, was eliminating real wilderness. What good was it to get away from it all, only to find "it all" replicated, within earshot, on the next lake over?[16]

In 1964, Congress passed the Wilderness Act, defining wilderness in nearly poetic terms: "an area where the earth and its community of life are untrammeled by man, where man himself is a visitor who does not remain," a place where "the imprint of man's work [is] substantially unnoticeable." In short, this bill prohibited roads, buildings, vehicles, and motors and thrilled canoeists but alarmed those who had had access to the Boundary Waters by motorboat and logging truck. The Boundary Waters Canoe Area (BWCA) was included in the act, but because of its history of mixed use it already showed the inroads of machines and logging. Secretary of Agriculture Orville Freeman appointed a committee to make recommendations. The committee heard impassioned arguments for and against limiting further non-wilderness uses of the area. Many Minnesotans, like Olson, "saw logging as a violation of sacred space and outboard motors as a disruption of a sacramental experience."[17]

Lodge owners and outfitters saw the end of their livelihoods. Some county officials worried, too, about so much land being taken off the tax rolls. The result was an increase in the no-cut zone and an increase in the number of portages opened to motorboats and snowmobiles. Power logging near canoe routes was banned during the summer months. In 1971 the state tightened the motorcraft regulations, and in 1972 the Minnesota Public Interest Research Group (MPIRG) sued the U.S. Forest Service to prevent logging. The case landed on the docket of District Judge Miles Lord, who ruled in favor of MPIRG, banning the logging of virgin forests. The next year the appeals court reversed his decision but only temporarily. The end of wilderness logging was in sight.[18]*

*

George Selke, who had served under Governor Freeman as state commissioner of conservation, chaired the committee.

A few women helped build Hubert's house. Though never elected to public office, they were politically active for decades. When the Red Wing activist Eugenie Anderson sought advice about how she might effect change in the world after World War II, she came to Professor Humphrey, whom she had heard speak on the radio. She was an avid student and he a talented teacher and she a good ally in his reorientation of the DFL in 1948. They went together to the 1948 Democratic convention, she as a national committeewoman. In 1949 President Harry S Truman appointed her ambassador to Denmark, at which she was a great success—intellectually, strategically, and socially, learning to speak Danish with skill, the first woman to be named ambassador for the United States. She was unsuccessful, however, in her bid for the 1958 DFL nomination for Senate, the nod going that year to Congressman Eugene McCarthy. Later, President Kennedy sent her to Bulgaria; afterward she served as a U.S. delegate to the United Nations.[19]

Geri Joseph met up with Humphrey in 1945, when she was a University of Minnesota journalism student and managing editor of the *Minnesota Daily* and he was a mayoral candidate. He bounded into her office to let her know what he was going to do as mayor as well to tell her that the *Daily* should campaign for housing for returning veterans. He won her over, and she moved wholeheartedly into the Humphrey camp. She went on to work for the *Minneapolis Tribune*. She chaired the state party and attended several Democratic national conventions, becoming the first woman to chair a major committee. Presidents Kennedy, Johnson, and Carter named her to presidential commissions; Jimmy Carter also appointed her ambassador to the Netherlands. Fittingly, she spent ten years at the Hubert Humphrey Institute of Public Affairs at the University of Minnesota at the end of her career (Art Naftalin settled there, too).[20]

Though not early enough to support or defend Coya Knutson in her political aspirations in the 1950s, the women's movement forced changes in the DFL in the 1960s and later. In 1949, the DFL encouraged Cornelia Gjesdahl Knutson—a hotelkeeper and local political activist from Oklee—to run for the state legislature. This Julliard-trained farmwoman sang her way to success in 1950 and 1952. In 1954, however, when she set her sights on Congress, the DFL backed another (somewhat more conventional and less Norwegian- and rural-accented) candidate. Knutson defied the party, ran, and won; she was the first woman from Minnesota to serve in Congress (and the last until Betty McCollum took her seat in 2001). She also won the admiration of Speaker of the House Sam Rayburn, who, Coya remembered, told her when she arrived in Washington that "she did the impossible, so she can have whatever committee she wants." She chose the powerful Agriculture Committee, reflecting one of her two key legislative interests—protection of family farmers and student loans for college students.[21]

Coya showed her independence again in 1956, when she refused to support Adlai Stevenson's bid to become the Democratic presidential nominee. She didn't care that he might pick Humphrey as his running mate (he didn't); she thought his agricultural ideas were not as good as those of Estes Kefauver, whom she did support. Humphrey, who valued loyalty beyond almost everything else, did not forgive or forget. In 1958, just before the election, a letter purportedly written by Coya's husband appeared in newspapers all over the state:

> Coya, I want you to tell the people of the 9th District this Sunday that you are through in politics. That you want to go home and make a home for your husband and son. As your husband I compel you to do this. I'm tired of being torn apart from my family. I'm sick and tired of having you run around with other men all the time and not your husband. I love you, honey.

The DFL did not come to her aid or defense, and Coya lost by just under a thousand votes. She did not run again—nor did she return to what had for a long time been a very unhappy home for her.[22]

Eugene McCarthy, too, stood on the periphery of this group and always had ambivalence about it. He was not part of the University of Minnesota cohort, and he was not a political scientist. He was a Catholic, a poet and philosopher. They were Minneapolis; he was St. Paul. Where Humphrey was gregarious and warm, McCarthy was private and aloof, "little given to public emotion," according to his biographer. He always kept himself a bit distant from, even a bit above, in his own estimation, the Humphrey crowd. Even so, he had cooperated with Humphrey and the others who exiled the communists in 1948 and accepted (though he did not easily acknowledge) Humphrey's support in his congressional campaigns.* Their politics—until 1968—were similar. McCarthy's triumph over Eugenie Anderson for the DFL endorsement for Senate in 1958 had to have rankled Humphrey, but it didn't come close to McCarthy's failure to endorse Humphrey in 1968.

Everything seemed to change in 1968. As Bob Dylan described it, "America was wrapped in a blanket of rage." Paul Ehrlich's book *Population Bomb* portrayed growth as dangerous and promised starvation would stare us in the face. A group of women formed the National Abortion Action Rights League, while other groups "raised consciousness" and protested their relegation to domestic tasks (second-class citizenship) in the civil rights and other movements. In 1967, Tom Wolfe's *Electric Kool-Aid Acid Test* told of LSD use and culture. Were drugs really everywhere? Malcolm X had been assassinated in 1965. Martin Luther King, Jr.'s assassination in 1968 threw the civil rights movement into disarray and brought rioters into the streets of most major northern cities. The Black Power version of the movement showed itself at the Olympics that year when, during the American national anthem, two victorious African American athletes stood with gloved right fists raised in a Black Power salute.[23]

*

McCarthy's biographer writes that Humphrey supported the McCarthy campaign, though McCarthy himself never mentioned it. Humphrey's biographer writes that the Humphrey campaign even gave McCarthy money in 1968 (no doubt for a mix of generous and anti-Kennedy strategic reasons).

Out of a meeting in Minneapolis in 1968 the American Indian Movement was born with the aim of improving conditions, resisting harassment, fighting discrimination. Urban Indians especially—Ojibwe and Dakota primarily but not exclusively—agreed to act in community to bring changes. The leaders included Clyde Bellecourt (White Earth), Dennis Banks, George Mitchell, and Patricia Bellanger (Leech Lake), and Eddie Benton-Banai (Lac Courte Oreilles). In addition to helping each other, AIM in Minnesota and a growing web of AIM groups in other urban places focused on the revival of Indian culture, especially Indian spirituality.[24]

The Tet Offensive in January shocked Americans; the North Vietnamese showed themselves to be strong, effective, and resilient. A greater shock was the revelation of the slaughter of Vietnamese civilians in what came to be called the My Lai Massacre. The shooting of four Kent State students by members of the American National Guard was still in the future, as was the bombing of a math building at the University of Wisconsin. But an antiwar movement was coalescing.

Eugene McCarthy broke with the leaders of the national Democratic Party—and with President Johnson—when he declared his candidacy for the Democratic nomination for president in 1968. His issue? The end of the war. His brand of poetic and philosophic politicking appealed to students, who shaved and cleaned up—went "Clean for Gene"—and threw themselves into the work of the New Hampshire primary. McCarthy surprised the political pundits, the party, Lyndon Johnson, probably even himself when he garnered 42 percent of the vote to Johnson's 49. In March, Johnson declared he would neither seek nor accept nomination for the presidency in November. This was the chance Hubert Humphrey, who by then was vice president, had waited and planned for, dreamed of for twenty-five years; only Gene McCarthy and Robert Kennedy were challenging his nomination.[25]

Robert Kennedy's assassination in June 1968 left only Humphrey's old friend McCarthy barring Humphrey's path to the Oval Office. But Humphrey could not bring himself to break with Johnson on the war—to do so would be disloyal to his friend and president. He simply could not do it.

In the midst of literally bloody battles outside the convention hall in Chicago and figuratively bloody battles on the convention floor, the 1968 Democratic National Convention did indeed nominate Hubert Humphrey for the presidency. McCarthy did not, like the Dixiecrats twenty years earlier, walk out of the hall and the party, but neither did he give up his own campaign for the presidency. So, there they stood—McCarthy and Humphrey—face to face. They both lost, and Richard

Nixon won the presidency in November. The only unity the two men enjoyed after 1968 was the certainty of each that the other had foiled his political ambitions. The two men were identical in their bitterness.[26*]

In 1973, *Time Magazine* ran a cover story titled "Minnesota: A State That Works," which filled pages with accounts of the great state: "Some of the nation's most agreeable qualities are evident there: courtesy and fairness, honesty, a capacity for innovation, hard work, intellectual adventure, and responsibility." Clean politics, clean companies (Honeywell, Control Data, Univac, 3M), the Mayo Clinic ("a secular Lourdes"), the Tyrone Guthrie Theater, a tradition of civic activism and public philanthropy. Sure, "its winters are as hard as the Ice Age," its mosquitoes "seem half the size of dive bombers," and its Native Americans are "the most poverty-stricken residents," but Minnesotans had a passion for trying to fix things and believed that fixing was possible. Moreover, they were willing to pay for it. Following the 1967 riots in North Minneapolis, a group of Minneapolis people created the Urban Coalition to do something about it. Minnesota's voters had recently elected as governor Wendell Anderson, who campaigned on a promise to raise taxes so as to equalize public education funding in the state. Minnesota was a state that believed in taxation![27]

The picture was true and also too rosy. The Vietnam War and the 1968 election certainly rent the DFL in Minnesota; so did other wars of the 1960s and 1970s. Riots in North Minneapolis had resulted in the election of former police chief and Republican and conservative Charlie Stenvig as mayor in 1969. In attempts to make the Minnesota caucus system (and the state and national Democratic parties) more representative, the party changed the rules for the selection of delegates. The effect was to emphasize and institutionalize intra-party differences and polarize the party. George McGovern, the 1972 Democratic presidential nominee, from South Dakota, lost the vote in every state except Massachusetts.

The environmental movement appealed to many Minnesotans. It also divided the DFL's urban/range coalition. In 1974 the voters of Minnesota's Eighth Congressional District in northern Minnesota elected Jim Oberstar, who largely sided with the land and business owners in battles over the BWCA. Congressman Don Fraser, representing the interests of his largely middle-class, urban constituents, had enthusiastically supported the preservation and restricted use of the BWCA. He received the DFL nomination for the Senate in 1978 but was defeated in the party primary by Robert Short, a rich Minneapolis businessman who pleased the sportsmen and the traditional DFLers on the Iron Range but alien-

*

To Humphrey, loyalty was the most important value; to McCarthy, principle. Neither ever forgave the other.

ated pro-choice and equal rights members in the Twin Cities. That split
paved the way for the election of Republican Al Quie.

However, the issue that delivered the most severe blows to the house
that Hubert built was abortion. In 1973, in the *Roe v. Wade* decision written by Justice Harry Blackmun (from St. Paul) and concurred by four
others including Chief Justice Warren Burger (friends since childhood
with Blackmun), the Supreme Court ruled that, while not unqualified,
"the right of personal privacy includes the abortion decision." The DFL
coalition had been made up of urban liberals, Scandinavian leftists, and
working-class and African American women and men who shared
Humphrey's vision of government as an instrument of good. The
Supreme Court decision incinerated the ties that bound the coalition.
Catholic DFLers committed themselves to electing people at the national,
state, even local levels who would work to criminalize abortion. Feminist DFLers committed themselves to electing people at the national,
state, and local levels to uphold the court's decision. All other DFLers had
to array themselves somewhere between the two camps, but no "somewhere" could be found. Neither side could countenance a middle position, and virtually no politician (or voter) could find one. One moderate
and thoughtful state legislator, John Brandl (an economics professor and
later dean of the Humphrey Institute of Public Policy at the University
of Minnesota), proposed an abortion compromise in 1990 that did succeed in uniting the two sides—against his proposal.[28]

Humphrey's death in 1978 played a role in ending this phase of DFL
dominance in Minnesota—in part by removing his leadership and his
vote-getting strength at the top of the ticket. Mondale was also out of the
state. In 1976, Democratic presidential nominee Jimmy Carter asked
Senator Walter Mondale to join his ticket as the candidate for vice president. After Carter agreed to his proposal to energize the position—in
effect, to reinvent the job of vice president—Mondale agreed. In November 1976, American voters turned out Gerald Ford (who had taken office
after Nixon's resignation in 1974) and elected Carter and Mondale. Mondale had toyed with the idea of running himself but discarded it, so Minnesota did not yet have a president, but it had its second vice president
in twenty years.[29]

Arrogance and ambition played roles in the fall of the house of
Humphrey, too. Wendell Anderson made a serious misjudgment—and
destroyed his own political future—when he resigned as governor in
1976, paving the way for Lieutenant Governor Rudy Perpich to succeed
him and appoint him to complete Mondale's term in the Senate. If he
had waited, he would almost certainly have been elected to the Senate
in 1978. Hubert Humphrey had returned to the Senate in 1970 and served

until his death in early 1978; Governor Perpich appointed Humphrey's widow, Muriel, to serve the remaining eleven months of her husband's term.

In 1978, then, both of Minnesota's U.S. Senate seats as well as the governorship were open. The voters of Minnesota—in a greater than 70 percent turnout—elected Republicans to all three positions. Al Quie became governor. Rudy Boschwitz and Dave Durenberger were the new senators. In addition, the Minnesota House went from a 103–31 DFL majority to a dead balance of DFLers and Independent Republicans (IR, as the Minnesota party identified itself), with a Republican speaker of the house.[30]

The DFL never had a lock on Minnesota politics. Various strong and thoughtful Independent Republicans, from Harold Stassen through Luther Youngdahl to Charlie Stenvig, C. Elmer Anderson, and Dave Durenberger, have appealed to Minnesota voters. In 1975—after the Watergate scandal capsized Richard Nixon's presidency—and for twenty years, Minnesota's Republicans took "Independent Republican" as their statewide designation. Perhaps they also wanted to have their own name—as the DFL did.[31]

The Independent Republicans, especially under Governor Arne Carlson (1991–99) and Senator Dave Durenberger (1978–95), found just the right combination of economic and social positions to please and to speak for the majority of the voters. Economic restraint and active social policy were the two wheels of the bicycle they rode.

Minnesota state politics—like American politics more generally—crashed at the intersection of a newly reawakened religious consciousness and a new brand of partisan politics. Many Catholics in the "traditional" DFL alliance could not tolerate the legalized abortion that resulted from the 1972 *Roe v. Wade* Supreme Court decision; the feminist caucus could not abide an anti-abortion plank in the state DFL platform. The two sides fought out their battles in precinct, district, and state caucuses and then in state elections, leaving the Democratic Party wounded and bleeding. As more and more people who defined themselves as religiously conservative moved into the Republican ranks, the Republican Party also moved to the right. Its social conservatism caught up with its financial conservatism. Moderate Republicans found themselves less and less at home in the new Republican Party but without many choices about where they would go, either. Both parties tried to bridge what was turning into a widening crack in the ice.

Humphrey had been wildly successful, and many of the most important, talented, and experienced DFLers followed him into federal office, leaving the state DFL slightly understaffed and under equipped to sustain the party from the 1970s through the 1990s. Walter Mondale might have had the skills to do it, but after a time in the Senate he was elected as vice president under Jimmy Carter. Orville Freeman went to Washington; Eugenie Anderson to Copenhagen. And so on.

Carleton College political scientist Paul Wellstone emerged as a firebrand on the political landscape in the 1980s. He was elected to the U.S. Senate in 1990 and again in 1996 as the result of an unconventional campaign run out of a green bus and outside of full DFL supervision. As a relative newcomer and as a Jewish man not from Minnesota, Wellstone had some ability to maneuver among the issues. A master politician, he put together what was, in effect, a Wellstone coalition. He didn't ride other coattails, nor did he have coattails that could carry others into office.

In 1998, Hubert Humphrey III, Mike Freeman, and Ted Mondale all sought the DFL nomination for governor. They ran against Norm Coleman, a former DFLer who was the sitting, Republican mayor of St. Paul. Among "my three sons" in the primary, Humphrey advanced to carry the DFL banner. Coleman picked up the Republican nomination; professional wrestler Jesse Ventura emerged as the Independent candidate. Perhaps reflecting the disarray in Minnesota's political parties, or Minnesotans' openness to third parties, or the brilliance of Ventura's campaign, Minnesota voters elected Ventura. He found the political wrestling more irritating and exhausting than the professional kind. He didn't say it in public, but he must have thought it easier to get pummeled by other men in costumes than by politicians and journalists in suits and dresses. He bruised easily in those contests.[32]

The election of this surprisingly thoughtful wrestler/showman—and his ability to draw votes from both Republicans and Democrats—left people in Minnesota and elsewhere puzzling over the state's political legacy and future. Perhaps he provided a distraction from the Humphrey legacy and a pause in the state's tortures over abortion. He thought his wife—thrust into the role of governor's wife—should be paid a salary. He did not care about the sexual preferences of his staff: that was their business, not his. He didn't have many negotiating skills and had to work with a Democratic state senate and a Republican house. He lowered taxes on cars and fishing licenses and gave tax rebates to the voters when the state found itself with a surplus. But the public spotlight on the governor's office shone harsher and more critical than the light that had shone on the ring. He resented the attention the media paid to his children and to his life away from St. Paul. At the end of one term, he gave up political office and largely disappeared from Minnesota. He was succeeded by a conservative Republican, Tim Pawlenty, who promised no new taxes and took a solid line on conservative issues: anti–gun control, anti-abortion, anti–gay rights. He was narrowly reelected in 2006, signaling the solidification of a rightward shift in Minnesota politics that had been in the works for some time.

Having promised to stay in the Senate for not more than two terms, Wellstone changed his mind and ran again in 2002, believing the Senate needed the voice of what he called "the Democratic wing of the Democratic party" in a nation that continued to move right and that, on the eve of the election, was moving into war. His death in a plane crash just days before the election left the DFL scrambling for a candidate. Their best bet: the former senator and vice president Walter Mondale, who had, most recently, served as U.S. ambassador to Japan. He agreed to run but was defeated by St. Paul mayor Norm Coleman.

In 1978, *Time Magazine* declared that Hubert's house had tumbled. Senator-elect Dave Durenberger predicted: "It's going to take a few years for the D.F.L to react to the loss of Hubert, and then it will be back." Whatever else the last thirty years might demonstrate, they tell loud and clear that the DFL of Hubert Humphrey will not be back. Senator Amy Klobuchar, the first woman elected by Minnesotans to hold a Senate seat in her own right, may have some of Humphrey's skills, but she is part of a new party, in a state with a changing political alignment.[33]

16

Walleye Quesadilla
& the New Minnesota

IN 2005, CHEF BARRY MEYERS took over the kitchen at the Gunflint Lodge at the Canadian end of the Gunflint Trail—forty-three miles inland from Grand Marais, another two hours and a bit from Duluth, five from the Twin Cities, seven from Rochester, eight from Pipestone. Only about two hundred people live year-round on the trail, not enough to keep the restaurant—Justine's—in business. So most of Meyers's customers were vacationers from the Gunflint, Hungry Jack, Golden Eagle, or other lodges. Or from local B&Bs, private cabins, campgrounds, or the BWCAW (Boundary Waters Canoe Area Wilderness).

The restaurant takes its name from Justine Kerfoot (1906–2001), whose plans to go to medical school collapsed when the Great Depression plunged her family into financial ruin and sent them to the north woods. The 1920s camp they found there had neither electricity nor telephone and could be reached only by a dirt track or, better, by water. It served mostly fishermen and deer hunters and sold groceries to local Indian trappers. It wasn't the first of the vacation camps "up north," but it and they shared a relatively small clientele of people who wanted to get away, to rough it, to be in nature. Falling in love with the place, Justine stayed, married, and ran the lodge for over fifty years, first with her mother, then with her husband, Bill, then with their son and daughter-in-law, and most recently with their grandson.[1]

Today dozens of lodges, camps, and retreats serve those vacationers (with only the occasional Indian trader) who hunger for the woods and lakes "up north." Sitting down there in Marshall, my Minnesota friends plotted how they could steal a weekend or a few days to get up there. It was like they had to fill their tanks with some fuel that was only available north of Hinckley. A walk in the woods—or more likely on the prairie nearby—or a weekend at Camden State Park helped, but only a little and not for long. Maybe it was the magic potion of pine and birch?

Every weekend (it used to be in the summer and now it's most of the year), the roads to northern Minnesota—Duluth then Grand Marais, Ely, Brainerd, Bemidji, Blackduck, Alexandria, Nevis, or just "the lake"—are clogged with traffic.* Some of the cars (or vans or SUVs) are pulling powerboats or bass boats, snowmobiles or dirt bikes, Airstreams or Winnebagos; others are loaded with canoes or bicycles or cross-country skis, tents, and sleeping bags.

Some of the people, like Justine Kerfoot in the old days, want the thrill of imagining that they might set foot where no other human ever has. They want to rough it by hiking or paddling in, by carrying their supplies and tent in a pack. They want to walk on the edge of danger. These people tend toward the northeast, the Boundary Waters Canoe Area, Superior and Chippewa national forests.

Others prefer a few more creature comforts. A "rustic" cabin (or what passes in the twenty-first century for rustic, with indoor bathrooms and heat and stove and refrigerator, at least), perhaps close enough to Lake Superior to skip stones and watch the iron ore boats at a distance, but no television or phones. They might go, for example, to Fenstad's in Little Marais, a small family-run operation that has jigsaw puzzles and games and sells bundles of wood so you can make your own fire on the beach.

Still others flock to resorts that cater to Americans' more modern vacation interests: gift shops, TVs, DVD and CD players, saunas, whirlpools, modern bathrooms, restaurants, activities for children, paddleboats, fishing off the dock. In the northeastern part of the state, Clearwater Lodge, for example, promises queen-sized beds and showers; Bearskin Lodge, gas fireplaces; Rockwood, popcorn poppers and coffeemakers. Hungry Jack provides a high-speed wireless Internet hotspot. Ruttger's Bay Lake Lodge—the "oldest family-owned resort in Minnesota," which celebrated its centennial in 1998—and Cragun's and Madden's near Brainerd, Arrowwood near Alexandria, and other resorts in the north-central part of the state offer, in addition, golf courses and waterskiing, tennis and fitness centers.[2]

Still more people go to their own lake cabins or camps or piece of property in the woods, their summer mobile home or vacation spot. For some, the place just next to heaven is where they can get away from it all; for others, it is where they can be freed of the restraints of "civilization" and glide through the woods on their snowmobiles or dirt bikes.

These outdoors people, then, don't all agree on what they want in the northland (a lake quiet enough to hear the loons or open enough to water ski, a retreat or a social gathering). For both kinds—and the mul-

*

"Up north" is not an expression that is used generally to talk about going to Moorhead or Ada or East Grand Forks or Crookston—those are every bit (and some more than a bit) farther north—but they are the farming north, not the land of pine and birch. As such, they don't excite the Minnesota imagination in the same way as the northeast and north-central parts of the state.

tiple variations in between—the outdoors promise enough adventure to make it interesting: moose, eagles, wolf, or cougar. Enough bears still live in these parts that one must be careful about leaving food around. And, wherever one goes up north, there is always fishing. Some people might do it out of a bass boat, others from a canoe, in a secret spot, with a guide. Some might just drop in a line off the dock. But fishing seems to bridge many differences.

The Department of Natural Resources issued about 630,000 licenses to Minnesota residents in 1957; in 2005 nearly 720,000 Minnesotans paid for the pleasure of fishing. Minnesotans will fish for whatever they can catch: 90,000 people paid additional fees to add a trout stamp to their license, and the smelt run in Lake Superior attracts thousands of eager anglers every spring. Still, no fish has quite the allure of the walleye.[3]

The walleye—one is tempted to say "the lowly walleye," but there is nothing lowly about this fish in this state—isn't the biggest Minnesota fish by a long shot. The prize for the biggest fish caught in the state goes to the 94-pound sturgeon netted in the Kettle River in 1994. Someone caught a 70-pound catfish in the St. Croix River; someone else, a 55-pound carp in Clearwater Lake (Wright County). The biggest walleye, caught in Seagull River in Cook County, weighed in at only 17½ pounds.[4]

But in Minnesota a small walleye is a prize far superior to these other, bigger fish, even superior to fish that are more fun to catch (a trout, of course, or a bass that will fight all the way into the boat); the walleye gives up as soon as it takes the hook. A few naysayers whisper that northerns (northern pike) taste better, but no serious walleye angler will ever agree. Walleyes, they declare, are the best fish to eat because they have fewer bones and don't taste as fishy.

In 1965, Governor Karl Rolvaag signed state legislation naming the walleye the state fish. The fishing season usually opens in mid-April for trout, late May for bass, June for muskies (muskellunge). When most Minnesotans talk about the fishing opener, however, they're referring to the walleye and northern opener that routinely falls on Mother's Day weekend. No self-respecting governor would sit out the opener to spend the weekend with mother. Instead, even those governors who don't fish before or after their terms of office cast a line to show they're regular guys (we haven't had a female governor yet) and true Minnesotans. The newspapers and local TV stations always report on whether the governor lands a walleye.[5]

Fishing serves to unite people; it has also deeply divided Minnesotans. An especially controversial and important set of court cases testing the meaning of nineteenth-century Indian treaty rights has focused on fishing rights. In the mid-1960s, several bands of Pacific Northwest Indians—led especially by a group of very savvy Native American women—began the work of reclaiming their fishing rights by staging fish-ins in the Puyallup River and pursuing their case through the courts. In 1974 federal judge George Boldt ruled that Washington could legally limit the fishing rights of non-Indians but not of Indians. On appeal, both the Ninth Circuit and the U.S. Supreme Court upheld the basic provisions of the Boldt decision. Various bands of Ojibwe people in Minnesota and Wisconsin began to pursue the reinstitution of their treaty rights in the 1980s.[6]

In 1990 the Mille Lacs Band of Ojibwe in Minnesota filed suit to regain its treaty-guaranteed fishing and hunting rights. In Washington, the battle was fought over salmon; in Minnesota, over the walleye and especially walleye fishing at Mille Lacs, considered by many to be "the best walleye habitat in the world." The case tested the meaning of 1837 and 1854 treaties between the U.S. government and the Ojibwe people. The 1837 treaty stipulated "The privilege of hunting, fishing, and gathering the wild rice, upon the lands, the rivers and the lakes included in the territory ceded, is guaranteed to the Indians, during the pleasure of the President of the United States." The 1854 treaty repeated the provision, in slightly different words: "Such of them as reside in the territory hereby ceded, shall have the right to hunt and fish therein, until otherwise ordered by the President." No president ever ordered a change in these provisions, but in the intervening years the Indians' rights to fish and hunt eroded through the whites' passion for fishing, state regulation, and the poverty and racism that kept Indians from fighting back.[7]

The prospect of Indians fishing at will and without limits provoked conflict threatening to turn into open warfare in 1994, when district judge Diana Murphy handed down her ruling in *Mille Lacs Band of Chippewa Indians et al. v. State of MN et al*. She ruled for continuation of the fishing and hunting rights reserved to the Mille Lacs band in the 1837 and 1854 treaties.[*] In a second phase of the trial, Judge Michael Davis ruled three years later that the Ojibwe were entitled to establish their own rules for hunting and fishing on reservation lands.[8]

Led by the former—and popular—Minnesota Vikings coach Bud Grant, an army of dedicated fishermen and resort owners in Wisconsin and Minnesota opposed the lifting of restrictions on Indian fishing, claiming that differing rules for whites and Indians was unconstitutional. They focused their objections, however, on Indians' spearing and netting during walleye-spawning season and argued that, if left to their own regulations, Indians would destroy walleye fishing—and the tourism industry—in northern Minnesota and Wisconsin. "It's 1 percent of the

*

The treaty provisions reserved fishing and hunting rights for the bands, not necessarily for individual Indians, so when individual Indians hunt or fish off-reservation they are subject to the same limits and regulations as white anglers. This was a point often misunderstood by the treaty-rights opponents.

population exercising their rights to the detriment of 99 percent," argued one of the protestors.[9]

Indians in Minnesota—and in the United States—faced new circumstances in the 1990s; the Mille Lacs Band's decision to pursue the lawsuit made both financial and social sense. The development of Indian gaming and the explosion of its casino business provided the Mille Lacs Band the cash reserves to pursue a suit. This was a new phenomenon to the Ojibwe (and the Dakota in other parts of the state), who had for so long been among the state's poorest people.

Long subject to racism, both covert and overt, Indians had largely been excluded from the national debate about civil rights, which to most Americans involved only African Americans. Indians did not vanish as Edward Curtis's photos suggested they would at the end of the nineteenth century, but they had become largely invisible to most white Americans and most white Minnesotans. The U.S. Supreme Court ruling that allowed Indian gaming subjected some Indians to too much visibility and vulnerability, anger and envy, all related to the increasing wealth of many of the bands.

Racism continued to infect Minnesotans, but there were also signs of change in dominant American attitudes toward Indians. As early as Earth Day 1971, Keep America Beautiful, Inc., created a public service announcement in which a traditionally dressed Indian (Iron Eyes Cody) paddled his canoe solo through littered water, then stepped onto a trash-strewn shore. The voice-over intoned: "Some people [read: Indians] have a deep, abiding respect for the natural beauty that was once this country, and some people [anyone who litters, presumably whites] don't." The closing shot showed Cody with one big tear rolling down his face, the narrator saying, "People start pollution; people can stop it." Keep America Beautiful reports that the commercial dramatically reduced litter—by as much as 88 percent in three hundred communities, thirty-eight states, and several countries. Environmental groups often turned to Indian images and motifs to sell a new environmental consciousness.[10]*

*

One might well argue that whites have long paired two ideas about Indians—that they were savages and that they were noble. In the nineteenth century and for most of the twentieth, the "savage" version triumphed; in the late twentieth century, the "noble" version took over in the public iconography.

Spirituality groups, too, found much to emulate in what they understood to be Indian culture, adopting a pastiche of Indian spiritual practices—sweat lodges, sage smudges, drumming, and dream catchers. Hollywood moviemakers rediscovered Indians and created a new kind of western in which Indians were wise and smart and whites careless and stupid (at best) or brutally ruthless (at worst). After decades of westerns portraying whites in white hats and Indians as bad guys (while not allowing Indian actors to play the roles), Thomas Berger's *Little Big Man* (novel 1964, movie 1970) poked fun at everyone, but none so much as the hapless George Armstrong Custer. This comedic western was followed in 1991 by Kevin Costner's more serious and romantic *Dances with Wolves,* which portrayed Indians as spiritual, both parents to and heirs of the American frontier tradition, trying to defend their land against encroachment. Costner's film did away with "Kemosabe," "Ugh," and "How," instead providing subtitles for the Lakota- and Paiute-speaking characters, presenting Indians as intelligent and intelligible.

In 1991, *Dances with Wolves* won seven Oscars, including the award for Best Picture. Movie critic Roger Ebert noted the sociological value of the film:

> The movie makes amends, of a sort, for hundreds of racist and small-minded Westerns that went before it. By allowing the Sioux to speak in their own tongue, by entering their villages and observing their ways, it sees them as people, not as whooping savages in the sights of an Army rifle. This is one of the year's best films.

The movie traveled on the road of changing attitudes toward Indians and paved the way for others to travel farther.[11]

While many white anglers stood with Bud Grant to oppose Indian treaty rights, a great many white Minnesotans and Wisconsinites stepped in to defend and protect both Indians and Indian rights. White volunteers stood between Indian and white anglers, trying to prevent violence and to smother some of the fire surrounding the issue. Judge Murphy's decision, upheld through the Supreme Court, settled the legal issues, anyway.

Walleye fishing did not disappear; neither did the tourism industry. The bands regulated the Indian harvest; the state continued to enforce limits on other sport and commercial fishermen and, in addition, stocked Minnesota lakes with 41 million walleye fry in 1999 and another 32 million fry in 2001, which helped relieve tension and provide enough walleye for one of Barry Meyers's best concoctions—walleye quesadilla.

The walleye is essentially Minnesotan; so, increasingly, are the quesadilla and burrito, sushi and teriyaki, pad thai and pho, Asian eggplant, bulgogi, injera, and lemongrass. Minnesota's largest immigrant groups in the nineteenth century—Germans and Scandinavians—shaped much of the early infrastructure and character of the state. The St. Cloud–born Coen brothers highlighted and lampooned that character in their movie *Fargo* (1996), in which the players' naiveté—emphasized by their broad Scandinavian-German accents—made murderous men seem ineffectual and the intelligence of a pregnant sheriff surprising (how can someone who sounds so dumb and sweet be so smart?).

Minnesota radio personality and novelist Garrison Keillor locates his Lake Wobegon in Fargoland, too. Much of the humor of his monologues (and novels) derives from pitting his radio-show *Prairie Home Companion* characters' lack of guile against a more sophisticated and ironic world, where more often than not innocence and earnestness triumph. Bob's Bank in the mobile home operates just fine, thank you, as does the Side Track Tap. If Bob's Pretty Good Grocery doesn't have it, Keillor tells us, you don't need it.[12]

Sinclair Lewis's *Main Street* is only a few miles from Lake Wobegon, so the two authors are imagining virtually the same people, a half century apart. The people haven't changed much, but the narrator has—from Lewis's bitter indictment in 1920 of the self-satisfied people who populated Main Street to Keillor's more affectionate lampooning of their self-righteousness and admiration of their upright sturdiness.[13]

Howard Mohr, one of the regulars on Keillor's *A Prairie Home Companion* in the 1980s, published *How to Talk Minnesotan,* including some pieces he wrote for *PHC.* His lessons are overdrawn, of course, and stores shelve the book in their humor, not their regional sections. Even so, Mohr captures a language and culture that Minnesotans, especially those in or from the west-central and southern parts of the state, recognize.

Outsiders do need some translation of idioms like "that's different" and "not too bad." If, as Mohr recommends, you don't accept food until it's offered three times and don't stand too close or ask too many questions, you do have a better chance of being considered polite. Both rural and urban Minnesotans recognize Mohr's attention to reserve and restraint: If you say, "Oh, great, just wonderful, terrific. I love it!" he warns, "you might as well paste a bumper sticker on your forehead that says I'M NOT FROM AROUND HERE."[14]

Perhaps having learned from Keillor, Mohr, and others that these ways of talking and acting are not "normal" (even if they seem common), Minnesotans in the last several decades have begun to identify a vaguely defined set of cultural characteristics as "Minnesota Nice." The set usually includes a polite friendliness, an aversion to confrontation, a tendency toward understatement, a disinclination to make a fuss or stand out, emotional restraint, and self-deprecation. If those characteristics describe you and you're a Minnesotan, you likely think Minnesota Nice is benign, even nice. If, however, you wave your arms when you talk or blow up, ask too many questions, tell too much, talk too much about yourself—you may not applaud Minnesota Nice. The pro-Minnesota Nicers think that nice makes the world work a little better, smoother, more easily. Words said cannot be unsaid; hurt people hurt people, so why not save the words and hold back the hurt? But critics of Minnesota Nice call this behavior passive-aggressive and bridle at never knowing for sure what Minnesotans think. Nicers, they say, pretend consensus where none exists and fail to express disagreement or emotion directly; the reserve feels cool, even cold. Racist, too.[15]*

The roots of the concept of Minnesota Nice may rest with or in response to Garrison Keillor and others, but many of the behaviors almost certainly relate to the state's ethnic, religious, and political history.

Scandinavians have a reputation for being reserved. *Babette's Feast*, both in Danish writer Isak Dinesen's short story and the movie, tells of a French woman cooking a miracle of a meal for a dozen pietistic Danes who refuse to (or cannot) relish or give into the pleasures of her magnificent food. Philosopher Søren Kierkegaard's work and life express a similar holding back. The films of Swedish director Ingmar Bergman take as a recurring theme the inability of his Swedish characters to break from their solitary silence. Swedish artist Edvard Munch painted the loudest silent scream in modern art.[16]

The Norwegian American Minnesotan Thorstein Veblen invented the phrase "conspicuous consumption" to describe Americans' increasing use of things in the late nineteenth and early twentieth centuries to denote identity (and status). To say his description should not be mistaken for praise would be Minnesota-like understatement.[17]

People often ascribe Scandinavian spiritual darkness to the physical darkness that descends from mid-October to mid-April. Perhaps Minnesota's brighter and longer winter days lightened that Scandinavian darkness or kept it from settling in this new place. The Scandinavian restraint, though, seeps into Minnesota's culture.

Lutherans of the nineteenth and early twentieth centuries had a reputation for restraint—from consuming alcohol, dancing, playing cards and games—disdained by the more liberal synods of the Lutheran fellowship. Norwegian Lutherans in Minnesota and nationally fought energetically and persistently for the prohibition of the sale and manufacture of alcohol. Unlike many other religious women, who worked through the Women's Christian Temperance Union, most Norwegian women organized through their churches. Their opposition was both social and religious.[18]

Andrew J. Volstead, Norwegian American congressman from west-central Minnesota for twenty years, gave his name to the prohibition legislation that outlawed the manufacture and sale of alcohol in the United States from 1919 to 1933. Throughout the Midwest, temperance and prohibition campaigns divided communities along ethnic and religious lines (Irish and Bavarian Catholics on one side, Scandinavian and German Lutherans on the other).[19]

Everywhere in the United States, more Scandinavian immigrants—

*

A recent billboard ad for Minneapolis's deeply Scandinavian Thrivent, Inc., formerly Lutheran Brotherhood, made fun of itself with this tagline: "Lutherans Swear By Thrivent—okay, maybe they don't actually swear..."

63 percent of Norwegians and 46 percent of Swedes in 1900—opted for rural rather than urban lives. In Minnesota, it was 72 percent of Norwegians and 62 percent of Swedes. The second-generation Norwegians and Swedes were even more rural than the first. Norwegian American historian Odd Lovoll reads this rural preference among Norwegians as evidence and opportunity for them to maintain, even intensify, their ethnic identity. As late as the 1950s, the Norwegian language could be heard in normal conversation in various small towns in west-central and south-central Minnesota.[20]*

* *While it's true that more Scandinavians than Germans migrated to Minnesota, the Scandinavians include Swedes, Norwegians, Danes, and sometimes Finns. Divided up by nationality, more Germans arrived than any single Scandinavian group.*

No doubt much of Minnesota Nice is rooted in this Scandinavian, Lutheran, and rural soil. Keillor's and Mohr's Minnesotans are country people who say things like "Uf dah" and "You betcha" and "that's different," with a Scandinavian accent.

Scandinavians are not the only contributors to Minnesota Nice. When Father Louis Hennepin wrote about his time around the Great Lakes in the 1680s, he observed the difficulty in knowing when Indian people were persuaded, "For their civility hinder[s] them from making any objection or contradicting what is said to them." This sounds a lot like Minnesota Nice, too.[21]

Germans, too, contributed. They do not have a reputation for reserve or "niceness." Germans reputedly are direct (even with their often long and complex German sentences). There's no particular darkness ascribed to the German approach to life: no one would accuse Beethoven (or Mozart) of understatement; Wagner's operas thrive on emotional excess. Germans share in some of the piety of Scandinavians, but when they divided themselves into Lutheran and Catholic, their religious expressions and rules took separate direction. Lutheran German Americans shared the pro-temperance attitudes of their co-religionists. Catholic German Americans, however, actively opposed attempts at prohibition and ran some of the best breweries in Minnesota (public and private)—Hamm's, Schell's, and so forth.

German immigrants and German Americans for several generations enjoyed (and still enjoy) polka bands, dancing, Gast houses, and skat games. They knew how to enjoy themselves and did. German immigrants may have learned a bit about restraint from living around and among Scandinavian neighbors, but they no doubt learned more about restraint, withdrawal, and the danger of differences during World Wars I and II.

World War I forced many German Americans into silence or compliance, certainly into keeping their views to themselves and their differences hidden. Better to smile and avoid conflict. The quick turn from World War I to World War II must have kept German Americans on the defensive, too. They volunteered and accepted the draft in both wars; German Americans at home sacrificed and contributed to the home front efforts as enthusiastically as other Minnesotans.

While Scandinavian Minnesotans turned their numbers into votes and their ethnic unity into political power, German Minnesotans could not. The Catholic/Lutheran/Free Thinker/Amish/Mennonite division led German American voters to different political alliances. Besides, there was no "Germany" to emigrate from until after German unification in 1871, only Saxony, Bavaria, Prussia, and other regions of German-speaking people. No German political bloc formed. The list of Minnesota governors is full of Scandinavian names, empty of German ones.[22]

The language—that they did have in common. Even Mrs. Court—that German American woman who lived out the Depression years in rural Stearns County—was careful into her eighties (in the 1980s) about where she spoke German. She and husband Pete never taught or encouraged their own sons and daughter to speak it. People made fun of them when they went into town, she said, even though the town was St. Cloud—itself predominantly German American throughout Mrs. Court's life.

Germans and Scandinavians were never the only immigrants to Minnesota, but the time of their arrival, their group movements and settlement patterns, and their large number set the tone and determined the overall contours of the state. Two-thirds of Minnesotans in 1900 had roots in Germany, Norway, or Sweden. Other immigrants in much smaller numbers had made their way to Minnesota in the nineteenth century. Croats, Finns, Serbians, Lithuanians, and others flooded onto the Iron Range, where they could find jobs and often relatively better-paying work.[23]

In the early twentieth century, Italians, Russians, and Jews settled in the state. African Americans and Central Americans and Mexicans in increasing numbers moved to Minnesota. In the late twentieth century, Minnesota became home to the largest Hmong population outside of Laos and California, the largest population of Somalis in the United States, and one of the largest Liberian populations outside of Liberia. In 1900, nearly 70 percent of Minnesotans had arrived from Germany, Sweden, or Norway. In 2000, 77 percent of new immigrants had come from Asia, Latin America, and Africa.[24]

Non–Northern Europeans have been Minnesotans for a century. These immigrants—many now citizens—have contributed essential work to the mines in northern Minnesota, to meat- and beet-processing plants, to farming, to small businesses (and big ones, too), to the state's political identity and leanings. Their numbers have swelled and enlivened the congregations of existing religious communities, and newcomers have

built their own churches, synagogues, temples, and other places of worship. They have brought their music to the airwaves and to the streets.
They have brought their food preferences to newly invigorated farmers'
markets and grocery stores all over the state.

My mother specialized in meat and potatoes (always served with an
iceberg lettuce salad and a canned or frozen vegetable: corn, peas, or
green beans), chicken noodle and tomato soups, chicken potpies, and
macaroni and cheese. My dad worked at a meat-packing plant, so we ate
a lot of meat—"cervelat" sausage, hamburger, pork chops, pot roasts, and
bacon. In season, we ate a lot of tomatoes and watermelon, cantaloupe,
corn on the cob, and jelly that my mother put up from the grapes in the
backyard. That was a "normal" diet in our neighborhood and among our
friends. My mother's herb and spice shelf included salt, pepper, cinnamon, nutmeg, allspice, onion salt, chicken and beef bouillon, bay leaf,
Lowry's Seasoned Salt, and chili powder for one of her five ethnic spe-
cialties—chili. Her four other ethnic dishes were potato dumplings,
chow mein, goulash, and Chef Boyardee spaghetti. My mother learned
how to make the dumplings from her mother, who had learned from
her Norwegian-born mother. She had not grown up eating the other
dishes but had discovered, enjoyed, and found ways to fix what would
satisfy her family. Except for the dumplings, these ethnic meals bore
only a distant resemblance to their origins.

Garrison Keillor, among others, has long teased Minnesotans about
eating white as in bland (Wonder Bread and Uncle Ben's Instant Rice),
white as in color (cream of mushroom soup, tuna-noodle casserole, and
mashed potatoes), and white as in ethnic origin (krumkake, potato
dumplings, lefse, and lutefisk). But the eating preferences of newer
immigrants have invigorated the foods available to all Minnesotans.
Already in the nineteenth century, Chinese restaurants offered chow
mein and chop suey (hardly native, definitely adapted dishes). Italians
taught Minnesotans about spaghetti with meatballs, lasagna, and ravi-
oli, which became available in Italian restaurants and then on menus of
non-Italian establishments and then in cans on grocery-store shelves.
Oh, and don't forget pizza.

Mexican food, too, has had a profound effect on what and how Minnesotans eat: corn chips and salsa, guacamole, jicama, and jalapenos are
sold regularly in otherwise "white" stores. McDonald's, responding to
American hunger for slightly lighter fare (from time to time), first offered
wraps—of no clear ethnic derivation but clearly not typically "American." Then, when McDonald's developed and customers flocked to Chip-
otle's, the ethnically inspired culinary revolution became clear. The phe-

nomenon has affected different parts of the state in different ways.* The causes of the culinary shift are many but must be credited to ethnic groups that have brought and taught other ethnic groups about their culturally important—and tasty—foods.[25]

Most of the newer "ethnic" restaurants are in the Twin Cities, but the greatest change in Minnesota foodways in the past two decades has occurred in the opening of Mexican restaurants in Willmar, Melrose, Hutchinson, and Fairmont and Thai and Vietnamese places in Jackson, Baxter, and Two Harbors. Wherever Hmong people have settled in the United States, they have reinvigorated or reinvented farmers' markets— in San Francisco, Los Angeles, and Stockton, California, in Vancouver, Lowell, and Marblehead, Massachusetts; in Seattle and in Minnesota. Several programs in Minnesota explicitly assist the intensely rural Hmong people in raising culturally relevant foods—and flowers—for themselves and to sell in a wider market.[26]

Mexican Minnesotans and other Central and South American people have been part of the state's fabric for nearly a hundred years. More than 60 percent of the Latino people in the state are United States born. The number of Latinos in Minnesota grew from 54,000 in 1990 to more than 175,000 in 2004. In Pelican Rapids and St. James—home to many more recent immigrants who work in chicken- and turkey-processing plants, especially—one in four students in the public schools does not speak English at home. Somalis and Sudanese, Vietnamese, Hmong, and Liberians came—some of them directly from refugee camps—fleeing homelands at war. How much more traumatized these immigrants must have been than were Vilhelm Moberg's or Ole Rølvaag's Scandinavian immigrants, certainly forced from their homes by limited opportunity but hardly refugees of war. And Russians, especially Russian Jews, slipped through cracks in the Iron Curtain.[27]

Some Minnesotans, especially exurbanites—like many white Americans—are troubled by these new groups. Fear of ethnic groups seems to go hand in hand with downturns in the economy—even if those who are frightened are not themselves under particular threat. A Hmong population in St. Cloud, for example, faced enough resistance, even violence, that they abandoned Stearns County for friendlier surroundings. Mexican Minnesotans who have lived in the state for two generations are presumed new and feared to be illegal immigrants. Virtually none of the 16,000 Asian Indians in the state has received public assistance, but they are often presumed to be living off the state's generosity. Forgetting perhaps that their own ancestors also seemed unlikely to assimilate and forgetting that they may have resisted learning English themselves, many

*

The small town of Avon only recently "welcomed" its first McDonald's (the townspeople are divided over whether it represents a step forward or backward).

whites fear for the future of the state. What new Minnesota will Germans and Scandinavians, Irish and Croatians, Lithuanians, Lebanese and Russians, Latin Americans, Asians, and Africans make together?[28]

One of the greatest changes in Minnesota over the last two decades is related not to the state's ethnic composition but to its political orientation. Most of that has been the work not of the "new" Minnesotans but of the "old" moving right on the political spectrum. In the 1980s, Minnesota liberals—like liberals elsewhere in the United States—came to be called "card-carrying liberals," using the language that had discredited so many on the left in the 1950s under Wisconsin senator Joseph McCarthy. Conservative social policy—anti-abortion, anti-sex education, anti–stem cell research, and anti–gay rights—encouraged conservative economic policy. Minnesotans, who had long paid some of the highest taxes in the nation, in 2002 elected Republican Tim Pawlenty, who ran on a pledge of "no new taxes." Good to his word, he did not raise taxes, so education and social services—two causes for which Minnesotans had long been willing to pay high taxes—experienced deep cuts.

The international war on terrorism seemed a long way away, except to airline passengers and Somali immigrants—mostly Sunni Muslims—who found themselves under direct and indirect suspicion, their financial assistance for family and friends at home scrutinized and sometimes halted to ensure that none of their funds supported terrorists. Evidence of change back showed itself, perhaps, in 2006 when Keith Ellison became the first African American from Minnesota and the first Muslim from anywhere elected to Congress. That he had Catholic roots in Minneapolis certainly helped but does not negate the significance of his election.

Some critics of Minnesota Nice charge that it is a cover for deep-seated resistance to change. They see evidence of its passive-aggressive side in attempts by dominant-group Minnesotans to be "nice" to minority-group Minnesotans—stroking the hair of an African American child ("oh, isn't that pretty"), not noticing that the child and mother recoil from the touch. Or in the white students in my college class who claim not to notice that Hmong and Bahamian students are different from themselves (to notice would be racist, they explain) and so show no interest in their cultures and lives. Or in the ignorance of many Minnesotans that keeps them from seeing the riveting poverty that damages citizens and newcomers in both rural and urban Minnesota.

Whether it is Minnesota Nice or religiously inspired social justice, it is also the case that Minnesota Lutheran Social Services and Catholic Charities have sponsored many of these new immigrants, helped pave their way, offered them assistance, and worked hard to remind traditional

Minnesotans of the value and contributions of these new immigrants to the state's economic, social, even culinary well-being. The Minneapolis Foundation has made a special commitment to assisting new immigrants. The Minnesota Humanities Center has organized a Somali reading program. The American Refugee Committee (headquartered in Minneapolis) and Common Hope (headquartered in St. Paul), the Center for Victims of Torture, and dozens of other secular and sectarian organizations— funded by hundreds of thousands of donations from the state's businesses and citizens—have dedicated themselves to learning from, teaching to and about, healing, welcoming, and promoting new Minnesotans, supporting both a wider worldview and a closer attention to the world that is within the state's boundaries, the world that lives in Minnesota.

Barry Meyers, the former Gunflint chef, is neither historian nor sociologist, but rather an imaginative chef who has drawn on the best in Minnesota to create his signature dish: a walleye quesadilla. In it, Barry combines pieces of fried walleye, wild rice, smoked Gouda, and his own special and secret sauce, all folded into a tortilla. The new Minnesota, like the walleye quesadilla, brings together the customs and traditions of Europeans, American Indians, Latin Americans, and others. Minnesota has been made more interesting, more imaginative, and a bit spicier. It's a good thing.

TIMELINE

Dates Tell a Story, Too

Historians care a lot about time—when things happen and why they happen at a particular time and not at another—and we often organize what we know by time, in general, and by dates, in particular. Attending to dates offers a way to see the broad sweep of the past. Alone these dates don't tell the whole story, but together they walk us from the past to the present, and together they can provide a structure for knowing about the past of this place. As in each other chapter in this book, I'm offering here another version: not all the dates, but the ones that highlight the state's variegated, mixed, and multilayered past and offer an overview of the development of this place that became Minnesota.

1670	Hudson's Bay Company chartered
1679–83	Sieur du Lhut sets up trading posts on north shore of Lake Superior
1680	Father Louis Hennepin names the Falls of St. Anthony
1680	Mdewakanton, Wahpekute, Wahpeton, and Sisseton Dakota live at and around Mille Lacs
1736	Ojibwe live near Pigeon River (Grand Portage)
1763	British claim upper Great Lakes region from the French
1777	2,431 voyageurs licensed in Montreal and Detroit
1787	Northwest Ordinance declares "There shall be neither slavery nor involuntary servitude in the said territory"
1792	Grand Portage becomes central depot for North West [Fur] Company
1808	American Fur Company chartered by John J. Astor
1816	British abandon posts in upper Great Lakes region
1819	Indian agent Lawrence Taliaferro arrives at Fort Snelling
1823	First steamboat arrives at Fort Snelling
1825	Treaty of the Sioux (Treaty of Prairie du Chien) establishes boundary between Dakota and Ojibwe

1830 Reverend and Mrs. Frederick Ayer establish outpost at La Pointe, on Madeline Island

1830s–40s American Fur Company active in Minnesota

1832 Philander Prescott records first white visit to Pipestone quarries

1834 Henry Sibley and Alexis Bailly arrive at Mendota

1834 Samuel and Gideon Pond establish school at Lake Calhoun

1836 Dred Scott brought by his owner, Dr. Emerson, to posting at Fort Snelling

1837 157 white people not associated with Fort Snelling live around the fort

1837 Smallpox epidemic

1837 Stephen and Mary Riggs and family settle at Lac qui Parle

1837 Dakota and Ojibwe land divided by treaty

1838 Franklin Steele founds the town of St. Anthony

1838–39 Joseph Nicollet explores between Minnesota and Mississippi rivers for U.S. government

1839 Bishop Mathias Loras from Dubuque, IA, counts 185 Catholics around St. Paul; sends Father Lucien Galtier to tend that flock

1839 Gospel of Mark printed in Dakota language

1839 Joseph Nicollet records seeing herds of buffalo "covering the plains around us; we heard them passing us all through the night."

1841 Father Lucien Galtier renames Pig's Eye St. Paul

1841 Joseph Nicollet's map of region between Minnesota and Mississippi rivers published

1842 American Fur Company collapses

1842 Treaty of La Pointe divides Anishinaabe into Chippewa of the Mississippi and Lake Superior Chippewa

1845 Hidatsa move near Fort Berthold

1848 Land around St. Paul offered for sale

1849 James M. Goodhue publishes first edition of *Minnesota Pioneer* newspaper

1849 Minnesota Territory admitted to the union

1849 Minnesota Historical Society incorporated by legislature

1850 Forty African Americans and African American mulattos reside in St. Paul

1850 Voyageurs' way of life finished

1851 Treaties of Traverse des Sioux and Mendota signed

1852 Father Francis Pierz, an Austrian priest, is at work in central Minnesota

1853   Parker Paine organizes first private bank in Minnesota

1853   St. Paul Fire and Marine Insurance incorporated by territorial legislature

1854   Treaty of La Pointe establishes first reservations for the Lake Superior Chippewa

1855   Soo Canal joins Lakes Superior and Huron

1856   German settlement founded at Beaver Bay

1856   Ignatius Donnelly and Philip Rohr publish *Emigrant Aid Journal*

1856   James J. Hill settles in St. Paul by happenstance

1856   Mount Zion Hebrew Association founded in Minneapolis

1857   Banking and commercial collapse in Minnesota

1857   Inkpaduta and renegades terrorize southwestern Minnesota

1857   Jane Grey Swisshelm begins publishing *St. Cloud Visiter*

1857   Joe Rolette disappears for five days with official copy of legislation that would have removed state capitol from St. Paul to St. Peter

1857   *Minnesota Posten* (in Swedish) published in Red Wing

1857   Saint John's Abbey and Saint Benedict's Monastery founded in Stearns County

1858   First Minnesota state banking act

1858   *Folkets Röst* (in Norwegian) published in St. Paul

1858   Henry Sibley elected state governor

1858   Minnesota becomes the thirty-second state

1858   *Neu-Ulm Pionier* (in German) published

1858   Old Settlers Association of Minnesota founded

1858   State legislature passes "An Act to Encourage Emigration"

1859   Henry Whipple consecrated as bishop of Minnesota

1861   First Minnesota volunteers raised for Civil War service

1862   Dakota War and hanging of thirty-eight at Mankato

1862   Railroad between St. Paul and St. Anthony complete

1862   St. Paul and Pacific Railroad recruits Irish laborers

1863   School for the Deaf opens in Faribault; admits blind in 1864; "feeble-minded" in 1879

1864   Freedman's Aid Society founded in Owatonna

1864   Railroad between St. Paul and Anoka complete

1866   George Stuntz discovers ore deposits on the Vermilion Range

1866   Red River carts still passing through Anoka

1867   White Earth Reservation created

1867   Hans Mattson appointed state director of immigration

1867   St. Paul Chamber of Commerce organized

1867   White Earth Reservation formed

1869   Lake Superior and Mississippi Railroad Company builds Immigrant House in Duluth for Swedish railroad workers

1870   Duluth and St. Paul linked by rail (sixteen-hour ride)

1870   St. Andrew's Society founded in Duluth

1870s   Minneapolis Baseball Association formed

1870s   Patrons of Husbandry (Grange) local groups form

1871   Thirty-five Minnesota Irish march north to strike a blow against the British in Winnipeg

1871   Lakewood Cemetery Memorial Park (Minneapolis) founded

1871   Ship canal opens in Duluth

1872   Minneapolis and St. Anthony merge into Minneapolis

1873   Economic panic and collapse

1873–78 Grasshopper plagues in southwestern and central Minnesota

1874   Martin County's English immigrants fox hunt, red coats and all

1874   St. Olaf School (Northfield) opens; becomes college in 1899

1875   John Ireland founds Irish Catholic Colonization Association

1875   *St. Paul Pioneer Press* and *St. Paul Daily Press* merged by Joseph A. Wheelock into *Pioneer Press*

1878   Explosion in Washburn A Mill (Minneapolis) kills eighteen workers

1880   Washburn Crosby flour earns "Gold Medal" at Millers' Exhibition

1881   Army Corps of Engineers builds dams on the Upper Mississippi to control waterpower at the Minneapolis falls, flooding Ojibwe burial grounds and ricing areas at Leech Lake Indian Reservation

1881   Duluth is home to six locals of the Noble and Holy Order of the Knights of Labor

1881   Minnesota Woman Suffrage Association forms

1882   Edward D. Neill's *History of Minnesota* published

1882   Ladies Musicale Society forms in St. Paul; later becomes Schubert Club

1882   State's first intercollegiate football game: Hamline versus U of M

1883   Northern Pacific line completed; over 900 miles of track laid between 1879 and 1883

1883   Red Wing and St. Paul linked by telephone

1883 Stone Arch Bridge (Minneapolis) across the Mississippi opens to rail travel

1884 Charlemagne Tower finances the mining of the Vermilion Range

1884 Duluth Ladies' Relief Society forms to aid local poor

1885 Unskilled laborer in Duluth earns $500, young businessman, $1,000; cost of living: $720

1886 Sears, Roebuck founded

1887 James J. Hill sends his own immigration agent to Norway and Sweden

1888 John Ireland named Roman Catholic archbishop of St. Paul

1889 August Schell Brewing Company opens in New Ulm

1889 Captain Alexander McDougall introduces lake freighter on Lake Superior

1889 First school opens in Ely

1889 Great Northern Railway built out of the remains of the St. Paul, Minneapolis and Manitoba Railway

1889 Nelson Act, "For the relief and civilization of the Chippewa Indians in the State of Minnesota," passed by U.S. Congress

1890 Pocket of iron ore located near Ely; later becomes Mountain Iron Mine

1890 Forty-three nationalities present in Minnesota

1890 Weyerhaeuser Company buys timberland on upper Mississippi and builds mill at Little Falls; opens second mill in 1892

1890s Heyday of dining rooms as part of house design

1891 James J. Hill house (St. Paul) completed

1892 Ancient Order of Hibernians, St. Jean Baptiste Society, the Polish National Benevolent Society, and the St. Boniface Society celebrate St. Patrick's Day

1892 High Bridge over Mississippi River in St. Paul completed

1892 Trip from St. Paul to Seattle takes four days

1893 The Merritt Brothers lose control of their northern Minnesota mines to John D. Rockefeller and what will become U.S. Steel Company

1893 American Protective Association—to protect against Catholicism—controls Duluth City Council

1893 Weyerhaeuser headquarters move to St. Paul

1894 St. Thomas College (St. Paul) founded

1894 Washburn-Crosby employees strike for a ten-hour day

1895 Small waists going out of style

1896 Sabrie Akin begins publishing *Labor World* in Duluth

1897 Danes organize dairy cooperative at Lake Benton

1897   White Bear Yacht Club forms

1898   Minnesota State Art Society founded (the second state government–supported arts organization in the United States)

1898   Armed battle at Sugar Point on Leech Lake reservation counted as last of the nineteenth-century Indian wars

1898   Women are eligible to cast votes in school board elections

1898   Olof Ohman unearths Kensington runestone in his farmyard

1899   Ada Comstock (later Notestein) appointed to Rhetoric Department at University of Minnesota; becomes first dean of women in 1907

1899   Electric streetlights replace gaslights in Two Harbors

1899   Governor John Lind signs "Act to Regulate the Importation of Dependent Children"

1899   John Beargrease and his sled dog mail delivery system between Two Harbors and Grand Marais replaced by stage delivery

1899   Minnesota State Forestry Board created

1899   State legislature creates Itasca State Park

1900   250,000 tons of ice cut at Green Lake (winter is not cold enough to build St. Paul's ice palace)

1900   Andrew Carnegie's income $23 million; James J. Hill's income $20 million

1900   Forty-five bicycle repairers in St. Paul

1902   Dayton's Department Store opens in Minneapolis

1902   Minnesota Mining and Manufacturing Company (3M) founded

1903   Citizens Alliance, a union of Minneapolis business owners, forms

1903   Minneapolis Symphony Orchestra conducted by Emil Oberhoffer

1903   *Shame of the Cities* by Lincoln Steffens includes chapter on Minneapolis

1903   Workers at Washburn Crosby mills strike for eight-hour day

1904   American Swedish Institute opens in Minneapolis

1904   Gratia Alta Countryman named head of Minneapolis Public Library; holds position until 1936

1904   Handicraft Guild forms in Minneapolis

1904   Merger of Great Northern, Northern Pacific, and Chicago, Burlington and Quincy railroads set aside by Supreme Court in Northern Securities Case

1905   Aerial Lift Bridge opens in Duluth

1905 College of St. Catherine (St. Paul) founded

1905 Hennepin County Territorial Pioneers rescue Ard and Harriet Godfrey house from demolition

1905 Minnesota State Capitol (St. Paul; Cass Gilbert) complete

1905 Red Wing Shoe Company opens

1905 The *Amboy,* a three-masted schooner, is caught in a storm and sinks in Lake Superior just off Taconite Harbor; wreck added to National Register of Historic Places in 1994

1906 Finnish Socialist Federation meets in Hibbing

1906 Paul Bunyan story appears in Michigan newspaper

1907 84.5 percent of Oliver Mining Company's 12,000 employees are foreign born

1908 Glensheen Mansion (Duluth) built

1908 Lake Harriet Rose Garden (Minneapolis) opens

1908 National Farmers' Bank (Owatonna; Louis H. Sullivan) opens

1909 Sunshine Club of Virginia (MN) forms to visit the sick

1910 Lakewood Cemetery Memorial Chapel (Minneapolis; Harry Jones) completed

1910 Minnesota's iron ranges supply two-thirds of all iron ore mined in the United States

1910 Split Rock Lighthouse (Ralph R. Tinkham) lighted

1911 5.5-pound hailstone falls in Pipestone

1911 Cuyuna Range opens

1911 Fort Ridgely State Park opens

1911 St. Olaf choir begins touring

1912 Eighty-two units of the Ancient Order of Hibernians active in Minnesota

1912 Duluth streetcar workers strike to defend right to organize

1912 Gitchi Gammi Club (Duluth) built

1913 Duluth iron-ore dockworkers strike for safer working conditions

1913 University Club (St. Paul) opens

1914 Minneapolis Institute of Arts (McKim, Mead and White) opens

1914 Ninth Federal Reserve District headquartered in Minneapolis

1915 *Irish Standard* published in the Twin Cities

1915 Cathedral of St. Paul (Emmanuel L. Masqueray) completed

1915 Como Park and Conservatory (St. Paul) open

1915 Duluth Clinic founded

1915 Greyhound Corp. founded

1915　North East Neighborhood House (one of many settlement houses) opens

1915　Zlota Rivka Svidelesky founds Women's Free Loan Association

1916　*Nowiny Minnesockie* (in Polish) published in Twin Cities

1916　State Child Welfare Commission appointed

1916　Iron Range miners strike

1917　Minnesota Historical Society Building (600 Cedar St., St. Paul) completed

1917　Senator Charles A. Lindbergh opposes American entry into World War I

1917　Twin Cities streetcar strike

1918　Flu epidemic causes 10,000 to 12,000 deaths in Minnesota

1918　Forest fires burn from Cloquet to Moose Lake

1918　Nonpartisan League growing in Minnesota

1918　Tornado levels Tyler

1919　Duluth Citizens' Alliance formed to protect open-shop (nonunion) hiring

1919　Woman suffrage amendment ratified by Minnesota Legislature

1920　MIAC (Minnesota Intercollegiate Athletic Conference) founded

1920　Minneapolis mills produce more flour than any other city

1920　Three African American men lynched in Duluth

1920　Virginia and Rainy Lake Lumber Company employs 2,000 men, 900 horses, 13 locomotives

1921　Betty Crocker "born"

1921　Bran flake invented by Washburn Crosby Company

1922　Haralson apple introduced and named for director of University of Minnesota Fruit Breeding Farm (later merged into Minnesota Arboretum)

1922　University of Minnesota receives license to operate radio station WLB

1923　English made the official language of the Swedish Lutheran Church in Minnesota

1924　By legislative decree, all Indians become U.S. citizens, subject to federal and state laws

1924　KKK chapters founded in Owatonna and elsewhere in Minnesota

1924　WCCO radio station begins broadcasting

1924　WEBC, the first radio station in northern Minnesota, begins broadcasting from Duluth

1925   3M diversifies with the invention of masking tape and the first of Scotch adhesive tapes

1926   Farmer-Labor Party rejects communist members

1927   Anti-evolution bill introduced in state senate and fails

1927   Charles A. Lindbergh completes nonstop flight from New York to Paris

1927   Williams Arena opens at University of Minnesota

1928   General Mills forms out of the Washburn Crosby Company and four other mills

1928   Mayo Clinic (Rochester) opens new building

1928   Suburban World Theatre (Minneapolis) opens

1929   First Bank and Northwest Bank holding companies form

1929   Foshay Tower (Minneapolis) complete

1929   Naniboujou Lodge (Grand Marais; Holstead and Sullivan; ceiling mural, Antoine Gouffee) opens

1929   Northwest Airlines founded

1930   Minneapolis public relief caseload is 1,000, 7 relief workers; in 1935, caseload is 21,000, 350 relief workers

1931   Duluth longshoremen strike to protest wage cuts

1931   Ramsey County Courthouse (St. Paul) completed

1932   30 percent unemployment in Duluth; 70 percent of Iron Range workers unemployed

1932   Hunger march on Minneapolis City Hall

1933   Thirteen state forests created from tax-delinquent lands

1934   Indian Reorganization Act transfers to tribal governments more administrative authority, curtails further land allotments to individuals, encourages tribes to create written constitutions

1934   Minneapolis truckers' strike; followed the next year by Strutwear workers' strike

1935   Eric Sevareid publishes *Canoeing with the Cree*

1935   Hotel and Restaurant Employees International Union, the state's first integrated union, forms

1935   Women linen supply workers in Duluth strike for right to organize

1936   Minnesota Chippewa Tribe organized into corporate entity, which includes White Earth, Nett Lake, Leech Lake, Grand Portage, Fond du Lac, and Mille Lacs

1937   Lumberjacks strike

1937   Paul Bunyan and Babe statues erected on the shores of Lake Bemidji

1938   Harold Stassen elected governor (youngest at thirty-one)

1938   Northern League professional baseball includes Duluth
       Dukes, Eau Claire Bears, Fargo-Moorhead Twins, Grand
       Forks Chiefs, Superior Blues, and Winnipeg Goldeyes

1939   Meridel Le Sueur publishes *The Girl*

1940   Armistice Day blizzard

1940   James Ford Bell Museum of Natural History (Minneapolis;
       Clarence H. Johnston, Jr.) opens

1940   Margaret Ann Hubbard publishes *Little Whirlwind*

1940   Pipestone National Park founded

1940s North Star Woolen Mill—specializing in blankets since
       1869—in decline

1941   Clarence (Cap) Wigington designs St. Paul ice palace

1945   The last of fifteen prisoner of war camps, housing German
       and Italian prisoners, opens in Minnesota

1946   Cary McWilliams labels Minneapolis as capital of anti-
       Semitism in *Common Ground* magazine

1946   Grace (Holmes) Carlson and Dorothy (Holmes) Schultz run
       for senate and congress on the Socialist Workers Party
       ticket

1947   Northwest Airlines' first flight to the Orient

1948   Mayor's Council on Human Relations charged by H. H.
       Humphrey to study discrimination in Minneapolis

1949   Earl Bakken and Palmer Hermundslie form Medtronic

1949   Antal Dorati named conductor of the Minneapolis Sym-
       phony Orchestra

1949   Lutsen Lodge opens

1950   Several Jewish doctors, refused hospital privileges in Min-
       neapolis, found Mount Sinai Hospital

1953   Super Valu agrees to use Curt Carlson's Gold Bond stamps,
       helping launch Carlson Companies

1956   Modern lock and dam completed just below St. Anthony
       Falls

1957   Reserve Mining begins shipping taconite

1957   Control Data makes initial public offering

1957   Dr. C. Walton Lillehei (University of Minnesota Medical
       School) and Medtronic engineers develop pacemaker

1958   Archibald MacLeish gives poetry reading at University of
       Minnesota

1958   Evelyn Raymond's sculpture of University of Minnesota ed-
       ucator Maria Sanford unveiled in U.S. Capitol Statuary Hall

1959   Bob [Zimmerman] Dylan graduates from Hibbing High
       School

1959   St. Lawrence Seaway opens

1960   Arctic Cat snowmobiles for sale

1961   Minnesota Twins start playing baseball in Minneapolis

1961   Saint John's Abbey Church (Collegeville; Marcel Breuer) built

1962   First Target store opens in Minneapolis

1962   Republican Elmer L. Andersen elected to a second term as Minnesota governor by 149 votes; in a recount, DFL candidate Karl Rolvaag wins by 91 votes

1963   First skyway opens in downtown Minneapolis

1963   Tyrone Guthrie Theater (Minneapolis) opens

1964   Number of miners employed by Mesabi mines declines by nearly 25 percent in previous six years

1966   Duluth Entertainment and Convention Center opens

1967   Minnesota Public Radio's first station signs on air

1968   Reiko Weston opens Fuji-Ya on the ruins of the Columbia Mill on the west bank of the Mississippi River (Minneapolis)

1969   Dayton and Hudson corporations merge

1969   Peter Nelson Hall begins renovation of Pracna on Main on east bank of the Mississippi River (Minneapolis)

1969   Vine Deloria, Jr., publishes *Custer Died for Your Sins: An Indian Manifesto*

1969   Warren Burger named chief justice of the U.S. Supreme Court

1970   Mary Tyler Moore television situation comedy located in Minneapolis

1972   Walker Museum (Minneapolis) opens new building

1973   Governor Wendell Anderson appears on the cover of *Time Magazine*

1973   IDS Tower (Minneapolis) completed

1974   Garrison Keillor's *Prairie Home Companion* goes on the air

1976   Penumbra Theater (St. Paul) founded by Lou Bellamy

1976   Walter Mondale elected vice president of the United States

1977   Minnesota Vikings defeated 32–14 by Oakland Raiders in Superbowl XI

1978   Horst Rechelbacher founds Aveda Corporation

1980   Leeann Chin owns and operates Leeann Chin, Inc.

1980   SuperValu buys out Cub Foods

1983   Best Buy founded by Richard M. Schulze

1983   Harvey Mackay (CEO of Mackay Envelope Corporation) publishes *Swim with the Sharks Without Being Eaten Alive*

1983   Ignatia Broker publishes *Night Flying Woman: An Ojibway Narrative*

1984   Louise Erdrich's *Love Medicine* wins National Book Critics Circle Award

1984   Mollie Hoben and Glenda Martin found Minnesota Women's Press

1987   Dunn Bros. Coffee founded

1987   Minnesota Twins win World Series

1988   Minneapolis Sculpture Garden (Edward Larrabee Barnes) opens

1989   Pillsbury Corporation acquired by Grand Metropolitan, PLC

1989   William McGuire, MD, heads United HealthCare

1990   Esperanza Guerrero-Anderson named president/CEO of Milestone Growth Fund

1990   Evelyn Fairbanks publishes *Days of Rondo*

1990   Tim O'Brien publishes *The Things They Carried*

1992   Mall of America (Bloomington) opens

1992   Minnesota History Center (St. Paul; Hammel, Green and Abrahamson) opens

1993   Frederick R. Weisman Art Museum (Frank O. Gehry and Associates with Meyer, Scherer and Rockcastle) opens on University of Minnesota campus

1993   Minnesota North Stars hockey team moves to Texas

1993   Sharon Sayles Belton elected first African American and first woman mayor of Minneapolis

1993   Theatre de la Jeune Lune (Minneapolis) opens new building

1994   Confederation of Somali Community in Minnesota established

1994   International Wolf Center (Ely; Thorbeck Architects with Architectural Resources) opens

1995   Hebrew Immigrant Aid Society helps resettle Jews from the Soviet Union

1997   First Bank System acquires U.S. Bancorporation

1998   Masjid Abu-Bakr Al-Sidique Mosque (Rochester) opens

1998   Norwest Bank acquires and takes name of Wells Fargo

1998   Jesse Ventura elected governor

1999   106 software companies in Minnesota

2001   Merger of banks creates U.S. Bancorp, headquartered in Minneapolis

2000   Dayton-Hudson renamed Target Corporation

2001   General Mills acquires Pillsbury

2001   Lutheran Brotherhood and Aid Association for Lutherans become Thrivent Financial for Lutherans

2002   Leo Omani leads the first Dakota Commemorative March in honor of the Dakota people removed from Mankato to Fort Snelling in 1862

2002   Mai Neng Moua publishes *Bamboo Among the Oaks: Contemporary Writing by Hmong Americans*

2002   Mee Moua is the first Hmong person elected to the Minnesota State Legislature

2003   Mill City Museum (Minneapolis) opens

2004   Pillsbury A Mill (Minneapolis) closes

2005   Immigrants make up six percent of Minnesota's population, down from 29 percent in 1910

2005   Walker Art Center (Minneapolis) renovated; Minneapolis Institute of Arts renovated; Children's Theatre (Minneapolis) renovated

2006   Minneapolis Public Library renovated

2006   Journalist Gregg Aamot estimates the Minnesota population includes 175,000 Hispanics and Latinos, 60,000 Hmong, 25,000 Somalis, and 25,000 Vietnamese

2006   Amy Klobuchar elected first women senator from Minnesota

2006   Keith Ellison elected first African American congressman from Minnesota and first Muslim in the U.S. House of Representatives

2006   Northwest Airlines files for bankruptcy

2006   New Guthrie Theater built; old Guthrie Theatre torn down (Minneapolis)

2007   Northwest Airlines exits bankruptcy

With special thanks to Tom Joyce; Gregg Aamot, *The New Minnesotans: Stories of Immigrants and Refugees* (Minneapolis: Syren Book Company, 2006); AIA Minnesota, *100 Places Plus 1: An Unofficial Architectural Survey of Favorite Minnesota Sites* (Minneapolis: AIA Minnesota, 1996); William D. Green, *A Peculiar Imbalance: The Fall and Rise of Racial Equality in Early Minnesota* (St. Paul: Minnesota Historical Society [hereafter MHS] Press, 2007); June Drenning Holmquist, ed., *They Chose Minnesota: A Survey of the State's Ethnic Groups* (St. Paul: MHS Press, 1981); Richard Hudelson and Carl Ross, *By the Ore Docks: A Working People's History of Duluth* (Minneapolis: University of Minnesota Press, 2006); Lucile M. Kane, *The Falls of St. Anthony: The Waterfall that Built Minneapolis* (1966;

repr., St. Paul: MHS Press, 1987); Grace Lee Nute, *The Voyageur* (1931; repr., St. Paul: MHS Press, 1987); Linda Mack Schloff, *"And Prairie Dogs Weren't Kosher": Jewish Women in the Upper Midwest Since 1855* (St. Paul: MHS Press, 1996); David A. Walker, *Iron Frontier: The Discovery and Early Development of Minnesota's Three Ranges* (St. Paul: MHS Press, 1979); Workers of the Writers' Program of the Work Projects Administration of the State of Minnesota, comp., *WPA Guide to the Minnesota Arrowhead Country* (1941; repr., St. Paul: MHS Press, 1987).

EPILOGUE

Synecdoche

AT A SPELLING BEE held at Plymouth Church in Minneapolis in 1875, even the good spellers had a hard time with *niece, strychnine, reparable, seraglio,* and *synecdoche.* I haven't had many occasions to use *seraglio,* but *synecdoche* is one of the watchwords of this book. Film buffs use *synecdoche* to describe the technique of using a detail to conjure up the whole—a cracked headlight instead of the crashed car, or the silky bathrobe slipping to the floor, the screen fading to black. Each tells the essential story; both leave much to the imagination.

This history of Minnesota employs the device of synecdoche in that same way. Obviously, no one person's life does or could stand for all others. Little Crow and Ann North and Joe Campbell's lives differed from those of the timber barons in the northern woods, the miller in Marine on St. Croix, the railroad worker in Sauk Rapids, and the farmer in Lyon County, whose farm life differed, too, from a Red River Valley or cutover district farmer. When we keep looking, we see even more contrast: the lives of individual farmers in the Red River Valley varied depending on their ethnicity, age, and class, the soil type on their farm, their skill with their hands, their luck. One farmer lost crops to hail; another down the road didn't. Within the same family, experiences differed by age and gender, by aptitude and temperament, by health. No story can capture all of these individual historical experiences.

So, I don't intend to suggest, nor do I intend for you to think that all of these people and John S. Pillsbury and Governor Lucius Hubbard and James J. Hill had the same kind of impact on Minnesota. Gauging impact is not my ultimate goal. I seek instead something more elusive: understanding, indeed, historical understanding. By looking over the shoulder of a Native American person, of the Campbells, of Gertrude Braat, of Albert Ruger and the photographers, the sugar beet farmers, the furniture dealer in Staples, the Gunflint Lodge chef we can see a Minnesota that was steeped in water, shaped by trees, sometimes eager for the future and other times damaged by what the present demanded. By trying to see Red Wing and Minnesota and even the United States as Mary Gillett did, we can know many of the key issues facing Minnesota and Minnesotans in the 1880s—industrialization, the spread of the railroads, the change in the age and marital status of immigrants. We can see changes in women's lives percolating and brewing some new opportunities (and responsibilities). Mary's life suggests something about the expanding world and social life of single people in Minnesota towns and villages. Through her eyes we can see the power of James J. Hill, the paths cut by Drs. William Worrall Mayo and Charles Eastman and Martha Ripley; we can envision the consequences of their actions on other individual lives. We can see, too, the passing of the "old" Minnesota of Stephen Riggs and Harriet Bishop and how small a role Indian people were accorded in the new Minnesota. She becomes the means by which we crack open the coconut of the past and are fed by its insides. Mary Gillett's experience doesn't give us all the answers—history never does—but it does give us the feel, the texture, the context; and it challenges us to make connections to construct the answer that imagination allows and that the evidence supports.

When former poet laureate and always wonderful poet Billy Collins tells his friend in the poem, "Litany," "You are the dew on the morning grass, and the burning wheel of the sun. You are the white apron of the baker, and the marsh birds suddenly in flight," and when he calls himself "the shooting star, the evening paper blowing down an alley and the basket of chestnuts on the kitchen table," he's speaking metaphorically, of course, and his words take us to larger truths about the complex and funny ways of relationships. He leaves it up to us, though, to make the connections.[1]

As another poet, Mary Oliver, reminds us, "All narrative is metaphor," so Mary Gillett and all the other individuals who inhabit this book are metaphors. My job as author is to offer the images and to suggest the connections. At the end of this book, the baton of story-making power is passed, then, to you, the reader. What is this place to you? What is your story here? Where do you get silenced and where do you have voice? Where are you an actor and where are you an observer? What's the sense, finally, that you make out of this place—its water, its people, its past that is both glorious and shameful, its ability to be home and haven for some and painful outpost for others?[2]

I leave the next chapter to you.

A WORD TO THE WISE

Thank You

Books get done only because of the generous help of family, friends, colleagues, student workers, stack attendants, Kinko's staff, deans, department chairs, librarians, archivists—more than I can name, but some helped so much I can't not thank you in print.

Saint John's University and the College of Saint Benedict have, through multiple kinds of faculty development opportunities and support (grants, sabbaticals, the Michael Blecker Professorship, and the Flynn Professorship), helped me find the time to write. I am grateful to all the donors to those funds who recognize the value of scholarship in a liberal arts college. I was also the grateful recipient of an NEH Summer Stipend for College Teachers and thank the American taxpayers for their continued support of government programs for scholarship. The Minnesota Historical Society provided me with a carrel for years as well as a variety of kindnesses that didn't add up to much in dollars but constituted a treasure for me.

My history and other colleagues (and friends) at Saint John's University and the College of Saint Benedict helped me in innumerable ways. I'm especially grateful to those who read and commented on chapters: Dave Bennetts, John Brandl, Julie Davis, LtC James Fischer, Gloria Hardy, Eva Hooker csc, Louis Johnston, Ken Jones, Norma Koetter, Brian Larkin, Derek Larson, Ozzie Mayers, Rene McGraw OSB, Bev Radaich, Pam Reding, Greg Schroeder, and Hilary Thimmesh OSB. My CSB/SJU Faculty Writing Club, the 4 o'clock writing group, and my writing retreat pals created a community of writers that I found encouraging and sustaining. There have been legions of students workers, too, who have helped in thousands of ways big and small. Thank you, thank you.

Historians and friends in other places read and improved many of the chapters and saved me from more than one embarrassment: Walter Nugent, Suellen Hoy, Jim Madison, David Rich Lewis, Chuck Rankin, Brenda Child, Clarke Chambers, Bob Barrows, Stephen Nelson, Michael

Murphy, Bob Close, Judge Diana Murphy, Joe Campbell (Prairie Island), Kirsten Fisher and the University of Minnesota Early American History Workshop, Colette Hyman, Donald Fixico, Brendan Henehan, Dr. Thomas Reichert, William Lass, and Linda Shopes. They all pushed me to do the "even more" that improves a manuscript. Marge Barrett did an especially helpful reading of the manuscript.

The person who has walked most patiently and helpfully with me through the manuscript (and then again) has been Ellen Green. A first-rate editor, a sympathetic reader, a knowledgeable critic, Ellen kept the manuscript (and me) on the right track. Her help was invaluable. (If you need an editor, call her: she lives in St. Paul.)

Minnesota Historical Society staff really made the book—and my work on it—possible and pleasurable: Marcia Anderson, Debbie Miller, Brian Horrigan, Ann Regan, Alan Woolworth, Tim Hoogland, Tracey Baker, Earl Gutnik, John Lindell, Hamp Smith, Anne Kaplan, Marilyn Ziebarth, and dozens of others asked probing questions, provided helpful leads, answered a zillion questions, ate lunch with me. More than that, they and their colleagues do the daily work of collection, conservation, cataloging, and research that allows for the study of Minnesota's past.

Greg Britton, director of the MHS Press, Shannon Pennefeather, my editor, and Will Powers, the book's designer—as well as the marketing staff—have taken extraordinary care with this manuscript and me and have offered kindness along with their expertise.

Friends—many of whom I've already named—have listened to my stories of Minnesota as well as stories of my writing. As someone who thinks best out loud, I've given my friends' ears a real workout. Kathy Paden, Patsy Murphy, Les Bendtsen, Amy Levine, Peg Meier, Sanya Polescuk and Nigel Higgins, Jane and Robert Norbury, Jane Curry, Gretchen Kreuter, Anne Webb, Chris Anderson, Jim and Candy Beery, Don and Lois Ross, and Jackie and the late Bill Harrison have my thanks and my affection.

So, too, do the members of my various families: my dad, brothers, and sisters; Jeffrey and Ryan Cartwright; Ellen and Anne Joyce, Cliff Johnson, and Seamus and Alex Joyce-Johnson. My husband Tom Joyce has been running his own private faculty development program on my behalf for years. He's been my loving companion, helped me buy down my contract, read the manuscript multiple times, and in the last few months only sometimes minded when I had, yet again, to work on the book.

I am a lucky woman to be surrounded by such warmth, support, love, and wisdom. I thank you all.

NOTES TO PREFACE

1. William Watts Folwell, *A History of Minnesota*, 4 vols. (1921–29; repr., St. Paul: Minnesota Historical Society [hereafter, MHS] Press, 1956–61). Theodore Blegen, *Minnesota: A History of the State* (1963; repr., new chapter by Russell Fridley, Minneapolis: University of Minnesota Press, 1975). William E. Lass, *Minnesota: A History,* 2nd ed. (New York: Norton and American Association of State and Local History, 1998). Minnesota is blessed with a first-rate historical society, founded before the territory became a state and for its entire history having conducted an active program of scholarly and popular publication. In addition, the University of Minnesota Press has taken an active interest in state and regional history, so the shelves are full of varied and valuable secondary works on the history of the state—enough of it recent enough to support the writing of a state survey.

2. Some of the best of these monographs include Elizabeth Faue, *Community of Suffering and Struggle: Women, Men, and the Labor Movement in Minneapolis, 1915–1945* (Chapel Hill: University of North Carolina Press, 1991); Linda Mack Schloff, *"And Prairie Dogs Weren't Kosher": Jewish Women in the Upper Midwest Since 1855* (St. Paul: MHS Press, 1996); David Vassar Taylor with Paul Clifford Larson, *Cap Wigington: An Architectural Legacy in Ice and Stone* (St. Paul: MHS Press, 2002); Barbara Handy-Marchello, *Women of the Northern Plains: Gender and Settlement on the Homestead Frontier, 1870–1930* (St. Paul: MHS Press, 2005); Jennifer A. Delton, *Making Minnesota Liberal: Civil Rights and the Transformation of the Democratic Party* (Minneapolis: University of Minnesota Press, 2002); Odd S. Lovoll, *The Promise of America: A History of the Norwegian-American People* (Minneapolis: University of Minnesota Press, 1999); Gary Clayton Anderson, *Little Crow: Spokesman for the Sioux* (St. Paul: MHS Press, 1986).

3. Meanwhile, traditional historians, legislators, and school boards sometimes find the new histories dismaying or alienating. Are there no heroic stories? Isn't citizenship best taught by emphasizing the rise of freedom and the triumph of democracy? Shouldn't the pre-earthquake story be safeguarded? In Minnesota, the issuing of new K-12 state standards for the social sciences provoked a storm of controversy. Professors Sarah Evans and Lisa Norling noted errors of fact in the standards issued under the leadership of the state department of education but more importantly objected to the definitions and limitations of the history that was being mandated. See their column in the Organization of American Historians newsletter at http://www.oah.org/pubs/nl/2004nov/evans-norling.html (accessed Mar. 4, 2007).

4. Henry Glassie, *Passing the Time in Ballymenone: Culture and History of an Ulster Community* (Philadelphia: University of Pennsylvania Press, 1982), 86.

NOTES TO CHAPTER 1

1. Hildegard Binder Johnson, *Order Upon the Land: The U.S. Rectangular Land Survey and the Upper Mississippi Country* (New York: Oxford University Press, 1976). John R. Borchert, *Minnesota's Changing Geography* (Minneapolis: University of Minnesota Press, 1959).

2. On bonanza farms, see Gilbert C. Fite, *The Farmers' Frontier, 1865–1900* (New York: Holt, Rinehart and Winston, 1966).

3. Tree Bounty Payment Records, 1882–1915, Minnesota State Auditor's Office Papers, MHS, St. Paul. See especially Vol. 1: 1886–91, Vol. 2: 1891–97, and Vol. C: 1898–1905. See also Misc. Records,

Chippewa County, Auditor's Papers, MHS. Antona Hawkins Richardson, "Tree Planting Bounty Payments, 1890 and 1891," *Minnesota Genealogical Journal* 24 (Sept. 2000), 2315–20.

4. Percy C. Records, "Tree Planting for Shelter in Minnesota" (St. Paul, MN: State Forestry Board, 1913), 6.

5. See David Nass, "The Rural Experience," in Clifford E. Clark, Jr., ed., *Minnesota in a Century of Change: The State and Its People Since 1900* (St. Paul: MHS Press, 1989), 130. Janet Timmerman, "Draining the Great Oasis: Claiming New Agricultural Land in Murray County, 1910–1915," in Anthony J. Amato, Janet Timmerman, and Joseph A. Amato, eds., *Draining the Great Oasis: An Environmental History of Murray County, Minnesota* (Marshall, MN: Crossings Press, 2001), 125–41, quote, p126.

6. "The Scandinavian Sell and Other Quirks of Minnesota Advertising," *[Minneapolis] Star Tribune,* Aug. 18, 1991, E1.

7. Many geologists, geographers, and ecologists argue for three regions: prairie, deciduous trees, and coniferous trees. I'm focusing instead on "treed" and "not treed"—a distinction that is meaningful for a South Dakotan. See Thomas John Baerwald, *Glaciation in Minnesota* (St. Paul: Geography Department, Science Museum of Minnesota, 1983). Minnesota Geological Survey, "Minnesota at a Glance: Quaternary Glacial Geology" (St. Paul: University of Minnesota, 1997). For a wonderful map of the three regions, see "Come to Minnesota!: The Bread and Butter State: You'll Do Better on a Minnesota Farm" (St. Paul: 10,000 Lakes–Greater Minnesota Association, [1930]). The state department of natural resources has created a rich and full description of the three regions: see Minnesota Department of Natural Resources, "Natural History–Minnesota's Geology," www.dnr.state.mn.us/snas/naturalhistory.html (accessed Mar. 11, 2003).

8. Waters Section, Division of Waters, Soils, and Minerals, "An Inventory of Minnesota Lakes," Bulletin 25 (St. Paul: Minnesota Conservation Department, 1968).

9. See "Wetland Plants and Plant Communities of Minnesota and Wisconsin," www.npwrc.usgs.gov/resource/1998/mnplant/intro.html (accessed Mar. 10, 2003). "Water, Water Everywhere, But Is It Fit to Drink?" *[Minneapolis] Star Tribune,* Jan. 5, 1992, D2.

10. Grace McDonald, *With Lamps Burning* (St. Joseph, MN: Sisters of St. Benedict, 1957), and Incarnata Girgen, *Behind the Beginnings: Benedictine Women in America* (St. Joseph, MN: St. Benedict's Convent, 1981). Colman Barry, OSB, corroborates the story in his *Worship and Work: St. John's Abbey and University, 1856–1980* (Collegeville, MN: St. John's Abbey, 1956).

11. See www.ushockeyhall.com (accessed Apr. 2, 2003). The Hockey Hall of Fame has closed since I wrote this and is looking for a permanent home, perhaps in the Twin Cities.

12. Waters Section, "Inventory of Minnesota Lakes," and "Alphabetical Index of Minnesota Lakes & Streams," prepared under the direction of the Hydrologist of the Division of Water Resources and Engineering of the Department of Conservation by the Works Progress Administration (St. Paul, MN: Department of Conservation, [1941]).

13. "Summers at Clark Lake," manuscript, MHS.

14. Paul Arthur Swenson, "Family and Personal History," manuscript, MHS. Willis H. Raff, *CCC Days in Cook County, 1933–1942* (Grand Marais, MN: Cook County Historical Society, 1983). Ben Thoma remembered the mosquitoes especially: Ben Thoma, *The Civilian Conservation Corps and Itasca State Park* (Lake Itasca, MN: Itasca State Park, 1984).

15. Robert Bly, "Summer, 1960, Minnesota," *Silence in the Snowy Fields* (Middletown, CT: Wesleyan University Press, 1962), 31. Robert Frost, "Nothing Gold Can Stay," *New Hampshire: A Poem with Notes and Grace Notes* (New York: Henry Holt and Co., 1923), 84.

16. In their recent study, "The Rise of Exurbia: The Changing Shape of Minnesota," authors Stan and Anna Greenberg and Julie Hootkin found that the state's natural resources are "the greatest source of pride for residents statewide" (St. Paul: Hubert H. Humphrey Institute for Public Affairs, Minnesota Community Project, Dec. 14, 2004), 15.

NOTES TO CHAPTER 2

1. The Eastern (Santee or Dakota), Middle (Yankton and Yanktonai, or Nakota), and Western (Teton or Lakota) all speak a Siouan language and were the people referred to by others as *Sioux,* derived from a description of their method of moccasin making or from a word meaning "snake," in either case a name affixed to them originally by their Ojibwe adversaries and picked up by the French, British, and then Euro-Americans. See Roy W. Meyer, *History of the Santee Sioux: United States Indian Policy on Trial* (rev. ed., Lincoln: University of Nebraska Press, 1993). See also Karen Ordahl Kupperman, *Indians and English: Facing Off in Early America* (Ithaca, NY: Cornell University Press, 2000).

2. Donald L. Fixico, *The American Indian Mind in a Linear World: American Indian Studies and Traditional Knowledge* (New York: Routledge, 2003),1. Clara Sue Kidwell, "Native American Systems of Knowledge," in Philip J. Deloria and Neal Salisbury, eds., *A Companion to American Indian History* (Oxford: Blackwell, 2002), 87–102, quote, p87.

3. See Father Louis Hennepin's description of how he was taken care of by various Indian people. L[ouis] Hennepin, *A New Description of a Vast Country in America* (London: privately printed, 1699).

4. See, for example, Ignatia Broker's *Night Flying Woman* (St. Paul: MHS Press, 1983) as well as Fixico's *American Indian Mind* for different approaches to telling Indian history.

5. For some of the rage—or righteous anger—as well as some fine contemporary Native American writing, see, for example, *The American Indian Quarterly* during the editorial tenure of Northern Arizona State University historian—and Choctaw—Devon Mihesuah. Conversations with and comments from Winona State University historian Colette Hyman, as well as her work on Dakota women, has helped me see better, too. Notes in author's collection.

6. The authors of *We Look in All Directions* argue that traditional Ojibwe culture did value a kinship kind of relationship with the earth that was/is different from traditional "subdue" attitudes found in European culture. See Thomas Peacock and Marlene Wisuri, *Waasa Inaabidaa: We Look in All Directions* (Afton, MN: Afton Historical Society Press, 2001). Francis M. Carroll and Franklin R. Raiter, *The Fires of Autumn: The Cloquet–Moose Lake Disaster of 1918* (St. Paul: MHS Press, 1990), ch. 2.

7. The most effective germ carriers may have been Hernando DeSoto's pigs, which escaped after DeSoto died from fever in 1542 on the banks of the Mississippi River (probably in what is now Arkansas). Neither scholars nor storytellers relate an exact point of contact, but all agree that smallpox and other European diseases decimated the native population one wave at a time, from east to west. The disease reached the western Great Lakes by the late eighteenth century at least, probably earlier. It reached epidemic proportions again in the 1830s. White and indigenous scholars and storytellers continue to disagree among themselves about the size of the Indian population before 1492. William McNeill, *Plagues and People* (rev. ed., New York: Anchor, 1977). Alfred W. Crosby, *The Columbian Exchange: Biological and Cultural Consequences of 1492* (30th anniversary ed., New York:

Praeger, 2003). Charles C. Mann, *1491: New Revelations of the Americas before Columbus* (New York: Knopf, 2005). Linea Sundstrom, "Smallpox Used Them Up: References to Epidemic Disease in Northern Plains Winter Counts, 1714–1920," *Ethnohistory* 44:2 (Spring 1997), 305–43. See also Guy Gibbon, *The Sioux: The Dakota and Lakota Nations* (Oxford: Blackwell Publishing, 2003).

8. The site www.savewildrice.org is tended by the White Earth Land Recovery Project: see http://www.nativeharvest.com (accessed Mar. 16, 2007). Anishinaabe writer Winona LaDuke tells how in the distant past a duck led a hungry Nanaboozhoo to "manoomin." See details on Gemageskik dig at www.fromsitetostory.org (accessed Apr. 25, 2007). Peacock and Wisuri, *Waasa Inaabidaa;* Elsie M. Cavendar, Lorraine Cavendar-Gouge, and Mary C. Riley, drawings by Chet Kozlak, *Dakota Indians Coloring Book* (St. Paul: MHS Press, 1979). See also Walker D. Wyman with Kurt Leichtle, *The Chippewa: A History of the Great Lakes Woodland Tribe over Three Centuries* (River Falls: University of Wisconsin–River Falls Press, 1993); Broker, *Night Flying Woman;* Ella Cara Deloria, *Waterlily* (Lincoln: University of Nebraska Press, 1988). Janet D. Spector, *What This Awl Means: Feminist Archaeology at a Wahpeton Dakota Village* (St. Paul: MHS Press, 1993).

9. Archaeologists dated the residue on potsherds found near Rice Lake. See Johann Georg Kohl, *Kitchi-Gami: Life Among the Lake Superior Ojibway* (1859; repr., with new introduction by Robert Bieder, St. Paul: MHS Press, 1986).

10. Thomas Vennum, Jr., *Wild Rice and the Ojibway People* (St. Paul: MHS Press, 1988).

11. Resources for Indian Schools, "U.S. Indian Art: Minnesota Indian Artists," www.kstrom.net/isk/art/art_minn.html (accessed May 1, 2007).

12. See Anne Webb, "Both Sides of the Frontier: Native and White Women in the Midwest," unpublished manuscript.

13. Samuel W. Pond, *The Dakota or Sioux in Minnesota as They Were in 1834* (1908; repr., St. Paul: MHS Press, 1986).

14. Jack Weatherford, *Indian Givers: How the Indians of the Americas Transformed the World* (New York: Crown, 1988), especially 59–78.

15. The bag is featured in Christian F. Feest and Sylvia S. Kasprycki, *Peoples of the Twilight: European Views of Native Minnesota, 1823 to 1862* (Afton, MN: Afton Historical Society Press, 1999), 200. The account is in Deloria, *Waterlily,* 22–23.

16. Hennepin, *New Description,* XLVII, 165.

17. The substance of the MHS's collection of Indian material culture belonged to the Ayer Family of the Ayer Trading Post at Mille Lacs. Where the traditional pieces melt into the sale pieces isn't a categorical line that can be simply determined.

18. 104 Stat. 3048 Public Law 101–601 (Nov. 16, 1990).

19. Timothy R. Pauketat and Thomas E. Emerson, eds., *Cahokia: Domination and Ideology in the Mississippian World* (Lincoln: University of Nebraska Press, 1997); Thomas E. Emerson, *Cahokia and the Archaeology of Power* (Tuscaloosa: University of Alabama Press, 1997). See http://www.cr.nps.gov/worldheritage/cahokia.htm (accessed May 3, 2007).

20. Colin Calloway, *One Vast Winter Count: The Native American West before Lewis and Clark* (Lincoln: University of Nebraska Press, 2003).

21. See http://www.anishinaabemdaa.com/clans.htm (accessed May 3, 2007). "Figures on the Landscape: Effigy Mounds National Monument, Historic Resource Study," prepared for the National Parks Service by HRA Gray & Pape, Aug. 1, 2003, ch. 4, p5. Available: www.nps.gov/efmo/web/hrs/hrs4.htm (accessed May 1, 2007).

22. Bruce M. White and Alan R. Woolworth, "Oheyawake or Pilot Knob: Preliminary Summary of the Evidence," Turnstone Historical Research, Jan. 3, 2003.

23. Native peoples long had their own reasons to jostle and push and fight each other, and they did. After 1492, the warfare intensified with pressure exerted from the east and south by European explorers, then by settlers (from one perspective) or invaders (from another) and by fur traders and missionaries. The Anishinaabe knew about Frenchmen long before they encountered any. Oona, the central character in *Night Flying Woman*, Ignatia Broker's account of her great-grandmother, and her people moved and moved again to escape the "strangers." Competition for trade certainly provoked wars among native tribes. The Iroquois and Huron sought to control the trade and pushed out of the way other tribes wanting in.

Their moving thrust change in domino-like fashion upon other bands. So did changes on the land, increases and decreases in animals, colder or warmer temperatures, better or poorer growing seasons. Historians disagree about how the Dakota came to leave the woodlands and move onto the more open prairies—were they pushed by the Anishinaabe or pulled by better hunting opportunities? What's clear is that by 1800 Dakota people had moved away from Mille Lacs and other woodland lake areas and Anishinaabe people had moved in. Yes, whites pushed and pressured Native Americans all across the continent; Native Americans, too, pushed and fought with each other over territory, both before and after 1491. Gary Clayton Anderson, "Early Dakota Migration and Intertribal War: A Revision," *Western Historical Quarterly* 11:1 (Jan. 1980): 17–36.

24. Daniel K. Higginbottom, "Projectile Points of Minnesota: A Brief Introduction," http://www.tcinternet.net/users/cbailey/lithic1.html (accessed May 3, 2007). Stats from *Harper's Magazine* 312: 1868 (Jan. 2006): 11.

25. See Frances Densmore, *Chippewa Customs*, 2nd ed. (St. Paul: MHS Press, 1997), and William Warren, *History of the Ojibway People* (repr., St. Paul: MHS Press, 1984). Basil Johnston, *Ojibway Tales* (repr., Lincoln: University of Nebraska Press, 1990). Peacock and Wisuri, *Waasa Inaabidaa*. Samuel W. Pond, *Dakota Life in the Upper Midwest* (repr., with new introduction by Gary Clayton Anderson, St. Paul: MHS Press, 2003). Gary Clayton Anderson, *Kinsmen of Another Kind: Dakota-White Relations in the Upper Mississippi Valley, 1650–1862* (Lincoln: University of Nebraska Press, 1984). See also Fort Snelling army officer Seth Eastman's view of the Dakota people in the 1830s: Marybeth Lorbiecki, *Painting the Dakota: Seth Eastman at Fort Snelling* (Afton, MN: Afton Historical Society Press, 2000).

26. Hennepin, *New Description*, 40. Anderson, *Kinsmen of Another Kind*. See also Folwell, *History of Minnesota*, vol. 1.

27. See Kathy Davis Graves and Elizabeth Ebbott for the League of Women Voters of Minnesota, *Indians in Minnesota*, 5th ed. (Minneapolis: University of Minnesota Press, 2007), Table 1.1.

NOTES TO CHAPTER 3

1. A place that historian Richard White would identify as the Middle Ground. See Richard White, *The Middle Ground: Indians, Empires, and Republics in the Great Lakes Region, 1650–1815* (Cambridge: Cambridge University Press, 1991).

2. Mary Wheelhouse Berthel, *Minnesota Under Four Flags* (St. Paul: MHS Press, 1963). The 1850 U.S. Census reports Scott's age as fifty-two, which would put his birth date at 1798: Patricia C. Harpole and Mary D. Nagle, *Minnesota Territorial Census, 1850* (St. Paul: MHS Press, 1972), Ramsey County, 58. The "Register of Claims under the . . . Treaty . . . 1837" in Special Files, U.S. Office of In-

dian Affairs Papers (available on microfilm at the MHS), gives his birth date as 1792. John Wozniak in his genealogy of the Campbell family gives 1790: *Contact, Negotiation and Conflict: An Ethnohistory of the Eastern Dakota, 1819–1839* (Washington, DC: University Press of America, 1978), 120.

3. Jennifer S. H. Brown, *Strangers in Blood: Fur Trade Company Families in Indian Country* (Vancouver: University of British Columbia Press, 1980); Sylvia Van Kirk, *"Many Tender Ties": Women in Fur-Trade Society in Western Canada, 1670–1870* (Winnipeg: Watson & Dwyer, 1980); Susan Sleeper-Smith, *Indian Women and French Men: Rethinking Cultural Encounter in the Western Great Lakes* (Amherst: University of Massachusetts Press, 2001); Michael Lansing, "Plains Indian Women and Interracial Marriage in the Upper Missouri Trade, 1804–1868," *Western Historical Quarterly* 31 (Winter 2000): 413–33.

4. Van Kirk, *"Many Tender Ties,"* 6–7, 36–37. Donald Dean Parker, ed., *The Recollections of Philander Prescott: Frontiersman of the Old Northwest, 1819–1862* (Lincoln: University of Nebraska Press, 1966), 56. Philander Prescott was not a trader but was involved in the business. He, too, had a Dakota wife and talked about buying her, as was the custom. Lawrence Taliaferro, the longtime Indian agent at Fort Snelling, in his autobiography used the language of whites buying native wives. Lawrence Taliaferro, "Autobiography of Major Lawrence Taliaferro, Written in 1864," *MHS Collections* 6 (1894): 249. I'm grateful to Alan Woolworth, research specialist, MHS, for helping me sort out the Campbells and for opening his biography files to my use, especially his "Notes on the Family of Duncan Campbell" gathered in part from the "Lake Pepin Half Breeds" Special Files, U.S. Office of Indian Affairs Papers (available on microfilm at the MHS), manuscript in Woolworth's possession. See also Alan Woolworth, "Scott Campbell and His Many Frontiers," manuscript in Woolworth's possession.

5. Like his brother Scott, Duncan married a native woman. Following a not uncommon pattern in the mixed-blood community, one especially evident among Scott's daughters later, his sisters married white men and lived near Fort Snelling. One of his sisters, Margaret Campbell Pegano, died in childbirth in 1838 at the Indian Agency. Taliaferro Journals, Sept. 18, 1838, p92–93, typescript, MHS. William Joseph Snelling, the son of the fort's second commander, estimated that there were between 4,000 and 5,000 "half-breeds" and reported that "Each speaks French and the language of the mother." William Joseph Snelling, *Tales of the Northwest* (1830; repr., New York: Dorset Press, 1985), 78. See also Peter Lawrence Scanlan, *Prairie du Chien: French, British, American* (Menasha, WI: Collegiate Press, 1937), 170; Wozniak, *Contact, Negotiation and Conflict,* 118–21.

6. Roy Meyer repeats the Lewis and Clark story in his *Santee Sioux,* 37. In 1836 Taliaferro noted in his journals that the Campbell family was making sugar: Mar. 19, 1836, p40. It's not clear when or from whom Campbell learned to speak Ojibwe, but Taliaferro noted at various times in his journal that Campbell had interpreted in Ojibwe and in Dakota: see June 1, 1835, p3, for example. On May 20, 1836, p81, Taliaferro reported his "Interpreter for the Sioux . . . also talks Chippewa and other languages."

7. Scott Campbell met Long on this expedition. When Long stopped in Prairie du Chien to hire an interpreter and guide, Campbell served as the witness to their contract. See Lucile M. Kane, June D. Holmquist, and Carolyn Gilman, eds., *The Northern Expeditions of Stephen H. Long: The Journals of 1817 and 1823 and Related Documents* (St. Paul, MHS Press, 1978), 2. Paul C. Phillips, *The Fur Trade,* 2 vols. (Norman: University of Oklahoma Press, 1961), 2:87.

8. Harpole and Nagle, *Territorial Census,* Ramsey County, 58.

9. Gary Clayton Anderson and Alan R. Woolworth, eds., *Through Dakota Eyes: Narrative Accounts of the Minnesota Indian War of 1862* (St. Paul: MHS Press, 1988). J. Fletcher Williams identified Margaret as a Menominee half-breed: "A History of the City of St. Paul and of the County of Ramsey, Minnesota," *MHS Collections* 4 (1876): 134. So does Alan Woolworth, "Patoile, Marguerite Campbell," biography file, in Woolworth's possession.

10. Taliaferro Journals, May 12, 1826.

11. Taliaferro and his staff lived just outside the walls of the fort. See Nathaniel West, *The Ancestry, Life and Times of Honorable Henry Hastings Sibley* (St. Paul, MN: Pioneer Press Publishing Co., 1889).

12. Taliaferro Journals, Aug. 19, 1821, p15, June 17, 1836, p112–13.

13. Wozniak, *Contact, Negotiation and Conflict.* Taliaferro Journals, Aug. 19, 1821, p16; Oct. 21, 1821, p59, 65; June 1, 1835, p3; Feb. 13, 1825, p3.

14. Taliaferro Journals, July 25, 1838, p45–46. One charge made about the treaties in later days was that the interpreter—Scott Campbell being the only one listed officially on the treaty document—was being paid by the government and would,

therefore, have had loyalty to the government and so was an undependable interpreter. Taliaferro reported, however, that in 1838 the representatives of five villages "called at the agency on business relative to their Treaty stipulations." Among those stipulations the headmen included a salary of $450 per year for Campbell that was to come out of their own money. This document was signed by twelve men and, interestingly, witnessed by Scott Campbell, among others. Taliaferro Journals, Feb. 6, 1822, p74–75.

15. The only evidence of conflict between Taliaferro and his interpreter surfaced around the trade. In 1822 Campbell tried to mix his work as interpreter with work in the trade. Taliaferro objected and revoked Campbell's pay for the period from January to March 1822, during which time his work has overlapped. Forced to choose, Scott abandoned trading and kept at translating. His brother Duncan made a different choice. Duncan for a time also interpreted for Taliaferro and for a time served as subagent for Taliaferro, but in the mid-1820s he moved more fully into the trade, following his father's lead. He worked independently until the mid-1830s and then joined up with the American Fur Company. Taliaferro Journals, Feb. 8, 1822, p76, Aug. 1, 1835, p97, Oct. 13, 1835, p167, 174. Taliaferro remarked on issues of identity in relation to Joseph Renville: "His being an Indian—wearing the garb of a white man, & insisting on being of Mixed blood . . ." Taliaferro Journals, 1836, p72. See also Gertrude W. Ackerman, "Joseph Renville of Lac Qui Parle," *Minnesota History* 12 (Sept. 1931): 231–46. Williams, "History of the City of St. Paul," 266.

16. Meyer, *Santee Sioux*, 37–38. See also Pond, *Dakota or Sioux in Minnesota*, 339–41.

17. Williams, "History of the City of St. Paul," 266.

18. Article 13, "Treaty with the Sioux, etc. 1825," at http://digital.library.okstate.edu/Kappler/Vol2/treaties/sio0250.htm (accessed May 1, 2007). The treaty gave the land description in this way: "ARTICLE 7. It is agreed between the Winnebagoes and the Sioux, Sacs and Foxes, Chippewas and Ottawas, Chippewas and Potawatomies of the Illinois, that the Winnebago country shall be bounded as follows: south easterly by Rock River, from its source near the Winnebago lake, to the Winnebago village, about forty miles above its mouth; westerly by the east line of the tract, lying upon the Mississippi, herein secured to the Ottawa, Chippewa and Potawatomie Indians, of the Illinois; and also by the high bluff, described in the Sioux boundary,

and running north to Black river: from this point the Winnebagoes claim up Black river, to a point due west from the source of the left fork of the Ouisconsin; thence to the source of the said fork, and down the same to the Ouisconsin; thence down the Ouisconsin to the portage, and across the portage to Fox river; thence down Fox river to the Winnebago lake, and to the grand Kan Kanlin, including in their claim the whole of Winnebago lake; but, for the causes stated in the next article, this line from Black river must for the present be left indeterminate." From the manuscript document at http://www.wisconsinhistory.org/turningpoints/search.asp?id=1620 (accessed May 9, 2007).

19. Taliaferro's Indian wife was the daughter of Cloud Man. Their daughter Mary was born in 1828. She married Warren Woodbury and was herself a Dakota War captive. Eliza Taliaferro, the Pennsylvania wife, must also have known about her husband's daughter but never mentioned her. Rena N. Coen, "Eliza Dillon Taliaferro: Portrait of a Frontier Wife," *Minnesota History* 52 (Winter 1990): 150. Mary Riggs made this observation in a letter to her mother in July 1837. Stephen R. Riggs, *Mary and I: Forty Years with the Sioux* (Chicago: W. G. Holmes, 1880), 24.

20. Pond, *Dakota or Sioux in Minnesota*, 340. Theodore C. Blegen, ed., "Two Missionaries in the Sioux Country," *Minnesota History* 21 (Mar. 1940): 26–27.

21. See Don E. Fehrenbacher, *Slavery, Law and Politics: The Dred Scott Case in Historical Perspective* (New York: Oxford University Press, 1981), 122. Other Africans Americans lived around the fort. James Thompson, who had been brought to the fort as a slave, was purchased by Reverend A. Brunson and then freed and put to work. Thompson reportedly "talked Sioux first rate," so Brunson enlisted him to help with his missionary work. Another trader, Alexis Bailly, was also reported to have had slaves. Williams, "History of the City of St. Paul," 46. Taliaferro, "Autobiography," 235.

22. It was to their school that Taliaferro sent his daughter and with whom he left her when he returned to Virginia. Riggs, *Mary and I*, 15. No doubt some of these missionaries came to Minnesota with a real commitment to converting the Indians. But for some the Indians were simply a group of people in need of salvation, much like other groups in need of salvation. Frederick Ayer, for example, worked among the Ojibwe and after the Civil War moved to Tennessee to work among the freed

slaves. One son of Stephen and Mary Riggs stayed in the Midwest and worked among the Dakota people, even accompanying them to Nebraska after the Dakota War, but one of their daughters took up missionary work in China, her new frontier. See "Frederick Ayer, Teacher and Missionary to the Ojibway Indians, 1829 to 1850," *MHS Collections* 6 (1894): 429–37. Isabella Riggs Williams, *By the Great Wall: Letters from China, 1866–97* (New York: Fleming H. Revell Co., 1909). Sometimes, too, the mission fields might have been the place to which people fled hoping to convert, yes, but hoping perhaps to find freedom themselves. Stephen Riggs refers to two women who "were anxious to engage in mission work. They preferred to go to the Indians, as they desired to labor together. It was a David and Jonathan love that existed between Miss Mary C. Collins and Miss J. Emmaretta Whipple." Riggs, *Mary and I*, 303.

23. Charlotte O. Van Cleve, "*Three Score Years and Ten*": *Life-long Memories of Fort Snelling, Minnesota, and Other Parts of the West* (Minneapolis, MN: Harison and Smith, 1888), 46. Riggs, *Mary and I*, 126. John H. Bliss, "Reminiscences of Fort Snelling," *MHS Collections* 6 (1894): 347. See also James H. Baker, "Address at Fort Snelling," *MHS Collections* 7 (1908): 291–301.

24. Shortly after arriving at St. Peter's, Henry Sibley wrote to Ramsay Crooks, the American Fur Company president, a letter brimming with hope and ambition, wanting in various ways to "command the trade with the Indians." Sibley to Crooks, Nov. 1, 1834, Sibley Papers, MHS. Few men have received as careful and sensitive a treatment as Sibley does at the hands of Rhoda Gilman: *Henry Hastings Sibley: Divided Heart* (St. Paul: MHS Press, 2004).

25. See "A Sioux Store in the War," *MHS Collections* 6 (1894): 382–400, and Gilman, *Henry Hastings Sibley*.

26. Meyer, *Santee Sioux*, 70.

NOTES TO CHAPTER 4

1. Minisota details, William Lass to author, Feb. 2007, in author's possession.

2. With the admission of Missouri and Maine in 1820, Congress set a course of admitting states in pairs, one slave and one free, to keep a balance of northern and southern senators. Arkansas and Michigan joined as a pair in 1836–37. In 1845–46, Congress admitted Florida, Texas, and Iowa; Wisconsin followed in 1848. Soon the rush to gold propelled California into quick eligibility for statehood and resulted in the devil's bargain that was the Compromise of 1850 (and the long fuse to the Civil War). The Fugitive Slave Law that was part of the Compromise enraged Northerners, and its disregard angered Southerners. The lines that separated north and south hardened, and opponents faced off first in Kansas and Nebraska in the 1850s and then in 1861.

3. Baker, "Address at Fort Snelling," 298. Nancy Goodman and Robert Goodman, *Joseph R. Brown: Adventurer on the Minnesota Frontier 1820–1849* (Rochester, MN: Lone Oak Press, 1996). See also Folwell, *History of Minnesota*, 2:406.

4. According to historian Merlin Stonehouse, Steele "owned more of Minnesota than any other man in history": *John Wesley North and the Reform Frontier* (Minneapolis: University of Minnesota Press, 1965), 24.

5. Folwell, *History of Minnesota*, 1:365–76.

6. Stonehouse describes Steele in that way: *John Wesley North*, 24. Gilman, *Henry Hastings Sibley*, 88–89.

7. Fehrenbacher, *Slavery, Law, and Politics*.

8. Mary Riggs letter, Riggs Papers, MHS.

9. Grace Lee Nute, "Wilderness Marthas," in Rhoda R. Gilman and June Drenning Holmquist, eds., *Selections from Minnesota History: A Fiftieth Anniversary Anthology* (St. Paul: MHS Press, 1965), 55. See also Rebecca Marshall Cathcart, "A Sheaf of Remembrances," *MHS Collections* 15 (1909–14): 515–52, and Lucy Leavenworth Wilder Morris, ed., *Old Rail Fence Corners: Frontier Tales Told by Minnesota Pioneers* (1914; repr., St. Paul: MHS Press, 1976).

10. Evadene A. Burris Swanson, "Keeping House on the Minnesota Frontier," *Minnesota History* 14 (Sept. 1933): 263–82. Barbara Stuhler and Gretchen Kreuter, eds., *Women of Minnesota: Selected Biographical Essays*, rev. ed. (St. Paul: MHS Press, 1998), 7, 9–13.

11. See Warren Upham and Rose Barteau Dunlap, comps., *Minnesota Biographies, 1655–1912* (St. Paul: MHS, 1912), 392, 615.

12. Ann North to her parents, July 7, 1851, microfilm, John Wesley North Papers, MHS.

13. The Norths were among the New Englanders and East Coasters fired by republican and religious fervor in the 1830s and 1840s who set out to fix the world in general and the United States in particular. These Yankees' passionate and undoubting commitment to enacting their vision of what the United States ought to be did much to shape the Minnesota of then and later. The early territorial legislatures passed stringent laws limiting what could occur on Sundays and liquor laws that re-

quired a seller's license and limited sale to Indians. The Land Ordinance of 1785 specified that the proceeds of the sale of one section of every township would be dedicated to schools. The Oregon Principle enlarged that provision to two sections, and it was applied to Minnesota. The territorial legislature incorporated the state historical society (1849), and the university (1851).

It wasn't that these Yankees weren't also ambitious, land hungry, racist, and self-serving, but theirs was a complex set of motives and drives. They were neither one nor the other. That's what makes them interesting. Historian Joel Sibley—no relation to Henry Hastings Sibley—argues that these Yankees were engaged in their own version of cultural imperialism. They recoiled from the new immigrants, particularly the Irish and Catholic and poor who showed up in large numbers in the mid-1840s. It is difficult to know whether it was the immigrants' nationality, religion, or class that most distressed the Yankees, but facing the trio, they galvanized to protect what they knew and were themselves. Though not Yankees, strictly speaking, Sibley and Rice and Steele certainly shared their values and mores—and after 1848, especially, more and more of their style.

14. Linda Peavey and Ursula Smith, *Women in Waiting in the Westward Movement: Life on the Home Frontier* (Norman: University of Oklahoma Press, 1994), ch. 5 on Harriet Burr Godfrey.

15. Ann North letter, Oct. 20, 1849, microfilm, North Papers.

16. Ann North to her parents, Sept. 8 and 15 and Oct. 6, 1850, microfilm, North Papers.

17. See Gilman, *Henry Hastings Sibley*, 125; Anderson, *Kinsmen of Another Kind*, 181–89; Anderson, *Little Crow*, Folwell, *History of Minnesota*, 1:282–305.

18. Elizabeth Ebbott for the League of Women Voters, *Indians in Minnesota*, 4th ed. (Minneapolis: University of Minnesota Press, 1985).

19. Blegen, *Minnesota*, 171–73.

20. Ayako Uchida, "The Protestant Mission and Native American Response: The Case of the Dakota Mission, 1835–1862," *Japanese Journal of American Studies* 10 (1999): 153–76, see 164–65. Clifford Allen, Joy Knutson, Vince Pratt, Arlene Stuart, Paul Stuart, and Dwayne Weston, *Dakotah: A History of the Flandreau Santee Sioux Tribe* (Flandreau, SD: Tribal History Program, Flandreau Santee Sioux Tribe, Sept. 1971), 26–27.

21. Anderson, *Kinsmen of Another Kind*, 216; Allen, Knutson, Pratt, A. Stuart, P. Stuart, and Weston, *Dakotah*, 26–27. U.S. Census, 1860, Redwood

Agency, Brown County, and Yellow Medicine Agency, Yellow Medicine County. In the 1860 census, Mr. and Mrs. Patois are recorded as Francis and Mary Patwell. Joseph R. Brown served as the Indian agent at Yellow Medicine by 1860 and lived there with his wife and their eight children, including their youngest son, named "Sibley." Susanna is identified in the census as "m," the choices being "White, black or mulatto."

22. See Bruce M. White, "The Power of Whiteness: Or, The Life and Times of Joseph Rolette Jr.," *Minnesota History* 56.4 (Winter, 1998–99): 178–97.

23. See especially "Sioux of the Mississippi," part of the *Report of the Commission of Indian Affairs for the Year 1857* (Washington, DC: William A. Harris Printer, 1858), 61–112. See also Folwell, *History of Minnesota*, 2:225, 231, 415.

24. Upham and Dunlap, *Minnesota Biographies*.

NOTES TO CHAPTER 5

1. The Campbells were only one of many families that stood in this middle ground. Theresa M. Schenck tells the story of William Warren, an Ojibwe man the age of Antoine Joseph Campbell, and his adept steering through these racial waters. See Theresa M. Schenck, *William W. Warren: The Life, Letters, and Times of an Ojibwe Leader* (Lincoln: University of Nebraska Press, 2007).

2. Whether Madeline held on to Indian customs and stories and passed them to her children is impossible to know from the outside. The trajectory of her public life, however, landed her firmly in what became white territory, even when it was "Half-Breed Tract" near Lake Pepin. The 1850 Territorial Census identified these two families with the French versions of their names; in 1860 they had become the Roscoes and the Youngs.

3. The Dalton rumor appeared in print only in 1865. [Isaac F. V. Heard], "The Campbell Family," *St. Paul Pioneer Press*, May 7, 1865. Cecelia Campbell Stay, "Reminiscence," Manitoba Archives, Winnipeg [copy in Alan Woolworth Papers, MHS].

4. U.S. Census, 1860, Brown County; Anderson and Woolworth, *Through Dakota Eyes*. Stay, "Reminiscence."

5. Folwell, *History of Minnesota*, 2: 400–15, on Inkpaduta, see 2:415. See also Lucius Hubbard and Return I. Holcombe, *Minnesota in Three Centuries, 1655–1908*, 3 vols. (New York: Publishing Society of Minnesota, 1908), 3:263–300. K. Pritchette noted that Campbell's "efforts to harmonize these heathens and remove their feelings of disaffection were unremitting and successful. He was also active and

serviceable in forming the expedition against the Spirit Lake murderers, taking charge himself of the expedition and exposing himself in the attack at the Dry Wood Lake, where several of the marauding band were killed. I would recommend him as worthy a pecuniary recompense." For another version, see William Cullen, Superintendent of Indian Affairs, noting that the annuity Indian fighting force sent after Inkpaduta was "under the command of Little Crow; as an assurance to me of their good faith, I had placed my interpreter, A. D. Campbell in charge of them, with six reliable half-breeds," in *The Commissioner of Indian Affairs, 1857* (Washington, DC: GPO, 1858), 51–52, 87–98.

6. My presumption is that Joe—like most other mixed bloods—generally dressed white, as did his wife and his brother Baptiste on the gallows. Barbara T. Newcombe, "Sioux Sign a Treaty in Washington in 1858," *Minnesota History* 45 (Fall 1976): 82–96.

7. *An Act To Suppress Insurrection, To Punish Treason and Rebellion, To Seize and Confiscate the Property of Rebels, and for Other Purposes,* http://www.history.umd.edu/Freedmen/conact2.htm (accessed Mar. 18, 2007). See also Mark Grimsley, *The Hard Hand of War: Union Military Policy Toward Southern Civilians, 1861–1865* (New York: Cambridge University Press, 1995).

8. Anderson, *Little Crow;* Anderson, *Kinsmen of Another Kind;* Anderson and Woolworth, *Through Dakota Eyes.*

9. Sylvia Hoffert, "Gender and Vigilantism on the Minnesota Frontier: Jane Grey Swisshelm and the U.S. Dakota Conflict of 1862," *Western Historical Quarterly* 29.3 (1998): 342–62. See also Sylvia Hoffert, *Jane Grey Swisshelm: An Uncommon Life, 1815–1884* (Chapel Hill: University of North Carolina Press, 2004).

10. Anderson and Woolworth, *Through Dakota Eyes,* 56, 152. Stay, "Reminiscence." Another casualty of that first day was a white trader named Francois Patoille, the second husband of Joe Campbell's widowed mother.

11. Cecilia Campbell Stay, in Anderson and Woolworth, *Through Dakota Eyes.* M. P. Satterlee, *The Court Proceedings in the Trial of Dakota Indians Following the Massacre in Minnesota in August 1862* (Minneapolis, MN: Satterlee Printing Co., 1927), 47. Kurt D. Bergemann, *Brackett's Battalion: Minnesota Cavalry in the Civil War and Dakota War* (St. Paul, MN: Borealis Books, 2004). The Sibley Papers (MHS) include letters sent by Henry Sibley responding to the fears of his wife. See also *St. Paul Pioneer Press,* which in late August and early September was full of graphic stories of settlers' deaths and the perceived threat to the whole state.

12. Other of the Campbell brothers could have translated, but apparently Joe was the only one who could read and write in English. On 1857 affidavits both Baptiste and Jack signed with an "x" while Joe signed his name. Oct. 15, 1858, addressed to W. Cullen, Supt. of Indian Affairs, in "Claims for goods and services furnished in the expedition against Inkpadutah in 1857," Special File 132, Roll 26, Office of Indian Affairs Papers, RG 75, National Archives, Washington, DC. See Anderson and Woolworth, *Through Dakota Eyes.* Gilman, *Henry Hasting Sibley;* Court of Claims, No. 22524, *The Sisseton and Wahpeton Bands of Sioux Indians v. The United States,* Evidence for Claimants, Part II, 255–65 (photocopy from Alan Woolworth). Stay, "Reminiscence"; Bergemann, *Brackett's Battalion.*

13. Satterlee, *Court Proceedings,* 46–47. Trial Transcripts, Congressional records, National Archives.

14. Isaac F. V. Heard, *History of the Sioux War and Massacres of 1862 and 1863* (New York: Harper & Brothers, 1865), 283–90, quote, p290.

15. This distinction between mixed-blood and Dakota men is rarely made in recent retellings of the story. See for example the reference to "38 Santee were executed" at http://www.thenicc.edu/SanteeSiouxTribeHistory.htm (accessed Jan. 21, 2004).

16. William Seeger, "Interesting Reminiscence," *The [Mankato] Review,* Feb. 16, 1897; Bergemann, *Brackett's Battalion.*

17. Samuel Brown, in Anderson and Woolworth, *Through Dakota Eyes,* 132; "Startling News!! More Indian Murders!!," "Blood for Blood!!" and "The Campbell Family—Sketch of John Campbell," *St. Paul Pioneer Press,* May 4, 5, 1865. *[Mankato] Record,* May 6, 1865. The *St. Peter Tribune* (May 10, 1865) identified Jack's mother as a "full-blood squaw" who threatened his death would be avenged.

18. Some Dakota people had, after 1863, disassociated themselves from the majority of their bands. A few stayed around Faribault; a few others around Wabasha. Some—who did not take part in the war or who could be shown to have helped save whites—stayed behind through the intervention of Bishop Whipple and Alexander Faribault. But, as historian Roy Meyer relates, some white Minnesotans fought the presence even of these. An 1865 resolution in the Minnesota Legislature expressed

the objections of many white Minnesotans: "The experience has shown that even under ordinary circumstances a settlement of Indians in a body among whites is very detrimental and injurious both to the Indians and whites." Meyer, *Santee Sioux*, 258–72, quote, p263. Motier A. Bullock, *Congregational Nebraska* (Lincoln, NE: Western Publishing and Engraving Company, 1905), 271.

19. Meyer, *Santee Sioux*.

20. Sioux Half Breed Census, 1856, Entry 378, Vol. 2, RG 75, National Archives; *Minnesota in the Civil and Indian Wars* (St. Paul, MN: Pioneer Press Co., 1898); Minnesota State Census, 1865. http://www.rootsweb.com/~mnwabbio/wab7.htm (accessed Dec. 6, 2002). *History of Wabasha County* (Chicago: H. H. Hill and Co. Publishers, 1884), 1272. U.S. Census, 1870, Pepin, Reeds Landing, Wabasha County, Reel 11, p1; U.S. Census, 1880, Reel 635, p426. Minnesota State Census, 1895. *The [Wabasha] Standard*, Mar. 25, 1899, 1:4; *Minneapolis Journal*, Mar. 27, 1899, 3:2. In her book *Indian Women and French Men*, Susan Sleeper-Smith argues that in the 1830s Indian people found "adaptive strategies" to resist removal. Perhaps blending in at Lake Pepin was a latter-day version of that for the Campbell women. They stayed where they were—what it allowed or cost them we cannot calculate. A brother who had been wounded in a gunshot accident lived for some years at the St. Peter State Hospital. He was a "quiet and inoffensive" man who developed "acute mania" within a few years. The case notes report: "The patient is a filthy and obstinate one and will not do anything voluntarily." St. Peter State Hospital Case Book, Vol. 2, 1868–71, p237, manuscript, MHS.

21. Minnesota 1860 Federal Population Schedule, p32; U.S. Census, 1870, St. Paul, M593 10, p1346, image 179 (both http://www.ancestry.com). "Andreas' History of the State of Nebraska: Knox County," http://www.kancoll.org/books/andreas_ne/knox/knox-p1.html (accessed Mar. 5, 2004), p5. The Annuity Pay Rolls are useful for following many of the Campbells. From these records one can determine age, "blood," address, and, by implication, the race of the spouse (spouses ineligible for annuities because they were not part Indian did not appear on the rolls). One can also determine, by their absence, which eligible people did not apply. See, for example, Annuity Pay Roll, 1899, M405, MHS.

22. "Interesting Letters from Paul Campbell," *St. Peter Tribune*, May 10, 1865. "Catholic Cemetery at Santee," http://www.rootsweb.com/~neknox/cemeteries/catholic.htm (accessed Mar. 5, 2004), p1.

23. *St. Peter Tribune*, May 1, 1865. The most useful source for tracking people at Santee Reservation is the Census of Santee Indians. See, for example, the 1886 census, which includes Joseph Campbell and his two sons (and their families), Margaret Campbell, Harriet Young (and her family). I followed these until 1910, the last one in which Joseph Campbell appears and in which his sons and dozens of other Campbells also appear. Census of Santee Indians, M559, Roll 475, MHS; Bullock, *Congregational Nebraska*, 271. Knox County, NE, Marriage Index, http://www.rootsweb.com/~neknox/marriage/index.htm (accessed Mar. 5, 2004), p3. Campbell may have married two different women named Louise. He is listed as married to Louise Frienier in January 1889. The ages and different Indian names listed in two Santee censuses suggest the existence of two Louises. Knox County Farmers Listing includes A. J. Campbell as a farmer in 1890–91: http://www.rootsweb.com/~neknox/farmers.htm (accessed Mar. 5, 2004), p3.

Much of the information about Antoine Joseph Campbell's family comes from his daughter Celia Campbell Stay's reminiscences. One version is included in the Dakota War Manuscripts, Reel 1 (Campbell in alphabetical order); another, "The Massacre at the Lower Sioux Agency, August 18, 1862," is in the Manitoba Archives, copy in Woolworth Papers. Still another (also in the Woolworth Papers), "A Captivity Narrative of Celia Stay," was recorded in 1924 by a New Ulm committee visiting Mrs. Stay in Montevideo. The only published parts of her accounts (outside of newspapers) appear in Anderson and Woolworth, *Through Dakota Eyes*, 44–52, 135–38, 249–54. According to Stay, St. Joseph's Catholic Church in Montevideo, where she lived, was named for him.

24. Minnesota Land Records, document 7631, http://ancestry.com (subscription; accessed May 4, 2007). So many Roscoes stayed so long in Wabasha County that they are relatively easy to find in census returns. They were prominent enough for mention in county histories and for local newspapers to carry obituaries detailing their ancestors and survivors. These Roscoes led remarkably long lives—many into their eighties. Finally, their stability made locating their death certificates possible. That the records on their lives are so accessible is a function of their movement into white society. See for example, *History of Wabasha County*, 1272, on Oliver Rosicot; Minnesota Scrapbook, Vol. 1, p160, MHS;

U.S. Census, 1870, Pepin Township, Wabasha County, Roll 11, p1; 1880, Reel 635, ED 177, p15; Minnesota State Census, 1895, Reel 102, p10; *Marshall County Banner*, Feb. 23, 1911; death certificates for Eli Roscoe, Feb. 20, 1911, William Roscoe, Feb. 11, 1920, Mrs. Josephine Roscoe Shaw, June 19, 1943, Clemence Derosier, Jan. 6, 1918, Louise Ann Pritchard, Sept. 2, 1939; "Wm. Roscoe, Sr., Passed Away Wednesday Morning," *Pipestone Leader*, Feb. 12, 1920; "Mrs. Levi Derosia," *The [Wabasha] Standard*, Jan. 10, 1918, "Sand Prairie Woman Buried at Minneiska," *Wabasha County Herald Standard*, Sept. 7, 1939; "Mrs. Shaw 91, Reads Oldest Resident, Dies," *Wabasha County Herald Standard*, June 24, 1943.

25. *Marshall County Banner*, Feb. 23, 1911. Meyer, *Santee Sioux*, 165, 242, 256. U.S. Census, 1930. The Roscoes—except Samuel—made the transition, at least in the public record, to a white world. The youngest son of Madeline and Oliver, Samuel moved to an explicitly Indian community: Flandreau, in what would become South Dakota. The town was largely settled by Dakota people fleeing the Santee Reservation to homestead in Dakota Territory in 1869. In the late 1880s and early 1890s an Indian boarding school grew up there, serving mostly Dakota and Ojibwe children. In 1920 Samuel, age fifty-nine, lived in Flandreau with his son's family—all identified as white, living among "full-bloods." Ten years later his son had moved, but Samuel stayed there in a rooming house, his connection to that community apparently stronger than to family. As mixed bloods, the Roscoes were entitled to annuities. Madeline collected them until her death in 1899. Her daughters did not. Neither did her sons in Pipestone and Marshall counties. Samuel Roscoe, like his mother, accepted annuities despite his being recorded in Flandreau as white. See Annuity Pay Roll, M405, MHS.

26. Margaret Labathe is the most difficult to track both during and after the war. In 1855 she and her mixed-blood husband Joseph Labathe were at the Lower Sioux Agency; he was almost certainly a Dakota scout. There were at least two Joseph LaBaths. Labathes, Labat, LaBathes, and LaBaths all show up in the historical record, in Minnesota and federal census returns and on the Birch Coulee annuity rolls. Meyer, *Santee Sioux*, 198–200, ch. 10.

27. U.S. Census, 1910, ED 119, p15. These sons, too, received annuities. At least one married a full-blood Indian woman. "Schedule of Sioux Claimants, [1916–1923]," RG 75, National Archives.

28. Anderson and Woolworth, *Through Dakota Eyes*, 136 (Emily's Indian name). U.S. Census, 1860, Redwood Township, Brown County, Minnesota (many photocopies, and Heritage Quest), Series 653, Roll 567, p250. Heard, "Campbell Family."

29. Frank Stay folder, Biography Files, Woolworth Papers. "Frank Jetty's Life—related by himself to the Grey Nuns," in C. Stay folder, Woolworth Papers. See "Frank Jetty's Life," reel 1, Dakota War Manuscripts, MHS. See also: http://ftp.rootsweb.com/pub/usgenweg.mn/lacquieparle/cemetery/stayfarm.txt (accessed Mar. 18, 2007).

30. U.S. Census, 1930, Montevideo City, Chippewa County, ED 12–15, p12-B. U.S. Census, 1900, Camp Release Township, Lac qui Parle County, ED 121, F6, Roll 772, p9608; 1905, Roll 131, ED 15; 1900, Roll 709. *[Montevideo] Commercial*, Jan. 17, 1913.

31. Roediger, David, *The Wages of Whiteness: Race and the Making of the American Working Class* (New York: Verso, 1999); Matthew Frye Jacobson, *Whiteness of a Different Color: European Immigrants and the Alchemy of Race* (Cambridge, MA: Harvard University Press, 1998); Noel Ignatiev, *How the Irish Became White* (New York: Rutledge, 1995); Peter Kolchin, "Whiteness Studies: The New History of Race in America," *Journal of American History* 89 (June 2002): 154–73.

NOTES TO CHAPTER 6

1. For this number I'm grateful for the help and advice of Hamp Smith, the MHS staff member most knowledgeable about the Civil War in the state. Because Minnesota was such a new state, who counted as a "Minnesotan" is neither straightforward nor easy to quantify. For example, the Christie brothers, whose letters are excerpted on the MHS website, enlisted when they were in Wisconsin but spent the late 1860s and 1870s in Minnesota (except for their time in school at Beloit College in Wisconsin). While their father and sister stayed in the state for several decades more, one of the brothers moved to Montana, one to seminary and then to missionary work in Turkey, one to employment in Washington, DC. Do they count as Minnesotans? See http://www.mnhs.org/library/Christie/intropage.html (accessed Mar. 18, 2007). Minnesota's census reported population in 1860 as 172,023; in 1870 as 439,706. See Table Aa4242–4304, "Minnesota population by race, sex, age, nativity, and urban-rural residence, 1850–1990" in *Historical Statistics of the United States Millennial Edition Online, Part A: Population*, http://hsus.cambridge.org/

HSUSWeb/toc/showPart.do?id=A (accessed May 3, 2007).

2. Alfred Carpenter, July 30, 1863, in "A Civil War Journal: Company K, 1st Minnesota Volunteer Infantry Regiment," A Winona County Historical Society Education Project, at www2.smumn.edu/deptpages/~history/civil_war (accessed May 2, 2007).

3. Kenneth Carley, *Minnesota in the Civil War: An Illustrated History* (1961; repr., St. Paul: MHS Press, 2000). Richard Moe, *The Last Full Measure: The Life and Death of the First Minnesota Volunteers* (1993; repr., St. Paul: MHS Press, 2001).

4. Quoted from Christopher C. Andrews, *Recollections: 1829–1922*, ed. by Alice E. Andrews (Cleveland, OH: Arthur H. Clark. 1928), 147–90.

5. Madison Bowler to Lizzie Caleff, July 31, 1862, in Carley, *Minnesota in the Civil War*, 91.

6. A. C. Smith, *A Random Historical Sketch of Meeker County, Minnesota, from its First Settlement to July 4th, 1876* (Litchfield, MN: Belfoy and Joubert, 1877), 69–78.

7. Judson Bishop, "Narrative of the Third Regiment," *Minnesota in the Civil and Indian Wars*, 1: 174–90.

8. Mary Dillon Foster, *Who's Who Among Minnesota Women* (St. Paul, MN: The Author, 1924), 115, and manuscript census reports 1860, 1870, 1880 (as Garber), 1900. The Garvers' military companies are listed at the ancestry.com service records website. See also announcements of the golden wedding anniversary celebrations for Dr. and Mrs. James A. Garver in Minnesota Scrapbook, 17:35, MHS.

9. Jane E. Schultz, *Women at the Front: Hospital Workers in Civil War America* (Chapel Hill: University of North Carolina Press, 2004).

10. Here and following taken from a selection of the Bowler letters reprinted in Carley, *Minnesota in the Civil War*, 90–93; the full collection of letters is held at the MHS.

11. Mary Livermore, *The Story of My War* (Hartford, CT: A. D. Worthington and Co., 1888). See "Activities and Accomplishments of the Commission," *Iowa Journal of History and Politics* 16:2 (Jan. 1918), part of the Iowa History Project, at http://iagenweb.org/history/IJHP/IJHP2IA10.htm (accessed May 3, 2007).

12. Wendy Hammond Venet, "The Emergence of a Suffragist: Mary Livermore, Civil War Activism, and the Moral Power of Women," *Civil War History* 48:2 (2002): 143–64, see especially 146, 153–60. See J. Matthew Gallman, "Voluntarism in Wartime: Philadelphia's Great Central Fair," Maris Vinovskis, ed., *Toward a Social History of the American Civil War: Exploratory Essays* (New York: Cambridge University Press, 1990), 93–116.

13. For Miller's and Eggleston's call, see http://edinborough.com/Learn/Civil_War_Life/NW%20Fair.htm (accessed May 3, 2007). Minnesota Quilt Project, *Minnesota Quilts: Creating Connections with Our Past* (Stillwater, MN: Voyageur Press, 2005), 25.

14. Casualty figures come from MHS Civil War specialist Hamp Smith. Gary Paulsen, *Soldier's Heart: A Novel of the Civil War* (New York: Delacorte Press, 1998).

15. Amy Holmes, "'Such Is the Price We Pay': American Widows and the Civil War Pension System," in Vinovskis, ed., *Social History of the Civil War*, 191–75. See also Carol Reardon, "Gettysburg: A Turning Point in Memory," in James A. Rawley and Kenneth Winkel, eds., *Turning Points of the Civil War*, 2nd ed. (Lincoln: University of Nebraska Press, 2006).

16. James Alan Marten, "Exempt from the Ordinary Rules of Life: Researching Postwar Adjustment Problems of Union Veterans," *Civil War History* 41:1 (2001): 57–70, quote, p60. Trevor Plante, "National Home for Disabled Volunteer Soldiers," *Prologue: Journal of the National Archives and Records Service* 36 (Spring 2004), http://www.archives.gov/publications/prologue/2004/spring/soldiers-home.html (accessed May 4, 2007). See also Eric T. Dean, Jr., *Shook Over Hell: Post-Traumatic Stress, Vietnam, and the Civil War* (Cambridge, MA: Harvard University Press, 1997). Dean looked at Indiana veterans who were considered insane and found many examples of what in a later generation we would identify as PTSD, ranging from anxiety and sleeplessness to survivor guilt and depression.

17. The foundation of the Women's Christian Temperance Union (WCTU) nationally in 1873 and its first local in Minnesota in 1876 may simply have been a resurgence of prewar prohibitionism, but more likely it reflected what appears to have been a growing problem with alcohol—and violence—and not just in the national asylums. Some nativists blamed the problem on increased immigration after the war. More likely it was the war's lingering effect. By its second annual convention in 1878, the WCTU of Minnesota included twenty-four local chapters ranging in membership from twenty-one to one hundred. The WCTU also advocated laws to protect children from various temptations and influences and promoted woman suffrage. Perhaps Mary Livermore was not the only woman whose

Civil War experiences encouraged her into suffragist ranks. Foster, *Who's Who*, 350–54.

18. Frank H. Heck, "The Grand Army of the Republic in Minnesota, 1866–1880," *Minnesota History* 16.4 (Dec. 1935): 427–44. On the Daggett GAR Post, see http://www.litch.com/gar/History.htm (accessed Apr. 24, 2007). See stereography, loc. no. U3.4 r25, in MHS visual collections. See also Stuart McConnell, "Who Joined the Grand Army? Three Case Studies in the Construction of Union Veteranhood, 1866–1900," in Vinovskis, ed., *Social History of the Civil War*, 139–70.

19. In St. Paul in 1865, women ran boardinghouses, worked as bonnet bleachers and pressers, operated one of the book and stationery stores, one of the dry goods stores, one of the furriers, one of the grocery stores, and one of the ice cream "saloons." The two midwives were women, as were seven of the eight milliners and one of the music teachers. They ran four schools, including the St. Joseph Academy and the school of the Sisters of Charity. Men worked as architects, bankers, barbers, blacksmiths, boot and shoe manufacturers, brewers, carpenters, carpet weavers. They manufactured carriages, chairs, and cigars. They were bell hangers, civil engineers, coopers, coppersmiths, distillers, druggists, locksmiths, masons, meat dealers, merchants, notaries public, photographers, physicians, real estate agents, tinsmiths, and undertakers. *McClung's St. Paul Directory and Statistical Record for 1866* (St. Paul: J. W. McClung, 1866). Foster, *Who's Who*, 359.

20. See 1900 census returns. Bruce is recorded there as white, as are all the other "inmates." His wife and two of their children were still living in St. Paul. Here and below, see Leslie A. Schwalm, "'Overrun with Free Negroes': Emancipation and Wartime Migration in the Upper Midwest," *Civil War History* 50:2 (2004): 145–74. Abraham L. Harris, *The Negro Population in Minneapolis: A Study in Race Relations* (Minneapolis, MN: Minneapolis Urban League and Phyllis Wheatley Settlement House, 1926). Race in the federal censuses was an inexact indicator, and blacks then and now have seemed more invisible than others to census takers, so such figures should be read skeptically.

21. For an excellent account of the complexity of race issues in this period, see William D. Green, *A Peculiar Imbalance: The Fall and Rise of Racial Equality in Early Minnesota* (St. Paul: MHS Press, 2007).

22. Harris, *Negro Population in Minneapolis*.

23. Bergemann, *Brackett's Battalion*.

24. C. F. MacDonald, "Narrative of the Ninth Regiment," in *Minnesota in the Civil and Indian Wars*, 1:416–54. On Campbell see Bergemann, *Brackett's Battalion*, 112–19. See also Carley, *Minnesota in the Civil War*, p163 especially.

25. Brenda J. Child, *Boarding School Seasons: American Indian Families, 1900–1940* (Lincoln: University of Nebraska Press, 1998). See also David Wallace Adams, *Education for Extinction: American Indians and the Boarding-School Experience, 1875–1928* (Lawrence: University Press of Kansas, 1995), K. Tsianina Lomawaima, *They Call it Prairie Light: The Story of Chilocco Indian School* (Lincoln: University of Nebraska Press, 1994), and Melissa L. Meyer, *The White Earth Tragedy: Ethnicity and Dispossession at a Minnesota Anishinaabe Reservation, 1889–1920* (Lincoln: University of Nebraska Press, 1994).

NOTES TO CHAPTER 7

1. Immigration historian Victor Greene identified Mattson as one of about twenty immigrant leaders and described how enthusiastically Mattson and the others became American, indeed middle-class Americans. See Victor R. Greene, *American Immigrant Leaders, 1800–1910: Marginality and Identity* (Baltimore, MD: Johns Hopkins University Press, 1987). For an overview of some of the selling of Minnesota—including Mattson's—see also Lars Ljungmark, *For Sale—Minnesota: Organized Promotion of Scandinavian Immigration, 1866–1873* (Chicago: Swedish Pioneer Historical Society, 1971). Ljungmark also demonstrates the various ways in which Mattson benefited from his selling.

2. See Hans Mattson, *Reminiscences: The Story of an Emigrant* (St. Paul, MN: D. D. Merrill Co, 1892); see also James B. Hedges, "The Colonization Work of the Northern Pacific Railroad," *Mississippi Valley Historical Review* 13:3 (Dec. 1926): 311–43.

3. Here and below: John Fletcher Williams, *The Minnesota Guide: A Hand Book of Information for the Travelers, Pleasure Seekers and Immigrants* (St. Paul, MN: E. H. Burritt, 1869). As William Lass points out, these were not the Chinese Ringneck pheasants common in Minnesota in the twenty-first century, but prairie chickens.

4. Both the MHS and the Library of Congress have extensive collections of these maps. John R. Hebert, "Panoramic Maps of American Cities," *Special Libraries* (Dec. 1972): 554–62. "Texas Bird's-Eye Views," from Amon Carter Museum, www.birdseyeviews.org/history.php (accessed May 5, 2007). See also Bettina A. Norton, *Edwin Whitefield: Nineteenth-Century North American Scenery* (Barre, MA: Imprint Society, 1977). John W. Reps is the real

master of these maps and has written about them extensively, especially as indicators of town growth in the post–Civil War years. "The itinerant urban viewmakers who roamed America . . . chronicled for us the swiftly changing appearance of the country's towns and cities" is one of his main themes. See John W. Reps, *Bird's Eye Views: Historic Lithographs of North American Cities* (New York: Princeton Architectural Press, 1998), 17. See also John W. Reps, *Views and Viewmakers of Urban America: Lithographs of Towns and Cities in the United States and Canada, Notes on the Artists and Publishers, and a Union Catalog of Their Work, 1825–1925* (Columbus: University of Missouri Press, 1984), and John W. Reps, *Cities of the Mississippi: Nineteenth-Century Images of Urban Development* (Columbia: University of Missouri Press, 1994).

5. Robert Earnest Miller, "War Within Walls: Camp Chase and the Search for Administrative Reform," *Ohio History* 96 (Winter-Spring 1987): 33–56, quote, p34, mortality numbers, p54. For a copy of the map, see http://memory.loc.gov/ammem/pmhtml/panart.html (accessed Apr. 30, 2007). Ruger is recorded in Summit County, Ohio, in the 1850 U.S. Census, Roll M432-732, p. 435, image 342; in 1880, he was an artist, married to English-born Charlotte, and located in Summit County. John W. Reps argues that "What was distinctively American about nineteenth-century lithographic viewmaking was the sheer number of images drawn, printed, and published . . . The views were thus a democratic art form in that they reflected conditions in urban places of all types." Reps, *Views and Viewmakers*, 3. He includes a chart of where and when Ruger drew maps on p202.

6. Reps, *Bird's Eye Views,* 17. The Library of Congress "Panoramic Maps Collection" offers an excellent introduction to Ruger and the other bird's-eye view mapmakers and includes over a thousand maps. See http://memory.loc.gov/ammem/pmhtml/panhome.html (accessed Apr. 30, 2007).

7. The MHS owns many of the maps that Ruger drew. They don't exactly conform to Reps's list of maps (he shows Ruger drawing only a Minneapolis map after 1870, but the MHS collection includes one of Stillwater in 1879). The MHS maps include Stillwater, Minneapolis and St. Anthony, St. Paul, St. Peter, Mankato, St. Cloud, Faribault, Anoka, Northfield, Red Wing, and Hastings.

8. W. J. T. Mitchell, "What Is an Image?," *New Literary History* 15:3 (Spring 1984): 503–37, quote, p504.

9. Charles S. Bryant, *History of Freeborn County,*

Including: Explorers and Pioneers of Minnesota, and Outline History of the State of Minnesota, by Rev. Edward D. O'Neill (Minneapolis: Minnesota Historical Co., 1882).

10. June Drenning Holmquist, ed., *They Chose Minnesota: A Survey of the State's Ethnic Groups* (St. Paul: MHS Press, 1981).

11. Here and below, Gertrude Braat Vandergon, *Our Pioneer Days in Minnesota* (Holland, MI: Holland Letter Service, 1949), quotes, 29–30, 50–52.

12. See my book-length account of the grasshopper plagues and the rural poverty they caused, *Harvest of Grief: Plagues and Public Assistance, 1873–1878* (St. Paul: MHS Press, 1984).

13. Apr. 27, 1869, quoted in Franklyn Curtiss-Wedge, *The History of Mower County, Illustrated* (Chicago: H. C. Cooper, Jr., and Co., 1911), 175; whole railroad story, p172–79.

14. See Gilbert Fite, *Farmers' Last Frontier.* Folwell, *History of Minnesota,* 3:44–74. Arthur P. Rose, *An Illustrated History of Nobles County, Minnesota* (Worthington: Northern History Publishing, 1908).

15. See George Pierson, *The Moving American* (New York: Knopf, 1973), and Linda Peavey and Ursula Smith, *Women in Waiting in the Westward Movement* and *The Gold Rush Widows of Little Falls: A Story Drawn from the Letters of Pamelia and James Fergus* (St. Paul: MHS Press, 1990).

NOTE TO SIDEBAR

1. Cecil O. Monroe, "The Rise of Baseball in Minnesota," *Minnesota History* 19 (1938): 162–81.

NOTES TO CHAPTER 8

1. Department of the Interior, Census Office, *Compendium of the Tenth Census,* Table III, "Showing the nativities of foreign-born population in the United States and in each state and territory: 1880" (Washington: GPO, 1885), 484–87. Holmquist, ed., *They Chose Minnesota.*

2. Department of the Interior, National Park Service, "Notice of Inventory Completion for Native American Human Remains and Associated Funerary Objects in the Possession of the Minnesota Indian Affairs Council, St. Paul and Bemidji, MN," *Federal Register* 64.141 (July 23, 1999), at http://www.cr.nps.gov/nagpra/fed_notices/nagpradir/nico281.html (accessed Apr. 23, 2007). In painfully uninflected language, the Reverend Joseph Hancock reported that he and his family landed at Red Wing in June 1851 and that "The first birth occurring among the whites was that of my son Willie, born August 25, 1850, and died Sept. 27, 1851. The

first death was that of Mrs. Nathan M. Hancock, mother of Willie, who died March 20, 1851. The remains of both now lie in Oakwood Cemetery." Hancock some years later told the story with more emotion: "The first white person known to have been buried within the limits of this county was the dear wife who accompanied me hither from our eastern home and shared in the labors and privations of the situation for the first two years." No mention of the death of the infant. A. T. Andreas, *Illustrated Historical Atlas of the State of Minnesota* (Chicago: A. T. Andreas, 1874), 235–36. J. W. Hancock, *Goodhue County, Minnesota, Past and Present* (Red Wing, MN: Red Wing Printing Co., 1893), 24–25, 51.

3. *Compendium of the Tenth Census (June 1, 1880)*, rev. ed., Part I: 189, 427–28, 457, 482–87, 513–14.

4. U.S. Census, 1880. Peg Meier located a house of prostitution in Virginia, Minnesota, which included a dance house keeper, a bartender, two watchmen, a violin and piano player, three gamblers, two cooks, one carpenter (all male), a dressmaker (female) and more than a dozen women identified as "demi-monde." Peg Meier, *Bring Warm Clothes: Letters and Photos from Minnesota's Past* (Minneapolis, MN: Minneapolis Tribune, 1986), 153. The income averages also come from Meier, 152. *Statistics of the Population of the United States at the Tenth Census (June 1, 1880)*, Tables 29–35 (Washington: GPO [1882]), esp. Table 33: "The Number of Persons in the United States Engaged in Each Special Occupation and Class of Occupations, By States and Territories, 1880," 762–64.

5. Edith Abbott, *Women in Industry: A Study in American Economic History* (New York: D. Appleton & Co., 1910), http://ocp.hul.harvard.edu/ww/outsidelink.html/http://nrs.harvard.edu/urn-3:HBS .BAKER:91795 (accessed May 3, 2007).

6. Martin Ridge, *Ignatius Donnelly: The Portrait of a Politician* (1962; repr., St. Paul: MHS Press, 1991), 211.

7. Marvin G. Lamppa, "From Art to Science: Mining at Soudan (1882–1924)," in Michael G. Karni, ed., *Entrepreneurs and Immigrants: Life on the Industrial Frontier of Northeastern Minnesota* (Chisholm, MN: Iron Range Research Center, 1991), 26–31, quote, p28.

8. See Hancock, *Goodhue County*, 216–26.

9. Marguerite Connolly, "The Disappearance of the Domestic Sewing Machine, 1890–1925," *Winterthur Portfolio* 34:1 (Spring 1999): 31, 32. See Stacy Lorraine Braukman and Michael A. Ross, "Married Women's Property and Male Coercion: United States' Courts and the Privy Examination, 1864–1877," *Journal of Women's History* 12:2 (2000): 57–80, quote, p58.

10. One of the great dangers of the nineteenth century was fire. In one particularly bad fire in 1882 in Red Wing, a "whole cluster of buildings was a seething mass of ruins" for blocks; "Misses G. Easterly and Tilda Carlson, sewing girls, . . . lost all their effects except one sewing machine." If even "sewing girls" had sewing machines, a seamstress certainly would have. See Hancock, *Goodhue County*, 209.

11. For a rich description of the life of a St. Paul dressmaker, see Judith Jerde, "Mary Molloy: St. Paul's Extraordinary Dressmaker," *Minnesota History* 47:2 (Fall 1980): 93–99. Martha McMurry, "Turn of the Century: Minnesota's Population in 1900 and Today" (St. Paul: Minnesota Planning, State Demographic Center, 1999), 15.

12. U.S. Census, 1880, Frankford, Mower, MN, roll T9_626; Family History film 1254626; p441.2000 ED 158; Image 0612 at www.ancestryLibrary.com, "1880 United States Federal Census" (accessed Apr. 20, 2007). The 1870 census return shows Mary at home with an older sister, in addition to all of the other siblings listed in 1880. The family name is spelled variously Gillet, Gillett, Gillette.

13. Sarah R. Mason, "The Chinese," in Holmquist, ed., *They Chose Minnesota*, 531. See also Sherri Gebert Fuller, "Mirrored Identities: The Moys of St. Paul," *Minnesota History* 57:4 (Winter 2000–2001): 162–81. Hancock, *Goodhue County*, 215–16.

14. Julia Bullard Nelson, from Red Wing, co-founded the Minnesota Woman Suffrage Association and was active, too, in the WCTU. The effects of malaria contracted during service in the Civil War killed her husband in 1868, within a few months of the death of their only son. On her own, she went to Texas. She later earned her living as a traveling lecturer for woman suffrage. As Goodhue County historian Frederick L. Johnson relates, she answered a critic who complained that women didn't bear arms, so they shouldn't vote, thus: "Women don't bear arms, but they bear armies." See Frederick L. Johnson, *Goodhue County, Minnesota: A Narrative History* (Red Wing, MN: Goodhue County Historical Society Press, 2000), 79–80, 139–41, quote, p140.

15. Jon Gjerde, *From Peasants to Farmers: The Migration from Balestrand, Norway to the Upper Middle West* (Cambridge, NY: Cambridge University

Press, 1985), and Odd S. Lovoll, *The Promise of America* and *The Promise Fulfilled: A Portrait of Norwegian-Americans Today* (Minneapolis: University of Minnesota Press, 1998).

16. All of these people appear in the Federal Manuscript Census returns, 1880, ED 170, Ward 1, Red Wing, Goodhue County, pp21–38. Other information is from the *Red Wing [Minnesota] Gazetteer,* 1883. By 1890 Mary Gillett had moved away from Red Wing or disappeared into a married name and the usual "keeping house" occupation that census takers assigned to married women (almost no matter what their work).

17. Federal Manuscript Census returns, 1880, ED 170, p29–30. See Steven Smith, writer and producer, "Song Catcher: Frances Densmore of Red Wing," a radio biography, http://news.minnesota.publicradio.org/features/199702/01_smiths_densmore/docs/index.shtml (accessed May 7, 2007). See also Nina Marchetti Archabal, "Frances Densmore: Pioneer in the Study of American Indian Music," in Stuhler and Kreuter, eds., *Women of Minnesota,* 94–115.

18. On literacy in Minnesota and the United States, see Table VII, "Illiteracy, by States and Territories, 1880," in *Statistics of the Population of the United States at the Tenth Census (June 1, 1880),* 919–25.

19. Another son, Charles, completed his medical training at Northwestern in 1888, and the Sisters and the Mayos opened St. Mary's Hospital in 1889. Eventually they also opened the Mayo Clinic, and their family way—and the Sisters' way—of working together, consulting with each other, developing specializations, and focusing on each patient—has served medicine (and patients) well in Rochester for over a hundred years now. Drs. Charles and Will Jr. stayed involved with the clinic until their deaths (within a few months of each other in 1939). The Mayos added their first non-family partner in 1892. In 1915 the Mayos opened the Mayo Graduate School of Medicine, and in 1972 the Mayo Medical School opened. For more information on the Mayo Brothers, see Helen Clapesattle, *The Doctors Mayo* (Minneapolis: University of Minnesota Press, 1941), and "History of Mayo Clinic," at www.diavlos.gr.orto96/ortowww/historym.htm (accessed May 7, 2007). See Anderson, *Little Crow.*

20. Winton U. Solberg, "Martha George Rogers Ripley," in Edward T. James, Janet Wilson James, and Paul S. Boyer, eds., *Notable American Women,* 1607–1950, 3 vols. (Cambridge: Belknap Press, 1971), 3:162–63.

21. Charles Eastman, *Indian Boyhood* (1902; repr., New York: Dover Publications, 1971), 288.

22. Meyer, *Santee Sioux,* 51–57.

23. S. R. Riggs, "Mythology of the Dakotas," *The American Antiquarian* V (1883): 148. See also Alan R. Woolworth, comp., ed., *Santee Dakota Indian Legends: Tales of the Santee (Eastern) Dakota Nation,* Vol. 2 (St. Paul, MN: Prairie Smoke Press, 2003).

24. Harriet E. Bishop, *Floral Home; or, First Years in Minnesota* (New York: Sheldon, Blakeman and Co., 1857), quote, p87. Norma Sommerdorf, "Harriet Bishop: A Doer and a Mover," *Minnesota History* 55: 7 (1997). See also Stuhler and Kreuter, *Women of Minnesota.*

25. Here and below: Marvin Richard O'Connell, *John Ireland and the American Catholic Church* (St. Paul: MHS Press, 1988).

26. James Shannon, *Catholic Colonization on the Western Frontier* (New Haven, CT: Yale University Press, 1957).

27. All immigrants felt pulled between old loyalties and new, and every immigrant had to decide what the right balance would be. What language will we speak, will our children speak, will we speak with each other? Will we live primarily with each other or with a mix? Do we celebrate St. David's Day and the Fourth of July or Bastille Day or May 5 or Santa Lucia or St. Nicholas or Christopher Columbus or Leif Erikson? McDonald, *With Lamps Burning.* Here and below: Charles R. Morris, *American Catholic: The Saints and Sinners Who Built America's Most Powerful Church* (New York: Vintage, 1998), 98–99. Thomas E. Hughes, ed., *History of the Welsh in Minnesota, Foreston and Lime Springs, IA* (Mankato, MN: Free Press Printing Co., 1895).

28. Michael P. Malone, *James J. Hill: Empire Builder of the Northwest* (Norman: University of Oklahoma Press, 1996); Albro Martin, *James J. Hill and the Opening of the Northwest* (1976; repr., MHS Press, 1991). Claire Strom, *Profiting from the Plains: The Great Northern Railway and Corporate Development of the American West* (Seattle: University of Washington Press, 2003). See Louis D. Johnston, "James J. Hill," in *The Oxford Encyclopedia of Economic History* (New York: Oxford University Press, 2003), 2:529–530.

29. In 1932, Robert L. Vann, editor of the *Pittsburgh Courier,* an important black newspaper, called on African Americans to turn Abraham Lincoln's picture to the wall, to abandon the Republican

Party and join the Democrats. Not an easy switch for many African Americans to make, given the deep racism of the Democratic Party in the South, but one that McGhee's shift so much earlier made easier. See Andrew Bunie, *Robert L. Vann of The Pittsburgh Courier: Politics and Black Journalism* (Pittsburgh, PA: University of Pittsburgh Press, 1974). See also Paul Nelson, *Fredrick L. McGhee: A Life on the Color Line* (St. Paul: MHS Press, 2001).

30. See http://webexhibits.org/daylightsaving/i.html (accessed Apr. 30, 2007).

31. Connolly, "Disappearance of the Domestic Sewing Machine."

32. Hiram Drache, *The Challenge of the Prairie: Life and Times of Red River Pioneers* (Fargo: North Dakota Institute for Regional Studies, 1970), and Mary Dodge Woodward, *The Checkered Years: A Bonanza Farm Diary, 1884–88,* ed. by Mary Boynton Cowdrey, with a new introduction by Elizabeth Jameson (St. Paul: MHS Press, 1989). See also Fite, *Farmers' Frontier.*

33. Edward Slavishak, "Artificial Limbs and Industrial Workers' Bodies in Turn-of-the Century Pittsburgh," *Journal of Social History* 37:2 (2003): 365–88. View photos of the Artificial Limb Company at http://collections.mnhs.org/visualresources/ to see both the mechanics and the variety of limbs available in Minnesota by the time of World War I. U.S. Census, 1900, *Manufacturing,* I: Vol. VII, Table 4.

34. Agnes Larson, *History of the White Pine Industry in Minnesota* (Minneapolis: University of Minnesota Press, 1949), 169. Photo of Magel in Vernard E. Lundin, *Hubbard Milling Company, 1878–1978: A Past to Remember, A Future to Build* (Minneapolis, MN: T. S. Denison, 1978).

NOTES TO CHAPTER 9

1. John McPhee, *Oranges* (1967; repr., New York: Penguin Paperback, 2004).

2. Jose Morilla Critz, Alan L. Olmstead, and Paul W. Rhode, " 'Horn of Plenty': The Globalization of Mediterranean Horticulture and the Economic Development of Southern Europe, 1880–1930," *Journal of Economic History* 59:2 (June 1999): 316–52, p316, 326.

3. Stonehouse, *John Wesley North,* 180–225. "Navel Oranges," *New York Times,* Jan. 21, 1907, p8.

4. W. W. Cumberland, *Cooperative Marketing: Its Advantages as Exemplified in the California Fruit Growers Exchange* (Princeton, NJ: Princeton University Press, 1917), 18.

5. Ronald Tobey and Charles Wetherell, "The Citrus Industry and the Revolution of Corporate Capitalism in Southern California, 1887–1944," *California History* 74 (Spring 1995). "[C]itrus built the foundations of the region's economic modernization before the great flood of defense funds began in World War II." This was not primarily an agricultural endeavor but an industrial enterprise. "Reclassified as manufacturing, the citrus industry in the first half of the twentieth century ranked among California's largest industries in terms of employees, wages, and revenues." p6, 8.

6. Ralph Joseph Roske, *Everyman's Eden: A History of California* (New York: Macmillan, 1968).

7. W. H. Hutchinson, *California: Two Centuries of Man, Land, and Growth in the Golden State* (Palo Alto, CA: American West Publishing Co., 1972), 184; Roske, *Everyman's Eden,* 399; Cumberland, *Cooperative Marketing,* 20. Matthew Garcia, *A World of Its Own: Race, Labor, and Citrus in the Making of Greater Los Angeles, 1900–1970* (Chapel Hill: University of North Carolina Press, 2001). Douglas Cazaux Sackman, *Orange Empire: California and the Fruits of Eden* (Berkeley: University of California Press, 2005).

8. See William A. McKenzie, *Dining Car to the Pacific: The "Famously Good" Food of the Northern Pacific Railway* (1990; repr., Minneapolis: University of Minnesota Press, 2004). See also Henrietta Larson, *The Wheat Market and the Farmer in Minnesota, 1858–1900* (New York: Columbia University Press, 1926).

9. All of these products were advertised for sale in the *St. Paul Pioneer Press* and *Minneapolis Journal* in 1898.

10. George Brown Tindall, ed., *A Populist Reader: Selections from the Works of American Populist Leaders* (New York: Harper & Row, 1966), 90–96.

11. Ridge, *Ignatius Donnelly.* Blegen, *Minnesota,* 149, 245, 292, 312, 397–99; see Steven L. Keillor, *Cooperative Commonwealth: Co-ops in Rural Minnesota, 1859–1939* (St. Paul: MHS Press, 2000).

12. H. Vincent Moses, "G. Harold Powell and the Corporate Consolidation of the Modern Citrus Enterprise, 1904–1922," *Business History Review* 69 (Summer 1995): 119–55, quote, p125.

13. Cumberland, *Cooperative Marketing,* 61. John William Lloyd, *Co-Operative and Other Organized Methods of Marketing California Horticulture Products,* University of Illinois Studies in the Social Sciences (Urbana: University of Illinois, 1919), 23. Garcia, *World of Its Own,* 18, 329. "Buried Under Oranges," *Minneapolis Journal,* Mar. 2, 1910, p10.

14. U.S. Census, 1920. *St. Paul Pioneer Press* obituaries for Andrew Schoch, June 11, 1925, p1, and Florence [Mrs. William] Schoch, Nov. 5, 1971, p41.

15. Stephen Nissenbaum, *The Battle for Christmas* (New York: Knopf, 1996), 7.

16. Simon Carter, *Christmas Past, Christmas Present: Four Hundred Years of English Seasonal Customs, 1600–2000* (London: Geffrye Museum Trust, 1997). Cynthia Hart, John Grossman, and Priscilla Dunhill, *Joy to the World: A Victorian Christmas* (New York: Workman Publishing Company, 1999). J. M. Goldby and A. W. Purdue, *The Making of the Modern Christmas* (London: B. T. Batsford Ltd., 1986). William B. Waits, *The Modern Christmas in America: A Cultural History of Gift-Giving* (New York: New York University Press, 1993). Penne L. Restad, *Christmas in America: A History* (New York: Oxford University Press, 1995). *New York Daily Times,* Jan. 2, 1856, p3.

NOTES TO CHAPTER 10

1. Daniel James Brown, *Under a Flaming Sky: The Great Hinckley Firestorm of 1894* (Guilford, CT: Lyons Press, 2006). Theodore Blegen, *The Kensington Rune Stone: New Light on an Old Riddle* (St. Paul: MHS Press, 1968).

2. Oscar W. Firkins, *Cyrus Northrup: A Memoir* (Minneapolis: University of Minnesota Press, 1925), 319, 321. The University of Minnesota's first undergraduates completed their degrees in 1873. The university awarded its first master's degree in 1880 and its first PhD in 1888. The university grew from 1,000 students in 1890 to 17,000 in 1939. As late as 1910, only about five percent of Minnesota's eighteen- to twenty-one-year-olds were in college. St. Scholastica, Saint Benedict's Academy, and St. Teresa's in Winona educated first high school–aged girls and gradually expanded into four-year colleges; Hamline, Augsburg, and Concordia colleges focused on the training of ministers and priests; Mankato and St. Cloud Teachers' Colleges on teacher training; the College of St. Thomas, Saint John's, and St. Mary's College on educating Catholic boys and young men. Here and below: Merrill E. Jarchow, *Private Liberal Arts Colleges in Minnesota: Their History and Contributions* (St. Paul: MHS Press, 1973). James Gray, *University of Minnesota, 1851–1951* (Minneapolis: University of Minnesota Press, 1951), and Stanford Lehmberg and Ann M. Pflaum, *University of Minnesota, 1945–2000* (Minneapolis: University of Minnesota Press, 2001).

3. Papers of the Work People's College, Immigration History Research Archives, Minneapolis, MN.

4. See http://www.ewestminster.org/sermon.asp?id=548 (accessed Apr. 26, 2007). See photos of the Chinese congregation and school, negs. 96900, 37895, 96901, in MHS collections. Marilyn Chiat, "'And a Sprinkling of Jews': Work and Faith and Minnesota's Jewish Merchants," *Ramsey County History* 28:1 (Spring 1993): 8. See also Fuller, "Mirrored Identities." Dave Kenney, *Walking Together in All God's Ways* (Minneapolis, MN: Plymouth Congregational Church, 2007).

5. McMurry, "Turn of the Century," 7, 9.

6. Foster, *Who's Who.*

7. See Gretchen Kreuter, "Kate Donnelly Versus the Cult of True Womanhood," in Stuhler and Kreuter, *Women of Minnesota,* 20–33.

8. George B. Engberg, "The Knights of Labor in Minnesota," *Minnesota History* 22 (Dec. 1941): 357–90. Rhoda R. Gilman, "Eva McDonald Valesh: Minnesota Populist," in Stuhler and Kreuter, *Women of Minnesota,* 55–76. Julia Wiech Lief, "A Woman of Purpose: Julia B. Nelson," *Minnesota History* 47:8 (1981): 302–14. Kim E. Nielsen, "'We All Leaguers By Our House': Women, Suffrage, and Red-Baiting in the National Nonpartisan League" *Journal of Women's History* 6:1 (1994): 31–50.

9. June D. Holmquist, Joseph Stipanovich, and Kenneth B. Moss, "The South Slavs," in Holmquist, ed., *They Chose Minnesota,* 386. Jeffrey David Kolnick, "A Producer's Commonwealth: Populism and the Knights of Labor in Blue Earth Country, Minnesota, 1880–1892." PhD diss., University of California, Davis, 1996. McMurry, "Turn of the Century," 17.

10. Paul H. Landis, *Three Iron Mining Towns: A Study in Cultural Change* (Ann Arbor, MI: Edwards Brothers, Inc., 1938).

11. *St. Paul Daily Pioneer,* Jan. 19, 20, 21, 1900.

12. John E. Haynes, "Revolt of the 'Timber Beasts': IWW Lumber Strike in Minnesota," *Minnesota History* 42:2 (Spring 1971): 163–74. Clark, *Minnesota in a Century of Change;* Holmquist, Stipanovich, and Moss, "South Slavs." Carl H. Chrislock, *The Progressive Era in Minnesota, 1899–1918* (St. Paul: MHS Press, 1971). William Millikan, *A Union Against Unions: The Minneapolis Citizens Alliance and Its Fight Against Organized Labor, 1903–1947* (St. Paul: MHS Press, 2001). Mary Lethert Wingerd, *Claiming the City: Politics, Faith, and the Power of Place in St. Paul.* (Ithaca, NY: Cornell University Press, 2001).

13. Faue, *Community of Suffering*, 47–50, 56–57.

14. Here and below Chrislock, *Progressive Era in Minnesota*.

15. Barbara Stuhler, "Organizing for the Vote: Leaders of Minnesota's Woman Suffrage Movement," *Minnesota History* 54:7 (Fall 1995): 290–303. Barbara Stuhler, *Gentle Warriors: Clara Ueland and the Minnesota Struggle for Woman Suffrage* (St. Paul: MHS Press, 1995). See also Ethel Edgerton Hurd, *Woman Suffrage in Minnesota: A Record of the Activities in its Behalf since 1847* (Minneapolis: Inland Press for the Minnesota Woman Suffrage Association, 1916).

16. Robert L. Morlan, *Political Prairie Fire: The Nonpartisan League, 1915–1922* (1955; repr., St. Paul: MHS Press, 1985). Kathleen Diane Moum, "Harvest of Discontent: The Social Origins of the Nonpartisan League, 1880–1922," PhD diss., University of California, Irvine, 1986. Karen Starr, "Fighting for a Future: Farm Women of the Nonpartisan League," *Minnesota History* 48:6 (Summer 1983): 255–62. Larry Remele, "Things as They Should Be: Jeffersonian Idealism and Rural Rebellion in Minnesota and North Dakota, 1910–1920," *Minnesota History* 51:1 (Spring 1988): 15–22.

17. Historians have long pointed to the MCPS with horror and dealt with it as a kind of Minnesota exception. But so many people in the state picked up its spirit—and its work—with such ebullient and terrifying enthusiasm that it was certainly a statewide and state-bred phenomenon. The MCPS could not have been so repressive so widely on its own. It had allies in nearly every town and village. Where did all of these allies come from? Were they simply the other side of the reform impulse, the shadow of progressivism, both growing from the same fear about the state of America? Carl H. Chrislock, *Watchdog of Loyalty: The Minnesota Commission of Public Safety During World War I* (St. Paul: MHS Press, 1991). See also Minnesota Commission of Public Safety Agency History Records, State Archives, MHS. For the full text of Governor Burnquist's address to the legislature, see *Alexandria Citizen*, Jan. 2, 1919.

18. Chrislock, *Watchdog of Loyalty*. See also Governor J. A. A. Burnquist, Report of Minnesota Commission of Public Safety, 1919, and MCPS Records, State Archives, MHS. Editorial, *Alexandria Citizen*, Apr. 3, 1919.

19. *Pine County Pioneer*, Jan 4, Feb. 8, Mar. 15, Apr. 15 and 19, May 10, Sept. 6 and 13, 1918.

20. Carl H. Chrislock points out the enormous political capital that could be made out of accusa-tions of disloyalty. Chrislock, *Watchdog of Loyalty*, 12.

21. Here and below, drawn from the Alien Registration and Declaration of Holdings, MHS.

22. Women's Committee of the Public Safety Commission, Women in Industry Survey Forms, microfilm, MHS.

23. *The [White Earth] Tomahawk*, Jan. 17, 24, 1918. See also Mar. 21, 1918. "Just now the public press is loudly protesting . . . against the rape of Belgium . . . yet we hear not a word of public protest against the wanton and profligate expenditure of Indian tribal funds or the confiscation of lands."

NOTES TO CHAPTER 11

1. Alan Trachtenberg, *Reading American Photographs: Images as History, Mathew Brady to Walker Evans* (New York: Hill and Wang, 1989). Martha Sandweiss, *Print the Legend: Photography and the American West* (New Haven, CT: Yale University Press, 2002). Shawn Michelle Smith, *American Archives: Gender, Race, and Class in Visual Culture* (Princeton, NJ: Princeton University Press, 1999). Miles Orvell, *American Photography* (New York: Oxford University Press, 2003).

2. See photographers' files, manuscripts, MHS. Hundreds of Briol's photos are available online at http://collections.mnhs.org/visualresources/. A larger collection is available on site. Most of the photos used in this chapter are available in the online collection and can be located by subject or by photographer. While there are hundreds of Briol's photos in the collections of the MHS, others are held by the Stearns History Museum.

3. See Clifford Peel Autobiography and photographers' files, manuscripts, MHS. The MHS holds thousands of Norton and Peel photographs. Which one took a particular photograph cannot be determined, so alike are the photos in tone and view.

4. Oliver Mining Co., photo album, 111.13.1, MHS.

5. Oliver Mining Co., photo album.

6. Janet Daly Bednarek, "The Flying Machine in the Garden: Parks and Airports, 1918–1938," *Technology and Culture* 46.22 (April 2005): 350–73.

7. The literature on labor in Minnesota is especially rich. One of the larger categories in the *Minnesota History* index is "strikes." See Haynes, "Revolt of the 'Timber Beasts.'"

8. Frederick Jackson Turner, "The Significance of the Frontier in American History," a paper originally read at the meeting of the American Historical Association in Chicago, July 12, 1893; pub-

lished first in the *Proceedings of the State Historical Society of Wisconsin,* Dec. 14, 1893. It is now widely available online and in American history source books, so much a staple has it become as part of the historians' repertoire.

9. John K. Sherman, *Music and Maestros: The Story of the Minneapolis Symphony Orchestra* (Minneapolis: University of Minnesota Press, 1952).

NOTES TO CHAPTER 12

1. Oral interviews with Magdalena Court, Luxemburg Township, Stearns County, Sept. 1980–85, notes in author's possession.

2. Magdalena Harren Court, "January Was a Month," ed. by Annette Atkins and Barton Sutter, *North Country Anvil,* Spring 1983. Mrs. Court, as she preferred to be called, never visited Germany, nor did her parents. Her grandparents migrated to Stearns County from Bavaria in 1858. She wrote about her days on the farm in English, but much of her writing reflected the German language patterns in which she felt most comfortable. She and Pete spoke German to each other. She prayed in German all of her life. She did not, however, speak German to her children. The times were changing, she said, and the two world wars made her careful about where and when she spoke her grandparents' native tongue.

3. Annette Atkins, "At Home in the Heart of the City," *Minnesota History* 58.5 (Spring/Summer 2003): 286–304.

4. U.S. Department of Agriculture, *Yearbook of Agriculture, 1937* (75th Cong., 1st sess., H. Doc. 28), p53.

5. See *Minneapolis Tribune* in June 1932, when grasshoppers made front-page news day after day in that first summer of infestations. The quote is from Meridel Le Sueur, *North Star Country* (1945; repr., Minneapolis: University of Minnesota Press, 1998). See also my book on the earlier grasshopper plagues in Minnesota, *Harvest of Grief.* In earlier hard times, farmers had found work off the farm. Laura Ingalls Wilder's novels about farm life, romantic in so many ways, tell of "Pa," who went to the pineries in the winter to earn some extra money, but with the depression conditions, those jobs were harder to come by. In 1929, over 20 percent of Minnesota farmers worked off the farm eighty days on average. In 1934, 32 percent worked, but for sixty days on average. Laura Ingalls Wilder, *On the Banks of Plum Creek* (1937; repr. ed., New York: HarperCollins, 2004); U.S. Census, 1940, *Agriculture,* State Table 9, p9.

6. In 1930, the U.S. Census Bureau for the first time published two volumes just on unemployment, reporting in extraordinary detail by city and county, by "period of idleness," and by occupation the numbers of unemployed. It gave two categories: "out of a job, able to work, and looking for a job" or "having jobs, but on lay-off without pay." I'm lumping those two categories together here. U.S. Census, 1930, *Unemployment Bulletin* (Washington, DC: GPO, 1931). Raymond L. Koch, "Politics and Relief in Minneapolis During the 1930s," *Minnesota History* 41 (Winter 1968): 153–70. Faue, *Community of Suffering,* 59.

7. D. Jerome Tweton, *The New Deal at the Grass Roots: Programs for the People of Otter Tail County, Minnesota* (St. Paul: MHS Press, 1988), 40–41. Donald B. Dodd and Wynelle S. Dodd, *Historical Statistics of the United States, 1790–1970* (Tuscaloosa: University of Alabama Press, 1976), Vol. II: Midwest.

8. Koch, "Politics and Relief in Minneapolis."

9. Reported in *Duluth Herald,* June 11, 1932. Here and below, see Faue, *Community of Suffering,* 62–63.

10. Eula T. Murphy with David V. Taylor, "Growing Up in St. Paul: Looking Back at the Black Community," *Ramsey County History* 27:4 (Winter 1992): 12–15.

11. Written for Gold Diggers of 1933 (New York: M. Witmark & Sons, 1933) See http://www.harrywarren.org/songs/0140.htm (accessed Mar. 27, 2007).

12. Based on Elizabethan Poor Laws: see Walter I. Trattner, *From Poor Law to Welfare State: A History of Social Welfare in America* (New York: Free Press, 1999).

13. For a contemporary statement (and critique) of this traditional system, see "Report of the Committee on Social Security and Public Welfare of the Minnesota State Planning Board," Aug. 1936, typescript, MHS, especially p8–9.

14. *Minneapolis Tribune,* June 4, 1933.

15. George Tselos, "Self-Help and Sauerkraut: The Organized Unemployed, Inc., of Minneapolis," *Minnesota History* 45 (Winter 1977): 307–20. Tweton, *New Deal at the Grass Roots,* 17.

16. *Minneapolis Tribune,* June 4, 1933.

17. The Minneapolis mayoral elections during the 1930s seesawed between parties, demonstrating the ambivalence of the voters: Republican William Kunze served from 1929 to 1931; Farmer-Laborite William Anderson from 1931 to 1933; Republican A. G. Bainbridge from 1933 to 1935; Farmer-Laborite Thomas Latimer from 1935 to 1937; Republican

George Leach from 1937 to 1941. Koch, "Politics and Relief in Minneapolis," 156–59.

18. Or "red agents" as the *Duluth Herald* also called them. A July 30, 1932, editorial after the violence between the protestors and the army was even more critical. It reported that many of the protestors were "bent on making trouble, many of them foreign-born agitators and Communists" and repeated Hoover's charge that "a considerable number were not veterans at all; many were Communists and persons with criminal records" who tricked and misled the real soldiers. *Duluth Herald,* June 13, July 30, 1932.

19. After World War I, and based on his European experiences, Herbert Hoover published *American Individualism,* in which he declared that after "Seven years of contending with economic degeneration, with social disintegration, with incessant political dislocation," he had emerged "an individualist—an unashamed individualist." Hoover, *American Individualism* (Garden City, NY: Doubleday, Page and Company, 1922), 8–9. Walter F. Dexter entitled his campaign biography *Herbert Hoover and American Individualism* (New York: Macmillan Co., 1932).

20. Magdalena Court, "Life on the Farm," ms. in author's possession.

21. David Nass, "Recollections of Rural Revolt," *Minnesota History* 44 (Winter 1975): 304–8.

22. See Tweton, *New Deal at the Grass Roots,* 28–29. See also D. Jerome Tweton, *Depression: Minnesota in the Thirties* (Fargo: North Dakota Institute for Regional Studies, 1981), 28–29. David Riehle, "Minneapolis Teamsters Strikes of 1934," *Labor Standard,* http://www.laborstandard.org/MN_Teamster_Festival/Dave_R_on_1934.htm (accessed May 7, 2007). This is a rich site for documents and information from the strikers' point of view. See also Charles R. Walker, *American City: A Rank and File History of Minneapolis* (1937; repr., Minneapolis: University of Minnesota Press, 2005), and Millikan, *Union Against Unions,* and George H. Mayer, *The Political Career of Floyd B. Olson* (1951; repr., St. Paul: MHS Press, 1987). The significantly more amicable relations between labor and management in St. Paul in this period is striking. Why in Minneapolis and not in St. Paul? St. Paul was already a union town by the 1930s. As Mary Wingerd argues in her excellent history, *Claiming the City,* Minneapolis was a national market city while St. Paul was more regional, which made for different cultures and different employee/employer relations. In 2004, over 1,000 union people (including

especially University of Minnesota clerical workers, Metro Transit workers, and nursing home aids), met to commemorate the seventieth anniversary of the strike. David Riehle, a Minneapolis labor organizer and historian who has almost single-handedly kept alive the memory of the truckers' strike, claimed for those 1934 strikers a "stubborn resentment toward authority and an illogical faith in justice." *[Minneapolis-St. Paul] City Pages,* July 28, 2004.

23. Tweton, *New Deal at the Grass Roots,* 33, 53. Faue, *Community of Suffering,* 100–125.

24. Tweton, *New Deal at the Grass Roots,* 35. Darragh Aldrich, *Lady in Law: A Biography of Mabeth Hurd Paige* (Chicago: R. F. Seymour, 1950), 303–12. Minnesotans elected four women to the legislature in the years immediately following the passage in 1920 of the woman suffrage amendment: Myrtle Cain, a young telephone operator from Northeast Minneapolis who was active in the Women's Labor Union and in a telephone strike; Sue Dickey Hough, also from Minneapolis, who dealt in real estate; Hannah Kempfer from Fergus Falls; and Mabeth Paige from Minneapolis. Kempfer and Paige served in the legislature for over twenty years and became fast friends and Republican allies. *Minneapolis Journal* reporter Vivian Thorp shared Hurd's and Kempfer's politics and worried: are we "to have a government by the elected representatives of the people or by a mob?" Quoted in Aldrich, *Lady in Law,* 314. Both Paige and Thorp's positions are presented with sympathy by Aldrich. It is difficult to tell where Paige's opinions and Aldrich's merge and when they divide. This was also Minneapolis. As Mary Wingerd demonstrates, St. Paul had long been a regional market town and bred a different kind of relationship between employers and employees than in Minneapolis. Long after St. Paul had become a union town, Minneapolis remained "open shop." The 1934 truckers' strike broke the control of the Citizens Alliance and turned Minneapolis more labor union. Wingerd, *Claiming the City.*

25. See Blegen, *Minnesota,* 528. Tweton, *New Deal at the Grass Roots,* 28, 30.

26. Aldrich, *Lady in Law;* Mayer, *Political Career of Floyd B. Olson.*

27. See http://content.lib.washington.edu/feraweb/essay.html (accessed Apr. 25, 2007).

28. The ambition of the middle classes to remake people in their own image runs like a powerful river through the American story—from civilizing Indians to Americanizing immigrants. The

tragedy of their efforts was that so much well intended work was so harmful to its recipients. The well intended could have thought themselves to a different approach, perhaps, but the rare instances in which it happened testify to the blinding power of the social context. See Stephen Neil Greengard, et al., "Ten Crucial Years: The Development of United States Government Sponsored Artists Programs, 1933–1943: A Panel Discussion by Six WPA Artists," *Journal of Decorative and Propaganda Arts* 1 (Spring 1986): 58.

29. H. S. Langland, Director, Minnesota State Planning Board, "Estimates of Unemployment, March 1933," typescript, MHS.

30. Court, "Life on the Farm."

31. The record of these accomplishments is bound into an untitled volume in the collections of the MHS. It includes photos of people at work plus a summary report, "Physical Accomplishments, Minnesota Works Progress Administration," from data provided by the Division of Statistics and Economic Research, Nov. 1, 1938. It includes, in addition, a summary of accomplishments from all of the states. The 1938 numbers are in Tweton, *New Deal at the Grass Roots,* 23.

32. Federal Writers' Project of the Works Progress Administration, *WPA Guide to Minnesota* (1938; repr., St. Paul: MHS Press, 1985). "Achievements of the Minnesota Writers' Project of the W.P.A. (The Final Report)," typescript, MHS. Historians continue to benefit from WPA projects. George Rawick, for one example, edited ten volumes of interviews of former slaves and published them with his own introductory volume, *From Sundown to Sunup: The Making of the Black Community,* a book that helped reimagine and better understand the American slave experience. In Minnesota, for a second example, Frances Densmore collected oral interviews from Native American people that are still of great value to historians. The catalog of county records put together by the Historical Records Survey helped me locate relevant documents for my doctoral dissertation and subsequent book, *Harvest of Grief.* Typescript, MHS. See also FWA, MWPA, University General Research Programs, 1935–1943, *Final Report,* University of Minnesota, typescript, Feb. 26, 1943.

33. Susan Ray Enler, "Art for a Democracy: WPA's Art Education Programs in Minnesota," PhD diss., University of Minnesota, 1990. Kenneth E. Hendrickson, Jr., "The WPA Federal Art Projects in Minnesota, 1935–1943," *Minnesota History* 53:5 (Spring 1993): 170–83.

34. See www.loc.gov. In an undergraduate thesis, College of Saint Benedict student Katie McCarney wrote about the 1930s murals and their different funders (the Treasury Department as well as the WPA hired artists to paint murals). The FSA and the WPA had different requirements for murals and required different levels of artistic accomplishment. Kathleen McCarney, "Art for a People: An Iconographic and Cultural Study of Mural Painting in Minnesota's New Deal Art Programs," undergraduate honors thesis, College of Saint Benedict/ Saint John's University, 2004. See Thomas O'Sullivan, "The WPA Federal Art Project in Minnesota: A Job and a Movement," *Minnesota History* 53:5 (Spring 1993): 184–95. See also Karal Ann Marling, *Wall-to-Wall America: Post Office Murals in the Great Depression* (Minneapolis: University of Minnesota Press, 1982). In an excellent undergraduate thesis, Jessica Haidet wrote insightfully about George Morrison's and Patrick DesJarlait's artwork, tracing the roots of their quite distinctive styles in the different Ojibwe cultures at Grand Portage and Red Lake. The Grand Portage Ojibwe lived more integrated with the white society around Grand Marais and, like many of his band mates, Morrison learned much about living (and working) in a white culture—one that he took a prominent place in for much of his career as an artist in a more European tradition. DesJarlait, by contrast, had learned his art within the Red Lake community, and his work reflects much of that culture in line, shape, and subject matter. Morrison's work shifted to more and more Indian themes and motifs as he spent more and more time at—and then relocated entirely to— Grand Portage as he got older. Jessica Haidet, "Approaches to American Indian Identity 1945–c.1970: An Analysis of the Art of Patrick DesJarlait and George Morrison," undergraduate honors thesis, College of Saint Benedict/Saint John's University, 2003.

35. Martha Davidson wrote in *ArtNews* in 1943, "a whole talented generation was enabled to remain at home, working steadily and relatively peaceably instead of being forced either to abandon skills, starve, or migrate East or to Europe." Quoted in O'Sullivan, "WPA Federal Art Project," p195.

36. O'Sullivan, "WPA Federal Art Project."

37. See www.ti.org/Parkstext.html (accessed Apr. 26, 2007). Roy W. Meyer, *Everyone's Country Estate: A History of Minnesota's State Parks* (St. Paul: MHS Press, 1991). See "Oral History Interview with Dewey Albinson" (1965), Smithsonian Archives of American Art, http://www.aaa.si.edu/collections/

oralhistories/transcripts/albins65.htm (accessed Apr. 26, 2007).

38. Not all New Deal programs took the needs of American minority groups into consideration, but the CCC–Indian Division "was perhaps the first measure to bring material aid to reservations, to encourage self-administration by Indians, and to conserve and even add to the Indians' considerable land resources . . . Within less than a year after the establishment of the CCC–Indian Division, then, a majority of nonurban Minnesota Indians, Chippewa and Sioux, were receiving some aid from the program . . . By providing financial assistance to working Indians to improve their most tangible asset—their land—the CCC had been a valuable program for American Indians." Calvin W. Gower, "The CCC Indian Division: Aid for Depressed Americans, 1933–1942," *Minnesota History* 43:1 (Spring 1972): 3–13.

39. Meyer, *Everyone's Country Estate*, 103–5.

40. See Thomas Dickson, "100 Years of Conservation," at http://www.dnr.state.mn.us/volunteer/janfeb00/100years.html (accessed Apr. 26, 2007). For a full accounting, see Meyer, *Everyone's Country Estate*, 103–5, 107–8, 112–13. See also http://www.dnr.state.mn.us/state_parks/gooseberry_falls/selftour_waterfallswalk.html (accessed Apr. 26, 2007). See Gordon Parks, *A Choice of Weapons* (1966; repr., St. Paul: MHS Press, 1986).

41. "Gooseberry Falls State Park," information brochure, July 2001, State of Minnesota, Department of Natural Resources.

42. U.S. Census, 1930, for both Berini and Cattaneo. See http://www.mnhs.org/places/nationalregister/stateparks/Gooseberry.html and http://www.mnhs.org/places/nationalregister/stateparks/index.html#PARKS (accessed Apr. 26, 2007).

43. Don Boxmeyer, "Their Labor Lives On," *St. Paul Pioneer Press*, Jan. 9, 2006.

44. Court, "Life on the Farm" and "January Was a Month."

45. P. Van Deraa, "REA Allotments and Loans," *Journal of Land and Public Utility Economics* 12:4 (Nov. 1936): 428. Tweton, *New Deal at the Grass Roots*, 136–45. Brian Q. Cannon, "Power Relations: Western Rural Electric Cooperatives and the New Deal," *Western Historical Quarterly* 31:1 (2000): 133–59.

46. Stuhler and Kreuter, *Women of Minnesota*.

47. As it did in thousands of businesses, the bottom dropped out of the recording business in 1929 (with a corresponding effect on musicians, recorders, arrangers, composers, and others involved in the music industry). From 1929 to about 1934, historian Kenneth J. Bindas argues, the recording industry languished, but Benny Goodman's 1934 tour revitalized it. "RCA Victor, Goodman's label, experienced a 300 percent sales increase from 1935 through 1936," he reports, and in 1937 and 1938 "most record companies were boasting profits that recalled the halcyon days of 1929." Employment of musicians rebounded to 1927 levels in 1936. Kenneth J. Bindas, *Swing, That Modern Sound* (Jackson: University Press of Mississippi, 2001), 5. Tweton, *New Deal at the Grass Roots*, 26.

48. Photos of all these bands can be found online at the MHS site and are worth a look. Alma Milch's band, the Queens of Syncopation, are all dressed in satin suits, including trousers, as are the members of the other "all-girl" band: see negs. 33847, 60968. The presence of women's bands testifies in part to the openness of the music world at the time (room for women musicians) but also to their being largely frozen out of the men's bands, except as the sexy torch singer. See Bindas, *Swing*, xviii.

49. Beth L. Bailey, *From Front Porch to Back Seat: Courtship in Twentieth-Century America* (Baltimore, MD: Johns Hopkins University Press, 1989). Sally Sommer, "Social Dance," in Eric Foner and John A. Garraty, eds., *The Reader's Companion to American History* (New York: Houghton-Mifflin, 1991). Lewis Erenberg, "From New York to Middletown: Repeal and the Legitimization of Nightlife in the Great Depression," *American Quarterly* 38:5 (Winter 1986): 761–78.

50. Through the 1920s, various marathons were interrupted by police trying to stop the dancing. "San Francisco Police Stop Record Marathon Dance on Doctor's Advice"—this after fifteen hours and six minutes. Dancers' endurance and police patience lengthened over the years, so that the police didn't stop the Tri-State Dance Marathon in Connecticut in 1923 until after sixty-nine hours. In 1928, Dr. Daniel Sable, Chief Surgeon of the Safety Department, put a stop to a Pittsburgh marathon dance, declaring the dancers "not in a fit condition to continue" as they started their 304th hour. In 1933, state legislators began introducing bills to outlaw marathon dancing entirely. A recent raid on a roadhouse in Pennsylvania had resulted in the arrest of forty-two dancers and one promoter for breaking the Sabbath law. These couples had been dancing for about two weeks, so the police waited, no doubt, until a Sunday so that they had some le-

gal authority to intervene. *New York Times,* Mar 21, 1910, Apr. 18, 1923, June 21, 1928, Feb. 2 and April 27, 1933.

51. See http://www.streetswing.com/histmain /d5marth2.htm (accessed Apr. 26, 2007). This site does not come with supporting documentation. I found both Callum DeVillier and Vonnie Kuchinski in the 1930 census returns, so I know that there were such people and that they had a connection. "Marathon Dancing Outlawed" and "Topics of the Times," *New York Times,* Apr. 27, p8, and Apr. 28, 1933, p16.

NOTES TO CHAPTER 13

1. Dave Kenney, *Minnesota Goes to War: The Home Front during World War II* (St. Paul: MHS Press, 2005), 230 for casualty figures. For a more detailed list of casualties, see http://www.archives.gov/ research/arc/ww2/army-casualties/minnesota .html (accessed Apr. 26, 2007).

2. See "U.S. Needs Farm Workers," www .farmworkers.org/usneedbp.html (accessed Apr. 26, 2007). Elizabeth Stawicki, "Women Vets Remember World War II," Minnesota Public Radio, May 30, 2005. *Contra Costa Times,* Nov. 16, 2004, at www.rosietheriveter.org (accessed Apr. 26, 2007).

3. Wayne G. Broehl, Jr., *Cargill: Trading the World's Grain* (Hanover, NH: University Press of New England, 1992), 671.

4. See women making parts for Twin City tractor line at Minneapolis Steel and Machinery Co., neg. 18555, and machine shop, Bohn Refrigerator Co., St. Paul, neg. 32940, MHS.

5. Clara Bingham and Laura Leedy Gansler's book *Class Action: The Landmark Case that Changed Sexual Harassment Law* (New York: Anchor Books, 2003) documents the experiences of a few women who thirty years after World War II wanted the good pay of mining work but met intense opposition to their presence in the mines.

6. Carl G. Ash, "Garden and Table," *[East Grand Forks] Weekly Record,* July 3, 1942.

7. Richard Dougherty, *In Quest of Quality: Hormel's First 75 Years* (St. Paul, MN: North Central Publishing Co., 1966), 177–203; oral interview with R. C. Atkins, manager, John Morrell and Co. plant, Sept. 15, 2006, notes in author's possession.

8. See http://minerals.usgs.gov/minerals/pubs /commodity/iron_ore/stat (accessed June 20, 2007).

9. As 3M historian Virginia Huck wrote, "wartime products had peace time applications." More than that, wartime products had the capacity in themselves to return big profits: 3M's annual sales doubled from 1941 to 1945. Loralee J. Bloom, "Mining the Archives," *Minnesota History* 58:3 (Fall 2002): 162–67, and Virginia Huck, *Brand of the Tartan: The 3M Story* (New York: Appleton-Century-Crofts, 1955), 226, 230, 231.

10. See Broehl, *Cargill,* 663–66, on dog food and soybeans.

11. Bloom, "Mining the Archives," and Huck, *Brand of the Tartan,* 226, 230, 231.

12. "General Mills in 2003," pamphlet available from General Mills website: http://www.generalmills.com/corporate/index.aspx (accessed Apr. 26, 2007).

13. See photos of Percy B. Christianson and Sigurd Moe at work on posters, 1944, loc. no. N1.1 r5, MHS. General Mills, "History of Innovation: Radio and TV," http://www.generalmills.com/corporate /company/hist_roots.pdf (accessed Nov. 14, 2006).

14. For illustration and contents of K rations "units," see www.usarmymodels.com (accessed Apr. 26, 2007).

15. The American sugar industry had received a lot of attention from the federal government over the decades. Tariffs on sugar in the nineteenth century did not protect domestic sugar so much as it raised revenue for the federal government. Not until the 1930s did the government use tariffs to protect domestic sugar growers from foreign competition. The Sugar Acts of 1934, 1937, and 1948 set foreign quotas, minimum wages, and child-protection rules for beet workers and paid benefits to growers. Jose Alvarez and Leo C. Polopolus, "The History of U.S. Sugar Protection," Dept. of Food and Resource Economics, Florida Cooperative Extension Service, Institute of Food and Agricultural Sciences, University of Florida (2002), EDIS document no. SC 019, http://edis.ifas.ufl.edu/SC019 (accessed May 3, 2007). Sidney W. Mintz, *Sweetness and Power: The Place of Sugar in Modern History* (New York: Viking, 1985); U.S. Bureau of the Census, *U.S. Census of Agriculture: 1954* (Washington, DC: GPO, 1956).

16. Mintz, *Sweetness and Power.* Terry L. Shoptaugh, *Roots of Success: History of the Red River Valley Sugarbeet Growers* (Fargo: North Dakota Institute for Regional Studies, 1997), 72. For figures on farms, acres, yields, see *U.S. Census of Agriculture: 1954,* Vol. 1: "Counties and State Economic Areas," Part 8: Minnesota. Sugar policy and tariffs and cravings both propelled and supported the African slave trade, Caribbean and Brazilian colonization, and the American Revolution. Sidney Mintz argues: "The first sweetened cup of hot tea to be

drunk by an English worker was a significant historical event because it prefigured the transformation of an entire society, a total remaking of its economic and social basis." The transformation of American society was no less profound, as consumption of refined sugar increased from 38 pounds of sugar per person per year to 63 pounds in 2003. Most of this sweet dynamite came from sugar cane until the 1920s, when sugar beets emerged as an alternate source. Mintz, *Sweetness and Power,* 72. The East Grand Forks *Weekly Record* reported on July 10, 1942, that sugar beets constituted "one of [the] most important crops" in the area.

17. Agricultural Census, 1954.

18. Oral interview with my father, Robert Atkins (born 1917; interviewed Sept. 10, 2006), who grew up on a farm outside Lennox, SD. He followed the harvests when his own family's farm proved too unproductive to need the help of more than one of the Atkins boys and the younger Alvin could manage.

19. James M. Booth, "An Autobiography," Feb. 27, 1950, American Crystal Sugar Company Papers, MHS.

20. According to the Governor's Interracial Commission, housing was better for workers around Chaska if they lived in "The Mexican Hotel," an accommodation run by the sugar company that "was good, even for winter use." Governor's Interracial Commission, "The Mexican in Minnesota (Revised): A Report to Governor C. Elmer Anderson of Minnesota" (1953), 6–7. See especially Jim Norris, "Bargaining for Beets: Migrants and Growers in the Red River Valley," *Minnesota History* 58:4 (2002–3): 196–209.

21. U.S. Census, 1910, Crookston Ward 4, Polk County, Roll T624-715, p3A, ED 194. R. I. Holcombe and William Bingham, eds., *Compendium of History and Biography of Polk County, Minnesota* (Minneapolis, MN: W. H. Bingham and Co., 1916). The Sinner family of sugar beet farmers, on the North Dakota side of the Red River Valley, employed the same families for years. Norris provides several examples of Mexican workers who also reported returning to the same families for many years running. See Shoptaugh, *Roots of Success,* 34–35; Norris, "Bargaining for Beets," 204.

22. Dionicio Valdés, *Mexicans in Minnesota* (St. Paul: MHS Press, 2005). U.S. Census, 1930, Roll 1107, Page 2B, ED 29. For other individual family stories, see Dionicio Nodin Valdés, *Barrios Nortenos: St. Paul and Midwestern Mexican Communities in the Twenti-*

eth Century (Austin: University of Texas Press, 2000), 98.

23. Antonia Castañeda, "'Que Se Pudieran Defender': Chicanas, Regional History, and National Discourses," *Frontiers* 22:3 (2001): 116–42, quote, p121. Governor's Interracial Commission, "Mexican in Minnesota," 8.

24. Norris, "Bargaining for Beets," 205. For the text of the official bracero agreement, see www .farmworkers.org/bpaccord.html (accessed Apr. 26, 2007). See www.farmworkers.org/migrdata .html (accessed Apr. 26, 2007) and W.A. Cornelius, "Mexican Migration to the United States," in W. A. Cornelius and J. A. Bustamante, eds., *Mexican Migration to the United States: Origins, Consequences, and Policy Options* (La Jolla, CA: Bilateral Commission on the Future of U.S.–Mexican Relations, 1989), 1–21. For an especially interesting article on the effects of the bracero program on Mexican fertility, see Susan B. Carter and Richard Sutch, "Mexican Fertility Transition in the American Mirror," paper delivered at the Economic History Society annual conference, Apr. 2004. See also Zadie M. Feliciano, "Mexico's Demographic Transformation: 1920–1990," in Michael R. Haines and Richard H. Steckel, eds., *A Population History of North America* (New York: Cambridge University Press, 2000). Governor's Interracial Commission, "The Mexican in Minnesota: A Report to Governor Luther W. Youngdahl" (1948), 11, 17. Mexican American men enlisted in large numbers. As they faced discrimination even during the war years, the service sometimes provided a more dependable income than they could secure at home. Successfully organizing in the 1930s, some Mexican and Mexican American workers made a place for themselves in the automobile plants. "They became a stable segment of the region's urban industrial workforce, and among Mexican workers in the Midwest, they most closely approximated the wartime American Dream of upward occupational mobility and a stable life." See Dionicio Valdés, "The Mexican American Dream and World War II: A View from the Midwest," in Maggie Rivas-Rodriguez, *Mexican Americans and World War II* (Austin: University of Texas Press, 2005), 116–40, quote, p123–24.

25. Anita Albrecht Buck, *Behind Barbed Wire: German Prisoner of War Camps in Minnesota* (St. Cloud, MN: North Star Press, 1998), 101.

26. Alan L. Olmstead and Paul W. Rhode, "Reshaping the Landscape: The Impact and Diffusion of the Tractor in American Agriculture, 1910–1960," *Journal of Economic History* 61:3 (Sept. 2001): 663–

98. Shoptaugh, *Roots of Success,* 82–85. Farmers received coupons for more gasoline than did their in-town neighbors; how many they got depended on their distance from town and other individual circumstances. The extent to which diesel fuel was rationed, I don't know.

27. D. Jerome Tweton, "The Business of Agriculture," in Clark, ed., *Minnesota in a Century of Change,* 263. On numbers of tractors, see U.S. Department of Agriculture, *Agricultural Statistics, 1950* (Washington, DC: GPO, 1950), 574.

28. Interview with Thomas Reichert, DDS, Oct. 2006, notes in author's possession.

29. Thomas Saylor, *Remembering the Good War: Minnesota's Greatest Generation* (St. Paul: MHS Press, 2005), 104, 101–2, 111.

30. Todd Tucker, *The Great Starvation Experiment: The Heroic Men who Starved so that Millions Could Live* (New York: Free Press, 2006) 37, 46, 36.

31. Tucker, *Great Starvation Experiment,* 191.

32. Tucker, *Great Starvation Experiment,* 202–13.

33. John Wranovics, "Weapon of Choice," *New York Times,* Jan. 8, 2006. Parks, *Choice of Weapons,* 94. Gordon Parks, *A Hungry Heart: A Memoir* (New York: Atria Press, 2005).

34. Parks, *Choice of Weapons,* 94.

35. In their article "Reshaping the Landscape," economic historians Olmstead and Rhode argue that "The decline in the farm population after 1940 represents one of the great structural shifts in American history," p665.

NOTES TO CHAPTER 14

1. Lizabeth Cohen, *A Consumer's Republic: The Politics of Mass Consumption in Postwar America* (New York: Knopf, 2003), explores nationally this story of mass consumption. She looks especially at how citizens in the 1920s had caught the consumerism virus and then could not act on it during the Depression and the war. It was ready to explode once prosperity returned. She argues further that the emphasis on consumption—and increasing the goods to be consumed—kept the focus off the redistribution of wealth or even economic equality.

2. Shirley Wajda, "Be It Ever So Humble: A Review Article," *American Quarterly* 41.3 (Sept. 1989): 568–76; Katherine C. Grier, *Culture and Comfort: Parlor Making and Middle-Class Identity, 1880–1930* (1988; repr., Washington, DC: Smithsonian Institution Press, 1997). James Madison, *Slinging Donuts for the Boys: An American Woman in World War II* (New York: Knopf, 2007).

3. See www.accessgenealogy.com/worldwar/ minnesota/todd1/htm (subscription; accessed May 2, 2007) as well as U.S. World War II Army Enlistment Records, 1938–46, at www.ancestrylibrary .com (accessed May 2, 2007).

4. U.S. World War II Army Enlistment Records, 1938–46. For population figures, see http://www.census.gov/population/cencounts/ mn190090.txt (accessed Apr. 26, 2007).

5. See James Gilbert, *Men in the Middle: Searching for Masculinity in the 1950s* (Chicago: University of Chicago Press, 2005).

6. Or more people dreamed about it, anyway. Historian Brian Horrigan shows how the thread of futurism passed through the fabric of the 1930s and 1940s, whatever the effects of depression and war. R. Buckminster Fuller designed a modernist/futurist house in this period. At the Chicago "Century of Progress Exposition" in 1933, architect Fred Keck exhibited his "House of Tomorrow," which would be built and furnished on the principles of the assembly line. This philosophy of "modern" housing got turned into "popular culture" in the 1950s. Brian Horrigan, "The Home of Tomorrow, 1927–1945," in Joseph J. Corn, *Imagining Tomorrow: History, Technology, and the American Future* (Cambridge, MA: MIT Press, 1986), 137–63. James T. Patterson, *Grand Expectations: The United States 1945–1974* (New York: Oxford University Press, 1996).

7. See Cohen, *Consumer's Republic,* and Elaine Tyler May, *Homeward Bound: American Families in the Cold War Era* (1988; New York: Basic Books, 1999).

8. People such as William Norris, who had been part of the navy intelligence operations during the war, at the conclusion of the war (and with navy encouragement and support) went off on their own and designed computers that in the 1950s had their most important impact on government and business. Their work pioneered the transistor, the Honeywell thermostat control, and, eventually, the home computer, but the effects of these trickle down and have most impact not in the 1950s but later. Jeffrey L. Meikle, *Design in the USA* (Oxford: Oxford University Press, 2005), 133.

9. Twenty years later, in response to a request from Nancy Willey of Minneapolis to recommend an architect, Wright himself designed a very modest "Usonian" house for her in 1934. Following the 1929 crash, Wright, like most other architects, found little work. So, he took on this very small project on a comparatively tiny budget. This house moved closer to the more popular version of the "modern" style, the rambler. For a view of the

house, see www.thewilleyhouse.com (accessed Apr. 26, 2007). Penny Sparke, *An Introduction to Design and Culture: 1900 to the Present* (1986; repr., New York: Routledge, 2004); Thomas Hine, *Populuxe* (New York: Knopf, 1986); Meikle, *Design in the USA.* Oral interview with Sanya Poleschuk, Sanya Poleschuk Architecture, Inc., Feb. 7, 2006, notes in author's possession. Breuer got the central idea for his tubular steel chair from his bicycle handlebars; the Eames from the bentwood splints that they had made on contract for the army to help wounded soldiers. For fifty years designers had objected to objects made to look like something they weren't: clocks that looked more like lamps than timepieces; painted surfaces that were supposed to look like carved wood. Their objections did not result in the elimination of such fakes. Until there were suitable replacements, the fakes continued to appeal to many buyers and manufacturers. Alcoa was manufacturing chairs in the 1920s. One model had the shiny, satiny surface of aluminum, but most of the chairs were instead painted walnut, mahogany, and oak. What Breuer meant by "honest" is that the material should be what the material is, not some material made to look like something else. No fakes was his aspiration. Clive Edwards, "Aluminum Furniture, 1886–1986: The Changing Applications and Reception of a Modern Material," *Journal of Design History* 14:3 (2001): 207–25, quote, p210. Breuer was in a tradition of anti-ornamentation that had begun with the rejection by both British and American designers of what they saw as Victorian excess and artifice. This objection—and the modernism that the International Style triumphed—can, according to design historian Penny Sparke, also be read as a stringently male movement whose intent, in part, and effect, in greater part, was to identify Victorianism with women (draperies, pillows, tablecloths, and knickknacks) and modernism with a male aesthetic. She makes a provocative argument. See Penny Sparke, *As Long as It's Pink: The Sexual Politics of Taste* (New York: Harper Collins, 1995).

10. See http://www.mnfiji.org/index.php?option=com_content&task=view&id=25&Itemid=73 (accessed Apr. 26, 2007). See also MHS biography file; *St. Paul Pioneer Press* obituary for William Yungbauer, July 1, 1935, p1. William Yungbauer, born in Bohemia in 1861, learned woodcarving as a boy; as a young man in Paris, he worked in both clay and wood. He was hired to help with the interior of railroad man Henry Villard's New York mansion. In 1888 he was sent to work on the interior and furnishing of James J. Hill's house on Summit Avenue

in St. Paul. He opened his own furniture and interior decoration business in St. Paul, married, and stayed put until he died in a house fire in 1935. By that time, his son William had taken over. While at the University of Chicago, William Jr. was certainly exposed to the work and, no doubt, the spirit of Frank Lloyd Wright.

11. *Staples World,* June 3, 1948.

12. Shelley Nickles, "'Preserving Women': Refrigerator Design as Social Process in the 1930s," *Technology and Culture* 43:4 (2002): 693, 727.

13. Design historian Nigel Whiteley distinguishes between "modernist" and "consumerist" design: "Consumerist society shifted the balance in design from a concern with solutions to utilitarian needs, to an emphasis on an object's emotional, psychological, and social role. Whereas modernist design had sought to unify people, consumerist design sought (and continues to seek) to differentiate individuals or groups." See Nigel Whiteley, "Pop, Consumerism, and the Design Shift," *Design Issues* 2:2 (Autumn 1985): 31–45, quote, p36.

14. In 1952, Gene and Dorothy Sylvestre approached University of Minnesota architect Carl Graffunder to design a small house for them in Minnetonka. It was built almost entirely by one man (Ray Sanford, a local builder) with weekend help from twenty-seven-year-old Gene and twenty-six-year-old Dorothy. They lived there—expanding the living space twice and raising four boys—until 1988, a total of thirty-six years. That house had all the hallmarks of a "modernist" house—open plan, wall of windows, natural materials. One especially ingenious design idea was a movable closet that could be pushed up against a wall until other children came along, after which it could be turned into a room divider. See photos—negs. 54566–54575—at http://collections.mnhs.org/visualresources/. Marcel Breuer did undertake two commissions in Minnesota in the 1950s, neither of them modest. Incorporating the principles of modernism that he had long heralded—open lines, industrial look, raw materials, and integration into setting—he designed a house of glass and steel with stunning views of Lake Superior. At about the same time, the Saint John's Abbey community began thinking about replacing its nineteenth-century church building. Abbott Baldwin and a monastic committee invited Breuer not only to build a church but also to make a hundred-year plan for the grounds of the abbey and university.

The Breuer church, planned and built between 1955 and 1961, looked like no other Catholic church in the state. Guided by some of the same churchmen who would later advise at the Second Vatican Council, it anticipated many of the liturgical changes that the council effected. When Pope John XXIII called on the church to open the windows to change, he both reflected and promoted the principles of modernism that were taking hold in architecture, design, and the lives of people in much of the first world.

See Victoria Young, "Design and Construction of Saint John's Abbey Church," in *This Place Called Collegeville: St. John's at 150* (Collegeville, MN: St. John's University Press, 2006).

15. Atkins, "Walk a Century in My Shoes: Minnesota 1900–2000," *Minnesota History* 56 (Winter 2000): 410–29.

16. The art community helped, too. In 1941 and again in 1947, the Walker Art Center in Minneapolis presented an exhibit that had at its center a completely furnished single-family home, intended to demonstrate what a well-designed house could and should look like. Furnished entirely with materials and items available locally, the exhibits encouraged visitors—over 90,000 walked through the door of Idea House I or Idea House II. A surprisingly large number of the items in Idea House II are still being manufactured, by Knoll, Herman Miller, and even Eva Zeisel. The exhibit garnered much attention locally and nationally, including from the Museum of Modern Art, which a year later mounted Breuer's "House in the Museum Garden." See Alexandra Griffith Winton, "'A Man's House is his Art': The Walker Art Center's Idea House Project and the Marketing of Domestic Design, 1941–1947," *Journal of Design History* 17:4 (2004): 377–96.

17. *Staples World*, Dec. 9, 1954. Traditional furniture manufacturers and retailers were slower to convert to new materials than they were to newer styles. Non-furniture manufacturers were, therefore, the first who "appreciated and exploited" metal's role in furniture. Not surprisingly: Alcoa, for example, had quite a vested interest in expanding the market for aluminum products, especially in the immediate postwar years when demand for aluminum was dropping. Edwards, "Aluminum Furniture," 209.

18. *St. Paul Pioneer Press*, Dec. 17, 1950; *International Falls Journal*, Dec. 4, 1950.

19. See "Television History: The First 75 Years," http://www.tvhistory.tv/1950–1959.htm (accessed Apr. 26, 2007).

20. "At 50, TV Dinner Is Still Cookin,'" *Christian Science Monitor*, Nov. 20, 2004.

21. For similar ads, see *Northfield Independent*, Dec. 1, 1949. No one "needed" the tail fins that car designers added in the 1950s. But they did, apparently, need what the fins stood for. They wanted to be seen—the fins were obviously intended more for the viewer than the viewed—in a big, luxuriant, powerful, forward-leaning, extravagant car. Many men wanted to show both that they could afford an Oldsmobile and that they belonged in one, too. Fins also conjured up missiles and rockets and said "speed" and "up-to-date." Even a woman could manage, and both Ford and Chevy described their cars (and their women drivers) as "sweet." (Chevy's phrase: "sweet, smooth, sassy.") Obviously, women's power looked different from men's.

22. See May, *Homeward Bound*, for a compelling argument about the relationship between domesticity and the Cold War.

23. *Rochester Post Bulletin*, Dec. 6, 1950, Nov. 29, 1959. Atkins, "Walk a Century in My Shoes." See May, *Homeward Bound*.

24. Except black veterans who were, more often than not, unable to get VA loans and assistance for their housing dreams, forced as they were by redlined real estate to specific and ineligible places. This constitutes one of the long-term effects of racism in the United States. The major form of individual wealth—and increase in wealth—in the United States has been the family home. Veterans and others who bought homes in the 1950s usually moved up the economic ladder by virtue of the increasing value of their homes. Black veterans, barred from such ownership, were confined to housing that did not increase in value or that, indeed, lost value. Many were forced to rent, not able to build or buy at all, and so never accumulated the nest egg that would have edged them into the American middle class.

25. For a cultural history of Levittown, see Peter Bacon Hales, "Levittown: Documents of an Ideal American Suburb," at http://tigger.uic.edu/~pbhales/Levittown.html (accessed Apr. 5, 2007).

26. Clifford E. Clark, Jr., "Ranch-House Suburbia: Ideals and Realities," in Lary May, *Recasting America: Culture and Politics in the Age of Cold War* (Chicago: University of Chicago Press, 1989), esp. p157. See also Barbara Berglund, "Western Living *Sunset* Style in the 1920s and 1930s: The Middlebrow, the Civilized, and the Modern," *Western Historical Quarterly* 37:2 (Summer 2006): 133–58.

27. Benjamin Spock, *Common Sense Book of Baby and Child Care* (New York: Duell, Sloan and Pearce, 1946). See Jane F. Levey, "Imagining the Family in

Postwar Popular Culture: The Case of *The Egg and I* and *Cheaper by the Dozen*," *Journal of Women's History* 13:1 (2001): 125–50.

28. Malcolm Gladwell, "The Terrazzo Jungle," *The New Yorker,* Mar. 15, 2004, 120–27. In a *New Yorker* article, Malcolm Gladwell concludes with this: "Victor Gruen invented the shopping mall in order to make America more like Vienna. He ended up making Vienna more like America." Frank Lloyd Wright hated Southdale: it had "all the evils of the village street and none of its charms." But to millions of Minnesotans—and others—shopping malls have provided just the evils and charms we've wanted. In 1992, the Mall of America opened with its 13,000 parking spaces; it has become one of the state's major tourist destinations. James Farrell, *One Nation Under Goods: Malls and the Seductions of American Shopping* (Washington, DC: Smithsonian Institute Press, 2003). Margaret Marsh, *Suburban Lives* (New Brunswick, NJ: Rutgers University Press, 1990); Kenneth T. Jackson, "All the World's a Mall: Reflections on the Social and Economic Consequences of the American Shopping Center," *American Historical Review* 101:4 (Oct. 1996): 1111–21.

29. See http://www.dot.state.mn.us/interstate50/ (accessed Apr. 5, 2007).

30. See Patricia Cavanaugh, "Politics and Freeways: Building the Twin Cities Interstate System" (prepared for the Center for Urban and Regional Affairs and the Center for Transportation Studies, University of Minnesota, 2006), 13.

31. Tom Lewis, *Divided Highways: Building the Interstate Highways, Transforming American Life* (New York: Viking, 1997).

32. In the 1930s, Rondo Avenue was at the heart of St. Paul's largest African American neighborhood. African Americans whose families had lived in Minnesota for decades and others who were just arriving from the South made up a vibrant, vital community that was in many ways independent of the white society around it. The construction of I-94 in the 1960s shattered this tight-knit community, displaced thousands of African Americans, and erased a now legendary neighborhood. In 1982, a small group of neighborhood residents conceived the idea to bring back a sense of community, stability, and neighborhood values; things they felt were lost when the old community of Rondo was destroyed. The Rondo Days Festival, founded in 1983, is held annually during the third weekend in July. It offers a multicultural celebration of art, music, and food and is attended by a diverse audience. The "Preliminary List of Na-tionally and Exceptionally Significant Features of the Federal Interstate Highway System," put together by the Federal Highway Administration of the U.S. Department of Transportation, included mention of the Rondo neighborhood: http://www.environment.fhwa.dot.gov/histpres/final_task4List.pdf (accessed Apr. 26, 2007). See also Evelyn Fairbanks's memoir of life in the Rondo neighborhood, *Days of Rondo* (St. Paul: MHS Press, 1990), and Brendan Henehan, writer and producer, "St. Paul's Past: River, Railroads, and Rondo" (video, St. Paul: Twin Cities Public Television, 1991).

33. Atkins, "At Home in the Heart of the City."

34. F. James Davis, "The Effects of Freeway Displacement on Racial Housing Segregation in a Northern City," *Phylon* 26:3 (Fall 1965): 209–15.

35. Albert Eisele, *Almost to the Presidency: A Biography of Two American Politicians* (Blue Earth, MN: Piper Co., 1972). Robert A. Caro, *Master of the Senate: The Years of Lyndon Johnson* (New York: Knopf, 2002).

36. Interview with Warren MacKenzie, Oct. 29, 2002, conducted by Robert Silberman, part of the Nanette L. Laitman Documentation Project for Craft and Decorative Arts in America, Smithsonian Archives of American Art. Online at http://www.aaa.si.edu/collections/oralhistories/transcripts/macken02.htm (accessed Apr. 5, 2007).

37. Much has been written on the rise of popular culture in the 1950s. See, for example Joanne Meyerowitz, *Not June Cleaver: Women and Gender in Postwar America, 1945–1960* (Philadelphia, PA: Temple University Press, 1994), Joel Foreman, ed., *The Other Fifties: Interrogating Midcentury American Icons* (Urbana: University of Illinois Press, 1997), Peter J. Kuznick and James Gilbert, eds., *Rethinking Cold War Culture* (Washington, DC: Smithsonian Institute Press, 2001); May, *Recasting America;* Douglas T. Miller and Marion Nowak, *The Fifties: The Way We Really Were* (New York: Doubleday, 1977); Stephen J. Whitfield, *The Culture of the Cold War,* 2nd ed. (Baltimore, MD: Johns Hopkins University Press, 1996).

NOTES TO CHAPTER 15

1. "The Liberal Flame," *Time Magazine,* Feb. 1, 1960. For the Ball story, see Carl Solberg, *Hubert Humphrey: A Biography* (1984; repr., St. Paul, MN: Borealis Books, 2003), 127. Eisele, *Almost to the Presidency;* Timothy N. Thurber, *The Politics of Equality: Hubert H. Humphrey and the African American Freedom Struggle* (New York: Columbia University

Press, 1999). In 1970, former vice president Humphrey visited the campus of Southwest Minnesota State College (as Southwest State University in Marshall was called then) and took time to talk to several students, including me. Two days later I received a note signed by Humphrey. It was a remarkable way to inspire affection even in those anti-authoritarian and rebellious days. I still have that letter.

2. The politics of the late nineteenth century has generated much discussion in the last generation as historians have tried to figure out why people voted as they did and in the numbers they did. Some of the questioning grew, I think, out of a comparison between the significantly lower voter turnout in the late twentieth century and that of the late nineteenth century. Historians wanted to understand how issues of the tariff and free silver and the gold standard could get voters to the polls when civil rights, women's rights, and the Vietnam War didn't. What they found was that people—white men, primarily, women not getting the vote in national elections until 1920—voted along lines that had more to do with ethnicity and religion and their local manifestations—alcohol regulations and public schools—than they did with national issues. Paul Kleppner, *The Cross of Culture: A Social Analysis of Midwestern Politics, 1850–1900* (New York: Free Press, 1970); Richard Jensen, *The Winning of the Midwest: Social and Political Conflict, 1888–1896* (Chicago: University of Chicago Press, 1971). For an even more local focus, see Lowell Soike, *Norwegian Americans and the Politics of Dissent, 1880–1924* (Northfield, MN: Norwegian American Historical Association, 1991), and, especially, the fine work of Jon Gjerde, *The Minds of the West: Ethnocultural Evolution in the Rural Midwest, 1830–1917* (Chapel Hill: University of North Carolina Press, 1997). Gjerde is no longer concerned so much with voter turnout in the late nineteenth century as he is with the role of religion in people's lives and decisions, including political ones. See also Hine, *Populuxe*. For an especially interesting essay on the role of religion—and its disappearance from contemporary historians' field of vision—see John T. McGreevy, "Faith and Morals in the United States," *Reviews in American History* 26:1 (1998): 239–54. On political party alignments, see an excellent overview article by Richard L. McCormick, "Political Parties in the United States: Reinterpreting Their Natural History," *History Teacher* 19:1 (Nov. 1985): 15–32. In a thoughtful essay, Patrick J. Kelly demonstrates even how Republican candidate William McKinley used the language and symbols of the Civil War to stress the importance of national unity (glossing over the Republicans' acquiescence in the limiting of black male voting in the south, labor/management issues in western mines, as well as farmers' grievances against big business). "Genuinely alarmed" in Kelly's words, by the prospect of a William Jennings Bryan victory in 1896, the GOP "waged [a] campaign of memory" that proved to be smart, compelling, and decisive. See Patrick J. Kelly, "The Election of 1896 and the Restructuring of Civil War Memory," *Civil War History* 49:3 (Sept. 2003): 254–80.

3. Republicans held the two Minnesota Senate seats from 1863 to 1923 and the governor's chair from 1860 to 1899, 1901 to 1905, and 1909 to 1931. The only Democrats who cracked this Republican dominance were John Lind, the Populist/Democratic Free Silver Party governor from 1899 to 1901, and John A. Johnson, the Democratic governor from 1905 to 1909. Charles A. Towne, a Democrat, was appointed to fill out the Republican senator Cushman K. Davis's term upon Davis's death in 1900. Winfield Scott Hammond held the office of governor—as a Democrat—from January to December 1915, when he died of food poisoning. What's surprising about Hammond is that he counted himself as a Democrat: by all exterior markers he would have been more at home in the Republican party—a Yankee and Civil War veteran who lived in St. James in southwestern Minnesota, which even he identified as a Republican stronghold. In any case, his election did not presage a significant shift in electoral politics in Minnesota, suggesting that the voters had elected the man and not voted the party. Jon Gjerde divides the political parties into Yankee (Republican) and Foreign (Democratic) minds and shows how people melded their ethnicity, religion, and party preferences into their political campaigns. In fact, he argues, the late nineteenth century political story is the poem that conveys the novel that was the social, ethnic, religious, and economic tale of immigrant groups and conflicts in the period. Gjerde, *Minds of the West*.

4. See Omaha Platform at http://history .missouristate.edu/wrmiller/Populism/texts/documents/Omaha_Platform.htm (accessed Apr. 10, 2007).

5. Duane Swanson, a longtime staff member at the MHS, tells of his mother walking into the polling place in Pine County in the 1940s and, on seeing a portrait of the deceased Floyd Olson hanging on the wall, demanding: "What's that Commu-

nist doing there!" As Duane tells the story, his father hustled his mother out of the courthouse and the two of them "hid out" as closet Republicans in a largely FL universe.

6. John Earl Haynes, *Dubious Alliance: The Making of Minnesota's DFL Party* (Minneapolis: University of Minnesota Press, 1984).

7. Hubert H. Humphrey to Secretary James B. Forrestal, Apr. 26, 1948, Papers of the Truman Library, available online: http://www.trumanlibrary.org/whistlestop/study_collections/desegregation/large/documents/index.php?documentdate=1948-04-26&documentid=81&studycollectionid=deseg&pagenumber=1 (accessed Apr. 6, 2007).

8. Delton, *Making Minnesota Liberal,* especially p14–17. On Humphrey's reception as well as on Humphrey and Johnson's relationship, see Caro, *Master of the Senate.*

9. May, *Homeward Bound.*

10. Grace Metalious, *Peyton Place,* new edition with foreword by Ardis Cameron (Boston, MA: Northeastern University Press, 1999). I am grateful to University of Minnesota professor Clarke Chambers for seeing this confluence of books and showing it to me.

11. Arthur F. Naftalin, "A History of the DFL," PhD diss., University of Minnesota, 1948.

12. Anthony Lewis, *Gideon's Trumpet* (New York: Random House, 1964), 1–11, 146–68. See also Yale Kamisar, Abe Krash, Anthony Lewis, and Ellen S. Podgor, "*Gideon* at 40: Facing the Crisis, Fulfilling the Promise," *American Criminal Law Review* 41.1 (2004):135. See http://www.oyez.org/oyez/resource/case/139/ (accessed Apr. 6, 2007).

13. In 1991 and 1992, Minnesota Public Television journalist Beth Friend recorded nearly ninety interviews with some Minnesota connections, from Native American activist Clyde Bellecourt to University of Minnesota surgeon John Najerian, from Minneapolis restaurateur LeAnn Chin to choreographer and dancer Loyce Holton. Copies of those tapes are archived—and available for viewing—in the MHS library. It was in his interview for this program that Miles Lord repeated his philosophy. Beth Friend, *Portrait* (St. Paul: KTCA, 1991–92).

14. See "The Legacy of the Reserve Mining Case," http://news.minnesota.publicradio.org/features/2003/09/29_hemphills_reservehistory/ (accessed Apr. 7, 2007).

15. Thomas Huffman, "Enemies of the People: Asbestos and the Reserve Mining Trial," *Minnesota History* (2005): 292–306.

16. Sigurd Olson, *The Singing Wilderness* (New York: Knopf, 1956). For an accounting of Olson's thinking and writing of this book, see an excellent website at http://www.uwm.edu/Dept/JMC/Olson/letters/The%20Singing%20Wilderness.htm (accessed Apr. 6, 2007).

17. David Backes, *A Wilderness Within: The Life of Sigurd F. Olson* (Minneapolis: University of Minnesota Press, 1997), 310.

18. R. Newell Searle, *Saving Quetico-Superior: A Land Set Apart* (St. Paul: MHS Press, 1977), 220–27.

19. Philip Nash, "Ambassador Eugenie Anderson," *Minnesota History* 59:6 (Summer 2005): 249–62.

20. Geri Joseph remarks, May 30, 2006, Leadership Awards Banquet at the Hubert Humphrey Institute for Public Affairs at the University of Minnesota. Full text available at http://www.hhh.umn.edu/img/assets/20890/hhhremarks_gerijoseph2006.pdf (accessed Apr. 6, 2007).

21. Friend, interview with Coya Knutson, *Portrait.*

22. Gretchen Urnes Beito, *Coya, Come Home: A Congresswoman's Journey* (Los Angeles, CA: Pomegranate Press, 1990).

23. Bob Dylan, *Chronicles,* vol. 1 (New York: Simon and Schuster, 2004), 113.

24. Julie L. Davis, "American Indian Movement Survival Schools in Minneapolis and St. Paul, 1968–2002," PhD diss., Arizona State University, 2004, 97–116. See also Paul Chaat Smith and Robert Allen Warrior, *Like a Hurricane: The Indian Movement from Alcatraz to Wounded Knee* (New York: New Press, 1996).

25. Here and below, see Dominic Sandbrook, *Eugene McCarthy: The Rise and Fall of Postwar American Liberalism* (New York: Knopf, 2004).

26. See Sandbrook, *Eugene McCarthy;* Solberg, *Hubert Humphrey;* Eisele, *Almost to the Presidency.* Interview with John Brandl, Nov. 2, 2006, notes in author's possession.

27. "The State That Works," *Time Magazine,* Aug. 13, 1973.

28. U.S. Supreme Court 410 U.S. 113. *Roe, et al. v. Wade,* District Attorney of Dallas County, Appeal from the U.S. District Court for the Northern District of Texas, No. 70–18. Jan. 22, 1973. Brandl interview.

29. Richard Moe, "The Making of the Modern Vice Presidency: A Personal Reflection," *Minnesota History* 60.3 (Fall 2006): 88–99.

30. E. Lester Levine, "Is Minnesota a Two-Party State Again," *Publius* (Winter 1979): 197–204, online

at http://publius.oxfordjournals.org/cgi/reprint/ 9/1/197.pdf (accessed Apr. 6, 2007).

31. Christopher P. Gilbert, "Christians and Quistians in Minnesota," *PS: Political Science and Politics* 28:1 (Mar. 1995): 20–23.

32. William Souder, "Minnesota Democrats Host 'My Three Sons' Slate for Governor," *The Washington Post*, Dec. 29, 1996, A3.

33. "Demise of Hubert's D.F.L.," *Time Magazine*, Nov. 20, 1978.

NOTES TO CHAPTER 16

1. Here and below, Justine Kerfoot, *Woman of the Boundary Water: Canoeing, Guiding, Mushing, Surviving* (1986; repr., with new afterword by Justine Kerfoot, Minneapolis: University of Minnesota Press, 1994).

2. All north woods resorts and lodges also have websites, online booking, photos of the accommodations: this information is drawn from such sites.

3. The state's population increased at a faster rate than did the issuing of licenses, but the state's methods of categorizing license buyers is not entirely comparable across the decades. In 1957, for example, the state issued more than 305,000 fishing licenses to nonresidents; in 1982, only 66,000. It seems more likely that the methods of issuing licenses changed than that there was such a dramatic drop-off in nonresident fishing. See http://files.dnr .state.mn.us/rlp/licenses/historical_licenses.xls (accessed May 2, 2007).

4. See "State Record Fish," http://www.dnr .state.mn.us/fishing/staterecords.html (accessed May 2, 2007).

5. See http://www.leg.state.mn.us/webcontent/leg/symbols/walleyearticle.pdf (accessed May 2, 2007).

6. See http://www.historylink.org/essays/ output.cfm?file_id=5282 (accessed May 2, 2007). Larry Nesper, *The Walleye War: The Struggle for Ojibwe Spearfishing and Treaty Rights* (Lincoln: University of Nebraska Press, 2002). Sonna Hightower Langston, "American Indian Women's Activism in the 1960s and 1970s," *Hypatia* 18:2 (2003): 114–32, esp. 122–24. See also Gerald Vizenor, "Minnesota Chippewa: Woodland Treaties to Tribal Bingo," *American Indian Quarterly* 13:1 (Winter 1989): 30–57.

7. *A Guide to Understanding Chippewa Treaty Rights, Regulation, and Resource Management*, Minnesota ed. (Odanah, WI: Great Lakes Indian Fish and Wildlife Commission, 1995). See http://www .leg.state.mn.us/lrl/issues/indian.asp (accessed Apr. 11, 2007). Full treaty text available at http:// digital.library.okstate.edu/kappler/vol2/treaties/ chi0491.htm and http://digital.library.okstate.edu/ kappler/vol2/treaties/chi0648.htm (accessed Apr. 11, 2007)

8. See http://www.leg.state.mn.us/lrl/issues/indian.asp (accessed May 2, 2007). Rick Whaley and Walter Bresette, *Walleye Warriors: An Effective Alliance Against Racism and for the Earth* (Philadelphia, PA: New Society Publishers, 1994). Judge Murphy's meticulously researched and written decision (nearly 150 pages long) offers a detailed history of Minnesota treaties with the Ojibwe and how treaty rights were eroded or negated. Her decision was upheld by the Federal Appeals and Supreme Courts. Interview with Judge Murphy, Nov. 2, 2006, notes in author's possession.

9. "Walleye War," *Time Magazine*, Apr. 30, 1990, p36.

10. See http://www.aded.org/exhibits/social _responsibility/ad_council/2278 (accessed May 2, 2007). See Philip Deloria, *Indians in Unexpected Places* (Lawrence: University Press of Kansas, 2004), and *Playing Indian* (New Haven, CT: Yale University Press, 1998).

11. See http://rogerebert.suntimes.com/apps/ pbcs.dll/article?AID=/19901109/REVIEWS/ 11090301/1023 (accessed May 2, 2007). Fifteen years later, Leech Lake Ojibwe writer David Treuer chafes against the representation of Indians in the *Dances with Wolves* mode, but even he admits that the movie had a dramatic impact on white viewers, most of whom have never themselves had a conversation with an American Indian that lasted as long as that film. As the *Washington Post* reviewer of David Treuer's new novel *The Translation of Doctor Appeles: A Love Story* wrote (and Treuer quotes on his own website), "David Treuer is sick and tired of dancing with wolves, throwing tea in the bay, hiding in the cupboard or weeping a single tear at the sight of a littered highway." See "Burning Wooden Indians," *Washington Post*, Sept. 17, 2006, http:// davidtreuer.com/wordpress/index.php (accessed May 2, 2007); interview with David Treuer, "Talking Volumes," Minnesota Public Radio, Sept. 29, 2006; David Treuer, *Native American Fiction: A User's Manual* (Minneapolis, MN: Graywolf Press, 2006).

12. Garrison Keillor's *Prairie Home Companion* has been broadcast on National Public Radio since 1975. The program in 2007 was broadcast on 581 stations. Many of his monologues have been pub-

lished on CD, which, with his nearly dozen books, has given him an international reputation. He draws a big crowd in Edinburgh, Scotland, for the Festival Fringe. His and Minneapolis master musician Philip Brunelle's *Young Lutheran's Guide to the Orchestra* played to a sold-out Royal Festival Hall London crowd in the fall of 1992. What most contemporary Londoners seem to know about Minnesota is that both Garrison Keillor and wrestler Jesse Ventura live there. (Not such an odd combination from that distance!)

13. In his *Babbitt* and *Arrowsmith* as well as in various short stories and other fiction, Lewis adopted the same authorial stance and critical tone regarding his townspeople. The Gopher Prairie people are smug and proud of it. In a *New York Times* review of a biography of Lewis, author Jane Smiley wrote that "The publication of 'Main Street' ranks with that of 'Uncle Tom's Cabin' as one of the few literary events in American history that proved to be a political and social event as well. The book sold hundreds of thousands of copies. As with the Stowe novel, Americans took up what appeared to be a violent critique of themselves with great enthusiasm, and were ready to read it, judge it and discuss it." Jane Smiley, "All-American Iconoclast," *New York Times,* Feb. 20, 2002. See http://query.nytimes.com/gst/fullpage.html?res=9905E7DE1139F933A15752C0A9649C8B63 (accessed Apr. 11, 2007).

14. Howard Mohr, *How to Talk Minnesotan: A Visitor's Guide* (New York: Penguin, 1987). Much of Mohr's and Keillor's humor is of the same wry, self-deprecating, dry kind. The "Minnesotan" they both love and lampoon is similar enough that either they have invented those Minnesotans together or they both have a similar take on the Minnesotans they characterize.

15. In her soul-searching and revealing book, *Beyond Good Intentions: A Mother Reflects on Raising Internationally Adopted Children,* Cheri Register shows the painful side of her own Minnesota Nice: "It is important to me to keep my family's emotions in check. After all, anger only stirs up trouble, and nobody likes a frowning face. I steer clear of sensitive subjects, like my child's birth parents or the fact that he looks different from the rest of us. I prefer to keep life smooth and comfy, to accentuate the positive and leave the negative unsaid. We all get along better that way." She reveals, then, what this niceness cost her son. Register, *Beyond Good Intentions* (St. Paul, MN: Yeong & Yeong Book Company, 2005), quote, p51.

16. *Babette's Feast,* the short story by the Danish Isak Dinesen (Karen Blixen), first appeared in *Ladies' Home Journal* in 1958 and was published as part of her collection *Anecdotes of Destiny* (New York: Penguin, 1958).

17. Thorstein Veblen, *Theory of the Leisure Class: An Economic Study in the Evolution of Institutions* (New York: Macmillan, 1899), includes one chapter on "Conspicuous Leisure" and "Conspicuous Consumption."

18. Odd S. Lovoll, *Norwegians on the Prairie: Ethnicity and the Development of the Country Town* (St. Paul: MHS Press/Norwegian-American Historical Association, 2006).

19. See Kleppner, *Cross of Culture.*

20. Lovoll, *Norwegians on the Prairie,* 4, 7.

21. Hennepin, *A Description of Louisiana,* translated by John Gilmary Shea (1683; Ann Arbor, MI: University Microfilms, 1966), ch. 15, p45.

22. See Kathleen Neils Conzen, *Germans in Minnesota* (St. Paul: MHS Press, 2003), 62.

23. Holmquist, ed., *They Chose Minnesota.*

24. "Immigration in Minnesota: Discovering Common Ground" (Minneapolis, MN: Minneapolis Foundation, Oct. 2004). The exact numbers are 40 percent from Asia, 24 from Latin America, and 13 from Africa. See the full text online at http://www.minneapolisfoundation.org/publications/ImmigrationBrochure.pdf (accessed Apr. 24, 2007).

25. See "Groceries Go Global: Korea, Iraq, Mexico, Vietnam, Italy and India," *[Minneapolis] Star Tribune,* Apr. 20, 2006, T1.

26. Devon Idstrom, "Linking New Immigrants to Farming Opportunities," *Community Dividend* 1 (Minneapolis: Federal Reserve Bank of Minneapolis, 2003), http://www.minneapolisfed.org/pubs/cd/03-1/farmers.cfm (accessed May 3, 2007).

27. Minneapolis Foundation, "Immigration in Minnesota."

28. Stan Greenberg, Anna Greenberg, Julie Hootkin, "The Changing Shape of Minnesota: Reinvigorating Community and Government in the New Minnesota," Report Prepared for the Minnesota Community Project, Greenberg, Quinlan, Rosner Research, Inc., Dec. 14, 2004, p23, 29.

NOTES TO EPILOGUE

1. Billy Collins's "Litany" appeared originally in *Poetry* 179:5 (Feb. 2002): 249.

2. Mary Oliver, "Three Prose Poems," in *New and Selected Poems,* Vol. II (Boston, MA: Beacon Press, 2005), 114.

Index

Page numbers in *italic* refer to illustrations.

abortion, 232, 233
advertising, xv, 106, 188, 209–12, 217
Aerial Lift Bridge (Duluth), 108, 256
African Americans: in CCC, 184, 186; in Civil War, 64, 68–69; discrimination against, 82, 95, 215–16, 296n24; excluded from census, 281n20; middle-class, xv, 95, 215, 296n24; migration to Minnesota, 69, 245; music, 167, 190; newspapers, 117; occupations, 69, 95, *134;* in politics, 248, 262, 263; in St. Paul, 95–96, 215–16, 252, 297n32; social services, 109; suffrage, 113; unemployment, 173; as "white," 60; in World War II, 192, 203, 207, 296n24. *See also* civil rights movement; lynchings; slavery/slaves
African immigrants, 245, 247–49, 262, 263, 301n24
agriculture. *See* farmers/farming
Albert Lea (Freeborn County), 177
Alcoa, Inc., 294n9
Alien Registration, 115–16. *See also* Minnesota Commission of Public Safety
American Association of University Professors, 108
American Crystal Sugar Company (Moorhead), 197, 198
American Fur Company, 32, 251, 252
American Gas Machine Company strike, 177
American Indian Movement, 230
Americanization, 94, 107–18, 164, 166, 207, 281n1, 289n28
American Protective Association (Duluth), 255
American Refugee Committee (Minneapolis), 249
American Swedish Institute (Minneapolis), 107, 256
Anawangmani, Simon (Dakota), 43–44
Ancient Order of Hibernians, 255, 257
Andrew Schoch Grocery (St. Paul), 105, 122
Andrews, Christopher Columbus (general and conservationist), 62–64, 69
Anishinaabe people. *See* Ojibwe people
annuities, 41, 43, 45, 50, 58, 82, 278n21, 279n25. *See also* Dakota War of 1862; Inkpaduta, uprising of
Anoka County, 213, 253
apartment buildings, 124, *160, 161,* 166
apples, 106, 258
architects/architecture: Bauhaus modernists, 208, 209; Barber, Edward, 185; Beaux-Arts style, 208; Breuer, Marcel, 209, 210, 294n9, 295n14; Close, Lisl and Winston, 209; Fuller, R. Buckminster, 294n6; Gilbert, Cass, 208, 257; Graffunder, Carl, 295n14; Gruen, Victor, 214, 297n28; Keck, Fred, 294n6; Lindquist, George C., 185; Masqueray, Emmanuel L., 257; Prairie style, 208; Sullivan, Louis H., 208, 257; Wright, Frank Lloyd, 208, 294n9, 297n28; Wigington, Clarence, 260. *See also* houses; modernism
Arctic Cat snowmobiles, 261
armbands, Native American, 16
Armistice Day blizzard, 260
arrowheads, 21–22
Arrowwood Resort (Alexandria), 237
art/artists, xii, xv, 16, 182–83; Albinson, Dewey, 184; Catlin, George, 22; DesJarlait, Patrick, *13,* 15, 182, 290n34; Fossum, Syd, 182; Haupers, Clem, 183; MacKenzie, Alixandra Kolesky, 217; MacKenzie, Warren, 216–17; Mairs, Clara, *183;* Morrison, George, 290n34; Raymond, Evelyn, 182
artificial limbs, 97–98
Asian immigrants, 245, 247, 263, 301n24; as "white," 60
Assiniboine country, 73
Aster Theater (Minneapolis), *126*
athletics, xvi; college, 108–9, 254; 1920s, 122, *141, 142, 143, 161*

Augsburg College (Minneapolis), 286n2

August Schell Brewing Company (New Ulm), 255

Austin (Mower County), 81

automobiles, 122, *144, 145, 146,* 166, 167, 188, 200; 1950s, xvi, 209, 210, 211–12, 214, 217, 296n21

Aveda Corporation (Blaine), 261

Avon Products, Inc., 247

Ayer family, 98, 272n17

baby boom, 223–24

Bailly, Alexis (settler, Wabasha), 252, 274n21

Ball, Joseph (candidate), 219

Bakken, Earl (inventor of pacemaker), 260

bands, musical, 122, *139, 140,* 161, 189, 291n47

banks, 253, 257; closing of, 171, 173, 176. *See also individual banks*

Banks, Dennis (Ojibwe), 230

barter, 170, 175, 201. *See also* trade/traders

baseball, 83, 260, 261, 262

beads/beadwork, 18, 35

Beargrease, John (mail carrier), 256

Bearskin Lodge (Grand Marais), 237

Beaver Bay (Lake County), 253

Beaver Creek Valley (Houston County), 184

Bellanger, Patricia (Ojibwe), 230

Bellecourt, Andrew (Ojibwe), 117

Bellecourt, Clyde (Ojibwe), 230

Beltrami County, photographs of, 122

benevolence, culture of, 68, 98–99, 231. *See also* charities; women, volunteer work

Benevolent League, 69

Benton-Banai, Eddie (Ojibwe), 230

Bergeron, John (logroller), 121, *128*

Berini, John (stonemason), 185

Best Buy Co. (Richfield), 261

Bierman, Bernie (coach), 109

Bird Island (Renville County), 10

bird's-eye view maps, 74–79, 81–83, 281n4, 282n5, n6, n7

Black, Hugo (Supreme Court justice), 225

Black Dog village (Dakota County), 73

Blackmun, Harry (Supreme Court justice), 232

Blandin Foundation, 99

blanket Indians, 44

Bloomington (Hennepin County), mounds in, 20

Bly, Robert (poet), 10

B'nai B'rith, 109. *See also* Jewish immigrants

boarding schools, Native American, 43–44, 70, 82, 279n25

Bohemian Flats (Minneapolis), 124

bonanza farms, 4, 97

Boschwitz, Rudy (senator), 233

Boundary Waters Canoe Area Wilderness (BWCA), 10, 227, 231–32, 237

Bowler, Lizzie and Madison: in Civil War, 63, 65, 68

Braat family (immigrants), 79–80, 265

braceros, 199. *See also* migrant workers

Brackett's Battalion, 70

Brandl, John, 232

Breckenridge (Wilkin County), 4

breweries, 244

British. *See* English immigrants; Great Britain

Brown, Joseph R. (trader), 30, 34–36, 48, 276n21

Brown's Valley Man, 18–19

Brown v. Topeka Board of Education, 216, 223

Bruce, Robert (barber), 68–69, 281n20

buffalo, 45, 53, 252

buildings. *See* apartment buildings; architects/architecture; houses

Bunyan, Paul, legend of, 257, 259

Burger, Warren (Supreme Court chief justice), 232, 261

burial mounds. *See* mounds, Native American

Bush Foundation, 99

business: government relations, xv, 102; growth of, 72–73, 163, 167; immigrant, 245; labor relations, 111, 289n22, 289n24. *See also specific businesses and types of business*

Cahokia mounds (Illinois), 19–20

Cain, Myrtle (legislator), 112, 289n24

California Fruit Growers Exchange (CFGE), 105. *See also* Sunkist oranges

Campbell family (mixed bloods), xv, 26–33, 49–60, 265, 273n6, 276n1; Antoine Joseph "Joe," 50–52, 54, 55, 57–59, 265, 276n5, 277n12, 278n23; Archibald John "A. J.," 26–27; Baptiste, 50, 54, 55–56, 59, 276n6, 277n12; Duncan, 273n5, 274n15; Jack, 50, 55–56, 57, 70, 277n12; Louise Frienier, 57–58, 278n23; Margaret Menagre (Patoile), 26, 30–33, 49, 51, 54, 55; Mary Ann Dalton, 50–51, 55; Mary Rainville, 50; Matias Scott, 50; Ninse, 26–27; Paul "Hippolite," 50, 55, 57; Rosalie Renville, 50; Scott, 26–33, 49, 51, 273n7, n14, 274n15

Camp Chase, Ohio, map of, 74, 77

Camp Release (Lac qui Parle County), xv, 55, 59, 183

Cannon River, 75

canoes, 5, 24

Cargill Company (Minneapolis), 193, 194

Carleton College (Northfield), 96, 108

Carlson, Grace Holmes (politician), 260

Carlson Companies (Minneapolis), 260

Carlson Furniture (Staples), 205, 209, 210, 212

Carpenter, George and Mary (settlers), 78

cars. *See* automobiles

Cass Lake Reservation (Cass County), 43

Cathedral of St. Paul, 257

Catholic Charities, 248

Catholic Colonization Bureau, 94

Catholics: American, 94–95, 223; in Duluth, 255; German, 15, 243–44; immigrant, 115; Irish, 46–47, 69, 94, 96, 243, 275n13; politics of, 219, 220, 232, 233; St. Paul, 39, 207, 252

Cattaneo, Joe (stonemason), 185

Cedar-Riverside neighborhood (Minneapolis), 224

census: 1850 territorial, 38–39, 276n2; 1930, 288n6; as historical sources, 38–39, 59, 89; race as category, 57, 281n20; spelling of names, 38, 50, 276n21

Center for Victims of Torture (Minneapolis), 249

chairs, 209, 210, 218

change, 222–24, 248

charities, 167, 174. *See also* benevolence, culture of; women, volunteer work

Charleston (dance), 167, 190

Chaska (Carver County), 196, 198, 293n20

Chicago, Milwaukee and St. Paul Railroad, 87

children: mixed-blood, 27, 30, 38, 54; protection of, 68, 112, 256, 280n17; raising of, 214

Children's Hospital (St. Paul), 188

Children's Theater (Minneapolis), 263

Chinese immigrants, 90, 95, *107*, 109, 115, 246

Chippewa County, 4, 184

Chippewa National Forest (Beltrami/Cass/Itasca counties), 10, 237

Chippewa people. *See* Ojibwe people

Chisholm (St. Louis County), 108

Christianity, Native American converts to, 44, 49, 55–56, 92

Christiansen, Melius (choir director), 109

Christianson, Theodore, gubernatorial campaign, *144*

Christie family, 78–79, 279n1

Christmas, 105–6

churches, 43, 47, 90. *See also* ministers, training of; missionaries; religion

Citizens Alliance, 112, 177, 186, 256, 258, 289n24

citizens/citizenship: delayed, 113, 115–16; for Native Americans, 44, 117, 258

city directories, as historical sources, 89

Civilian Conservation Corps (CCC), 9, 176, 179, 184–86; Indian Division, 184, 291n38

"civilization": escape from, 237; imposed on Native Americans, 44, 49, *52*, 56, 70, 82, 207, 289n28; white, 16, 31, 37–38

civil rights movement, xii, 95–96, 203, 216, 223, 229, 240; Hubert Humphrey's involvement in, 216, 221–22

Civil War, xv, 53, 61–71, 253, 275n2, 279n1; aftermath, 72, 77–78, 81–82, 95, 97, 103, 280n17, 281n4, 298n2; families during, 64–65, 67–68, 280n8; First Minnesota Volunteers, 61–62, 253; photography, 119, 162

class, division by, 216. *See also* specific classes

Clearwater County, 7

Clearwater Lake (Wright County), 238

Clearwater Lodge (Grand Marais), 237

Cloquet (Carlton County), 123, *154, 155,* 258

clothing: making, 87–88, 97; Native American, 35, 55; Native American–white combinations, 35, 45, 274n15, 276n6; white, 35, 38, 39, 47, *52*, 56, 188. *See also* washing clothes

Clovis period, 19

clubs, 109–11. *See also*

benevolence, culture of; women, clubs; *and individual clubs*

Cold War, 203, 212, 221, 222

Coleman, Norm (senator), 234, 235

Coleraine (St. Louis County), 123, *151*

College of Saint Benedict (St. Joseph), 108, 287n2

College of St. Catherine (St. Paul), 108, 257

College of St. Scholastica (Duluth), 108, 286n2

College of St. Teresa (Winona), 108, 286n2

Collins, Billy (poet), 266

Columbia Company (fur trade), 32

Columbian Exchange, 16

Common Hope (St. Paul), 249

communism/communists, 175, 177, 224, 259, 289n18, 298n5; DFL ouster of, 221, 229

Como Park and Conservatory (St. Paul), 257

Compromise of 1850, 46, 275n2

computer industry, 262, 294n8

Comstock, Ada (educator), 256

Concordia College (St. Paul), 286n2

conductors: Dorati, Antal, 260; Oberhoffer, Emil, 256; Verbrugghen, Henri, *125*

Congdon, Chester A. (lawyer), 108, 124

conscientious objectors, 201–2

conservatives/conservatism, 187, 233, 235, 248

conspicuous consumption, 123, 243, 294n1

consumerism, 212, 216, 217–18, 294n1, 295n13

Control Data Corporation, 231, 260

Cooke, Jay (businessman), 95, 103

Coon Rapids (Anoka County), 212–14

cooperation, 23, 24. *See also* white–Native American relations

cooperatives, 104, 109, 255

corn, 14, 15, 16, 20, 172
Cornish immigrants, 86
Corpus Christi Day strikers, 111
Countryman, Gratia Alta (librarian), 256
Court, Magdalene and Peter (farmers), 170–72, 176, 180, 186–87, 245, 288n2
Cowperthwait, Thomas (map maker), 73, 76–77
cradleboards, 17
Cragun's Resort (Brainerd), 237
Croatian Benefit Society, 114
Croatian immigrants, 207, 220, 245
Crocker, Betty, creation of, 258
Crookston (Polk County), 98, 113
Crosby, John (miller), 86, 99
Crow Creek Reservation (Dakota Territory), 56, 58
cultural strength, Native American, 12–13, 18, 25
culture(s): clash of, 24–25, 50; homogenous, 217, 223; industrial, 166; interpreter of, 29; intersection of, 49–50, 60, 106; popular, 209, 211, 294n6; youth, 224. See also Minnesota Nice
Cuyuna Range, 107, 257

Dakota County, French people in, 38
Dakota language, 44, 252, 270n1, 273n6; dictionaries of, 30, 31, 270n1; white speakers of, 27, 29, 31, 41
Dakota people, 11, 15–18, 22–23; casinos, 240; conversion of, 44, 85; dances, 189; hanging at Mankato, 54, 55–56, 57, 59, 93, 253; land ceded by, 35, 41–43; removal of, 44, 53, 56–57, 82, 93, 263, 272n23; treaties with, 30, 50, 252, 274n18; urban, 230; wars with Ojibwe, 5, 21, 29, 70
Dakota War of 1862, xv, 44, 52, 53–60, 63, 94, 253; aftermath, 66, 69–70, 72, 92
dams, 40, 50, 213, 254, 260
dances/dancing, 167, 188–91, 291n50

dancing the rice, 14
Danish immigrants, 84, 243, 244, 255
Danish Young People's Home, 143
Daughters of Rebekah, 90
Davis, Alice, Kate, and Mrs. George, 8
Davis, Michael (judge), 239
Dawes Act of 1889, 93
Dayton-Hudson Corporation (Minneapolis), 214, 256, 261, 262
Defenbacher, Daniel (Walker museum director), 182
DeGrood family, 122, 145
Democratic-Farmer-Labor Party (DFL), 221, 231–35. See also Farmer-Labor Party
Democratic Party, 46, 230, 235; civil rights and, 216, 221–22, 284n29; ethnic make-up, 219–20; governors, 298n3
depots, railroad, 81, 90, 103
depressions: 1857, 46; 1873, 80–81, 103; 1893, 92, 104. See also Great Depression
Derham, Hugh (philanthropist), 108
DeSoto, Hernando (explorer), 271n7
DeVillier, Callum, 172, 191
discrimination. See racism
dockworkers' strike, 111, 257, 259
dolls, Native American, 17
Donaldson, L. S., Company (Minneapolis), 161
Donnelly, Ignatius (politician), xiv, 91, 104, 110, 220, 253
Donnelly, Kate, 110
Douglas County, in World War I, 114
draft, military, 114, 192–93, 200
dressmakers/seamstresses, xv, 87–89, 96–97, 283n10
Duluth (St. Louis County): economy, 80; Italians in, 185; lynchings, 166, 258; photographers, 119; shipping, 107–8; strikes, 111–12, 257, 259; timber industry, 98; unemployment, 259

du Luth, Daniel Greysolon, sieur (explorer), 23–24, 251
Duluth, Red Wing and Southern Railroad, 87
Duluth Clinic, 257
Duluth Entertainment and Convention Center, 261
Duluth Ladies' Relief Society, 255
Dunn, Lorna, 122, 146
Dunn Bros. Coffee (St. Paul), 262
Dunwoody, William (businessman), 86, 99
DuPuis, Hypolite (businessman), 48
Durenberger, Dave (senator), 233, 235
Dutch immigrants, 79–80
Dylan, Bob (musician), 216, 224, 260

East Grand Forks (Polk County), 200; sugar-beet factory, 196, 197, 198
Eastman family, 92–93, 266
economy, 247–48; 1870s, 84–86; 1880s, 92; 1920s, 170, 171; 1950s, 212. See also depressions; poverty; wealth, disparities in
Edina (Hennepin County), 124, 159, 214
education, xii, 231, 248, 269n3. See also schools; teachers
Effigy Mounds National Monument, 20–21
Eggleston, Edward, 66
electricity, 186–87, 207, 256
Ely (St. Louis County), 10, 255
Emancipation Proclamation, 53
employment. See labor; occupations; unemployment
English immigrants, 23–24, 28, 69, 84, 251
English language, 31, 44, 86, 247, 258; Native American speakers of, 27, 29, 41, 51, 55, 277n12
environmental movement, 209, 223, 226, 231, 240
ethnicity, 192, 255; politics and, 219–20, 245, 298n2, 298n3; Prohibition and, 46, 164, 243,

244. *See also individual ethnic groups*

Euro-Americans, 28, 31, 69; farmers, 4, 12, 15–16

European languages, 24, 43, 245, 288n2

Europeans, 16–17, 271n6; diseases brought by, 12–13, 271n7. *See also* explorers; fur trade/fur traders; *and individual immigrant groups*

Eveleth (St. Louis County), 7

explorers, 5, 11–12, 23–24, 272n23

factories, 85, 87, 97–99, 194–95. *See also* industrialization

Fairbrother, Edward and Minnie, 100, 103–4, 106

Falls of St. Anthony (Minneapolis), 36, 251, 260

families, *120, 145, 150*, 161, 162, *169*

Faribault (Rice County), 75, *76*, 87

Faribault, Alexander (legislator), 48, 277n18

Faribault family, 39

Faribault Woolen Mills, 98

Farmer-Labor Party (FL), 178, 220–21, 259. *See also* Democratic-Farmer-Labor Party

Farmers' Alliance, 104

farmers/farming, xv, 46, 265; 1870s, 80–82, 97; 1880s, 85, 97–98; bonanza, 4, 97; Catholic, 15, 94; decline in, 107, 222, 294n35; Depression-era, 170–72, 175, 177, 178, 197; growth of, 72; immigrant, 245; milling and, 86, 104, 113; Native American, 15–16, 20, 42, 44, 122, *131;* organization by, 109; photographs of, *120, 121, 127;* World War II, 199–200, 203–4. *See also* soil

Farmers Holiday Association, 177

Farm Security Administration, 182

Farm Women's Co-operative, 175

fear, 58; of ethnic groups,

247–48; during World War I, 114–15, 117

Federal Art Project (FAP), 182–83

Federal Emergency Relief Administration (FERA), 179

Federal Highway Act of 1956, 215

Federal Music Project, 181

Federated Women's Clubs, 114

Federation of Negro Women, *136*

feminism, xii, 223, 232, 233

Fenstad's Resort (Little Marais), 237

Finnish immigrants, 111, 115, 207, *244*, 245

Finnish People's College and Theological Seminary (Minneapolis), 109

Finnish Socialist Federation (Hibbing), 257

fires, 12, 108, 119, 123, *154*, 258, 283n10

First Avenue Club (Minneapolis), 224

First Bank Systems (Minneapolis), 259

First Minnesota Volunteer Regiment, 61–62, 253

fishing, 300n3; Native American rights, 238–41

Fitzgerald, F. Scott (author), 216

Flandreau Reservation (Dakota Territory), 60, 82, 279n25

flophouses, 124, 171

floristic provinces (geology), 6

flu epidemic of 1918, 117, 198, 258

Fond du Lac Reservation (Carlton/St. Louis Counties), 70, 259

food: convenience, xvi; ethnic, 16, 241, 246; Native American, 14–17, 24. *See also* K-rations; starvation experiment; sugar

football, 109, 254, 261

Ford, Guy Stanton (educator), 109

forest fires, 12, 108; 1918, 123, *154*, 258

forests, 10; state, 259. *See also* parks, state; *and individual forests*

Fort Berthold, North Dakota, 252

Fort Gaines (Morrison County), 73

Fort Ridgely State Park (Nicollet County), 257

Fort Snelling (Hennepin County), 26–28, 47, 49, 73, 251; slaves at, 30–31, 36, 252, 274n21

Foshay, Wilbur B. (businessman), 173

Foshay Tower (Minneapolis), 125, 259

Foster, Mary Dillon: women's biographies compiled by, 110

Fox people, treaties with, 30, 274n18

France, 27, 53. *See also* French immigrants; French language

Frank Dagget Post (GAR), 68

Fraser, Donald (mayor), 224, 226, 231

Frederick R. Weisman Art Museum (Minneapolis), 262

Freedman's Aid Society, 253

Freeman, Mike (politician), 234

Free Soil Party, 46

freeways. *See* interstate highway system

French immigrants, 23–24, 39, 41, 47, 69, 94, 251

French language: Native American speakers, 29, 31, 41, 273n5; spelling of names, 38, 50, 276n21

frontier: closing of, 166, 184; women on, 37–38

Frost, Robert (poet), 10

Fugitive Slave Law, 275n2

furniture, xv, xvi, 208–14, 217–18, 266, 295n10, 296n16, n17

fur trade/fur traders, 5, 24, 26–28, 41, 59, 60, 84; decline of, 32, 34, 36, 49

Garver, Eliza and James A.: in Civil War, 64–65, 67–68, 280n8

gas stations, *120*

Gaultier de Varennes, Pierre, sieur de la Vérendrye (explorer), 24

gender roles: changes in, 214;

definitions, 15–16, 66, 68, 174; occupations based on, 122, 192–93. *See also* men, roles; women, roles

General Mills Company (Minneapolis), 172, 195, 259, 263

Geneva Township (Freeborn County), 78

geography/geology, 3–10

German immigrants, 60, 84, 94, 164, 165, 241; farmers, 15, 224; newspapers, 253; politics of, 219, 220, 243–45

Gettysburg, battle of: First Minnesota Regiment at, 61–62

GI Bill, 207, 212, 216, 222, 296n24

Gideon v. Wainwright, 225

Gillett, Mary (seamstress), 84, 85, 87–99, 266, 283n12, 284n16

Gitchi Gammi Club (Duluth), 257

glaciers, 4, 5–6

Glensheen Mansion (Duluth), 108, 124, 257

Godfrey, Ard and Harriet (settlers), 34, 39–41, 257

Gold Medal Flour, 86, 254. *See also* Washburn, Crosby and Company

Goodhue, James M. (newspaper publisher), 252

Goodhue County, 84–85, 90

Gooseberry Falls State Park (Lake County), 185

Gooseberry River (Lake County), *150*

government: reforms in, 112–14, 174–75; relations with business, 102; role of, xv, 179, 191, 222. *See also* relief programs

governors: Andersen, Elmer L., 261; Anderson, C. Elmer, 233; Anderson, Wendell, 231, 232, 261; Benson, Elmer, 177, 178, 220–21, 224; Burnquist, Joseph, 114; Carlson, Arne, 233; Davis, Cushman K., 298n3; Democratic, 232; foreign-born, 107, 245; Freeman, Orville, 222, 224–25, 227,

234; Gorman, Willis, 46; Hammond, Winfield, Scott, 298n3; Hubbard, Lucius, 91, 265; Johnson, John A., 107, 298n3; Kunze, William, 288n17; Latimer, Thomas, 288n17; Leach, George, 288n17; Lind, John, 162–63, 298n3; Miller, Stephen, 66; Nelson, Knute, 107; Olson, Floyd B., 177, 178, 220, 221, 298n5; Pawlenty, Tim, 234–35, 248; Perpich, Rudy, 232; Petersen, Hjalmar, 220; Quie, Al, 232, 233; Republican, 91, 233; Rolvaag, Karl, 238, 261; Stassen, Harold, xiv, 220, 233, 259; Towne, Charles A., 298n3; Ventura, Jesse, 234, 262, 300n12; Yankee, 107; Youngdahl, Luther, 233. *See also* Ramsey, Alexander; Sibley, Henry Hastings

Grand Army of the Republic (GAR), 68, 109

Grand Marais (Cook County), 10

Grand Portage Reservation (Cook County), 11, 70, 184, 251, 259, 290n34

Grange movement, 82, 254

Grant, Bud (coach), 239, 241

grasshopper plagues, 4, 80, 172, 254, 288n5

Great Britain, 27, 53. *See also* English immigrants; English language

Great Depression, xv, 162, 171–91, 197, 199, 212, 259, 288n5, 291n47; aftermath, 222, 294n1

Great Lakes, 27, 194, 251. *See also* Lake Superior

Great Northern Railroad, 95, 103, 255

Greeley School baseball team, *141*

Greyhound Corporation (Hibbing), 257

Groseilliers, Médard, sieur de (explorer), 23

Gunflint Lodge (Grand Marais), 236, 266

Gustavus Adolphus College (St. Peter), 108, *142*

Guthrie Theater (Minneapolis), 231, 261, 263

hailstone, record, 257

hair, cutting of, *52*

Halleck, Henry (general), 53

Hamline University (St. Paul), 90, 108, 286n2

Handicraft Guild (Minneapolis), 256

Harriet Island (St. Paul), 94

Hazelwood Republic, 43–44

Hebrew Immigrant Aid Society, 262

Hennepin, Louis (missionary), 18, 23, 24, 244, 251

Hennepin County Territorial Pioneers, 257

Hibbing (St. Louis County), 123–24, *153, 156*

Hidatsa people, 252

Hill, James J. (businessman), 95, 103, 106, 108, 253, 256, 265, 266; house, 124, 255, 295n1

Hill, Mary T., 95, 98, 124

Hinckley (Pine County), 108

Hispanic immigrants. *See* Latin American immigrants; Mexican Americans

Historical Records Survey, 290n32

history, study of, xi–xvi, 265–66, 269n3. *See also* methodologies; scholars on Minnesota

History of Minnesota (Neill), 254

History of Minnesota, A (Blegen), xi–xii

Hmong immigrants, 245, 247, 263

hobos, 173

Ho-Chunk people, 11, 30, 35, 43, 73, 274n18

hockey, 7

Hoge, Jane (social worker), 66

Homestead Act of 1862, 4, 52, 72

Honeywell, Inc. (Minneapolis), 195, 231, 294n8

Hoovervilles, 175

Hormel and Company (Austin), 177, 194

Hotel and Restaurant Employees International Union, 259

hotels, transient, 124, 171

Hough, Sue Dickey (legislator), 289n24

houses: 1890s, 255; 1920s, *120*, 124, *151*, *155*, *156*, *157*, *159*, 161; 1950s, 212–14, 294n9, 295n14; for miners, 164

Houston County, 115, 184

Hubbard, Margaret Ann (author), 260

Hubbard County, 7

Hudson's Bay Company, 32, 251

Huff Furniture Store and Funeral Parlor (Staples), 205, 209, 210

Humphrey, Hubert (vice president), xiv, xvi, 219–35; associates, 201, 224–29; as candidate for president, 230–31; civil rights and, 216, 221–22, 260; death of, 232–34

Humphrey, Hubert, III (politician), 234

Humphrey, Muriel (senator), 233

hunters/hunting, 28, 61, 73, 254; decline of, 34, 36, 42, 45, 47, 53; Native American, 15, 21–22, 239–40

Huron people, 272n23

idealism, 109, 221, 222, 224

identity: mixed-blood, 54–55, 277n15, 278n23, 279n25; Native American, 56–57, 69. *See also* Americanization; ethnicity; race

IDS Tower (Minneapolis), 261

Ihlen (Pipestone County), 122

Illinois Central Railroad, 81

images, xiii, 23, 77, 266. *See also* maps; photographers/photography

Immigrant House (Duluth), 254

immigrants/immigration: Americanization of, 94, 115–17, 284n27; in Civil War, 64, 68–69, 72; demographic changes, 198, 245–49, 266, 267, 301n24; education, 109; politics, 219–20, 243–45, 298n3; promotion of, 72–73,

79, 253, 255; in Red Wing, 90–91; restrictions on, 46, 220, 275n13; role of, xii. *See also* Braat family; Christie family; Turnblad, Swan and Christina Nilsson; *and individual immigrant groups*

Independent Party, 220, 234

Independent Republican Party, 233. *See also* Republican Party

Indian agents, 28–33, 41–42. *See also* Taliaferro, Lawrence

Indian Reorganization Act of 1934, 259

Indians. *See* Native Americans

individualism, 289n19

industrialization, 85–87, 90, 97–99, 104, 106, 166, 194–95, 266

Industrial Workers of the World, 111, 162

Inkpaduta, uprising of, 51, 253, 276n5

International Brotherhood of Electrical Workers, 112

International Falls (Koochiching County), 10

International Wolf Center (Ely), 262

interpreters, 28–29, 41, 55, 56

interstate highway system, 214–16, 297n32

Ioway people, 30

Ireland, John (bishop), 94, 96, 254, 255

Irish Catholic Colonization Association, 254

Irish immigrants, 16, 23, 84, 254; Catholic, 47, 69, 94, 96, 275n13; newspapers, 257; occupations, 95, 253; politics of, 207, 219, 220, 243

iron ore, 86, 194, 226, 253

Iron Range, 107, 119, 172, 231, 259. *See also* mines/mining; *and individual towns*

Iroquois people, 272n23

Ishpeming, Michigan, rest home, 124, 162

isolationism, 114, 116–17, 258

Italian immigrants, 16, 111, 185, 245, 246

Itasca County, 5, 7, 9

Itasca State Park (Clearwater County), 183, 256

Jackson, Henry (merchant), 50–51

jazz, 167

James Ford Bell Museum (Minneapolis), 260

Jefferson, Thomas, 27; tradition of, 166, 178

Jeffers Petroglyphs (Pipestone County), 22

Jewish immigrants, 109, 115, 216, 220, 245, 247, 260, 262

jobs. *See* labor; occupations

John Morrell and Company, 194

Johnson, Magnus (politician), 178, 220

Josefson, J. A. (legislator), 209

Joseph, Geri (politician), 224, 228

June 14 celebration (White Earth Reservation), *138*

Kamisar, Yale (lawyer), 225

Kampelman, Max (lawyer): in starvation experiment, 202

Kansas-Nebraska Act of 1854, 46

Kaposia (Dakota County), 27, 30, 49

Keillor, Garrison (author), 241–42, 243, 244, 246, 300n12, 301n14

Kelley, Oliver H. (farmer): and Grange movement, 82

Kempfer, Hannah (legislator), 289n24

Kensington runestone, 108, 256

Kerfoot, Justine (resort owner), 236, 237

Kettle River, 238

Keys, Ancel (researcher), 195–96, 201–3

Kidwell, Clara Sue (historian), 11

kinship: Native American–earth, 271n6; among Native Americans, 22–23, 29; white–Native American, 24, 26, 32, 36, 42, 50, 55–56, 59–60. *See also* mixed bloods

Kittson, Norman (businessman), 95

Kittson County, ccc in, 184

Klobuchar, Amy (senator), 235, 263

Knights of Labor, 110, 178

Know-Nothing Party, 46

Knutson, Coya (Congresswoman), 228–29

Kodak Brownie cameras, 121

K-rations, 195–96

Kuchinski, Vonnie (marathon dancer), 172, 191

Ku Klux Klan (KKK), 166, 258

Kvale, Ole J. (Congressman), 178

Labathe, Joseph and Margaret Campbell, 50, 57, 58, 279n26

labor: organization of, 111, 161, 177–78, 193, 259; relations with management, 111, 289n22,n24; wartime short-ages, 199–200. See also Farmer-Labor Party; strikes; working class

LaChapelle, Fred and Marie Campbell, 50, 57, 58

Lac La Croix (St. Louis County), 5

Ladies Musicale Society (St. Paul), 254

Lake Agassiz, 4, 10

Lake Calhoun (Minneapolis), school on, 31, 252

Lake City (Goodhue County), bird's-eye view map, 74, 75, 76

Lake Harriet Rose Garden (Minneapolis), 26

Lake of the Isles Congregational Church (Minneapolis), 137

Lake of the Woods (Lake of the Woods County), 5

Lake Pepin (Wabasha County), 74

lakes, 5–8, 10, 237–38

Lake Superior, 5, 251, 253, 257; pollution of, 226; tourism, 7, 237–38; wilderness areas, 10, 184

Lake Superior and Mississippi Railroad Company, 72, 254

Lakewood Cemetery Memorial Chapel and Park (Minneapo-lis), 257

Lakota Dakota, 270n1. See also Dakota people

land: distribution of, 3–5, 46, 102; Native American ceding of, 13, 30, 35–36, 42, 49, 51–52, 84, 93, 99, 239–40; Native American concept of, 10, 21–22; sales, 73, 79, 81. See also Homestead Act of 1862

Landis, Paul H. (sociologist), 111

Land O'Lakes Creameries, Inc. (Watertown), 104

language(s), 39, 77, 242. See also specific languages

Larpenteur, Auguste Louis (politician), 50, 51

La Salle, Robert Cavelier, sieur de (explorer), 23–24

Latin American immigrants, 245, 247, 263, 301n24

laws, alcohol-related. See Prohi-bition

Lea, Luke (Indian commissioner), 41–42

Leach, George (governor), 288n17

Leavenworth, Henry (colonel), 27–28, 29

Leeann Chin, Inc. (St. Paul), 261

Leech Lake (Cass County), 5, 15

Leech Lake Reservation (Cass County), 43, 70, 254, 259

Legend of Nanaboozhoo, The, 14

legislature. See Minnesota Legis-lature

leisure, xvi, 123. See also resorts

Lend-Lease Act of 1941, 194

LeSueur, Meridel (author), 80, 260

Lewis, Sinclair (author), 167, 242, 301n13

Lewis and Clark Expedition, 20

liberalism/liberals, 109, 221, 222, 224, 248

Liberian immigrants, 245, 247

Lillehei, C. Walton (surgeon), 260

Lincoln, Abraham (president), 53, 54, 55, 61, 66, 284n29

Lindbergh, Charles, Jr. (aviator), 125, 190, 259

Lindbergh, Charles, Sr. (legisla-tor), 115, 116–17, 178, 258

Lindy Hop (dance), 190

Litchfield (Meeker County), 68

literacy rate, 91

literature: 1950s and 1960s, 222–23, 226; 1980s, 262; Scandinavian, 243

Lithuanian immigrants, 245

Little Crow (Ta-o-ya-te-du-ta, Dakota), 41–43, 45–46, 50–51, 265; in Dakota War of 1862, 53–55, 59, 63, 275n5; village of, 27, 30, 49

Little Six, village of, 39

Livermore, Mary (social worker), 65–66, 280n17

lodges, bark, 22–23

log cabin, 148

logging. See timber industry

log rolling, 121, 128

Long, Stephen A. (surveyor), 27, 273n7

Loras, Mathias (bishop), 252

Lord, Miles (judge), 224, 225, 226–27

Louisiana Purchase, 27

Lower Agency (Redwood Falls) Reservation, 42, 45–46, 50, 51–52, 53, 57

Lundeen, Ernest (Congressman), 114–15, 220

Lutherans, 219, 243–45

Lutheran Social Services, 248

Lutsen Lodge (Cook County), 260

lynchings, 56, 166, 190, 258

Lynnwood Apartment Building (Minneapolis), 160

Lyon County, WPA in, 184

Macalester College (St. Paul), 108

McCarthy, Eugene (senator), xvi, 228, 229, 230–31

McCarthy, Joseph (senator), xvi, 206, 248

McCollum, Betty (Congresswoman), 228

McDonald's restaurants, 246–47

McGhee, Fredrick (lawyer), 95–96, 284n29

machinists' strike, 112

Mackay, Harvey (businessman), 261

McKinley, William (president), 112, 298n2

McKnight Foundation (St. Paul), 99

MacLeish, Archibald (poet), 260

McPherson, Aimee Semple (crusader), 167

Madden's Resort (Brainerd), 237

Mall of America (Bloomington), 212, 262, 297n28

Mankato (Blue Earth County): Dakota hanging at, 54, 55–56, 57, 59, 93, 253. *See also* North Mankato

Mankato Teachers' College, 108, 286n2

manufacturing, 85–87, 97–99, 194–95, 207–8

maple sugaring, 15, 273n6

maps, *viii, ix,* xv, *2,* 73–79; Nicollet's, *2,* 252; territorial, 73, 77. *See also* bird's-eye view maps

Mar, James (immigrant), *107*

marathon dancing, 190–91

Marine on St. Croix (Washington County), 86

marriages, 68, *107;* white–Native American, 26–27, 30, 32–33, 47, 51, 58–59, 273n5

Marshall (Lyon County), 9–10

Marshall County, 58

Martin County, 198, 254

Maternity Hospital (Minneapolis), 92

Mattson, Hans (immigrant recruiter), 64, 72–73, 79, 253, 281n1

Mayo, Charles (doctor), 284n19

Mayo, William Worrall (doctor), 92, 99, 266

Mayo Clinic and St. Mary's Hospital (Rochester), 231, 259, 284n1

mayors: Anderson, William, 288n17; Bainbridge, A. G., 175, 176, 288n17; Belton, Sharon Sayles, 262; Fraser, Donald, 224, 226, 231; Naftalin, Arthur, 224, 225, 228; Stenvig, Charles, 231, 233

Mazakutemane, Paul (Dakota), 43–44

Mdewakanton Dakota, 11, 27, 251; 1837 treaty, 32, 42, 43. *See*

also Dakota people; Dakota War of 1862

meatpacking plants, 173, 177, 194, 245, 247

Medicine Bottle (Wa-kan-o-zhan, Dakota), 41–43

Medtronic, Inc. (Minneapolis), 260

Meeker County, 68

Melrose (Stearns County), tornado in, 119

men, *143, 169;* occupations, 85, *135,* 184, 281n19; roles, 15, 68, 73, 211; World War II, 193, 203, 205–6

Mendota (Dakota County), 43, 47–48, 50, 252

Mendota Treaty of 1851, 21, 43

Menominee people, 28, 30, 73

Merritt Brothers (mine owners), 255

Mesabi Range, 107, 261

metaphors, 266

methodologies, xi, xiii, xvi, 265–66, 269n3; art as, 34–38; biography as, 84–99; dates as, 251–64; economy as, 170–91; fishing as, 236–49; food as, 100–106, 192–204, 236–49; furniture as, 205–18; genealogy as, 26–33, 49–60; maps as, 72–83; objects as, 205–8; photography as, 119–69; politics as, 107–18, 219–35; war as, 61–71. *See also* scholars on Minnesota

Metropolitan Stadium (Bloomington), 217

Mexican Americans, 184, 246–47; discrimination against, 207, 216; as migrant workers, 198–99, 293n21, n24

Meyers, Barry (chef), 236, 241, 249

middle class, 164, 190, 289n28; African American, xv, 215, 296n24; women, 110, 122

migrant workers, 197–99, 203, 293n18, n20, n21, n24

Mill City Museum (Minneapolis), 263

Mille Lacs Band of Ojibwe, 239–40

Mille Lacs Lake (Mille Lacs County), 5, 15, 239, 251

Mille Lacs Reservation (Mille Lacs County), 11, 43, 70, 259

milling, 50, 85–87, 98–99; flour, 81, 104, 109, 111, 113, 162, 195, 258; water-powered, 5, 36, 40–41

Milwaukee and Chicago Railroad, 87

Milwaukee and St. Paul Railroad, 75–76

Milwaukee Railroad, 81

mines/mining, 86, 123–24, *153,* 255, 261; immigrants in, 245, 257; strikes, 111–12, 162–63, 258; women workers, 193–94, 292n5. *See also* Iron Range

ministers: Bellows, Henry Whitney, 65–66; Mecklenburg, George, 175; Riley, William Bell, 167; training of, 108, 109, 286n2

Minneapolis (Hennepin County), 43, 289n22; African Americans in, 95, 231, 260; Gateway area, 171; manufacturing, 87; mayors, 113, 222, 262, 288n17; merger with St. Anthony, 254; photography, 119, 167; population, 223–24; railroads, 103; strikes, 111–12, 177, 186, 259, 289n22, n24; unemployment, 172–73, 175, 180; urban redevelopment, 215–16

Minneapolis and St. Louis Railroad, 87

Minneapolis Baseball Association, 254

Minneapolis Foundation, 249

Minneapolis Institute of Arts, 22, 99, 257, 263

Minneapolis Lakers basketball team, 217

Minneapolis Millers Association, 86

Minneapolis Public Library, 263

Minneapolis Symphony Orchestra, *127,* 256, 260

Minnehaha Park (Minneapolis), 183

Minnesota: borders, 5, 46; mobility within, 78–79, 82; name/ slogan, 5; northern regions, 9, 10, 236–38; prairie region, 4, 15; qualities of, xiv, 34, 167, 231; southern regions, 4, 5, 9, 10; statehood, xv, 34, 46, 224, 253, 275n2; western region, 4, 9. *See also* governors; Minnesota Legislature; Minnesota Territory; *and individual cities, counties, and towns*

Minnesota Arboretum (Chanhassen), 258

Minnesota Beet Sugar factory (Chaska), 198

Minnesota Bureau of Immigration, 72–73

Minnesota Commission of Public Safety (MCPS), 114, 115–17, 164, 287n17

Minnesota Federation of Labor, 111

Minnesota Historical Society (St. Paul), 22, 48, 73, 99, 252, 258, 262, 272n17

Minnesota Humanities Center, 249

Minnesota Intercollegiate Athletic Conference (MIAC), 108, 258

Minnesota Legislature, 184, 263, 298n3; territorial, 46, 48, 275n13; women in, 289n24

Minnesota Mining and Manufacturing Company. *See* 3M

Minnesota Museum of Art (St. Paul), 188

Minnesota Nice, 242–44, 248, 301n15

Minnesota Public Interest Research Group (MPIRG), 227

Minnesota Public Radio, 261

Minnesota Reformatory for Women (Shakopee), 121

Minnesota River, 4, 10, 35; confluence with Mississippi River, 26, 27–28; Native Americans living along, 15, 19, 42, 44, 50

Minnesota Soldiers' Home, 67

Minnesota State Art Society, 256

Minnesota State Capitol (St. Paul), 208, 253, 257

Minnesota State Child Welfare Commission, 258

Minnesota State Forestry Board, 256

Minnesota State Park System, 183

Minnesota State Planning Board, 171

Minnesota Territory, 34, 35–36, 252

Minnesota Twins baseball team, 217, 261, 262

Minnesota Vikings football team, 261

Minnesota Woman (formerly known as Minnesota Man), 18–19, 20

Minnesota Woman Suffrage Association, 254, 283n14

Minnesota Women's Press, 262

Minnetonka (Hennepin County), 208

missionaries, 13, 23–24, 37–38, 93–94, 274n21; Allouez, Claude, 23; Ayer, Frederick, 252, 274n22; Bishop, Harriet, 37, 93–94, 266; Brunson, A., 274n21; Collins, Mary C., 274n22; Galtier, Lucien, 252; Hancock, Joseph W., 84–85, 90, 282n2; Marquette, Jacques, 23; Peirz, Francis, 252; Ravoux, Augustine, 55–56; Whipple, J. Emmaretta, 274n22; Williamson, Thomas, 44, 48, 184. *See also* Hennepin, Louis; Native Americans, conversion of; Pond, Gideon and Samuel; Riggs, Mary; Riggs, Stephen R.; Whipple, Henry

Mississippi River, 5, 36; confluence with Minnesota River, 26, 27–28; damming of, 213, 254; maps of, 73, 74; Native Americans living along, 15, 18–20; shipping on, 86–87

Mitchell, George (Ojibwe), 230

mixed bloods, 49–60, 276n1; Bucier, Louis, 54; Boutwell, Hester Crooks, 38; in censuses, 39, 276n21; in Civil War, 61, 70; clothing, 274n15, 277n6; Courselle, Joe, 55;

hanging at Mankato, 54, 55–56, 57, 59, 93, 253; Quinn, George, 55; relations with full bloods, 273n5, 277n15, n18; Warren, William, 276n1. *See also* Campbell family; children, mixed-blood; identity, mixed-blood

modernism, xv, xvi, 205–18, 294n6, n9, 295n13, n14

Mohr, Howard (author), 242, 244, 301n14

Mondale, Ted (politician), 234

Mondale, Walter (vice president), 224, 225, 232, 234, 235, 261

Monks Mound (Cahokia), 19

Moorhead (Clay County), sugarbeet factory, 198

Moose Lake (Carlton County), fire in, 258

moraines, glacial, 5–6

Morrill Act, 52

motorcycles, 122, *147*, 167

motor vehicles, 122, 227. *See also* automobiles

Moua, Mee (legislator), 263

mounds, Native American, 19–21, 84

Mounds Park (St. Paul), 20

Mountain Iron Mine (Ely), 255

Mount Sinai Hospital (Minneapolis), 260

Mount Zion Hebrew Association, 253

movies, 167, 188–89, 240–41, 243, 300n9

mulattos, 91; as census designation, 39, 276n1. *See also* African Americans; mixed bloods

Munsingwear band (Minneapolis), 161

murals, 182, 290n34

Murphy, Diana (judge), 239, 241

music, 167, 189–90, 246, 291n47. *See also* conductors; dances/dancing; Dylan, Bob; songs, Depression-era

Muslims, 248, 263

Myrick, Andrew and Nathan (traders), 51, 53

Namakan Lake (St. Louis County), 5

Naniboujou Lodge (Grand Marais), 259

National Abortion Rights League, 229

National Association for the Advancement of Colored People (NAACP), 96, 114

National Farmer's Bank (Owatonna), 257

National Woman Suffrage Association, 110

Native American Graves Protection and Repatriation Act (NAGPRA), 18, 22

Native American languages, 21, 24, 45, 49, 50, 241, 273n5. *See also* Dakota language

Native Americans, xv, 11–26, 84–85; alcohol and, 29; casinos, 240; in CCC, 184, 291n38; citizenship, 44, 117, 258; clothing, 35, 45, 55, 274n15, 276n6; conversion of, 31, 44, 49, 55–56, 84–85, 92, 93, 274n22; crafts, 16–18, 35; culture, 28, 45, 49, 244; discrimination against, 69, 207, 216, 239–41, 266, 287n23; diseases among, 12–13, 24, 85, 271n7; excluded from census, 38–39; farmers, 4, 42, 44, 122; as interpreters, 24, 28–30, 32–33, 41, 49, 55, 56, 273n7, 274n15; kinship culture, 22–23, 24, 29; land ceded by, 13, 30, 35–36, 42, 49, 51–52, 84, 93, 99, 239–40; living spaces, 22–23; newspapers, 117; poverty of, 231, 239–40; removal of, 32, 34, 39, 42, 47, 85, 224, 272n23, 278n20; spirituality, 230, 240–41; strength of, 12–13, 18; trade among, 19, 20; transportation, 5; urban, 230; warfare among, 21–22, 29–30, 256, 272n23; in World War II, 203. *See also* boarding schools, Native American; Dakota War of 1862; fur trade/fur traders; treaties; white–Native American rela-

tions; *and individual people and tribes*

natural resources, 270n16

nature, 9–10, 271n6

Nelson, Julia Bullard (suffragist), 111, 283n14

Nelson Act of 1887, 93, 255

Nett Lake Reservation (Koochiching County), 11, 70, 259

New Deal, 176, 178–79, 182–84, 221, 291n38. *See also individual programs*

newspapers, ethnic, 107, 117, 253, 254, 257, 258

Niagara Movement, 96

Nicolet, Jean (explorer), 23

Nicollet, Joseph (explorer and mapmaker), 2, 37, 252

Nicollet Island (Hennepin County), 39–41, 43

Nineteenth Amendment (U.S. Constitution). *See* woman's suffrage

Ninth Minnesota Volunteers, 70

Noble and Holy Order of the Knights of Labor (Duluth), 254

Nonpartisan League (NPL), 113, 114–15, 117, 220, 258

non-treaty Indians, 51

Norris, William (businessman), 294n8

North, Ann and John (Northfield, St. Anthony Falls), 34, 39–41, 46, 48, 100–102, 265, 275n13

North Central Association of Colleges, 108

North East Neighborhood House (Minneapolis), 258

Northern Pacific Railroad, 72, 95, 103, 122, *134*, 205, 254

Northern Securities Case, 256

Northern States Power Company, 213

Northfield (Rice County), 48, 102

North Mankato (Goodhue County), 124–25

Northrop, Cyrus (second president, University of Minnesota), 39, 40

North Shore, 7. *See also* Lake Superior; up north

North Star Club (baseball), 83

North Star Woolen Mill (Faribault), 260

Northwest Airlines (Eagan), 259, 260, 263

Northwest Area Foundation (St. Paul), 99

Northwest Bank (Minneapolis), 259

North West Fur Company (Grand Portage), 32, 251

Northwest Ordinance of 1785, 3, 36, 251, 275n13

Norton and Peel studio (Minneapolis), *165*

Norwegian immigrants, 56, 84, 85; politics of, 207, 219, 220, 243–44

Oberstar, Jim (Congressman), 231

objects: Native American, 18–22, 272n17; as historical method, 205–8; storytelling with, xiii, xvi

O'Brien, Alice (philanthropist), 188

occupations, 47, 122, 167, 222; gender-based, 85, 193, 281n19; seasonal, 170–72, 197–99; traveling, 82

Ohman, Olof (farmer), 108, 256

Ojibwe language, 21, 273n5

Ojibwe people, 5, 14–16, 18, 22–23, 70, 251, 252, 272n23; burial grounds, 19–21, 84, 254; casinos, 240; culture, 16–18, 189, 271n6, 290n34; farmers, *131;* land ceded by, 35, 43, 93, 98; photographs, 122–23, *149;* on reservations, 82, 93; treaties with, 30, 32, 43, 239, 252, 274n18, 300n8; tribal incorporation, 259; urban, 230; wars with Dakota, 21, 29, 70

Old Bets (Asa-Ya-Man-Ka-Wan), 39, 47

Old Settlers' Associations, 109, 253

Oliver, Mary (poet), 266

Oliver Mining Company (Duluth), 123–24, *153, 156, 157,* 162, 167, 257
Olmsted County, 7
Olson, Sigurd (author), 223, 227
Olson's Studio (Cloquet), 123
oranges, 100–102, 104–6, 285n5
organizations. *See* clubs; cooperatives; labor, organization of; *and individual organizations*
Organized Unemployed, Inc. (Minneapolis), 175
Ortonville (Big Stone County), 4
Otter Tail County, 7, 19, 180
Owatonna (Steele County), bank building, 208
oxcarts, 81, 213, 253

pacifism, 114–15, 201–2
Paige, Mabeth Hurd (legislator), 112, 177–78, 289n24
Paleo-Indians, 19
Panic of 1873, 80–81, 103
Panic of 1893, 92, 104
Parker, Joseph (barber), 91
parks, state, 183–86
Patoille, Francois (husband of Margaret Menagre Campbell/trader), 277n10
patriotism, 206–7
Patrons of Husbandry. *See* Grange movement
Paulsen, Gary (author), 66
Peacock, Thomas (storyteller), 13
Pegano, Margaret Campbell (sister of Scott Campbell), 273n5
Pelican Rapids (Otter Tail County), 247
Pennington County, lakes in, 5
Penumbra Theater (St. Paul), 261
People's Party, 104
Phil Anderson's Our Own Hardware (Staples), 205, 209, 210
photographers/photography, xv, xvi, 119–69, 265; Brady, Mathew, 119, 162; Briol, 119, 121, 164, 166, 167, 168; Cameron, Julia Margaret, 119; Curtis, Edward, 119, 240; during Great Depression, 174, 182, 184; Hibbard, Charles, 121; Lange, Dorothea, 162; Parks, Gordon, 184, 203; Peel, Clif-

ford, 121, 164, 167; Riis, Jacob, 174; Stewart, James, 162; Vachon, John, 182
Phyllis Wheatley House (Minneapolis), 109
Pigeon River, 5, 251
Pigs Eye. *See* St. Paul, naming of
Pike, Zebulon (explorer), 27, 43
Pillsbury, Charles and John (businessmen), 86, 98, 99, 265
Pillsbury Company (Minneapolis), 86, 195, 262, 263
Pillsbury House (Minneapolis), 109
Pilot Knob (Dakota County), 21
Pine County, in World War, 114–15
pioneering, 70–71, 257. *See also* settlers
pipestone, 22
Pipestone County, 5, 22, 58, 252
Pipestone National Park (Pipestone County), 260
planned obsolescence, 210
Plessey v. Ferguson, 216
Plymouth Congregational Church (Minneapolis), 109
Polish immigrants, 91, *107,* 207, 220; newspapers, 258
Polish National Benevolent Society, 255
politics, xiv, 13, 112, 178, 260, 263, 289n24, 298n2, n3; 1880s, 91; 1960s, xvi, 219–35; DFL and abortion, 232–33; modern, 248; territorial, 41, 45–46, 48, 50, 51; traditional, 113. *See also* Democratic Party; ethnicity, politics and; governors; isolationism; mayors; Populism/Populists; reformers, political; religion, politics and; Republican Party
Pond, Gideon and Samuel, 15–16, 30, 31, 49, 252
poor people, xv, 174–76, 189, 191, 207, 255. *See also* poverty
Pope County, 7
population, 66; 1880s, 84; 1890s, 255; 1910s, 107; 1920s, 164; 1950s, 213; 1960s, 222–24; growth of, 300n3; Na-

tive American, 271n7; 1850s, 43
Populism/Populists, 104, 166, 178, 220, 224
Post Office (St. Paul), *132*
post-traumatic stress disorder (PTSD), 66–67, 206, 280n16
Pottawatomie people, 30, 274n18
poverty, 215, 223, 248; during Great Depression, 171, 174–76, 179, 187–88; Native American, 231, 239–40. *See also* poor people
Powell, G. Howard (pomologist): and California Fruit Growers Exchange, 105
power, xiii, xvi, 25, 211–12
powwows, 189
Prairie du Chien, Wisconsin, 20, 21, 26–27, 28
Prairie Island Reservation (Goodhue County), 82, 84
Prescott, Philander (trader), 39, 54, 252, 273n4
prison, state, 46
prisoner of war camps, 199, 260
Progressives, 112–18, 163, 174, 224
Prohibition, 46, 94, 164, 189–90, 243, 244, 275n13. *See also* Women's Christian Temperance Union
prosperity, 92, 109, 114, 224; 1950s, 207, 209, 222
prostitution, 85, 283n4
Pueringer, John (builder), 6
Pythian Sisters, 90

race: as census category, 38–39, 276n21, 281n20; occupations determined by, 69, 122; permeable boundaries, 49–50, 59–60; solidification of categories, 33, 56–57, 60, 82, 216
racism, 186, 192, 243, 248. *See also* African Americans, discrimination against; civil rights movement; Native Americans, discrimination against
radicalism, 178–79
radio(s), 187, 188, 211, 257

Radisson, Pierre (explorer), 23
railroads, xv, 87, 96–98, 113, *129*, 205; building of, 46, 52, 81–82, 102–4, 266; employment, 95, 173; mergers, 256. *See also* depots; *and individual railroads*
Rainy Lake (Koochiching County), 5
Ramsey, Alexander, 46, 48, 50; as governor, 36, 37, 41–43, 45, 54
Ramsey, Anna Jenks, 34, 37, 48, 68
Ramsey County, population of, 38. *See also* St. Paul
rationing, xvi, 200–201, 203, 207, 293n26
Read's Landing (Wabasha County), 50, 57
recall, system of, 112
Red Lake Reservation (Beltrami County), 11, 70, 122, *149*, 290n34
Red River Lumber Company (Crookston), 98
Red River of the North, 5
Red River Valley: farming, 97, 265; migrant workers, 293n21; oxcarts, 81, 213, 253; sugar beet industry, 198–99
Red Wing (Goodhue County), 20, 84–91, 99, 266, 282n2, 283n10
Red Wing Shoe Company, 87, 257
Red Wing Stoneware Company, 87
Redwood Falls Agency. *See* Lower Agency (Redwood Falls) Reservation
reformers, political, 109–10, 112–18, 163, 193; Yankee, 219, 224
relief programs: federal, 171, 172, 174–76, 179–80; private, 173, 174; state/local, 177, 259. *See also* benevolence, culture of; charities
religion, 16, 47, 90; politics and, 219–20, 232–33, 245–46, 298n2, n3. *See also* churches; missionaries
rendezvous, fur trade, 26, 47
Renville family, 39, 50

Republican Party, 95–96, 115, 233, 234; ethnic make-up, 219–20; founding of, 46, 102; governors, 91, 298n3
reservations, 11, 13, 82, 92, 93; establishment of, 41, 42, 44, 50, 253; fishing and hunting on, 239–40. *See also individual reservations*
Reserve Mining Company (Silver Bay), 226, 260
resorts, 236, 237, 259, 260, 266
restaurants, ethnic, 90, 245–47
Rice, Henry Mower (senator), 46, 48, 275n13
Riggs, Mary (missionary), 30, 31, 37, 43–44, 56, 93, 252
Riggs, Stephen R. (missionary), 31, 42–44, 49, 55–56, 93–94, 252, 266, 274n22
Ripley, Martha (doctor), 92, 93, 266
rivers, 5. *See also individual rivers*
Robinson, Harriet (slave), 31
Rochester (Olmsted County), 87, 92
Rock County, lakes in, 5
Rockefeller, John D. (businessman), 255
Rockwood Lodge (Grand Marais), 237
Roe v. Wade, 232, 233
Roleff family, *150*
Rolette, Joe (legislator), 46, 253
Rondo neighborhood (St. Paul), 215–16, 297n32
Roosevelt (Roseau County), *148*
Roosevelt, Franklin D. (president), 176, 179, 180, 221
Roosevelt Junior High School (Minneapolis), *135*
Roscoe, Madeline Campbell and Olivier (mixed bloods), 50, 51, 57, 58, 278n24, 279n25
Roseau County, 5
Ruger, Albert (mapmaker), 74–79, 81–83, 265, 281n5, n6, n7
rural areas, xv, 166–67, 171, 207, 220, 244
Rural Electrification Authority (REA), 186–87
Russian immigrants, 245, 247

Rust Iron Mine (Hibbing), *153*
Ruttger's Bay Lake Lodge (Deerwood), 237

Sac people, treaties with, 30, 274n18
St. Andrew's Society (Duluth), 254
St. Anthony (Hennepin County), 36, 38, 39–41, 43, 46, 48, 73, 251, 252, 260; founding of, 101, 252; merger with Minneapolis, 254
Saint Benedict's Monastery (St. Joseph), 6, 253
St. Boniface Society, 255
St. Cloud (Stearns County), 108, 245
St. Cloud Reformatory, 161; band, *139*
St. Cloud Teachers' College, 286n2
St. Croix River, 5, 36, 238
St. James (Watonwan County), 247
St. Jean Baptiste Society, 255
Saint John's Abbey and University (Collegeville), 6, 7, 108, 164, 253, 261, 286n2, 295n14
St. Louis County, 7
St. Louis County Farm Bureau Recreational Institute, *140*
St. Mark's Catholic Parish (St. Paul), 215
St. Mary's College (Winona), 286n2
St. Olaf College (Northfield), 108, 109, 254, 257
St. Paul (Ramsey County), 43, 51, 73, 87, *158*, 260, 289n22; African Americans in, 95–96, 215–16, 297n32; employment, 281n19, 289n22; Irish in, 39, 207, 252; mounds in, 20; naming of, 252; photography, 119; population, 38, 39; railroads, 46, 103, 253, 254; state capitol in, 46, 253; unemployment, 180
St. Paul, Minneapolis, and Manitoba Railway, 255
St. Paul and Pacific Railroad, 72, 95, 253

St. Paul Chamber of Commerce, 254

St. Paul Fire and Marine Insurance Company, 253

St. Paul Home for the Friendless, 68

St. Peter (Nicollet County): state capitol controversy, 46, 253; in World War I, 115

St. Peter Claver Catholic Church (St. Paul), 96

St. Peter's River. *See* Minnesota River

St. Thomas College (University of St. Thomas, St. Paul), 108, 255, 286n2

Sandstone (Pine County), World War I in, 115

Sandy Lake Reservation (Aitkin County), 43

Sanford, Ray (builder), 295n14

Santee Reservation (Nebraska), 57–60, 82, 270n1, 278n23

Savage (Scott County), shipbuilding yard, 194

Scandinavian immigrants, 60, 84, 224, 241, 243–45, 247. *See also* Danish immigrants; Norwegian immigrants; Swedish immigrants

Schoch, Andrew (grocer), 105, 122

scholars on Minnesota: Bindas, Kenneth J., 291n47; Blegen, Theodore, xi–xii; Broker, Ignatia, 13, 272n23; Castañeda, Antonia, 199; Child, Brenda, 13; Connolly, Marguerite, 87; Crosby, Alfred, 16; Deloria, Ella, 13, 17; Deloria, Philip and Vine, 13; DeMallie, Ray, 16; Densmore Frances, 91, 290n32; Evans, Sarah, 269n3; Faue, Elizabeth, 172; Fixico, Donald, 11, 13; Glassie, Henry, xiii; Greene, Jack P., xiv; Greene, Victor, 281n1; Higginbottom, Daniel, 21–22; Huck, Virginia, 292n9; Jenks, Albert, 19; Kidwell, Clara Sue, 11; Kleppner, Paul, 219; Lass, William, xi, 269n1; Lovoll, Odd, 244;

May, Elaine Tyler, 212; Meyer, Roy, 277n18; Mintz, Sydney W., 196, 292n16; Morlan, Robert, 113; Neill, Edward D., 254; Nickles, Shelley, 209; Nissenbaum, Stephen, 105; Norling, Lisa, 269n3; Nunpa, Chris Mato, 13, Patterson, James, 207; Peacock, Thomas, 13; Rawick George, 290n32; Reps, John, 281n4, 282n5, n6, n7; Richter, Daniel, xiv; Riehle, David, 289n22; Sibley, Joel, 275n13; Sleeper-Smith, Susan, 278n20; Sparke, Penny, 294n9; Turner, Frederick Jackson, 166, 183–84; Tweton, Jerome, 180; Veblen, Thorstein, 123, 243; Whiteley, Nigel, 295n13; Wilson, Waziyatawin Angela, 13; Wingerd, Mary, 289n24

School for the Deaf (Faribault), 253

schools, 94–95. *See also* boarding schools, Native American; teachers; *and individual colleges*

Schubert Club (St. Paul), 110, 254

Schultz, Dorothy Holmes (politician), 260

Scott, Dred (slave), 31, 252

Seagull River (Cook County), 238

seamstresses. *See* dressmakers/seamstresses

Sears, Roebuck and Company, 255

segregation. *See* racism

Selke, George (politician), 227

Selkirkers, 31

senators, direct election of, 112

Serbian immigrants, 245

settlement houses, 109, 254, 258

settlers, 12, 15–16, 41, 44, 72–73, 81, 84, 86, 109, 166, 224, 253. *See also* immigrants/immigration

Seventh Street Club (Minneapolis), 173

sewing machines, 87–88, 97,

283n10. *See also* dressmakers/seamstresses

sexual revolution, 223

Shattuck School (Faribault), 76

Shields, James (senator), 48

Ship Canal (Duluth), 254

shipping, 86–87, 194, 255

Shipstead, Henrik (senator), 178, 220

shipwrecks, 257

shopping malls, 214, 297n28

Short, Robert (candidate), 231

Shotley (Beltrami County), 123, *152*

Sibley, Henry Hastings, xv, 31–32, 34, 46, 49, 83, 98, 252, 275n13; in Dakota War of 1862, 54, 55, 57, 70; as governor, 47–48, 253; as territorial delegate to Congress, 36, 41

Sibley, Sarah Steele ("civilizer"), 34, 35, 37, 47–48

Silver Creek Township (Wright County), 79

Silver Lake (McLeod County), 10

single people, 91, 266

Sioux. *See* Dakota people

Sioux Falls, South Dakota, 3, 7, 10, 194

Sioux Uprising. *See* Dakota War of 1862

Sisseton Dakota, 11, 42, 50, 58, 60, 251

Sisters of Charity, 281n19

Sisters of St. Francis, 92, 284n19

skyways, 261

slavery/slaves, 37, 275n2; abolition of, 113, 224; escaped, 69; at Fort Snelling, 30–31, 36, 252, 274n21; freed, 53, 91; white, 68

Slavic immigrants, 220

Sleeper-Smith, Susan (historian), 278n20

Sleepy Eye (Brown County), 10

Sleepy Eye (Dakota), 42

Slovenian immigrants, 111, 220

smallpox, 252, 271n7

Snelling, Josiah, 28, 30, 37

social history, xvi

socialism/socialists, 113, 114, 221, 260

social justice, 248–49

Social Security, 176
soil, 4, 5, 43
soldiers: Balcom, Magdalene, 206; Bermon, Jeanne, 192; Beaulieu, Charles, 70; Bliss, John, 30, 31; Campbell, Inez, 206; Carpenter, Alfred, 61–62; Chievitz, Niels, 205; Densmore, Orin, 69; Kliem, Ralph, 205; Nalawaja, Phillip, 206; Rydeen, Phillip, 206; Taylor, Isaac and Patrick Henry, 62; Tonsager, Kenneth, 206; Tucker, Chester, 205; Wiebesick, Robert, 206. *See also* Bowler, Lizzie and Madison, in Civil War
Somali immigrants, 245, 247, 248, 249, 262, 263
songs, Depression-era, 171, 173, 190
Sons of Norway, 68, 114
Soo Canal, 253
Soudan mine strike, 111
Southdale Mall (Edina), 214, 297n28
Southern Minnesota Railroad, 81
Southern Pacific Railroad, 103
Spain, invasion of Mexico, 53
Spanish-American War, 108
Spirit Lake Massacre, 51, 276n5
Split Rock Lighthouse (Lake County), 257
Spock, Benjamin, 214
sports. *See* athletics; *and individual sports*
Staples (Todd County), 205, 207, 208–10, 217, 266
starvation experiment, 201–2
state history, xi–xvi
Stay, Celia Campbell (daughter of A. J. Campbell), 278n23
Stearns County, 15, 164, 170, 180, 187
Steele, Franklin (businessman), 34, 37, 46, 275n4, n13; milling business, 36, 40–41, 48, 252
Stillwater (Washington County), 46, 73
Stillwater Convention of 1848, 35, 36

stock market crash of 1929, 171, 173, 181, 189
Stone Arch Bridge (Minneapolis), 255
storytelling, xiii–xvi, 13, 265–66
streetcar workers' strike, 112, 257, 258
strikes, 111–12, 177, 186, 257, 258, 259, 289n22, n24
Strutwear Knitting strike, 177, 259
Stuntebeck Ford Authorized Sales and Service (Albany), 119
suburbs, 124, 216
Sudanese immigrants, 247
suffrage. *See* woman's suffrage
sugar, 193, 195–98; rationing, 200–201, 203, 207; tariffs on, 102, 292n15, n16
sugar beet industry, 196–200, 245, 265, 292n15, 293n20, n21
Sugar Point, battle of, 256
Sully expedition, 57, 70
Sunkist oranges, 105–6
Superior National Forest (Cook County), 10, 227, 237
SuperValu Stores, 261
survival, of Native Americans, 12–13, 18, 25, 230
Swede Hollow (St. Paul), 124
Swedish immigrants, 84, 85, 207, 254; newspapers, 107; politics of, 220, 244
Swedish Lutheran Church, 258
Swisshelm, Jane Grey (publisher), 54, 253
Sylvestre, Dorothy and Gene, 209, 295n14
synecdoche, 265–66

Taconite (St. Louis County), 123
Taliaferro, Eliza, 37, 274n19
Taliaferro, Lawrence (Indian agent), 28–33, 49, 50, 251, 273n4, n11, 274n15
Taliaferro, Mary, 274n19
Target Corporation (Minneapolis), 261, 262
tariffs. *See* sugar, tariffs on
taxation, 231, 248
teachers, 91; male, 85, *135;* training of, 108, 286n2

teamsters' strike, 112
technology, xvi. *See also* computer industry
telephone, 254
telephone workers' strike, 112
television, xvi, 209, 211, 217–18
Territorial Pioneers, 109
Teton Dakota, 270n1
Theatre de la Jeune Lune (Minneapolis), 262
Third Minnesota Regiment Volunteer Infantry, 62–64
Thompson, James (slave), 274n21
Thompson, Orrin (builder), 212–13
3M, 194, 195, 231, 256, 259, 292n9
Timber-Culture Act of 1873, 4
timber industry, 36, 50, 86, 98–99, 108, 123, 205, 227, 255; strikes in, 111, 259
time zone system, standardized, 96
tipis, hide, 22–23
tobacco, 16
Todd County, 205–6, 207
tornadoes, 92, 119, 258
tourism/tourists, 73, 123, 236–38, 239, 241
Tower, Charlemagne (businessman), 255
towns, small, 72, 204, 207, 220, 281n4
tractors, 199–200, 203
trade routes, 5; Native American, 19, 20
trade/traders: decline of, 34, 47, 50; trickery of, 41–42; white–Native American, 26, 31, 272n33, 274n15. *See also* barter; fur trade/fur traders
transportation, 77, 90. *See also* railroads; shipping; water, transportation on
trapping, 28. *See also* hunters/hunting
Traverse des Sioux (Nicollet County), 93
Traverse Lake (Traverse County), 5
Treasury Relief Art Project, 182
treaties, 30, 273n14; 1837, 32, 42,

43, 239; 1851, 42, 43, 44, 52,
    84; 1854, 239; 1858, 43, 51;
    rights under, 238–41, 300n8
Treaty of La Pointe, 252, 253
Treaty of Mendota, 43, 50, 84,
    252
Treaty of the Sioux of 1825
    (Treaty of Prairie du Chien),
    30, 32, 43, 251, 274n18
Treaty of Traverse des Sioux, 41,
    43, 50, 84, 252
trees, 4–6, 9–10, 86, 266, 270n7
Treuer, David (author), 300n9
truckers' strikes, 111, 177, 178,
    259, 289n22, n24
Turnblad, Swan and Christina
    Nilsson (American Swedish
    Institute), 107, 117–18
Twin Cities Jubilee Singers, 181
Two Harbors (Lake County),
    107–8, 111, 113, 256
Tyler (Lincoln County), tornado
    in, 258

unemployment, 171–76, 179,
    259, 288n5, n6
Union Mission (Minneapolis),
    173
Union Pacific Railroad, 102, 103
unions, 177. See also labor, organ-
    ization of
U.S. Bancorporation, 262
U.S. Hockey Hall of Fame, 7
U.S. Sanitary Commission (USSC),
    65–66
U.S. Steel Company, 255
Univac (St. Paul), 231
University of Minnesota, 48, 99,
    108–9, 200–201, 258, 259,
    286n2; founding of, 46, 101,
    224
up north, 10, 236–38
Upper Agency (Yellow Medicine)
    Reservation, 42, 43–45, 48, 50,
    53
urban areas, 107, 124, 166, 171,
    204, 216
Urban Coalition (Minneapolis),
    231
urbanization, xv, 90, 222
Usonian house, 294n9

Valesh, Eva McDonald (labor or-
    ganizer), 110–11
Valter family furniture, 209
values, American, 166–67, 174
Van Cleve, Charlotte Ouisconsin
    and Malcolm: at Fort Snelling,
    31
Vermilion Range, 107, 253, 255
veterans: Civil War, 66–68, 97;
    Native American, 280n16;
    World War I, 175, 289n18;
    World War II, 206, 296n24
Vietnamese immigrants, 247,
    263
Vietnam War, 223, 230, 231
Virginia (St. Louis County), 108,
    115
Virginia and Rainy Lake Lum-
    ber Company, 258
Vogland, Leonard (author), 181
Volstead, Andrew J.
    (Congressman), 243
voting rights. See African Ameri-
    cans, suffrage; woman's suf-
    frage
voyageurs, 34, 47, 60, 251, 252.
    See also fur trade/fur traders

Wabasha (Wabasha County), 58,
    87
Wade, C. P. (postmaster), 69
Wahpekute Dakota, 11, 42, 46,
    50, 251. See also Dakota people
Wahpeton Dakota, 11, 42, 50,
    251. See also Dakota people
Wahpeton houska (Long
    Trader). See Sibley, Henry
    Hastings
Wa-koo-tay, 41–43
Walker, Thomas B.
    (lumberman), 98, 181
Walker Art Center
    (Minneapolis), 181, 182, 261,
    263, 296n16
walleye, 238–39, 241, 249
Walseth, Henry (merchant),
    121–22, 130
Wa-pa-sha (Dakota), 41–43
war, xii, 167. See also specific wars
War of 1812, 27
war on terrorism, 248
warriors, Native American, xv,

42. See also Dakota War of
    1862
Washburn, Cadwallader and
    William (millers), 86, 99
Washburn, Crosby and
    Company (Minneapolis), 86,
    161, 162, 163, 254, 255, 258,
    259; strikes at, 111, 256
washing clothes, 187, 188
Washington County, 7
water, 5–8, 10, 266; transporta-
    tion on, 35, 73, 85. See also indi-
    vidual lakes and rivers
Watkins mansion (Winona), 123,
    151
wealth, 187–88, 190, 296n24;
    disparities in, 92, 171, 294n1
weather, 259, 260; droughts, 4,
    172; rainfall, 4; record
    hailstone, 257; tornadoes, 92,
    119, 258
Webb, Guy, repair shop, 122, 147
Wefald, Knud (Congressman),
    178
Wellstone, Paul (senator), 234,
    235
Welsh immigrants, 94
Western Federation of Miners
    (WFM), 111
Westminster Presbyterian
    Church (Minneapolis), 109
West St. Paul (Dakota County),
    48
Weyerhaeuser, Frederick (busi-
    nessman), 108
Weyerhaeuser Company (Little
    Falls), 98, 255; strike at, 111,
    177
wheat: milling, 50, 81, 86–87,
    104; prices, 97, 171, 175
Whig Party, 46
Whipple, Henry (missionary),
    54, 56, 93, 253, 277n18
White Bear Yacht Club, 256
White Earth Reservation
    (Becker County), 11, 70, 138,
    161, 253, 254, 259
white–Native American
    relations, xv, 23–25, 28–29,
    49–60, 93–94, 278n24,
    279n25; modern changes in,
    240–41; poisoning of, 32–33,
    41–43, 46, 277n18

white people: in CCC, 184, 185; fear among, 247–48; Prohibition's effects on, 164; racism of, 69, 203; unemployment among, 173, 181; unification among, 82. *See also* clothing, white

Wilder, Laura Ingalls (author), 288n5

wilderness protection movement, 10, 184, 223, 226–27, 231–32, 237

wild ricing, 14, 15, 239, 271n8

Wilkin County, 7

Willey, Nancy, 294n9

Williams Arena (Minneapolis), 259

Windom (Cottonwood County), 66–67

Windom, William (senator), 91

Winnebago people. *See* Ho-Chunk people

Winnibigoshish mounds, 21

Winona (Winona County), 73, 87, 108

Wisconsin, statehood, 35–36, 275n2

wives: multiple, 30, 32; Native American, 26–27, 39, 49, 54, 273n4, n5, 274n19; white, 37, 49, 63, 65, 68, 79–80

woman's suffrage, 66, 90, 92, 254, 280n17; ratification of, 110, 113, 161, 167, 256, 258, 289n24

women: African American, 161, 181; athletics, *142;* citizenship, 116; in Civil War, 61, 64–67; clubs, 68, 110, *136;* dancing, 167; education, 90, 108; middle-class, 110, 122; mixed-blood, 39; occupations, 85, 87, 88, 91, 122, *133,* 281n19, 292n5; in politics, 227–29, 260, 262, 263; property rights, 87; publishing, 54, 253, 255; roles, 15–16, 68, 78, 162, 211, 214, 266; strikes by, 259; traveling by, 82; unemployment among, 173, 180, 181; unmarried mothers, 92, 174; volunteer work, 98, 122, *137,* 174; white, 37–38; in World War II, 193, 203, 206. *See also* feminism

Women's Christian Association, 68

Women's Christian Temperance Union (WCTU), 68, 90, 110, 243, 280n17, 283n14

Women's City Club (St. Paul), 188

Women's Free Loan Association, 258

Women's Relief Corps (WRC), 68

Women's Trade Union League, 111

wood. *See* forests; timber industry; trees

Wood Lake, battle of, xv, 63

Workers' Alliance (Fergus Falls), 177

working class, 110–11, 164, 170–72, 190. *See also* migrant workers

Workmen's Compensation Act of 1913, 111

Works Progress Administration (WPA), 176, 179–83, 184–85, 290n32

World War I, 112, 114–17, 258; aftermath, 124, 164, 171, 198; German immigrants during, 244–45

World War II, xv–xvi, 192–204; aftermath, 202, 208, 212, 221, 222, 224; German immigrants during, 244–45

writers, xv. *See also* literature; *and individual writers*

Yankees, 35, 60, 90; governors, 107; politics of, 219, 224, 275n13, 298n3; social circle, 38–40, 50

Yankton/Yanktonai Dakota, 24, 270n1. *See also* Dakota people

Yellow Medicine Agency. *See* Upper Agency (Yellow Medicine) reservation

Young, Harriet Campbell (mixed blood), 50, 51, 57, 58

Young Women's Christian Association, 110

Yungbauer Furniture Manufacturers (St. Paul), 208, 295n10

Zimmerman, Robert. *See* Dylan, Bob

Creating Minnesota was designed by Will Powers and set in type at Phoenix Type, Milan, Minnesota, and at the Minnesota Historical Society Press. The text type is Clifford, designed by Akira Kobayashi. Printed by Friesens, Altona, Manitoba.